Designing Menus with DVD Studio Pro

Alex Alexzander, John Skidgel, & Ron Dabbs

SAN FRANCISCO, CA

Published by CMP Books
an imprint of CMP Media LLC
600 Harrison Street, San Francisco, CA 94107 USA
Tel: 415-947-6615; Fax: 415-947-6015

www.cmpbooks.com
e-mail: books@cmp.com

Managing editor: Gail Saari
Layout design: Brad Greene

Distributed to the book trade in the U.S. by:
Publishers Group West
1700 Fourth Street
Berkeley, CA 94710
1-800-788-3123

Distributed in Canada by:
Jaguar Book Group
100 Armstrong Avenue
Georgetown, Ontario M6K 3E7 Canada
905-877-4483

For individual orders and for information on special discounts for quantity orders, please contact:
CMP Books Distribution Center, 6600 Silacci Way, Gilroy, CA 95020
Tel: 1-800-500-6875 or 408-848-3854; fax: 408-848-5784
E-mail: cmp@rushorder.com; Web: www.cmpbooks.com

Printed in the United States of America
05 06 07 08 09 5 4 3 2 1

CMPBooks

ISBN: 1-57820-280-9

DEDICATIONS

To Christine Sabooni, a true writer whom has generously given me her time, friendship, and advice.

Alex Alexzander

For their unwavering support and love, I dedicate this book to my parents, Herbert and Blanca Skidgel, and to my wife, Allison.

John Skidgel

To my wife, Terry, my children Alex and Jennifer, and my parents Bud and Betty not only for being part of my dreams but also for helping me realize them.

Ron Dabbs

Contents

ACKNOWLEDGMENTS

The authors would like to thank Dorothy Cox, Gail Saari,
Damien Castaneda, Paul Temme, Sachie Jones,
and all the wonderful people at CMP Books for making this book possible.

—The Authors

To Zoe Heimdal, a true artist and friend for always being willing
to help on a moments notice.

To my good friends, Kathlyn and Ron Lindeboom of Creative Cow,
Michael Horton of LAFCPUG, and Ken Stone of Kenstone.net.
Each of these fine people have given me considerable help gaining an on-line audience.

Special thanks to Andrew Brother Elk of the Earth Dance Theater
for the use of their footage.

To my parents for allowing me to choose my own path, and to my brother Caesar
for his unwavering support. —Alex

Introduction

Developing a DVD requires several stages: acquisition, editing, menu design, linking, compression, quality assurance, usability testing, and replication. This book is about menu design with Apple DVD Studio Pro. You will learn how to create functional, aesthetically pleasing menus.

Menu design is a crucial part of the DVD authoring process because menus are the interface between viewers and the content stored on the DVD.

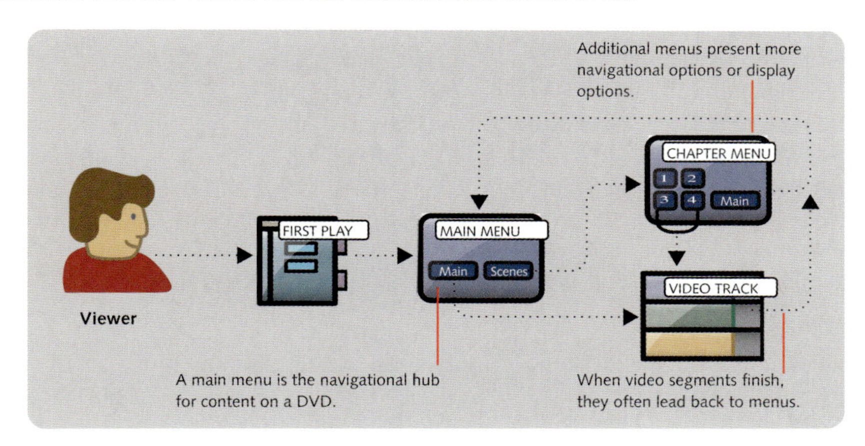

Figure 1.1 Relationship between the viewer and menus on a DVD

How this Book is Organized

To help you design better menus, this book explains all the facets of DVD menu design. The book is organized into four sections: Introduction, Designing for the Screen, Creating Still Menus, and Creating Motion Menus. A set of appendices, a glossary, and an index round out the book's offering.

Section One: Introduction

You're reading Chapter One, which gives you an overview of the book, tips on how to use the book, and hardware and software prerequisites.

Chapter Two discusses the DVD specification as it relates to menus. It covers the structure of a menu and the differences between still and motion menus, NTSC and PAL video formats, and normal and wide screen aspect ratios. It includes a descriptive list of the different types of menus you can create for projects at the end of the chapter.

Section Two: Designing for the Screen

Chapter Three explains interaction design for DVD menus. It includes strategies for gathering requirements, mapping interactions, and testing prototypes. If you're new to interface design, you'll want to read this chapter. Chapter Four covers graphic design for DVD menus. This chapter is a primer for visual design topics such as layout, color, typography, and imagery. Chapter Five details the process, principles, and common properties of animation.

Section Three: Creating Still Menus

Chapter Six gives you an insider's tour of the DVD Studio Pro interface, paying particular attention to menu design and editing functions. Chapter Seven gives tips for preparing images for menus. Chapter Eight guides you through the process of creating layered menus using DVD Studio Pro and Photoshop.

Section Four: Creating Motion Menus

Chapter Nine distinguishes between the different types of motion menus. You'll learn how still imagery or motion combine with sound to create different kinds of menus. You will also learn how to use transitional animations. At the end of Chapter Nine, you will use scripting to create a looping motion menu.

Chapter Ten shows you a quick method of creating a chapter index menu as well as methods of programming the remote control. Chapter Eleven demonstrates implementing a Setup Menu and Chapter Twelve provide guides to optimizing your DVD master. The last section concludes with an overview of building and formatting your final master.

Icon Glossary

Important information is separated from the main body of text by a light gray background, and several types of callouts (Figure 1-2) list the kinds of notes you will find throughout the book.

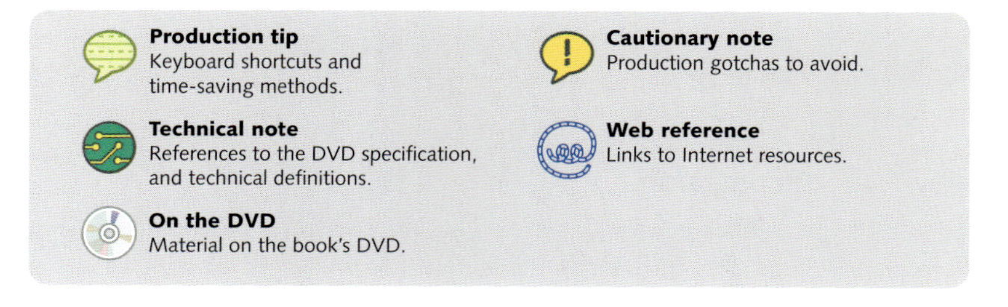

Figure 1.2
Icon Glossary

How to Use the Book and DVD

If you're new to digital video, design, and DVD authoring, read the entire book. It will give you a good foundation in this exciting new medium. If you are an experienced video editor or motion graphics designer, you should read Chapters Two and Chapters

Six through Nine. If you have DVD authoring experience but are new to DVD Studio Pro, Photoshop Motion, or After Effects read Chapters Six through Thirteen.

The DVD has a lot of resources on it, including templates for planning your project as well as assets for all the tutorials.

If you are looking for more reference material, book updates, and related information, go to www.apple.com/finalcutstudio/dvdstudiopro and www.cmpbooks.com/maillist.

Before You Begin

Apple DVD Studio Pro has several hardware and software requirements. The following pages list these requirements and offer additional advice in configuring your computer for DVD authoring.

Required Software

Apple DVD Studio Pro is a lot like a page layout application because it is the last leg of a publishing system. You create assets in other applications and then import them into DVD Studio Pro to "publish" a DVD. Adobe Photoshop, Apple's Motion, and Final Cut Pro have tight integration with DVD Studio Pro, and this book covers how to make the most of DVD Studio Pro with these applications. Figure Figure 1-3 shows the interaction between the applications.

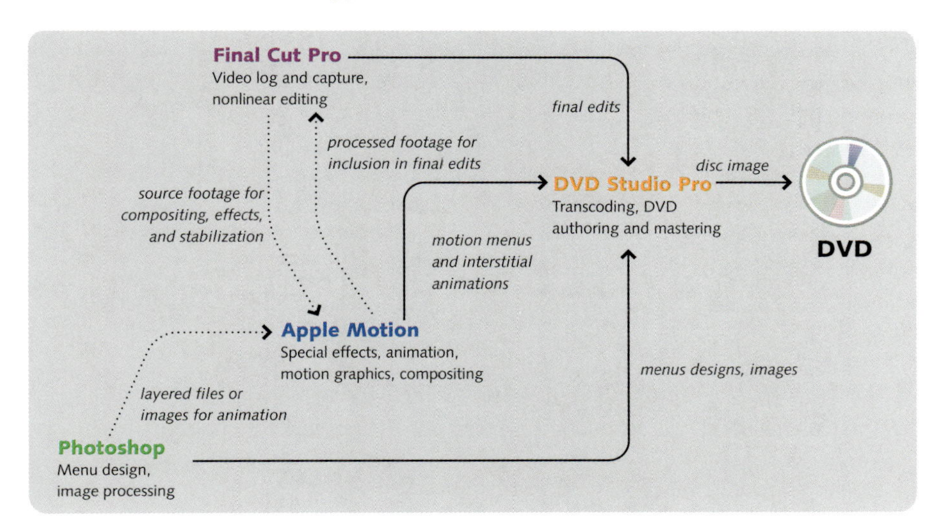

Figure 1.3 Applications used in DVD menu design

OPERATING SYSTEM

DVD Studio Pro 4 requires OS X v10.3.9 or later.

ADOBE PHOTOSHOP

Section Three explains how to use DVD Studio Pro with Photoshop; you will frequently switch between the two applications. If you plan to edit your menus outside of DVD Studio Pro or would like to use the Open In Editor feature, you will need Photoshop. Photoshop CS2 is referenced in this book.

APPLE MOTION

Section Four covers how to create motion menus with Apple's Motion. If you want to follow along with the lesson tutorial, you will need Motion.

Although some familiarity with Photoshop and Motion is expected, you don't need expert knowledge of either program to complete the tutorials.

Suggested Software

You do not need the following applications to run DVD Studio Pro, but they are incredibly helpful in producing a DVD. These are my recommendations, but feel free to use whatever you are most comfortable with.

NONLINEAR EDITOR

You use a nonlinear editor (NLE) to capture, edit, and output video for use in DVD Studio Pro. If you do not currently own a video editor, get Final Cut Pro because it has superb integration with DVD Studio Pro. For example, chapter markers can be embedded in MPEG-2 video files exported from Final Cut Pro and used in DVD Studio Pro. It also has many powerful features such as real-time video and audio editing. Final Cut Pro was used to capture and edit all the video content for this book.

A DRAWING OR DIAGRAMMING TOOL

Either OmniGraffle or Adobe Illustrator are great tools for creating planning diagrams, referred to as "flowcharts," of complex DVD projects. Use OmniGraffle if you want something that does not require a lot of computer drawing skills. Use Illustrator if you want the ability to customize your diagrams or want to integrate Photoshop files. Both files also can be used to create wireframes for complex and highly interactive DVD projects.

SPREADSHEET OR PROJECT TRACKING SOFTWARE

If you are managing DVD production, consider an application that helps with planning schedules. Microsoft Excel, Project, or OmniGraffle can be used for these tasks.

Required Hardware

Figure Figure 1-4 shows a typical hardware configuration for DVD menu design.

COMPUTER AND PROCESSOR

A G4 733MHz processor is the minimum requirement. I suggest purchasing the fastest

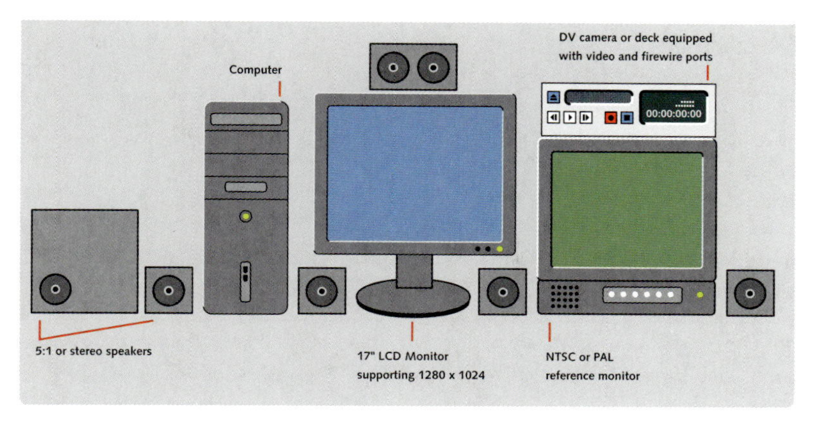

Figure 1.4
A typical computer configuration

G5 processor you can afford and consider purchasing a system with dual G5 processors. Menu rendering, video encoding, and disc burning all run faster with these processor enhancements.

 HD-DVD authoring requires a G5 processor.

MEMORY

Although DVD Studio Pro lists its memory requirements as 512 megabytes of RAM, 2 gigabytes is recommended to run DVD Studio Pro simultaneously with Photoshop and Motion. If you can afford more memory, go for it.

HARD DISK

Because DVD discs range from 4 to 18 gigabytes in size, large-capacity hard disks are a necessity for DVD authoring. DVD Studio Pro requires about 5 gigabytes of available space. Note that available space is the disk space left over after installing the operating system, all software, fonts, and other material—it is not the capacity of the hard disk. Ten gigabytes will fill quickly, and realistically, 10 gigabytes of available space will support authoring one project or at most two projects concurrently. If you plan to do a fair amount of DVD authoring, have 60 gigabytes or more of available storage. Add additional storage such as a second hard disk or a disk array if you plan to edit video on the same machine.

DISPLAY AND VIDEO CARD

Between designing menus, constructing tracks, and simulation, you should have at least one large (1280 x 1024 pixels) monitor. Two monitors are highly recommended. With two displays, you can spread DVD Studio Pro's windows out and quickly access items without having to close and reopen windows.

Your display card should support full color (referred to as "millions of color" or 24-bit color) at 1280 x 1024 pixels. The card should have at least 8 megabytes of video memory, however 32MB is recommended. If you plan to support two displays with a single card, I would recommend purchasing a card with 64 or 128 megabytes of video memory.

DVD-ROM DRIVE AND A SUPPORTED DVD BURNER

The software and additional content ships on DVD, so you need a DVD-ROM drive. If you plan to create DVDs, you'll need a DVD drive that burns DVDs.

SOUND REQUIREMENTS

Although you can hear audio while previewing a project in DVD Studio Pro through the computer's built-in speakers, you should consider purchasing external stereo speakers or surround sound speakers. DTS and surround sound require an external decoder which can be connected to the S/PDIF, FireWire, or USB ports.

A CCD is a charged-coupled device, an electronic component behind the lens that records color and light information.

Suggested Hardware

VIDEO CAMERA, VIDEO DECK

If you are producing video for DVDs, purchase or rent a three-CCD video camera equipped with FireWire and a high-speed cabling system for connecting video and storage equipment to computers. It is also known as Sony iLink or the IEEE 1394 standard. Cameras with three CCDs take better video because they capture color and detail better than a camera with a single CCD.

If you own a video camera already, consider purchasing a video deck to capture the video from the camera. A video deck saves wear and tear on your camera and saves you the time of reconnecting your camera to the computer.

A video tripod with a smooth fluid head and level rounds out your camera kit. Although hand-held shots are great, they are not meant for all shots. If you videotape scenery, interviews, or other B roll, a level tripod gives you steady footage and smoother pans and tilts.

A PROFESSIONAL VIDEO NTSC OR PAL VIDEO MONITOR

You should always use a professional television monitor to preview your broadcast video project, even if your computer has action- and title-safe guides. If you plan to design wide screen menus, look into a video monitor that can switch between 4:3 and 16:9 aspect ratios.

DVD PLAYER

One or more set-top DVD players are crucial for proofing test discs. I recommend purchasing a cheap DVD player so you can test the low end of DVD set-top players in addition to the fancier Sony, Panasonic, or Pioneer player that you might already own. The Sony PlayStation 2 and Microsoft Xbox are also great proofing systems.

DIGITAL CAMERA AND SCANNER

A scanner is useful when you want to input paper sketches, flow charts, illustrations, and photographic prints, negatives, and positives. A digital camera is a great resource for taking photos quickly and transferring photos to Photoshop for embellishment.

The DVD Menu

A menu is the user interface for a DVD. It contains hotspots, which are called buttons. Buttons play video, go to additional menus, display text subtitles, or switch audio streams. This chapter discusses both still and motion menus and the differences between the two.

This chapter presents the following topics.

- Menu structure
- Digital video and DVD menu design
- The differences between still and motion menus
- Types of menus
- Types of links

Menu Structure

To the viewer, a DVD menu appears to be a background image with buttons on top, but it is actually a single video frame without audio. As the user presses the arrows keys on the remote control, the selection moves among the buttons onscreen. The button's appearance changes as it is selected or activated. Pressing the Enter key activates a selected button and either goes to the button's link destination or executes a command, such as displaying subtitle text. Figure 2-1 shows the components of a menu.

Figure 2.1
A typical menu

Buttons

Although buttons go to links or initiate commands, they need not look like buttons in a software application. A button can be any combination of image, shape, and text. Most DVDs use only text with a simple rollover, as shown in Table 2-1.

BUTTON STATES

A button has three unique states—Normal, Selected, and Activated—triggered by selecting one button, or another button, and engaging the button after selecting it. Table 2-1 shows how the states are shown onscreen with the subpicture and corresponding state colors from the menu's color set.

Table 2-1: Button states from a one-color subpicture

PLAY	**Normal**	When a button is not selected.
PLAY	**Selected**	A selection is made with the arrow keys on a remote or with the cursor if played on a computer.
PLAY	**Activated**	Activation occurs when a button is selected and the viewer presses the Enter key on a remote or clicks on the button on a computer.

When DVD Studio Pro builds the DVD, it flattens the buttons and the background into one video stream, so the viewer interacts with hotspots on the video. The following items create this interaction.

- **Highlight region.** The highlight region is not a visible image—it is a list of screen coordinates specifying where each button, or hotspot, is located. It is analogous to an HTML image map, but note that it's only rectangular.
- **Subpicture.** This graphic is used to create the selected and activated button states. You see a piece of it when you select or activate a button. Subpictures are analogous to an HTML rollover effect.
- **Color set.** This is a color palette containing 16 colors. Each color also has an optional level of transparency. These colors are used to colorize the subpicture to show a button's state.
- **Button routing.** This comprises the navigational paths between buttons that are followed when the arrow keys on a remote control are pressed. It is analogous to Tab key order on an HTML form.
- **Button order.** This is the numerical ordering of buttons. Pressing the number keys on a remote control selects buttons on the basis of their button number.

> In DVD Studio Pro, you can specify that a button is automatically activated when it is selected. This Auto Action function is useful for touchscreen kiosks or for menus with more visually elaborate button states.

HIGHLIGHT REGION

The highlight region, or button outline contains X and Y coordinates that specify where buttons are and which portion of the subpicture to show for each button. Figure 2-2 is a representation of a menu's highlight region, but note that the highlight region is not an image stored on the disc.

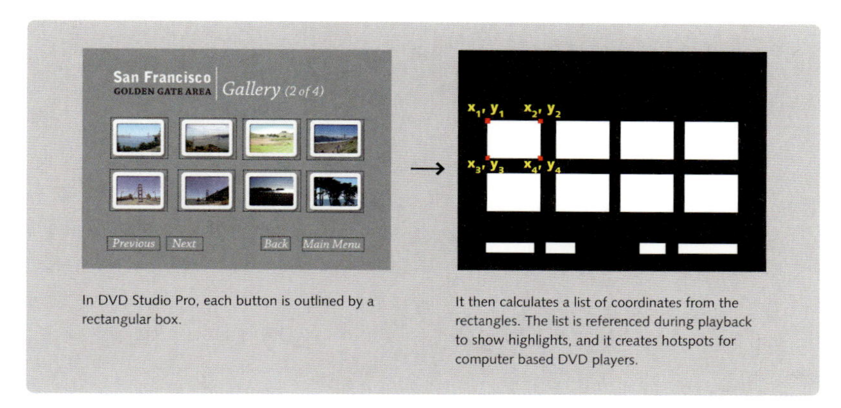

Figure 2.2 Highlight region

SUBPICTURES

A subpicture is a four-color (2-bit) image composited on top of a DVD menu or track during playback. Subpictures serve two purposes. For menus, they are the highlight that appears when a button is selected or activated. For tracks, they are the subtitle text. In both situations, one color is used for a matte, and the remaining colors (up to three) are for the fill. In most cases, a menu subpicture is only two colors: one for the matte and the other for the fill.

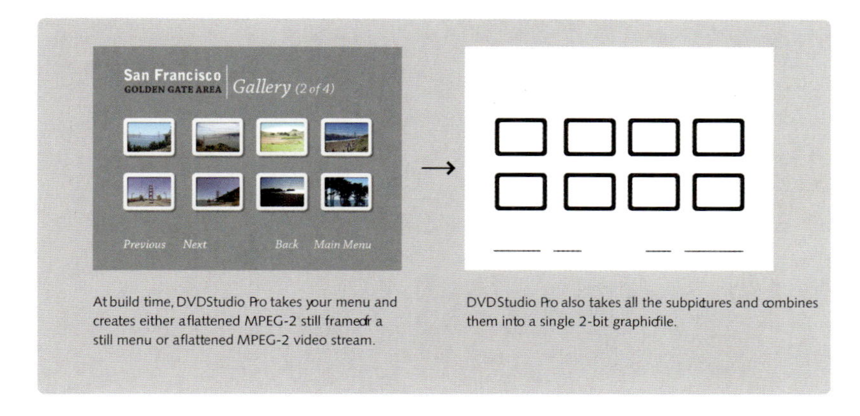

Figure 2.3 Subpictures

The rollover effect is created by the DVD player. The player shows the subpicture when the user selects or activates a button. The player can also change the color and opacity of the highlight so the selected state looks different from the activated state. When viewing this effect on an NTSC or a PAL television, it appears acceptable because television resolution is too low to show the aliasing. When viewed on a high-resolution computer display, the subpicture's crude aliasing is noticeable.

NTSC is the television standard used in North America and Japan whereas PAL is used in Europe.

The rollover effect on a DVD menu is less flexible than is possible with a Web page or Flash file. These other media allow full-color effects such as smoothly colored glows or animated rollovers. DVD rollovers are a simple color change because DVD players (especially old ones) have limited processing power to display menus and video without crashing.

MENU COLOR SETS

A color set provides the color information for button highlights. It has 16 color options specified in red, green, and blue (RGB). Each option also has an opacity value.

DVD Studio Pro offers two methods of mapping the overlay colors to the subpicture. One method is the Simple Overlay and the other is the Advanced Overlay.

The Simple Overlay provides one color and opacity setting for each button state, Normal, Selected, and Activated. The opacity level of the color for each button state can be adjusted from 0 to 16 with 0 being transparent and 16 completely opaque. Any white areas in the subpicture overlay are set as transparent and any black areas as mapped to the one of the colors in the color set. One of three color sets can be selected for each button.

The Advanced Overlay allows much more flexibility in menu design by mapping each of four colors or grayscales shades in the subpicture to one of the 16 colors in the color set. Like the Simple Overlay, the opacity of each color can be adjusted and each button can use one of three color sets.

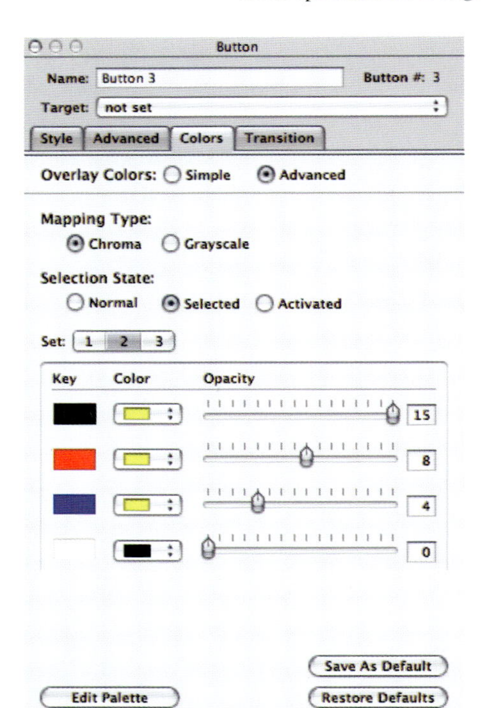

Figure 2.4 Menu color set

Antialiasing for button highlights can be created by using a multi-colored subpicture of similar color but varying levels of opacity.

In most menu designs, the Normal button state colors aren't used and are set to be fully transparent.

Because the activated state is only shown for a short period of time before the DVD advances to the button's target, there is the option to use the same color for both the selected and activated states.

One of three color highlight sets can be selected for each button, however all three color sets must use colors from the same color palette.

COMBINING THE SUBPICTURE, COLOR SET, AND HIGHLIGHT REGION

Although it might look like two or three unique graphics being swapped in and out while hovering over a button and activating it, only the single subpicture is dynamically colorized. Figure 2-5 shows how these elements are combined to create button states.

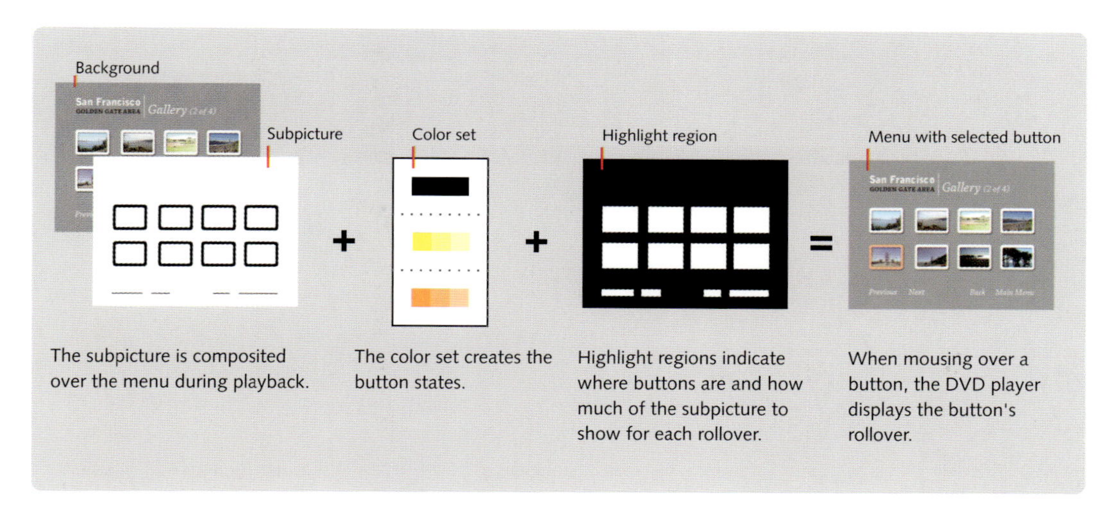

Figure 2.5 Menu video and subpicture graphics

DESIGNING SUBPICTURES

Although most DVD menu designers use only one color for the highlight, a multicolored subpicture with a varied color set offers more design possibilities.

NORMAL	SELECTED	ACTIVATED	EXPLANATION
Play	Play	Play	A single subpicture is used with different colors for the selected and activated states.
Play	Play	Play	The same effect as above, but instead of an underline, a copy of the text layer is used.
Play	Play	Play	Multi-colored subpictures are used with three colors for the selected and activated states.

BUTTON ROUTING

Button routing is the path designated between buttons. When a viewer presses the arrow keys on a remote control, the routing indicates which button is selected by pressing up, down, left, or right. DVD Studio Pro can determine the routing automatically, or you can set the routing manually if your menu layout is more complicated.

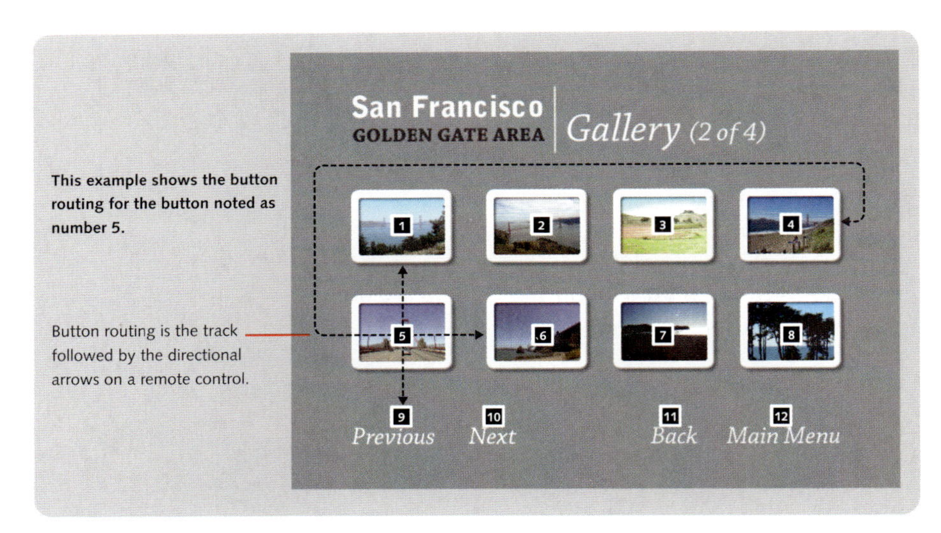

Figure 2.6a Button routing and numbering

DVD Studio Pro Allows Automatic Routing

Although DVD Studio Pro can automatically calculate this path for you, on occasion, you will want to do this yourself. You can change the automatic routing from Left to Right or Right to Left in the Menu settings of the Preferences Panel or you can adjust each button manually using the Advanced tab or the Button Inspector.

If your design is circular or does not adhere to a grid, automatic routing might not match your button layout. In these instances, disable automatic button routing and manually edit it.

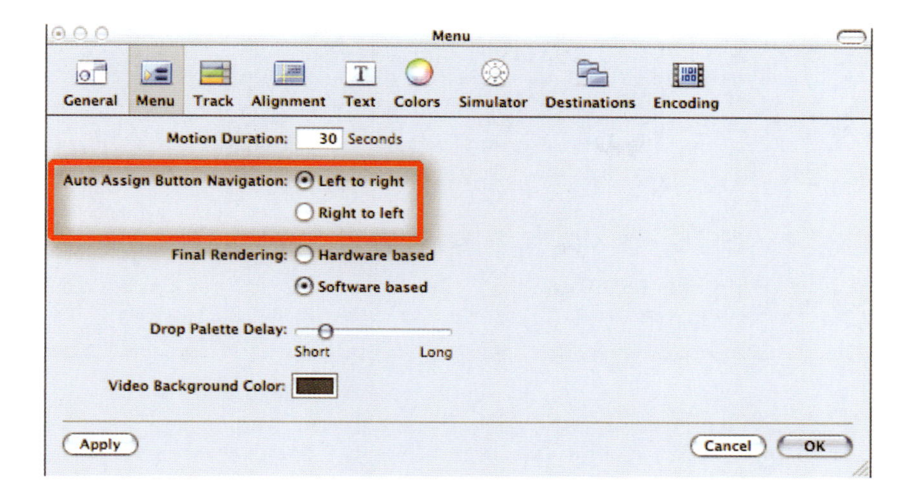

Figure 2.6b Change automatic button routing direction in the Preferences.

BUTTON ORDERING

A DVD menu can have up to 36 buttons and each button is numbered. These numbers are helpful for choosing buttons with the number keys on a remote control. The number for each button is shown in the upper right corner of the Button Inspector. If the menu has a 16:9 aspect ratio, only 18 buttons are allowed because two aspect ratios (4:3 and 16:9) are generated and the buttons need to display correctly when viewed in either aspect ratio.

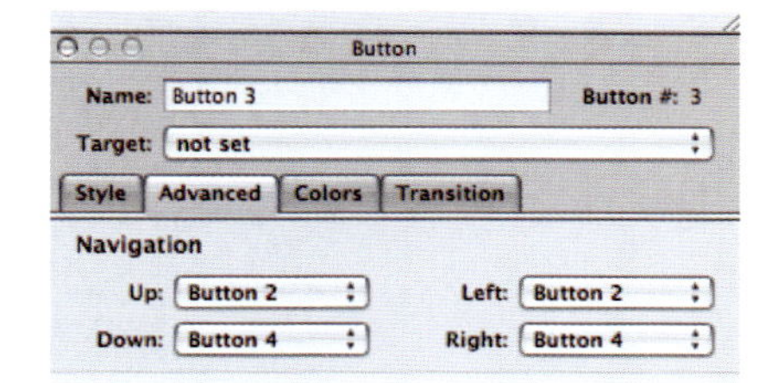

Figure 2.6c

Button ordering is important for enabling the numeric buttons on the remote control and button number 1 is the default button if no default button is selected. The button order can be changed using the Arrange buttons on the bottom of the Menu tab.

DEFAULT BUTTON

Every menu has a default button that is selected when the menu is initially displayed. For example, the main menu for a film DVD would mostly likely have the Play Movie button as the default.

The Default Button field on the Menu tab on the Menu Inspector is one way to set the default button. Using End Jump or scripts provides other methods of setting the desired menu button.

Digital Video and DVD Design

This section discusses the frame aspect ratio, resolution, and pixel aspect ratio for the NTSC and PAL video formats. Understanding the nature of these formats will make you a more technically savvy menu designer.

Video Formats

DVD Studio Pro can create video discs for either the NTSC or the PAL television standard. NTSC is the video broadcast standard used in the United States, Canada, and Japan. PAL is the video broadcast standard in Europe, but is used elsewhere too.

NTSC video plays at 29.97 frames per second (fps) at a resolution of 720 x 480 pixels. PAL video plays at 25 frames per second at a resolution of 720 x 576 pixels. Although NTSC has a slightly higher frame rate, PAL has slightly greater resolution and is closer to the frame rate of film, which is 24 frames per second. The two formats also have different pixel aspect ratios, which is discussed later.

A single DVD cannot support both PAL and NTSC standards. If you need to author for both standards, create separate PAL and NTSC projects.

MPEG-2

MPEG, pronounced m-peg, stands for Moving Picture Experts Group. MPEG is a collection of international standards for digitally compressing audio and visual information. The compression and decompression algorithm is often called a codec (compressor/decompressor). Compression is the method of shrinking the file size, and decompression is the method of reinterpreting the compressed file for playback. The MPEG collection of standards includes MPEG-1, MPEG-2, and MPEG-4.

DVDs use a strict form of MPEG-2. The strict rules define the frame size, frame rate, aspect ratio, GOP (group of pictures) length, and maximum bitrate. The frame sizes, rates, and aspect ratios allowed are listed in Table 2-3 on page 24. In DVD authoring, bitrate is widely defined as the amount of data in megabits (Mbits) read from the disc per second. The maximum video bitrate allowed for a DVD is 9.8 megabits per second. Bitrate is calculated from the video stream and all audio and subtitle streams. Video streams are the largest, followed by audio, and subtitle streams are the smallest of the streams. It is probably best to keep the bitrate under 8 megabits per second just so there is a little headroom for the player. Although there is not a set minimum bitrate for video, 2 megabits per second or less produces very poor video and should be avoided.

Like many digital video compression methods, MPEG-2 employs intraframe and interframe compression. Intraframe compression reduces the size of a single frame, whereas interframe compression looks at similarities across a range of frames to shrink file size. A GOP is the smallest range of frames in an MPEG-2 video stream and is composed of frames with more detail (I frames) and lesser detail (P and B frames). P frames contain more information than B frames. MPEG-2 video streams that are DVD-legal have GOPs that are up to eighteen frames long for NTSC and up to fifteen frames long for PAL.

The three important things to remember about MPEG-2 are: GOP placement, bitrates, and bit budgeting. Exceeding the bitrate can cause a DVD player to crash, and using high bitrates for all content on the disc can consume all the allocated space for the disc and leave you with no room for additional content.

GOP PLACEMENT

Knowing where GOPs are placed in a video stream is important when you set chapter points for a track in DVD Studio Pro. Since chapter points can only exist on the boundaries of a GOP, there are times when the exact frame you want to mark as a chapter is not available because it is within eighteen frames of the nearest GOP or another chapter.

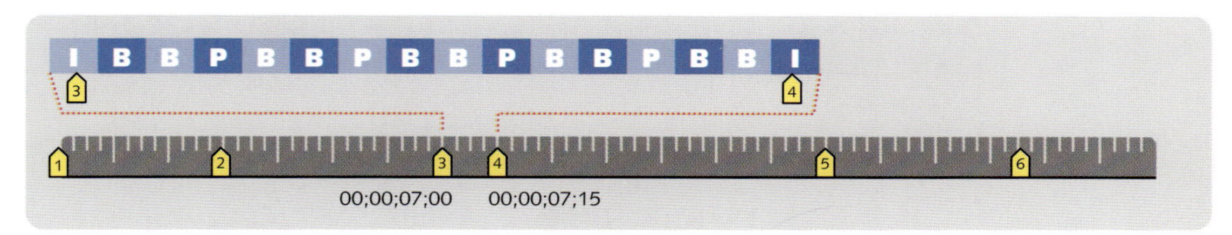

Figure 2.7 Legal locations for chapter points in an MPEG-2 DVD-videostream

If you set chapter markers before encoding video to MPEG-2, Compressor will place I-Frames where chapters occur.

CONSTANT AND VARIABLE BITRATES

With the constant bitrate compression method, the data rate is held constant regardless of what is being compressed. Portions that do not require the full data rate waste space, and portions that require more than the full data rate suffer in quality. By contrast, the variable bitrate method analyzes content in multiple passes and varies the data rate based upon specified data rate targets. Portions that need detail are given the maximum amount of bandwidth, and less detailed sequences are given lower amounts.

Figure 2.8 Comparing constant and variable bitrates

BIT BUDGETING

For short video clips such as an introductory animation or a motion menu, use a high bitrate, since it doesn't have additional audio streams and the short length ensures that a lot of disc space isn't consumed. In addition, video quality often benefits from a higher bitrate. If you have one long video clip (an hour or more) with multiple audio streams or several video clips of 10 minutes or more, use a smaller bitrate so that when audio and video bitrates are calculated together there is enough bandwidth available.

Frame Aspect Ratio

Frame aspect ratio is the proportional relationship between a video's width and height. Frame aspect ratio is a relative measurement, and it should not be confused with resolution, which is absolute. Nearly all NTSC and PAL video is created with a 4:3 aspect ratio. This means the width is one-third longer than the height. Your television set is most likely a 4:3 television screen. The 4:3 aspect ratio is referred to as the "standard" because it has been used for decades.

More televisions now support high-definition video (HD), which has a 16:9 aspect ratio. This aspect ratio is referred to as "widescreen" because it is closer to film aspect ratios. Although the DVD-Video specification and mini-DV camcorders do not support high-definition video, they do support standard definition video (SD) with a 16:9 aspect ratio.

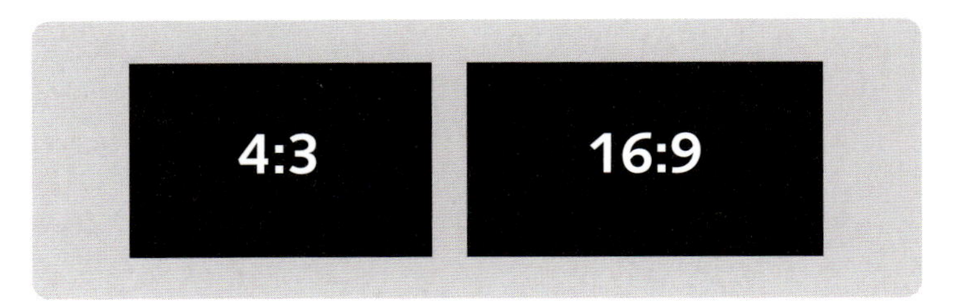

Figure 2.9 DVD-Video aspect ratios

Video footage at 16:9 is created by a video camera with a native 16:9 CCD or with an anamorphic lens adapter. The anamorphic process compresses the video image horizontally to a 4:3 video file that is stored on the DVD. During the production process, you flag the video as anamorphic and the DVD player uncompresses the video back to the 16:9 aspect ratio during playback. If the viewer owns a 16:9 television or watches the DVD on a computer screen, the video is shown in 16:9. If the television is 4:3, the DVD player will letterbox the video, that is, put horizontal black bars across the top and bottom so the video fills the television screen.

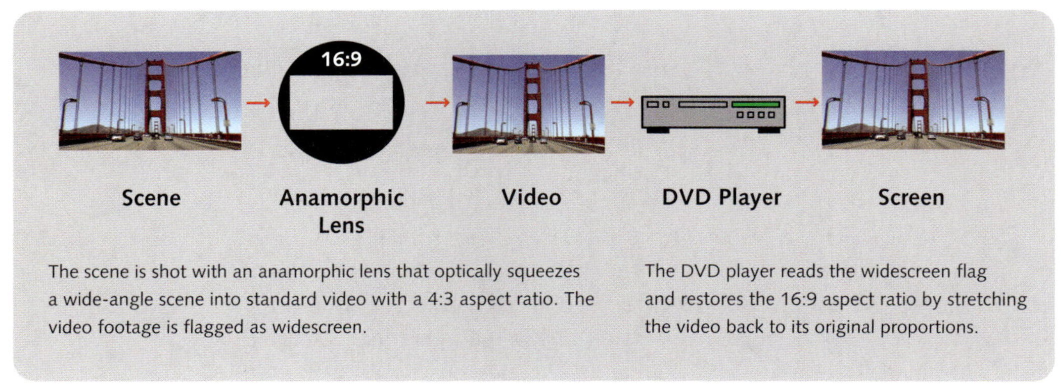

Figure 2.10 The anamorphic process

Resolution

Resolution is the number of pixels in an image. Resolution is often described as the number of horizontal pixels by the number of vertical pixels; for example, 720 x 480 for NTSC and 720 x 576 for PAL.

Pixel Aspect Ratio

Pixels (picture elements) are the tiny squares of color arranged on a two-dimen-sional grid that form an image. The aspect ratio of a single video pixel is its width relative to its height. One would imagine that video pixels would be perfectly square like the pixels on a computer screen. This could not be further from the truth! The NTSC and PAL digital video formats have rectangular (also referred to as nonsquare) pixels. A 4:3 NTSC video is 10 percent narrower than a computer's square pixel, whereas a 4:3 PAL video is roughly seven percent wider than a com-puter's square pixel. These formats have rectangular pixels because of recent broadcast technology. NTSC video used to be 640 x 480 or 648 x 486. In the 1990s, the NTSC D1 video standard was defined to be 720 x 486. By packing more discreet blocks of resolution, more detail was made available. Unfortunately when digital video and DVD were defined, 720 x 480 was considered preferable to 720 x 486. Table 2-3 lists the resolutions and pixel aspect ratios for 4:3 and 16:9 NTSC and PAL video.

Table 2-3: Resolution for NTSC and PAL television standards

TELEVISION STANDARD	FPS	RESOLUTION	PIXEL ASPECT RATIO
NTSC DV/DVD Standard (4:3)	29.97	720 x 480	0.9 x 1.0
NTSC DV/DVD Widescreen (16:9)	29.97	720 x 480	1.2 x 1.0
PAL DV/DVD Standard (4:3)	25	720 x 576	1.0666 x 1.0
PAL DV/DVD Widescreen (16:9)	25	720 x 576	1.422 x 1.0

When designing DVD menus and still graphics in Photoshop, you need to size files to accommodate pixel aspect ratio differences between video and computer screens. For more information, see the section on "Working with Adobe Photoshop" in Chapter Seven.

When you acquire footage from a DV camera, it will follow the settings listed above. You can directly import this footage and use it as a background for a motion menu. If you are creating animation, see if your animation software can output a file at this resolution. If it cannot, you can follow the size requirements of DVD-Video for still images, render your animation at this resolution, and use a program like Motion or Final Cut Pro to resize your animation.

DVD Links and User Operations

When designing DVD navigation, you are creating links between items. For example, you create links between buttons on a menu and chapter points in a track. The DVD also has global links that are accessed from a DVD remote control. This section is an overview on the types of links available in DVD authoring. For more information on designing user-friendly and intuitive navigation, see "Interaction and Navigation" in Chapter Four.

Five properties facilitate linking: the First Play, remote control Title button, remote control Menu button, Target, and End Jump. DVD Studio Pro also offers the ability to add some artifical intelligence to the navigation through the use of scritps

First Play

The first play is the first image shown when a DVD begins to play. In most DVDs, this is the FBI message that warns against illegally distributing the DVD's content. If you are not developing a DVD that requires this warning, the first play could be a company logo, a introductory video, or the main menu. First plays can be menus, tracks, stories, slideshows, or even scripts.

DVD Studio Pro, by default, uses the first menu created as the first play. You can set it to something else by selecting another target in the First Play field of the Disc Inspector-General Tab.

Remote Control Title Button

The Title button is on nearly every remote control and, generally speaking, is labeled Title, but occasionally it is labeled Home, or Top Menu. This property is set once for the entire disc and can be accessed from any menu or track. The Title button is best set to the disc's main menu or an introductory video segment that leads to the main menu. Think of it as being similar to the Home button on a Web page that sends you to the Web site's home page.

Remote Control Menu Button

The Menu button is also on nearly every remote control and is almost always labeled Menu. This is a track property and it sends the viewer back to the menu that is playing the current video or to a menu that allows the viewer to navigate to another item on the disc.

TARGET

Target is an object property. Targets link objects such as the First Play or buttons to other menues, tracks, stories, slideshows, scripts, and even markers. It is what the DVD player advances to the disc is inserted or when a button is activated.

END JUMP

An End Jump occurs at the end of an object such as a track or when a menu "times out." When a track completes playing, the DVD player will advance to the destination specified by the track's End Jump target, which should normally link back to the menu that called the track. However, a track's End Jump could also link to the next related track.

A menu can have an End Jump, but it cannot hold or loop forever. It must have a duration (still menu) or be looped a number of times (motion menu). If the menu holds or loops forever, the End Jump property is ignored. If you are designing a DVD public or tradeshow kiosk, you might want to set all the menus to time out and use an End Jump to reset the kiosk to an introductory video or menu. You can also create interactive quizzes that timeout with the Loop or Timeout properties and the Action target field.

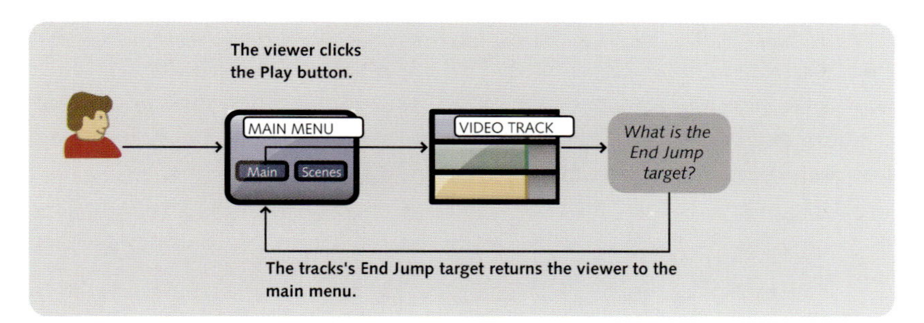

Figure 2.11 End Jump example

SCRIPTS

Scripting in DVD Studio Pro provides a method of creating interactive navigation. Scripts are a set of commands grouped into an object that can be set as a Target or an End Jump. The commands within the script are able to check certain parameters such as what button was last selected or whether a track has been played and execute other

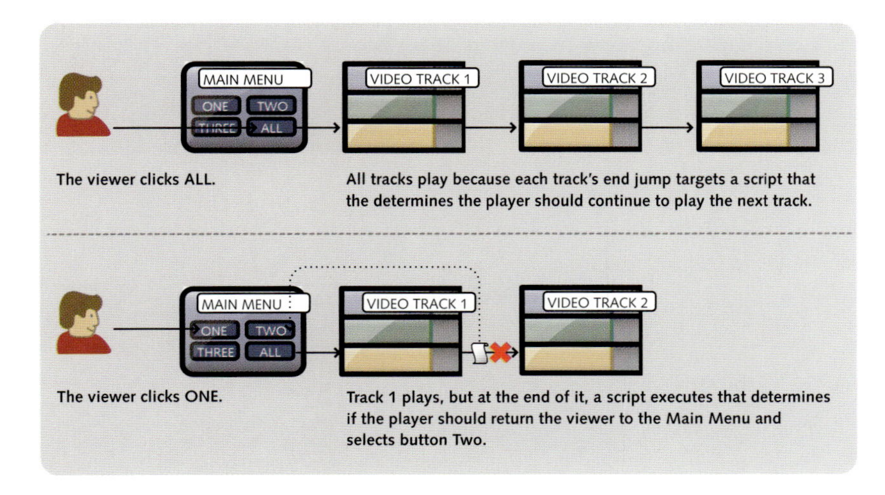

Figure 2.12 Script example

commands based on those parameters. The following example illustrates how scripting works.

The Main Menu has four buttons that allow the viewer to plays any one of the three available tracks and then return to the main menu or the viewer could choose a button to play all of the tracks before returning to the main menu. The script would determine which button the viewer had selected and target the menu or next track based on that selection.

User Operations

A disc, menu, track, and story all have user operation settings that permit or prohibit interaction between the user and the functions on a DVD remote control. For example, most Hollywood discs prohibit all user operations until after the FBI warning.

Tracks and Stories

Tracks

Menus are the interface to tracks on a DVD. Tracks contain the video content you shot, edited, and imported into DVD Studio Pro, as well as additional audio and subtitle streams. A DVD can have up to 99 tracks.

In DVD Studio Pro, there are nine video streams, eight audio streams, and 32 subtitle streams per track. Chapters within a track serve as shortcuts to scenes within the content. Upon completion, tracks can have an End Jump link that returns the viewer to the menu viewed prior to playing the track or to another object such as another track or menu.

Stories

A story is a selection of chapters that play in sequential order. The End Jumps for each track in a story are ignored by the program, and then one End Jump is observed for the entire story.

Creating stories allows for multiple paths through a DVD. For example, a video production company organizes its projects on a DVD by animation and live action, as well as corporate and music video. Certain reels would fall under animation or live action, but the selections for corporate and music video could contain both animation and live action pieces. In Figure 2-13, the same content is referenced in multiple stories to create alternative presentations.

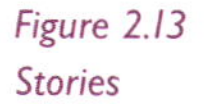
Figure 2.13
Stories

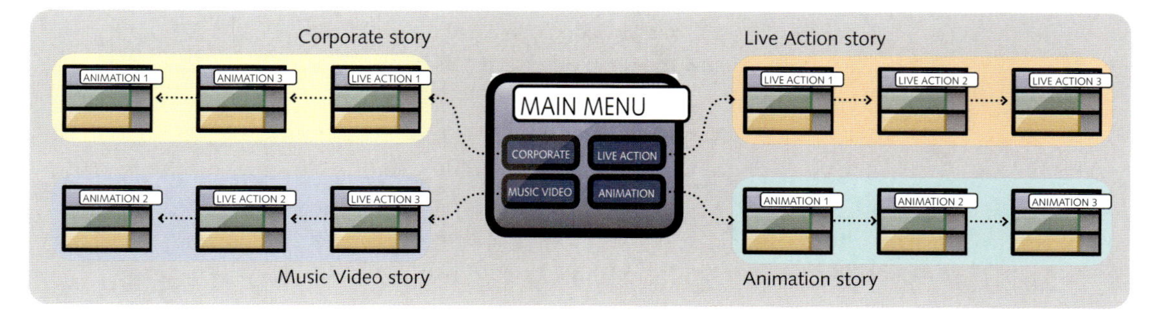

The Difference between Still and Motion Menus

There are two types of DVD menus, still and motion. A still menu is a single video frame without audio. It can be held indefinitely, waiting for user interaction, or it can time out and trigger an action. A motion menu, by contrast, is full-motion video with or without audio or is a single video frame with audio.

Still Menus

A still menu is a static frame of video with no motion or audio associated with it. It is simpler than a motion menu and is easier to create. Motion Still menus can be held onscreen indefinitely, or they can play for a set duration of time and then go somewhere else on the DVD (Figure 2-14). Still menus are often designed in Photoshop, but menus can also be created using the Menu tab In DVD Studio Pro.

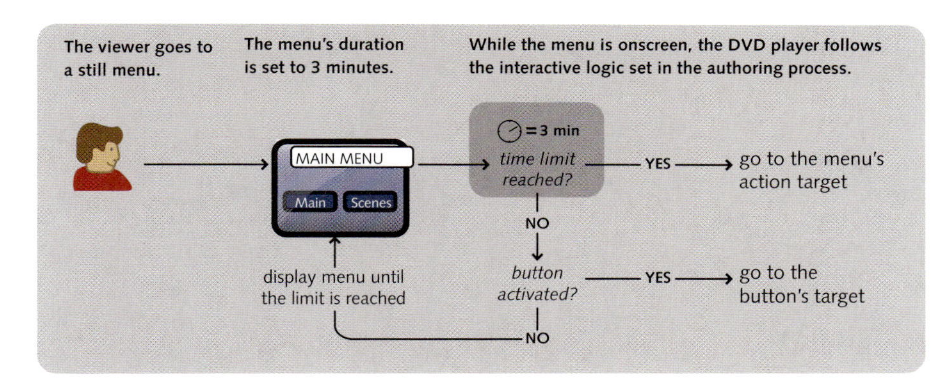

Figure 2.14 Still menu timing options

Motion Menus

A motion menu in DVD Studio Pro can be one of several combinations of still or motion video and audio.

- A still background with audio
- A motion video background with no audio
- A motion video background with audio

Motion menus are different from still menus with regard to timing. The Start, Loop Point, and End fields determine the video frame the loop begins and ends on as well as the frame that functions as the alternate starting frame once the loop has played through at once..

In DVD Studio Pro, a still menu that has video chapter buttons becomes a motion menu. DVD Studio Pro then renders live video from each chapter point into each button area.

More elaborate motion menus are created with Motion, Boris Red, or Adobe After Effects. Chapter Nine has information on using Motion for advanced motion menu creation.

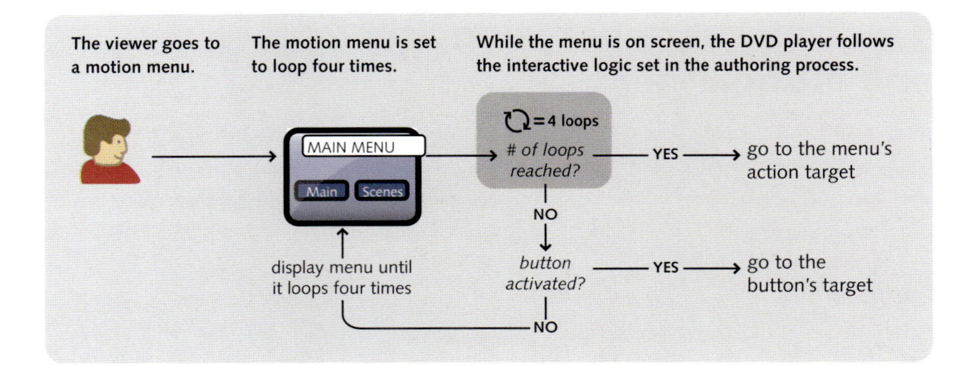

Figure 2.15 Motion menu timing options

Types of Menus

A typical DVD has a dozen menus. Most of these menus follow certain patterns of use that can be generically described and categorized. The DVD-Video specification defines a few types of menus: root, scene, subtitle, audio, and angle menus. Although you will undoubtedly create one or more of these menus, they do not necessarily give you a complete idea of the types of menus that will suit your content and your navigation needs.

For this reason, I provide a list of menus that are typically found in a DVD project, and I explain how they can be tailored for different purposes. All of these menus are not necessarily part of the DVD-Video specification, but knowing what they are and when to use them will help you prepare content and design DVD navigation.

Main Menus

A Web site's home page, after the introductory animation, provides links to the site's content. Main menus on a DVD are similar. You insert a DVD into your set-top player or computer and watch the FBI warning, film studio identity animation, and often a short transitional animation that leads to the main menu. On the main menu is a button to play the entire movie from start to finish, a button to special features, a button to chapter selections, and a button that links to a DVD configuration menu. The main menu is often the root menu. When you press the Title or Menu buttons on a DVD remote control, you will often see the main menu.

Although a DVD does not require a main menu—a DVD can simply have a video that plays immediately—it is highly recommended that you provide one to viewers so they can access the content areas of the DVD. Later in the book, I'll show you how to organize a main menu for simplicity and ease of use.

Secondary Menus

Nearly all menus other than the main menu are secondary menus. These menus present links to subsets of the DVD's content, offer options for configuring the viewer's DVD experience, or present content in and of itself, such as slide shows.

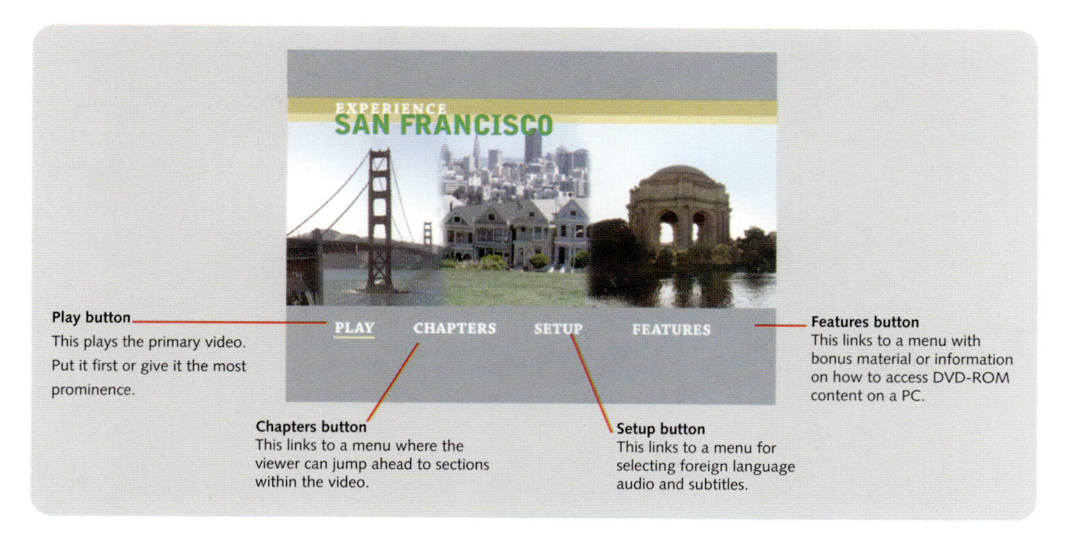

Figure 2.16 Sample main menu design

All secondary menus should have a link back to the main menu. When there are more than two levels of menus, provide buttons that go up a level from the current secondary menu.

CHAPTER SELECTION MENU

A chapter index or scene selection menu contains buttons that link to sequentially numbered chapter markers in a track. A DVD track can have up to 99 markers, so multiple chapter selection menus are possible. In this case, each menu will have Next and Previous buttons to switch between scene menus in addition to the chapter buttons.

Figure 2.17 Chapter section menu

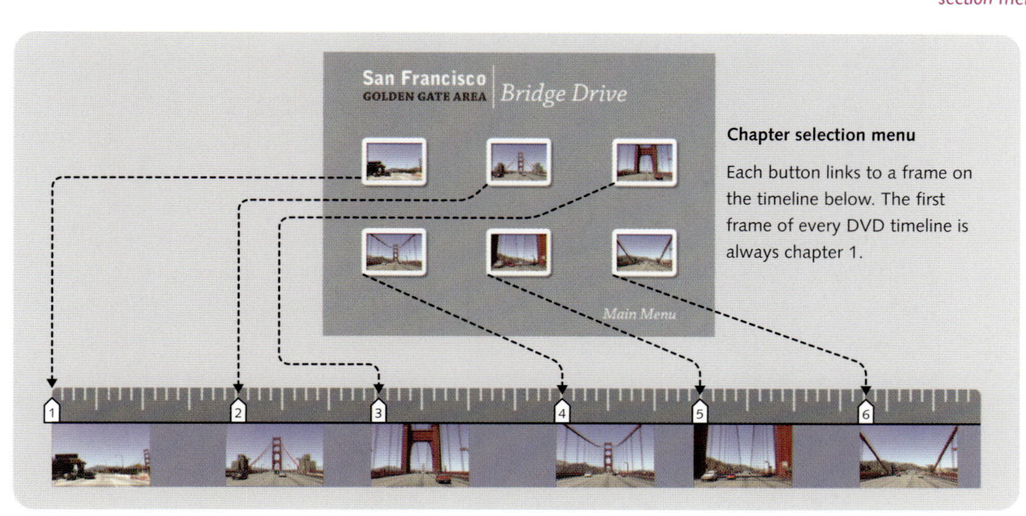

FEATURES MENU

When viewing a DVD from a major studio, a special features menu often contains links to trailers, a behind-the-scenes documentary, slide shows, help, DVD-ROM content information, or supplemental audio streams with narration from a director or actor. Additional menus could fall under the special features menu—it really depends on your content. If you are developing a DVD for another purpose, such as education, sales, or training, you can use elements of this type of menu to present slide shows, provide interviews with teachers, and present interactive quizzes.

DISC SETUP MENU

The Setup menu contains links to display subtitle text for foreign languages or to play auxiliary audio streams for foreign languages. The menu lists the languages that are available for subtitles and as audio streams. Selection of these links does not necessarily play the movie with the subtitles immediately. Often the designer will cre-ate a nearly identical menu with the word on next to the recently chosen subtitle or audio selection. Chapter Eleven provides a detailed look at scripting a Setup Menu.

Subtitle text is cheaper to produce than audio narration and occupies significantly less disc space. It depends on the budget, schedule, and available resources.

HELP MENU

Most DVDs are simple and straightforward enough that they do not need a Help menu. If you plan to provide a lot of content on the disc or are creating a set of DVDs, you might want to create a help menu. This menu can link to informative video tours of the DVD or provide a screen-to-screen instructional overview of the DVD with text.

Research, Interaction Design, and Usability

The three disciplines listed in the title of this chapter help you craft the viewer's experience when watching and interacting with a DVD. This chapter is a primer on how to plan the interface and apply good interface design principles.

This chapter presents the following topics.

- Conducting research
- Designing interaction and navigation
- Prototyping
- Usability testing

Process

When someone mentions process, others tend to yawn, myself included. Joking aside, a well-defined process shortens development and improves the quality of the overall project. Although the DVD production process covers many steps between inception and the shiny disc, I'm going to cover only the interface and visual design stages required for designing menus. This chapter covers interaction design, but Figure 3-1 on page 26 also shows the DVD authoring process.

Selling Process to Clients

If your client thinks a menu with a few buttons is all that is needed for a large DVD of video training materials, you might need to educate the client and tell them not all DVD projects are that simple.

For example, in the software industry, companies that make the effort to understand their users and the user's environment enjoy high levels of customer loyalty. They achieve this through user-centered design (a development methodology in which the customers' needs are put first). Although this is not a radical notion for someone in the design or retail industry, it was a radical idea for many software companies in the 1980s. And if I have not mentioned it yet, designing DVDs is very much like designing software. The more you understand the audience and the content you are presenting to them, the easier it is for them to navigate the disc. If they find your work user friendly and enjoyable, you gain repeat business, referrals, and good will.

When to Conduct Research, Do Design, and Test for Usability

You might wonder why I am covering user research and interaction design since most DVDs are fairly simple—one to two menus and perhaps one video. That may be true of some menus, but the vast majority of A-title Hollywood DVDs have a dozen or more menus and as many video segments. Training, sales, and education DVDs can be even more complex. The question to ask yourself is how complicated is the project going to be and what really needs to be done to make sure the disc is easy to use. If you are putting a lot of menus on the DVD, you will want to consider following these practices.

User Research

Gather Requirements

The first step is to gather requirements from the client. You need to know the subject of the project, the audience, the method of delivery, the budget, and the schedule. I will cover how to understand your client and your client's client, the viewer. If you are creating DVDs primarily for event videography, this step will be fairly straightforward, and you can streamline a few of these steps. If you are a consultant for hire, the steps will help you as you move from project to project.

Understand the Client

You should receive the majority of project information during the initial conversations with the client. For example, the tourism bureau of San Francisco wants to develop a city guide on DVD. They plan to play the DVD in hotels and sell the DVD in tourist bureaus. The DVD will have virtual city tours, interactive maps, and printed guides

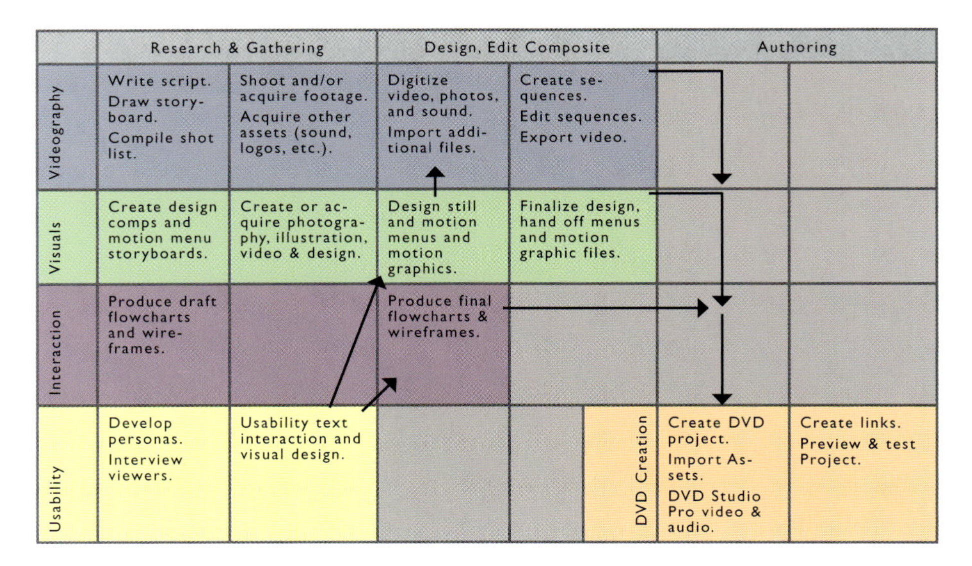

Figure 3.1 The DVD production process

on the DVD-ROM portion of the disc. Their goal is to have the disc completed and replicated in six months. With this information in hand, you know:

- The client—the tourism bureau of San Francisco.
- The project and scope—a city guide on San Francisco for tourists.
- The audience—tourists who are visiting San Francisco.
- The schedule—six months.

If you do not receive this information initially, ask for it. If the client is prepared, you will receive a Request for Proposal (RFP), a creative brief, or a one-page treatment, which outline the project goals, the scope, the content, and the schedule. An RFP is the most detailed of the three. It is your task to read this document, reply with a proposed budget and revised schedule, and perhaps pitch a few ideas on how to complete the project.

You might not want to show mock-ups because some clients will take your sketches and farm the idea out to someone who will work for less money. Whether or not to include sketches depends on the RFP requirements and your relationship with the client. If you have an established relationship, this is not a problem. If the client is new, show previous work; if the RFP requires a few sketches, keep them at the conceptual and wireframe level. Never overdeliver.

A questionnaire is located on the DVD-ROM in the Usability and Research folder.

Making Bad Clients Better

Perhaps you do work for hire and you have the best client list in the world. If so, you are lucky and you should write a book and share your secrets. However, if you are new to world of working with clients, here is a short list of how to make bad clients better.

Establish goals. Ask for a well written RFP or a clear definition of the project scope in a creative brief, storyboard, or outline.

Be proactive. You need to have them put you in touch with the right people, and have them get you what you need—whether it be content or a check!

Set realistic expectations. This is even more important if they are looking for a quick turn around.

Frame the discussion. While it is appropriate to be critical, discourage vague feedback like "make it jazzier, greener, or cool." Ask for qualifications and be receptive.

Understand the Viewer (the Client's Client)

The most obvious way to understand viewers is to talk to them. You learn what viewers need and what makes sense to them. Spending just one afternoon and talking to four people will often save you time and increase the project's chances for success.

Testing is shortened and further design and testing can often be eliminated because you are not designing in the dark.

Define the Audience

Once you know the nature of the project, find viewers who are likely to watch the DVD. Before you begin recruiting, however, work with the client to develop a list of personas or user profiles. Personas are fictional characters who best represent the audience. Give them names, give them a story, and create a simple chart listing the items listed in Figure 3-2. Then use these personas to recruit viewers who fit the description. Often you can base personas on real people you interview, or the persona can be a composite of several people.

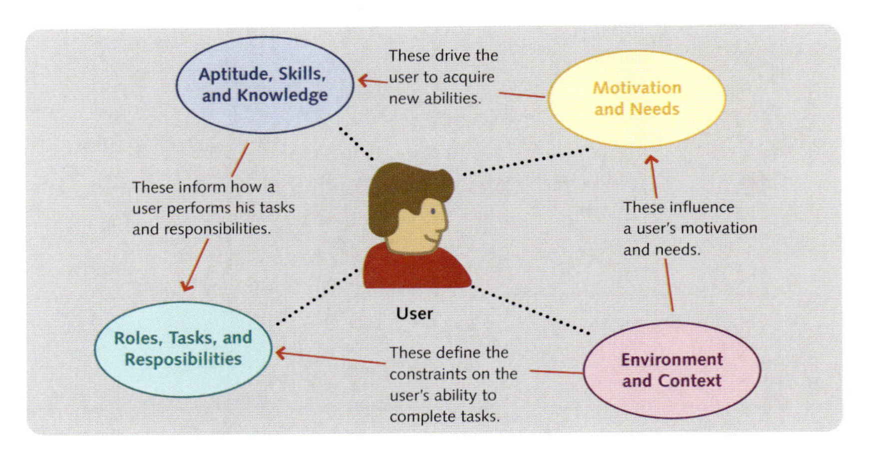

Figure 3.2
A persona

One important persona characteristic is how the user will view the disc. Will the user be watching the disc on a computer, on a television, or on both? I ask this because the way users interact with DVDs is noticeably different between the two platforms. On a computer, the user uses the mouse to point at and click on buttons. Although most software DVD players support keyboard navigation, most users rely on the mouse. By contrast, viewing a DVD on a set-top DVD player is more constrained because the user has to use the arrow buttons on a remote control. These buttons do not give the same immediate access to buttons. More importantly, these buttons follow the routing that is designated during the authoring process. Although the authoring algorithms in DVD Studio Pro do a great job, they might not work perfectly for complicated, circular button layouts. Therefore, it is important to view the button routing before burning the disc and to review the routing with viewers later in usability tests.

Keep your personas in mind when discussing features, design, and content. For example, Kay is a school teacher from Maine who wants to learn about cultural developments in San Francisco during the 1960s. She represents 30 percent of the audience. To accommodate this persona, you would want to include a brief segment on the Haight-Ashbury neighborhood or the area in North Beach around City Lights bookstore.

"Know your audience before you design" is the best advice I can give you. Designing with user research makes happier viewers. It also sets you apart from the competition, is something you can charge for, and makes you a better designer.

SCREENING PEOPLE TO INTERVIEW

Now that you know who will be using the DVD, you need to screen for real people who match the audience criteria and will talk with you. Talking with people who do not match the criteria does not fulfill your research needs. For instance, I would not interview many San Francisco residents for the DVD travel guide because although they might suggest wonderful places to visit, they do not have the same needs and experiences as the first-time San Francisco visitor.

An effective screening questionnaire will:

- Determine whether a person matches the audience criteria by collecting demographic information that qualifies potential subjects. Initial questions should be written so that people that do not match the audience criteria are eliminated quickly.
- Collect information regarding a subject's experience, attitudes, and affinities. This information helps researchers and designers understand a subject's responses during an interview or a test session.

A screening questionnaire is located on the DVD-ROM in the Usability and Research folder.

Conduct the Interview

WHO TO BRING

In most cases you can conduct the interviews by yourself. If you are talking with only one person, an additional person is acceptable if you need someone dedicated to taking notes while you are talking or if you need someone to handle a video camera. More than two people is often overwhelming, so bring no more than two people (and never go over five) when interviewing three to four people at the same time. If more than one person wants to take part, rotate them in as the note taker.

It is a great idea to bring team members and clients on interviews because they gain insights that they would not gain from your report. Their first-hand experience can sometimes be a rude awakening, humbling, and, at best, eye-opening. Their participation in the research and usability process makes it easier when it comes to getting agreements on important design decisions. You should, however, make it clear that they are there to observe and take notes—you are facilitating the interview. If they want to ask questions, they need to do it at the end and never interrupt. If they want to facilitate, switch off between interviews.

TELL THEM YOU WANT THEIR OPINION

When you begin, tell the viewer you want their candid opinion and advice. Let them know that everything is welcome and that they do not need to hold anything back. They can be as positive or negative as they want. All the advice they give will help create a better product. Tell them that you are there to listen and that you will encourage them to talk more if it is required.

GET CONSENT

When working on a commercial product, not only do people have to be willing to talk to you, but they have to give you permission, and sometimes they have to agree to keep what they have learned confidential—especially if you are testing a product that has competition. This is done by signing a consent form. By signing the form, the viewer understands the following points.

- The interview is for research and development purposes only. The information they share with you will be kept confidential and will not be used for marketing or other public use.
- They are free to stop the discussion at any time and they are not obligated to answer any questions they do not know or do not feel comfortable answering.
- They agree to keep the information they have learned from the discussion strictly confidential and not to discuss the product with third parties. Have two copies on hand for each participant. Have them sign both copies, and then sign both copies yourself. Keep one and give the other copy to the participant.

A consent form is on the DVD-ROM in the Usability and Research folder.

LET THE VIEWER DO THE TALKING

I refer to this as talking and not interviewing, because talking is more informal. You want the viewer to know that you are listening. Interviewing implies you are there to ask a lot of questions. Talking implies there will be a conversation. Although you might need to encourage the viewer to talk, you will learn more about the viewer if you listen and let the viewer talk more. It sounds simple, but it is rarely done!

KEEP THE DISCUSSION OPEN

Rather than lead with pointed questions on specific content planned for the DVD, ask the viewer qualitative questions like:

- What do you expect from the DVD?
- What do you need from it?
- What would you find valuable?

Pointed questions force people to say Yes or No and do not encourage long responses that yield the more important information. If you need straight answers, ask them later. If the viewer gives you a straight answer to a qualitative question, ask them to explain it—if something stinks, you need to know why.

Also, do not pose questions that imply a value judgement on your part. Appearing partial skews what the viewer will say. You are after the viewer's candid opinion.

ASK THE VIEWER TO COLLABORATE

Another way to learn from viewers is to ask them to design and collaborate with you. When they begin to describe something, ask them to sketch it for you. While they sketch, do not ask questions, but be quiet and offer encouragement. Even if you understand the design, keep listening and ask them to walk you through their explanations. Remember that the longer they talk, the more chances you have to learn new insights. If people do not feel comfortable sketching in front of you, give them a red pen and a sketch of the design. Ask them to improve it.

PHOTOS AND RECORDING

Bring a camera, and ask if you can take a photo. Tell them it is for research purposes only—it is not for public use. Add that having a photo helps you link your notes to what they say and that you need proof of your research. Do this at the end of the talk. In my experience, over the course of the talk, you build a rapport with the person and they do not mind having their photo taken. If anyone does not want to have their photo taken, respect their decision, and thank them for their time.

Recording the conversation on mini-DV or on a tape recorder can certainly help you with your notes and help if you are creating a presentation. If this is required, make sure you ask permission and make sure that the consent form states that they understand that the conversation might be recorded for research purposes only. Again, it is OK if they decline, just be sure to be taking notes.

THANK THE VIEWERS FOR THEIR TIME

When the time is up, thank the person for his time. Tell him that his opinion and advice has been helpful and that you value his involvement. Give him a business card and tell him that if he has any additional thoughts to feel free to e-mail you. It is also customary to pay the person for his time. Fifty dollars is an adequate amount for an hour of time. If you cannot offer a cash stipend, offer a small gift. In my experience, I have given users gift certificates and sometimes a tchotcheke (a cool item such as an "insider" T-shirt that was made for the development team). Leave them with a good impression, and you can come back to them when it is time to test your project.

WORKING WITH EXTERNAL AUDIENCES

If you are designing for an audience that is external to the client (a consumer, a corporate customer, a partner, or an investor) ask the client whether she has people in mind for the project. Often you can call people from a customer list or meet with someone the client knows. If she does not have these people handy, hiring a research recruitment firm can help you find people who match the user profiles.

WORKING WITH INTERNAL AUDIENCES

If you are designing for an audience that is internal to your company, the purpose of usability research and testing is the same as if you are creating a product for consumers. You need to find internal users who are most likely to benefit from the project and interview them. Scheduling time for interviews is significantly easier and cheaper than working with a recruiting agency because members of your audience may sit on the same floor as you. If you do not know the people personally, ask the manager of the audience who to interview. Run practice usability tests, advertise through mailing lists and post signs in the break and mail rooms.

If you are an outside consultant brought in to design material for an internal audience, you will need to ask the client to provide a list of names of employees to interview. Suggest to them that they advertise the interviews and tests internally. When you make contact with an internal audience, include them throughout the research and testing process and ask them whether they can recommend other employees for interviews.

WORKING WITH EVENT VIDEOGRAPHY CLIENTS

If you are an event videographer and produce DVDs for clients, your client is the audience, or at least an important part of it. Because you are creating the same project with slight variations, you do not need to do testing or research for every job. I would recommend that you extensively test your product at first and then do informal testing each time you introduce a new service.

Tailor your services to suit the majority of clients' needs. For instance, one client wants video that plays once the disc is inserted; another wants chapter points, motion menus, slide shows, or subtitles. Ask the client what media they have available or are willing to pay to have produced and show them what DVD authoring services you offer. Consider creating package deals and be ready to show clients examples of previous discs you have created for other clients. Like all projects, this can be an educational process.

GET TO KNOW THE PROJECT'S CONTENT

Although expert knowledge of the project's subject matter is not required, a general understanding helps you talk about it with clients and viewers, helps you design better navigation, and helps you design visuals that are relevant and appropriate to the audience.

CREATE A SCRAP BOOK

Usually when I begin any design project, I create a folder of material related to it. For example, if I were producing the travel guide DVD, I would go online, read book reviews of travel guides, and do searches on travelling to the San Francisco Bay area. Anything that interests me, I bookmark, save as a PDF file, and print. From there I would go to a book store and look for the books I found on the Internet, and I might buy a few. In addition, I look for documentaries on San Francisco, visit tourist information centers, and ask the staff what questions tourists frequently ask. I always have a camera ready to take pictures of things that might relate to the project. All of this goes into the folder.

WATCH THE VIDEO OR BE A PART OF IT

It should be obvious that you should watch the video and take notes. Look at the log notes and ask the editor for a dub so you can watch the material again and again. Look for small clips that you can meaningfully use in motion menu design or in a title sequence for the DVD's string of first play video. If you do not have access to the source tapes, schedule time to view them, write down the time codes, and create log notes for the clips you want to use in your designs. Then have the editor digitize and deliver them to you.

If the video has not been shot, you can play a crucial role because you have talked to viewers and read up on the subject, and you might have ideas you would like to use for menu design and disc content. Give these ideas to the production team so that they can be added to the shooting script.

Design Navigation and Interaction

DVDs are too often considered an output medium like VHS. Clients assume once the DVD is put into the player everything is fine. This oversight, however, perpetuates two myths: whatever is put on the DVD will be usable, and DVDs offer simplistic interaction. DVD-Video is obviously more interactive than VHS because the viewer can skip through content quicker, can access additional information, and has control over the viewing experience.

This section guides you through designing DVD navigation and interaction. I explain working methods and the tools used to create navigation. I introduce principles of DVD interaction, and I cover the navigation found typically on DVDs while pointing out things you can do to make your projects easier to implement and easier to navigate.

Process

I liken navigation, interaction, and visual design to creating structure, form, and finish to the DVD. Navigation is akin to Web information architecture. It is the structural categorization of content that creates meaningful paths to information for viewers. Interaction design gives the experience form through controls and models that help in accessing and understanding content. Visual design is the application of communication and motion design principles to speak to, delight, and support the viewer. A project is most successful when navigation, interaction, and visual design are created within a close team supported by research.

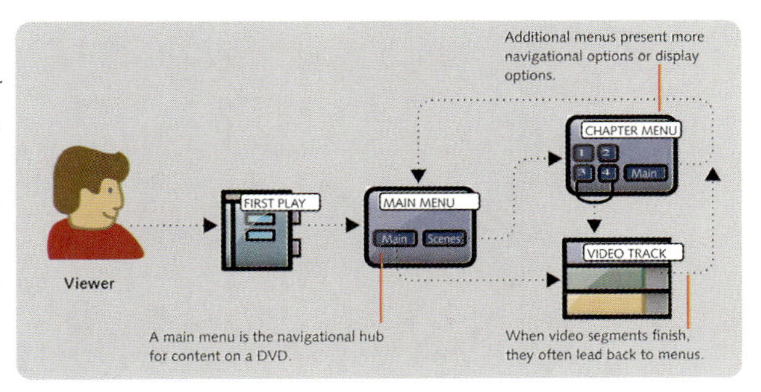

Figure 3.3 Relationship between navigation, interaction, and visual design

Interaction Design Deliverables

The two deliverables that document the navigation and interaction design are flowcharts and menu warerooms. These are similar to a Web site's site map and page schematics or warerooms.

Tools of the Trade

I have consistently used the following items to design DVDs, Web sites and software applications. They have been indispensable in the design process.

PENCIL AND PAPER

Getting excited over art materials reminds me of the hours I spent exploring a design school's art store. A high school English teacher told me Hemingway drew inspiration from sharpening pencils before writing. Well, I like soft number 2 Ticonderoga brand pencils; you know, the ones from the days of standardized tests. Coupled with a hearty plastic or rubber eraser, and you have nearly unlimited undos. Black felt pens are excellent for sketching because they photocopy and reproduce extremely well. For paper, I prefer bright white letter- and tabloid-size paper. I use letter-size for sketching wireframes and tabloid-size for flowcharts. Both photocopy extremely well, assuming you are using a copier that can copy tabloid-size originals.

To share ideas, quickly scan your drawings, place them in a page layout application, and create a PDF. I scan the drawings at 150 to 300 dots per inch and run simple level adjustments to improve contrast. Although photocopies are sufficient for reviews with local clients, this technique works very well with remote clients and, team members, looks a bit more professional, and if everyone uses the commenting features in Acrobat, helps you review the designs.

I have put an InDesign template that you can use to create these sketches. Use paper-sketches.indd in the Interaction Design folder.

WHITEBOARDS AND A DIGITAL CAMERA

Almost every workplace—whether it is a design firm or a tech company—has whiteboards in most rooms. Some rooms have whiteboards that cover the entire wall. The luxury of drawing with this much space can really liberate you. The downside is that someone can come in later and erase everything you have done, even if you have posted a save note.

Instead of taking a half hour to transcribe the design to paper, have a digital camera ready. The key in taking a photo of the sketch is to make sure that there is no glare on the white board and that you are getting all the details in the drawing. My advice is to take a photo and view it on the camera's LCD display. Zoom in to see if you are recording the white board properly. Take a few photos if you cannot capture it in one take—you can always stitch them together in Photoshop.

Flowcharts

A flowchart shows all the links between every menu and track on the disc, and because it is a bird's-eye view of the DVD, it is crucial to DVD production. For example, editors use the flowchart to create video segments; the menu designer uses it to produce designs for all the menus and menu transitions; authors use it to create all the necessary links and behaviors; and quality assurance engineers use it to write test plans, validate links, and check transcode quality. In addition, a flowchart helps familiarize new term members with a project and helps them to compare, create, and plan new projects.

Learning How to Learn by Novak and Gowin is an excellent book if you are looking to improve your flow charting and diagramming skills.

THE ELEMENTS OF A FLOWCHART

A flowchart usually contains the following elements: the first play item, menus, and timelines. The diagram also displays audio and subtitle track information and menu playback properties that indicate whether or not the a menus is timed, infinite, looped a number of times, or looped infinitely.

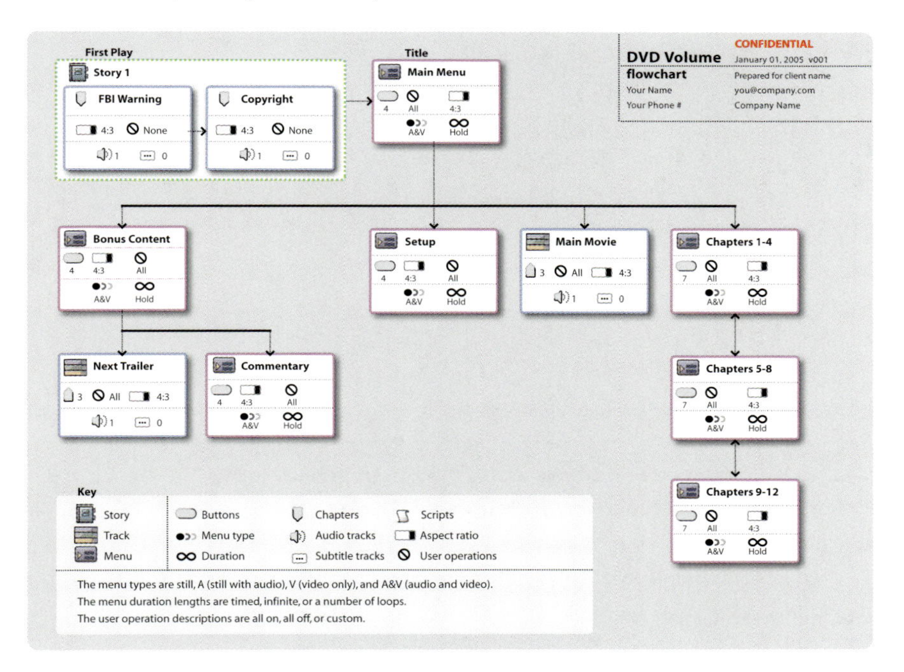

Figure 3.4 DVD Flowchart elements

All DVDs begin with a first play. As mentioned earlier, the first play is often the FBI warning video, or an introductory video, even the main menu. Because it is the first thing shown, it is placed prominently so people know where to begin examining the flow.

A flowchart does not need to show each button on a menu, but it should show the links created by the buttons. These links appear as one form of connection between menus and tracks. Likewise for tracks, it is often difficult to show every chapter point because a track has up to 99 chapter points.

CREATING A FLOWCHART FROM START TO FINISH

Developing a flowchart should begin soon after you understand the project's scope. I like to begin flowcharts early. When talking with the client, I will go up to a whiteboard and roughly sketch a flow. As I draw the diagram, I talk through it, asking the client questions as needed. Because it is all on the whiteboard, it is easy to erase one idea and sketch a new idea quickly. When the session is done, I take a picture of the whiteboard with a digital camera. I have found that a 2-megapixel or larger resolution camera works best. Be careful to not catch too much glare, or parts of the whiteboard will be obscured. Also, write legibly and use markers that create solid lines. Post the photograph for discussion. Save it as a PDF if you want people to add comments directly to it.

Figure 3.5

Once you have the flowchart recorded, draw it in a program like OmniGraffle or Adobe Illustrator. Having the flowchart in a digital form allows you to make frequent updates quickly, and you can reuse flowchart components again and again.

If you can, always sketch the initial flowchart. Although this sounds contradictory to the previous paragraph, a sketch is often faster to produce. It can be done anywhere and by anyone, and it is judged fairly because of its rough appearance.

The Graphical tab in DVD Studio Pro offers a quick way to develop flowcharts. Not only can the Graphical View be printed or saved as a PDF and annotated in another aplication such as Photoshop, it can also serve as the foundation of your DVD project.

A tryout version of OmniGraffle Professional is included on the DVD. It is located in the Interaction Design Folder.

Create headers and footers in the flowchart. In the header, include the modification date, the version, the project name, and the author's name and e-mail for questions. In the footer, include a key and footnotes. Another handy device is a short naming scheme for menus and tracks. Although this process is entirely optional, it facilitates the creation of large projects with more than one author. Conventions such as these are even better when everyone on the team understands and uses the conventions.

DVD-ROM CONTENT

DVD Studio Pro allows you to publish computer-readable files on a DVD by selecting a DVD-ROM folder. If you plan to publish HTML, PDF, or other computer files on the DVD, create a list of this content.

If you publish a large number of HTML and PDF documents on the DVD, the ROM portion of the disc might be another project.

Wireframes

As you develop the flowchart, you start to see all the menus and tracks that need to be created. For simple projects, a flowchart is sufficient. For large projects with many menus and tracks, wireframes help production in a few ways. It helps you prototype the disc quickly without having to shoot video, link up menus, and so on. And like a flowchart, wireframes help everyone on the team with their production tasks.

MENU WIREFRAMES

Menu wireframes detail all the content and interactive elements on a single menu. You should include the following items on a menu wireframe:

- The menu's name and a short descriptive name.
- A short description of the menu background.
- The menu buttons, and each button's target. If the menu has hidden buttons that link to "easter eggs," secret menus, or tracks, include these.
- The menu's timing and motion properties:
  - Is it held forever or does it have a duration?
  - Video or audio backgrounds. For instance the content in the menu (e.g., "short clip of dancer").
  - The loop point and number of loops.
  - Transitions that lead into or out of the menu.
  - End Jump targets and scripts, if applicable.
  - The default button.
  - Button routing.

Figure 3.6 Menu wireframe

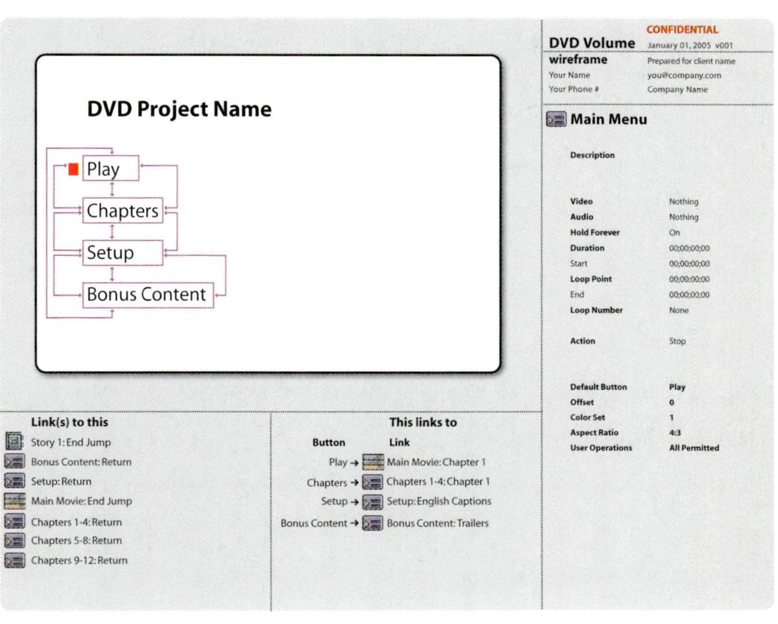

TIMELINE WIREFRAMES

Track wireframes should contain:

- The track's name.
- A short description of the track.
- The track chapters.
- The track's duration.
- The track's video clips and/or images.
- Audio stream content. The number of audio streams and each stream's content and language.
- Subtitle stream content. The number of subtitle streams and each stream's content and language.
- Remote Menu, End Jump Targets, and Scripts, if applicable.

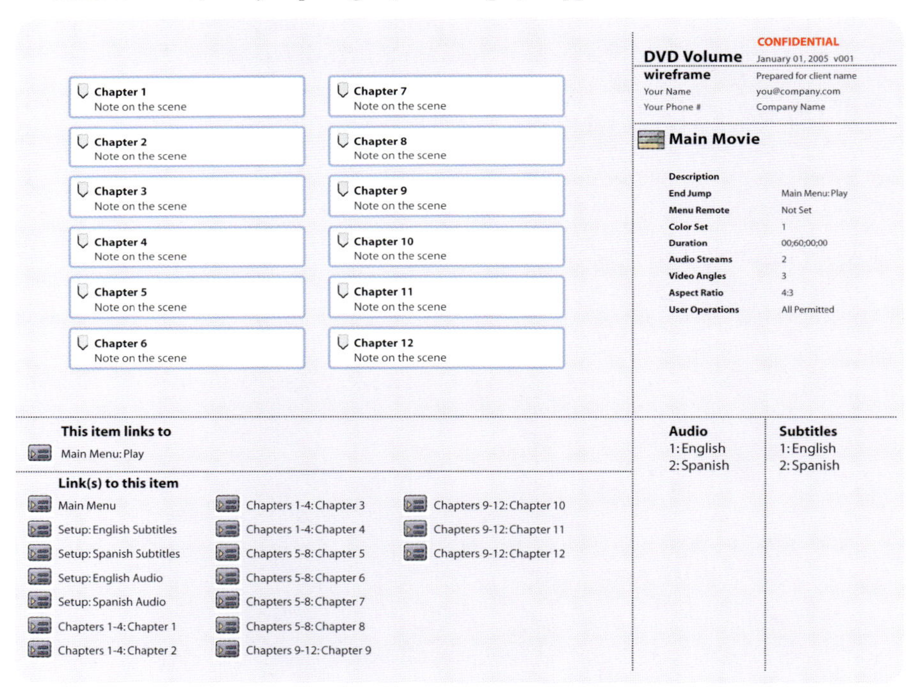

Figure 3.7 Timeline wireframe

STORY WIREFRAMES

Story wireframes should contain:

- The story's name.
- The chapters that are in the story.
- The story's End Jump.

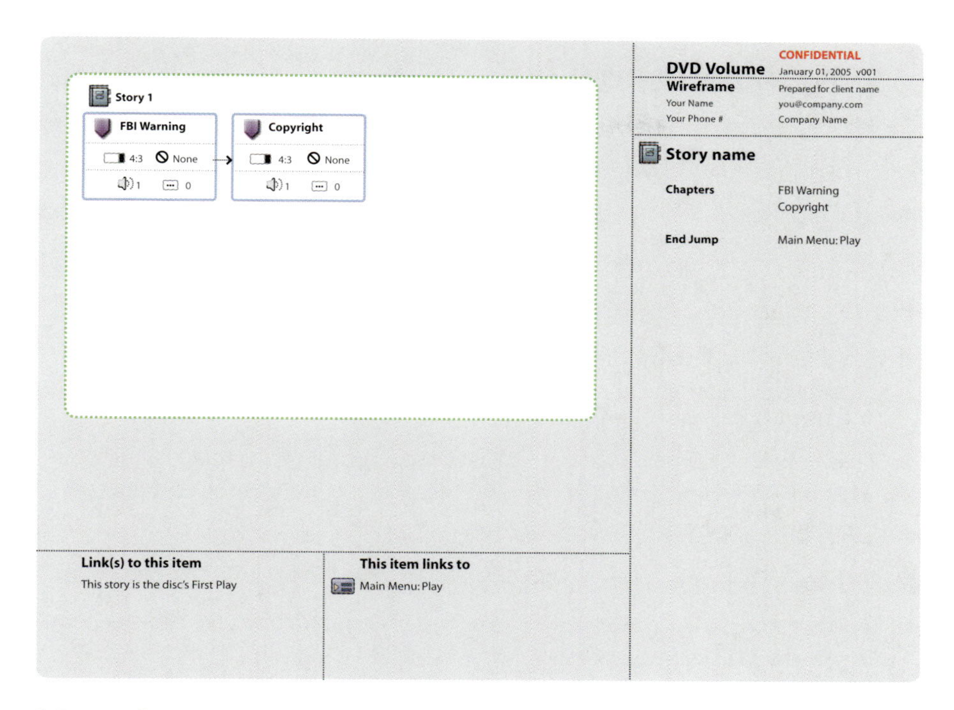

Figure 3.8 Stories wireframe

Helpful Questions

After conducting user research and watching the project's video, designing navigation and menu interaction is not always straightforward. When I have a hard time deciding what to design, I keep the viewer's needs in mind. I recall the user profiles and phrase questions in terms of what they need.

Flowchart Questions

- What is the most logical organization of the content? Does your project have one video segment? Are there ways to break it into logical chapters? If there will be more than one video, how many menus do you need to introduce to provide access to the video content?
- What does the viewer see after inserting the disc? This item is the first play. Every project should have one. It is usually the FBI warning, but in other cases, it could be the main menu, a company's logo animation, or a short video introducing the disc.
- What is on the main menu? Remember that you have a limit of 36 buttons and maybe fewer if you are designing for multiple aspect ratios. What can be on this menu versus what you can place on a secondary menu?
- What happens when the user clicks the remote control's Title button? The Title button is like a universal Home button on a Web site. The link for the Title button may not be the same item as for the first play, but it can be. Think of a Web site

with an animated introduction that plays before showing the home page. The animated introduction is shown first, but the home page is the primary way to access the site. On a DVD, the first play is like the animated introduction, and the main menu is like the home page.

Menu Questions

- On any menu, where is this most important button? Not only should this button be given additional prominence, but it should be the menu's default button. The default button is automatically selected when the menu is loaded.
- How much time should the user spend on this screen? Is the menu going to be a still menu and play forever until the user chooses a button, or will it time out and go somewhere else if no button is chosen?
- What links should be available at all times? In most cases, this should be the main menu, but if the project has many levels of menus, you need to provide buttons that go up a level as well as to the top level.

Track Interaction Design Questions

- Will the track have additional audio or subtitle streams? Will you provide menus to select these additional streams?
- Where will the track go after it plays? Will it go to another track, or will it return to the menu that played it?

Story Interaction Design Questions

- Is it desireable to construct multiple paths through the project? If it is, stories can help construct these paths.
- Where will the story go after it plays? Will it go to a track, a menu, or another story?

Interaction Design Tips

The following design rules can help you put into practice your navigation and interaction. They are not complete, and some can be broken, but like the previous set questions, they can bring order and clarity to wayward designs.

- Keep it simple. Remember that often, less is more. A cluttered interface is hard to use, and given the limited screen real estate on televisions, you cannot provide links to everything. Perhaps the one saving grace of the DVD specification is that it is far simpler than HTML. That said, do not fashion the DVD interface as a Web site, and do not fall into the trap many poor Web designers fall into by overloading the screen with too much stuff.
- Be consistent.
- Place buttons in the same place.
- Create consistent routing between buttons across menus.
- Keep selection and activation colors consistent across button groups.

- Set remote control menu button links in the same way.
- Use the same wording for buttons that have the same link.
- Provide adequate feedback. When a viewer selects a button, the visual state of the button should be unique from the other buttons. Treat selected buttons and nonselected buttons consistently.
- Use simple language that viewers understand. Do not succumb to irony and use clever wording that the viewer will not understand. For specialized projects, do research and ask participants what terminology and wording is understood in their community of interest.
- Provide links to the main menu on every menu. If the menu is a child menu under another menu, provide a link to the parent menu. For menus that are several layers deep, provide links to the main menu and the menu above the current menu.
- Create logical chapter points in tracks and create chapter menus. This gives the viewer the ability to continue when they are not able to watch the entire DVD in one session. If there are logical chapters in the video content, set them at the same interval and include the time interval on the chapter selection menu.
- Provide help. This can be a video or a short printed instructional booklet. If you cannot afford to print an insert to go with the disc, place a short video or still menu at the beginning of the disc explaining that there is an instructional file on the DVD-ROM portion of the disc.

Prototyping

Prototyping is creating a functional version of the project for evaluation purposes. The goal is to gain valuable feedback on the project's features before production. When prototyping a DVD project, you have the following options.

- Create a paper prototype from sketches, wireframes, or Photoshop files.
- Author a small subset of the project and build a DVD folder or disc.

PAPER PROTOTYPING

This option can be produced in a few hours. Usually you want to test to see whether people get the idea and purpose of the project, test your naming scheme, and test overall functionality. You can create prototypes at any stage of development, but prototyping with paper at the beginning has the most bang for the buck because paper prototypes are produced quickly and cheaply and yield a lot of valuable feedback. There is no need to make huge investments in production and design when an hour's worth of sketching and a few interviews will do.

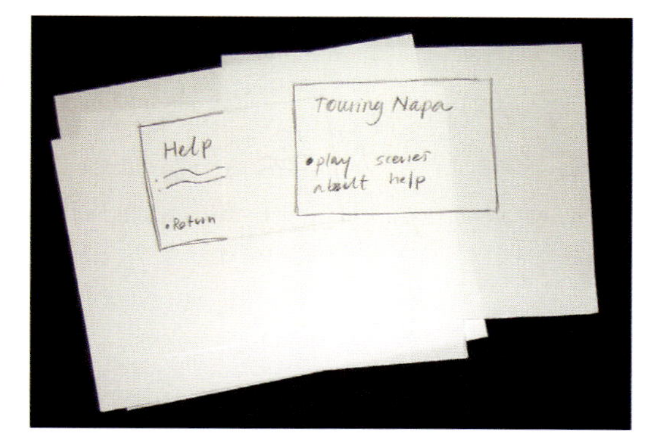

Figure 3.9

You can use either hand-drawn sketches or the wireframes for paper prototypes. I usually conduct two to three rounds of quick testing with paper sketches before moving to the more finished wireframes. If there is time, I will do two to three rounds of testing with more finished wireframes before beginning production.

Authoring a Functionally Limited DVD

Putting four to five menus with video on a disc is easy to do given DVD Studio Pro's simplified link creation tools. Determining what and how much video content to show should be determined early. If you include video for the sake of feedback on the presentation and content of the video, include as much as you need. If you are only testing menu design and navigation, include a small amount that makes moving between menus and video possible.

When you author a small test, your options are to burn the project to disc, build a DVD image, or build a DVD folder. A disc is flexible because it plays on both DVD players and computers. DVD players are cheap and easy to carry and connect to almost any television manufactured in the last several years. Using a DVD player is also important if the project is meant to be viewed on one. Viewing the prototype on a computer is more a matter of convenience. A DVD image or folder can only be guaranteed to play on a computer; not all DVD software players can play them. The advantage of the image or folder is that you save the expense and time of burning a disc.

When testing a functionally limited DVD, you test for the same things—does the viewer get the idea and purpose? More importantly, with the benefit of designing a few screens, you are testing whether the visual design makes interacting with the disc easy.

Usability Testing

Usability should not be left until the end because it is, hands down, the best method for discovering potential interface problems. Ideally it begins as up-front research and continues throughout production with testing. By testing iteratively, you learn from the viewers what makes the project easy to use and enjoyable. The usability testing process involves the following steps.

1. Planning. Write the screening questionnaire used in recruiting and the test plan, which covers the goals and content of the usability tests.
2. Recruiting. Contact or find test participants who match the audience criteria.
3. Testing. Run tests and make note of usability issues and opportunities to improve interaction.
4. Analyzing test results. Examine and report test results and make recommendations for improvements.

Planning and Recruiting

Remember when I talked about conducting viewer research at the onset of a project?

At that time, I described locating people who fit the audience's criteria for interviews. In some cases, you can test the people you interviewed because they are prequalified. The screening techniques used to locate these people are also used to locate people for usability testing. You rely on the user profiles that the screener originally created, and possibly updated after research to locate test participants.

WRITING THE TEST PLAN

The test plan is the framework written before testing begins. It is often a collaboration between the usability researcher, the designer, and a project manager. It is usually organized into the following sections:

- What are the test objectives? What areas will be tested, and how long will it take to complete tasks?
- Who is the audience for the tests? How many people need to be tested? Who are the test participants and what are their backgrounds?
- What will be the testing methodology? Will paper prototypes or a test build be used? Will it be recorded? Will the participant be asked to use the "talk aloud" principle, or will the session be an interview?
- When and where will the tests take place? What computer, audio, and video resources need to be acquired for the testing?
- What is the budget for testing? Include a breakdown for participant remuneration, facilitator salaries, and facility rental.

The test plan can benefit quality assurance teams because they can model their quality assurance plans on the same criteria.

Testing

If you are testing several people at one location, give each participant clear instructions to the test location, and have someone ready to greet and lead them to the waiting area before the test. Provide a few magazines, a glass of water, and a comfortable chair. While participants wait for their turn, it is a good time to have them sign consent forms and confidentiality agreements. Have phone numbers for each participant handy, and give them a courtesy call a day before to remind them about the time of their appointment and the location.

Renting research labs is not cheap. Have a few backup participants available to replace scheduled participants who fail to show or who cancel.

The procedure for nearly all usability tests begins by giving the user an orientation, a prequestionnaire, and a list of tasks, and ends with a postquestionnaire. A facilitator runs the test, and another person might be needed to take notes, to help with technical snafus, or to play the part of DVD player if paper prototypes are used.

ORIENTATION

In the orientation, the facilitator begins with introductions and tells the participant what she will be evaluating. It is important to stress that the product is being tested and that the product development team is looking for her candid and honest opinion. When I have run tests as an independent consultant, I tell the participant that I am not with the company and that she should feel free to tell me whatever she likes because I will not be offended. Tell the participant that the prototype is limited and does not do everything the final product will do. Continue by saying that you will point out when there are areas that are not fully functional.

A sample orientation script along with sample questionnaires and task lists are included in the Usability folder..

PREQUESTIONNAIRE

A prequestionaire can help verify information collected during the test screening, and it is a good place to collect additional information before the test begins and the participants have been exposed to the product. You can let them fill the form out, or you can ask the questions and fill the form out yourself. I tend to let them fill out the form, and after the test, I look for incomplete entries and ask for missing information.

TASK LIST

The task list is the set of tasks the participant will perform during the session. It should be no more than two pages, broken down by each screen shown in the test, and you should provide the participant with a scenario that frames a use of the DVD.

Before handing over the list, the facilitator needs to communicate that the participant need not complete all the tasks, that the facilitator cannot help with completing the tasks, and what the test protocol is—talk aloud, observation, or interview.

If the participant feels uncomfortable, tired, or wants to take a break, it is acceptable to stop the test. Ask the participant whether he needs a break or wants to stop the session. If he wants to stop, thank him for his time before he leaves.

If the participant does not understand a task, it is okay to explain it, but do not explain how to complete it. When the participant asks for help completing a task, say, "I am not allowed to help," and offer as much encouragement as possible.

You should never lead or help the viewer through the test because this defeats the purpose of objectively testing for usability.

For example, if a viewer was on a chapter selection menu and did not know that clicking a button labeled Back took them to the main menu, the facilitator should ask things like, "Where will the Back button go to?" If the viewer did not see the Back button, the facilitator might ask, "What links to the main menu?" Remember to always phrase questions that are open. Do not place judgement on the design, and do not make the viewer feel as if he is being tested.

Test methodologies include talk aloud (the most effective), observation, and interview. When following the talk aloud principle, the participant says out loud what he is thinking as he interacts with the prototype. He should say what he reads or sees, what assumptions and expectations he has about the interface, and how he feels about the interface as he experiences it. Tell the person that likes and dislikes are equally appreciated, and ask him not to hold back. If you use this method, tell the participant that you will ask him to speak up or to continue talking if he becomes silent. If the participant does not understand how to do this, give him an example. I usually say, "I am putting the DVD into the player. I see some text with the FBI warning on it. I guess I cannot copy this DVD for my own commercial use. Now I see the production company's logo. I like it. This is transitioning into a menu with the name of the movie across the top and five links on the menu, they are..."

With the observation method, the participant simply performs the tasks and the facilitator takes notes. The interview method will have more interaction between the participant and facilitator as the participant attempts and performs each task to completion. Personally, I like to mix talk aloud with some interview, but I encourage the participant to talk as much as possible.

If you are running a test in which there is a separate observation lounge, please tell any team members in the lounge to remain quiet during the test. It can make participants feel uncomfortable if they know there are other people watching and commenting on their decisions. One unfortunate but funny incident occurred when I was testing the Shutterfly Web site in New York. The home page text contained the words "click here," and unfortunately the spacing between the "c" and "l" was too tight. When the participant read the text aloud, she was not only confused, but a little offended. It was very hard to suppress the laughter that came from the observation lounge during that test!

If team members are observing you on video or from behind a two-way mirror, use hand signals to quiet them down.

OBSERVATION TIPS

During the test, you should play close attention to the interaction between the participant and the prototype. If it turns out that you cannot take notes and facilitate at the same time, your options are to tape the session and take notes later or to have a few people in an observation room taking notes for you. When observing users, note the following.

- Does the user complete each task successfully? What tasks are easy and which ones are hard? Note the time taken to complete each task.
- What is the participant saying at any given moment? Is the user confident, happy, frustrated, or confused?
- When and how frequently does the participant look for help or give up?
- Does the participant tell you about similar experiences with other DVDs, Web sites, or other products? Does she say she really likes the other approach or does she say the prototype has done a better job?

When interviewing, remember the advice given in Keep the Discussion Open on page 42—do not pass judgement and keep things open-ended.

POST-TEST QUESTIONNAIRE AND DEBRIEFING

After the tasks are complete or time is becoming short, tell the participant that time is running out, you would like him to answer a few questions about his experience, and you would like him to rate the product overall for ease of use and enjoyment.

This questionnaire should provide both a scale on which to rate answers and space to enter comments. The ranking provides you with data for compilation and statistical analysis. The free-form comments are more qualitative and provide good sound bites for the report. Again, if the user completes the questionnaire himself, remember to look it over quickly; if he has left questions unanswered, ask him to answer these questions before leaving.

After the participant leaves, I collect the questionnaire and make sure the participant's name is on all the forms and place them together. After all the sessions are complete, I photocopy my notes and organize them with the questionnaires. This makes writing the report much faster!

TESTING PAPER PROTOTYPES

When you test a paper prototype, it is best to have two people run the test with viewers. One person facilitates, and the second person plays the part of the DVD player. If you are the facilitator, introduce yourself and your colleague playing the role of the DVD player and explain your roles. The facilitator orients the viewer and leads the session. The DVD player shows and hides screens as the user "clicks" buttons.

The person playing the part of the DVD player should be very organized! Keep all the paper prototypes in order and be familiar with the test script. Often the designer or the DVD authoring engineer should play the role of the DVD player while someone else facilitates. The DVD player should not help the viewer and should never take screens away before the viewer is done. The person in this role needs to be patient and should not talk with the viewer. If the viewer asks the player a question, that person should say (with some bit of humor), "I am only the DVD player, I cannot answer any questions."

After the introductions, the facilitator begins the test by saying the viewer has hypothetically inserted the disc into the player; the person acting as the player begins to show the user the paper prototype and the viewer begins trying to complete the list of tasks.

EVALUATING TEST BUILDS

At the beginning of the session, hand the disc to the participant with the task list and have her insert the disc into the player. Remind her to be patient with the prototype since it is not fully functional and has a few rough spots. As with the paper prototype test, do not coach the participant. Only offer assistance when the participant accesses an area that is not functional or is not part of the test.

If you are using a DVD player, make sure there are fresh batteries in the remote. Place the DVD player so that there is a clear line of sight between the player and the remote. As with software or Web site testing, be sure to run through the test before the sessions in case you need to fix missing elements that are crucial to the test.

Analyzing Test Results

Write the report when the sessions are still fresh in your mind. You can forget a lot of useful information if you wait too long after the test. Although you can always watch the video tapes of the sessions, you probably won't unless you are going to include segments of them in your usability presentation or you are bursting to watch them.

ASSESSING THE RESULTS

When observing and reporting usability issues, consider how frequently something occurs in a test, and whether it is credible given the areas that are being tested, the users being tested, and the quality of the prototype. For instance, if every participant does not understand the wording of a button, most likely the wording should be changed. On the other hand, someone who is not part of the target audience and is not familiar with the subject matter does not understand or approve of the wording although other participants do, you should discount the opinion of the outside participant. Also, if participants become hung up on an area that is not fully fleshed out or is not part of the areas being tested, be ready to discount those findings too.

WRITING THE USABILITY REPORT

The usability report needs to summarize the test results, recommend design and functional changes, and then list the detailed findings from the test sessions. A report should have a table of contents with the following sections: introduction, summary, list of recommendations, and detailed findings.

A sample report template is located on the DVD in the Usability folder.

When summarizing the test, briefly describe the area of the project tested and who evaluated it. List the usability problems that occur most frequently and give an explanation of how the problem occurs and what occurs after the problem. Quotes from the participants can help stress the importance of specific usability issues. Use charts only when they show important trends or comparisons. Do not sugarcoat problems, and do not be completely negative. Write a fair assessment that recognizes strengths and weaknesses. The purpose of testing is to make the product better; it is not to pat the development team on the back or tell them they are doing a less than perfect job. If you do too much of either, they will not need or want to hire you again.

In making recommendations, correlate recommendations to usability issues and explain why they will address the issue. Identify what changes will make the biggest difference in overall usability. Also rate each recommendation on how expensive it is. Will it require a lot of work to be redone or is it a small change (e.g., a different link or word change)? Narrow the list to 10 major recommendations and then follow with the rest.

The detailed findings can be as long and as raw as you want to make them. Most people who review a report sadly read only the summary and recommendations. For a basic report, you can simply transcribe your notes and place the questionnaire answers after each subject heading. If you have more time, you can create a table that shows each task and the responses from several participants, or you can organize the findings into these areas: navigation, functionality, feedback, language, and consistency.

Design

In addition to interaction design, designing menus draws on several skill sets rooted in fine and applied art: typography, color, and image making.

This chapter presents the following topics:

- Graphic design principles
- Combining type and images
- Production tips

Graphic Design Principles

Graphic design communicates information visually. Successful design does this in a way that is functional, appropriate, consistent, crafted, and delightful.

- **Function.** Is the design functional? For instance, can people read it and do they understand what elements are interactive? Does it solve a problem?
- **Appropriateness.** Appropriate design speaks to an the audience effectively. It can share sentiment with the audience, create a sense of ease, or compel the audience to act. Appropriate design is not ignored.
- **Consistency.** Is the type set the same way? Are the buttons positioned in the same way? Inconsistency creates jarring experiences for viewers. The result can be confusion, irritation, or dissatisfaction.
- **Craft.** Good craft shows attention to detail, careful execution, consistency, high production value, and a fresh understanding of design principles.
- **Delight.** Design that delights satisfies the viewers for any number of reasons. It is a measurement of the overall quality of the experience. Delight can occur when the viewer finds humor or surprise in the design.

Successful design follows a process and develops visual language. The process is informed and guided by research. The visual language is a system for typography, color, imagery, and animation.The system is developed through sketches, color studies, storyboards, and animatics. The sketches explore strategies for creating hierarchy, contrast, and style.

Typography

Typography is the practice of arranging text for communication. If the text does not communicate, it is not typography, although it might be fine art or illustration. Typographic principles have been in place for centuries, but only within the past 20 years has typography been done by anyone with a personal computer. As powerful as these tools are, they do not guarantee clear communication, and a lot of bad design results because the tools are so accessible. Like many craft-oriented professions, typography has to be learned and practiced, so it is important that those lacking a design education learn typographic principles.

Figure 4.1

Parts of a Typeface

To understand the graphic form of type requires a look at the development of Roman, or Western, letter forms. As letter forms progressed from stone tablet to paper, the tools used to create them influenced their form and are the reason we have serif and italic typefaces and a number of display typefaces based on historical letter forms. The brush is the reason we have serifs, and the quill and nibbed pen are responsible for italics.

As movable type was invented, the forms were modified to suit printing. In 1471, Nicolas Jenson developed a single type family in which the uppercase from the Romans, namely the Trajan column, was combined with the uncial, or lowercase, letter forms from Carolingian miniscule. His letter forms were far more even in tone, and the combination of both cases improved legibility substantially.

Figure 4.2 The development of the modern alphabet of uppercase and lowercase letters

Although the graphic style of type has continuously been revised, the basic forms in Jenson's typeface are fairly close to today's serif typefaces. This is a testament to how radically different his design was from those of his contemporaries and how successful his contribution to typography has been.

Indentifying type is a useful skill when working with corporate design standards, choosing and purchasing type, and validating typographic consistency. Knowing the anatomical forms of type and the representation of these forms across varying typefaces helps indentify type.

To sharpen your indentification skills, quiz yourself on the typefaces you see. What is the name, who created it, and how is it classified?

THE PARTS

Given the number of uppercase and lowercase letters in typeface and the variations of typefaces that exist, many distinct parts create letter forms and unity within a typeface design (Figure 4-3).

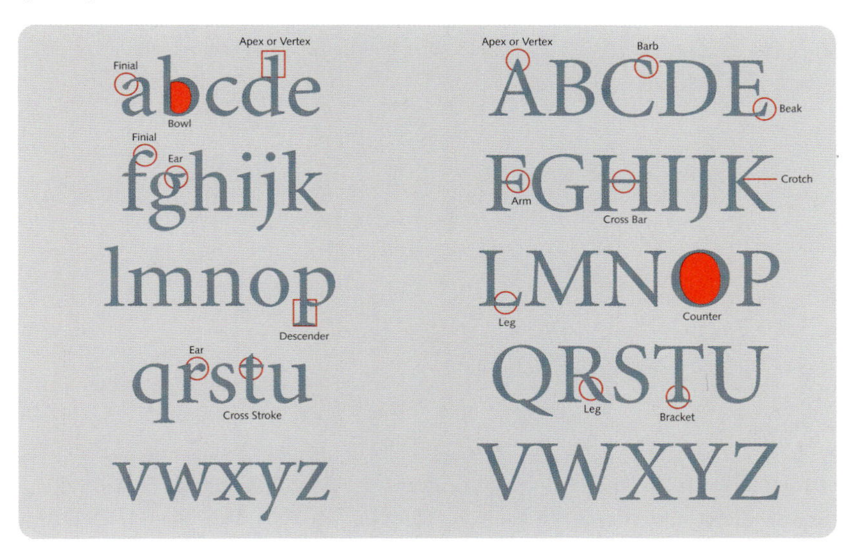

Figure 4.3 The parts of letter forms

VERTICAL PROPORTIONS

Almost all typefaces have a baseline, a median, an x-height, a cap height, an ascender height, and a descender height. These are all invisible guides that run horizontally and measure a typeface's vertical proportions. Type rests upon the baseline. The median is the top boundary of most lowercase characters (e.g., a, c, e, g, etc.). The space between the baseline and the median is the x-height, which as its name implies, is the height of the lowercase x. Cap height is the distance between the baseline and the top of the uppercase. Ascender height is the space between the baseline and the top boundary of

Figure 4.4 Vertical proportions

lowercase characters that ascend above the median (e.g., b,d,f,h,k,l). Descender height is the extent to which lowercase letter forms extend below the baseline (e.g., g,j,p,q,y).

Font Classification

Type families are classified by their graphic form and by their place in history. The major categories are serif, sans serif, and display. Each category has subcategories that classify type further.

SERIF

Serif type has its roots in the type that was carved in stone and drawn with an angled pen and brush. The serif is the product of the writing instrument completing a vertical or diagonal stroke. For 500 years, typeface designers have continued to vary strokes and serifs to create new typefaces. Today, serif typefaces are classified as Old Style, Transitional, Modern, or Slab Serif.

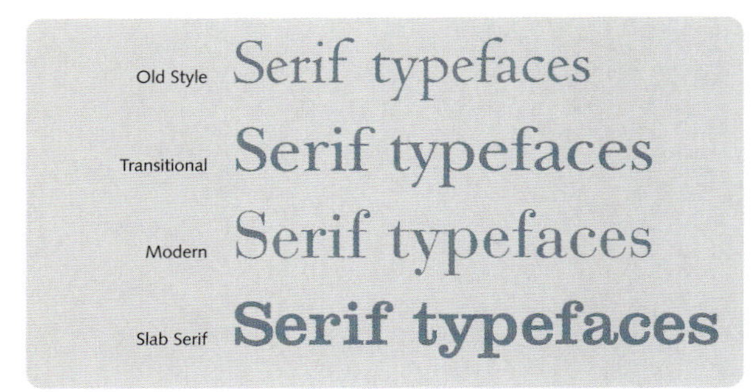

Figure 4.5 The serif

As mentioned earlier, Old Style typefaces were developed during the Renaissance in Italy and combined classical Roman uppercase and Carolingian lowercase. Centaur, a revival design by Bruce Rogers, and Bembo, designed by Francesco Griffo, are examples of Old Style from this period. In France, two notable Old Style typefaces were developed: Garamond and Granjon. Caslon, the last of the original Old Style typefaces, was developed in early 17th century England. Because Old Style type is derivative from written letter forms, it has bracketed asymmetrical serifs and a diagonal stress that creates contrast between horizontal and vertical strokes.

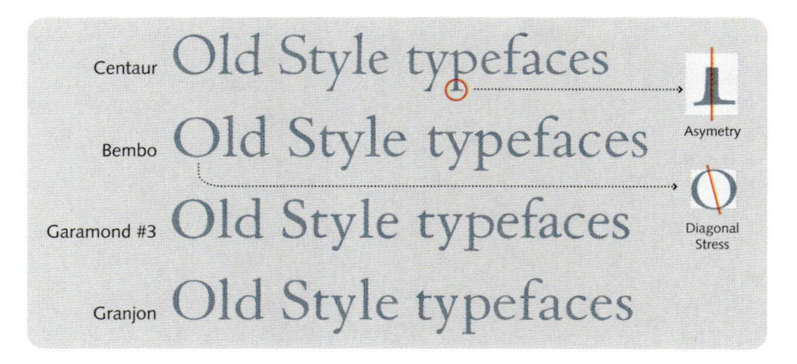

Figure 4.6 Old Style typefaces

Transitional typefaces lie between the hand-drawn quality of Old Style and the severe contrast of Modern typefaces. They were created because printing technology improved and made thinner serifs possible. In addition, the influence of handwritten letter forms decreased. Baskerville and Caslon are good examples of Transitional type. Transitional type has significantly less diagonal stress, and the serifs are more, but not perfectly, symmetrical.

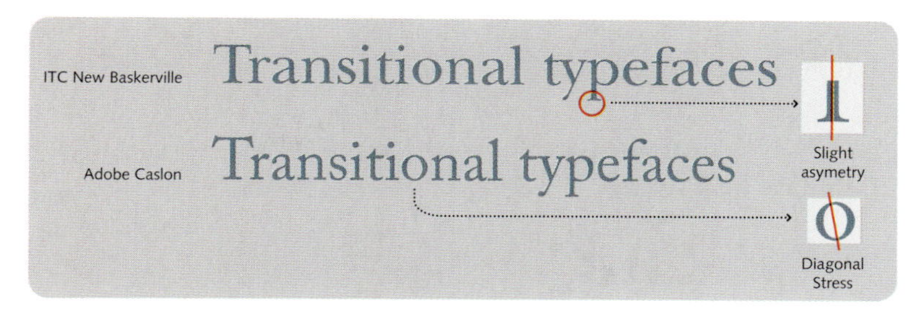

Figure 4.7 Transitional typefaces

Modern typefaces do not refer to type developed in the current day. Instead, they refer to type developed during significant printing advances in the late 18th century. Modern typefaces such as Bodoni are completely devoid of any reference to handwritten letter forms. The stress is perfectly perpendicular to the baseline. Modern is also referred to as Didot.

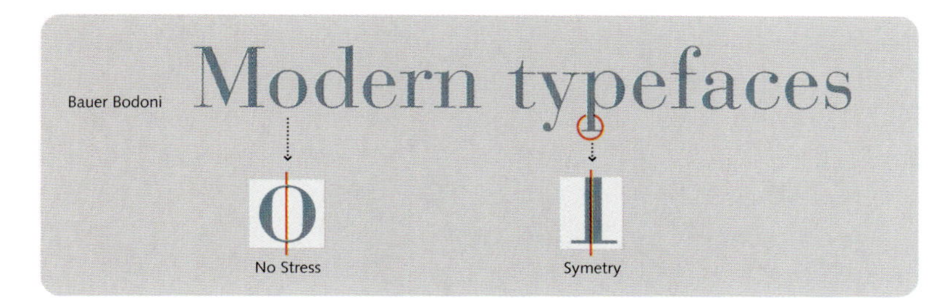

Figure 4.8 Modern typefaces

Slab Serif, or Egyption, typefaces were created in the late 18th century and were created for display purposes. Many people were critical of the design because Slab Serifs have less variation between stroke and serif and because the serifs are very thick slabs, hence the name Slab Serif. Although classifying these typefaces as Egyptian seems inappropriate, at the time, Egyptian antiquities were hip, and these type styles were promoted as being ancient, or Egyptian. Sometimes it is all about the marketing! Clarendon and Cheltenham are two fine examples of Slab Serif type.

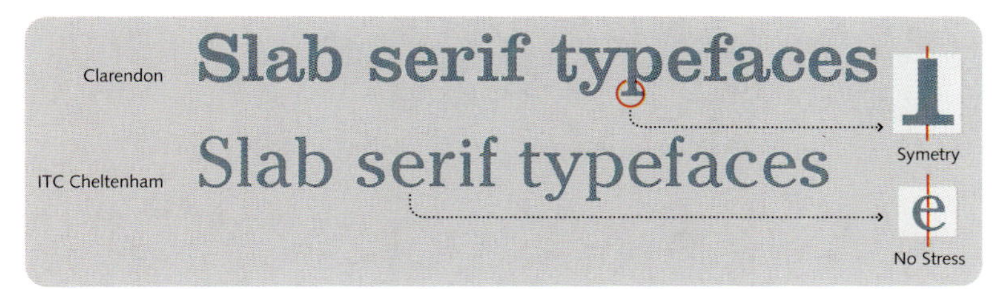

Figure 4.9 Slab serif typefaces

The best way to classify serif type is by the shape of the serif and by the amount of diagonal stress characters have from the y-axis.

SANS SERIF

In the early 19th century, sans serif typefaces were developed to mimic the lettering style seen in sign painting. Initially, sans serif type was available only in large sizes—Poster or wood type are excellent examples of early sans serif type—and was classified as Lineal, Humanist, and Geometric.

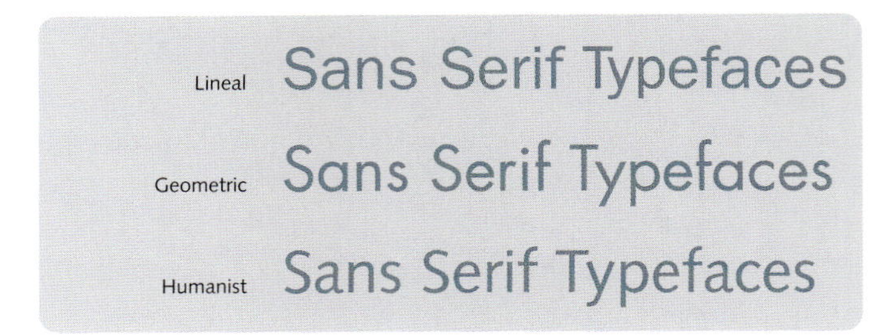

Figure 4.10 Sans serif typefaces

Lineal or ATypI, a term created by the international typography organization, depicts the early sans serif typefaces. I will refer to them as ATypI. These early sans serif types were called Antique, Gothic, Egyptian, and Grotesque. Some of the printers at the time thought the absence of serifs conjured ancient letter forms of Egypt and Greece. While they correctly related the design to antiquity, the terms have always caused confusion because Slab Serif type is also called Egyptian and because Gothic also refers to German black letter type. Another group of printers referred to the type as Grotesque because they thought the typefaces were less refined than serif types. Franklin Gothic, Monotype Grotesque, News Gothic, and Helvetica are examples.

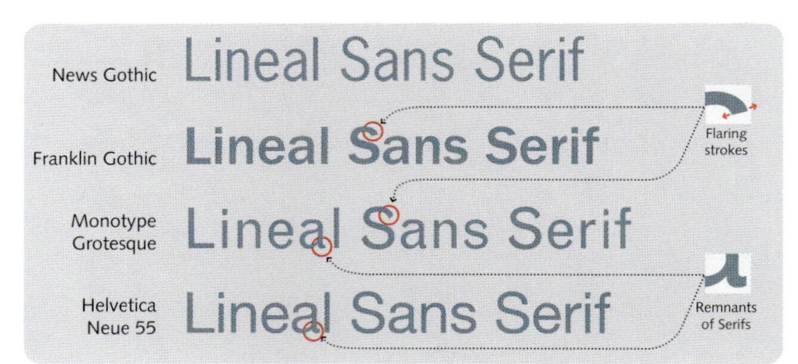

Figure 4.11 Lineal sans serif typefaces

Early 20th century modernism brought the Geometric class of sans serif type. This style was heavily influenced by the industrial and machine aesthetic started by the Bauhaus art school in Germany. Geometric typefaces are symmetrical and are constructed from straight lines and circles. Futura, designed by Paul Renner, is the most popular Geometric typeface, and Avenir and Avante Garde are two other examples.

Humanist sans serif faces were a response to Geometric sans serif typefaces. Rather than base the letter forms on geometry, Humanist type alludes to carved and handwritten letter forms. Humanist faces have proportions and a slight diagonal stress that are reminiscent of Old Style serif faces. Gill Sans was the first true Humanist typeface and Syntax, which this book uses, and Optima are examples.

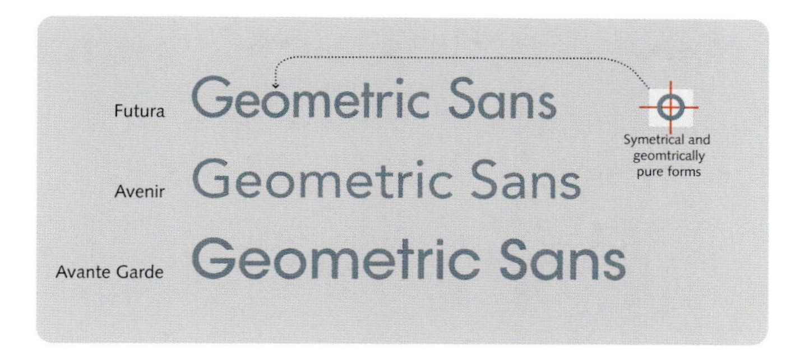

Figure 4.12 Geometric sans serif typefaces

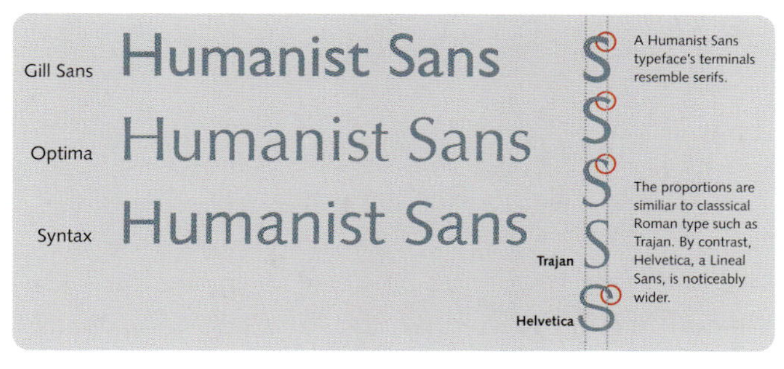

Figure 4.13 Humanist sans serif typefaces

The best way to classify sans serif type is by the amount of diagonal stress characters have from the y-axis, how uniform the strokes are, and how the strokes end.

BEYOND SANS AND SERIF TYPE

Black letter, monospaced, script, and display type are the other generalized type classifications. Black letter originated in Northern Europe and spread to France and England where it was quickly replaced with Old Style serif type. Black letter remained popular in Germany until the mid-20th century.

Figure 4.14 Black letter typefaces

Variable-spaced type has variable widths for each letter form. For instance, the lowercase "i" takes up less space than the lowercase "m." The majority of typefaces are variable width. Monospaced type has a fixed width for all letter forms and was developed for typewriters.

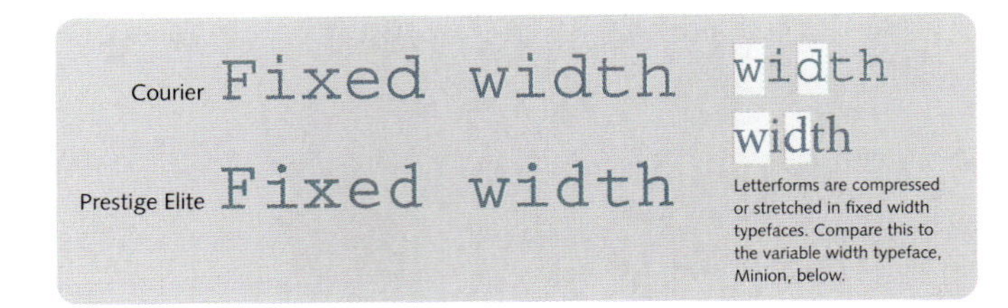

Figure 4.15 Variable-spaced and monospaced typefaces

SCRIPT

Script lettering styles developed in 17th century England. The master calligraphers took the italic lettering styles from Italy and made them more cursive by keeping the pen on the page and by using large, round strokes.

Figure 4.16 Script lettering examples

DISPLAY

Display is a catchall for all typefaces that are meant to be rendered at sizes larger than 14 points or pixels. Another kind of display type is poster type. Poster type is bold, very decorative, and not always easily classifiable as serif or sans serif because it is so ornate.

Display type was originally created for posters and advertisements, therefore you might hear display type referred to as poster type. Display typefaces can be based on classical roman letter forms, or they can take on entirely new shapes and forms.

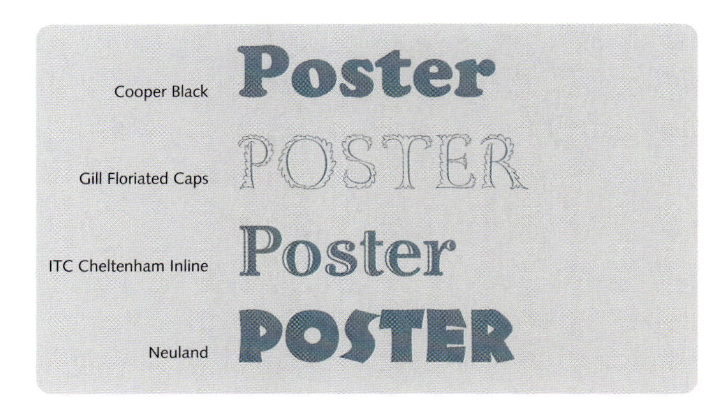

Figure 4.17 A variety of Poster typefaces

Display and Script types should be set larger than 14 pixels because they often have delicate and intricate forms that reproduce poorly at small sizes.

In addition, serif typefaces often have display versions. These tend to be proportionally the same as body text, except thinner and more severe looking. These display typefaces are used in headlines, titles, and mastheads.

Figure 4.18 Display typefaces

Typeface Families and Styles

A typeface family is a collection of styles that are similar in design and are meant to work together as a system when used for a book, signage system, or menu design. For instance, this book uses Syntax Roman for the body text, Syntax Bold for captions, and Syntax Black for the page number.

Both serif and sans serif typefaces often have additional type styles. The most common styles are roman, the normal typeface used for large passages of type; italic, the slanted or cursive version used for emphasis; and bold, the thicker version of the roman also used for emphasis and headlines. Although roman and italic designs are exclusive of one another, both roman and italic can have bold weights.

Also keep in mind that italics come in two forms. True italics is a separate design from the roman and follows the characteristics of cursive handwriting. Obliques are a version of the roman in which the type is slanted 10 to 15 degrees.

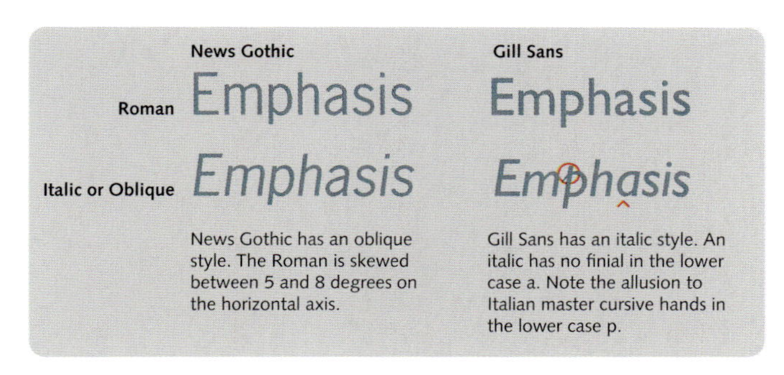

Figure 4.19 Italic and oblique typefaces

CASE

Most typefaces have uppercase and lowercase forms in a single style, but some typeface styles are only uppercase. Small capitals is a style in which both lowercase and uppercase letter sets have uppercase letter forms, but the lowercase letters comprise "smaller" capitals that are drawn at the x-height of the typeface. However, the smaller capitals are not merely a proportional reduction in size—they are drawn so that optically, they have the same weight or density as the uppercase form.

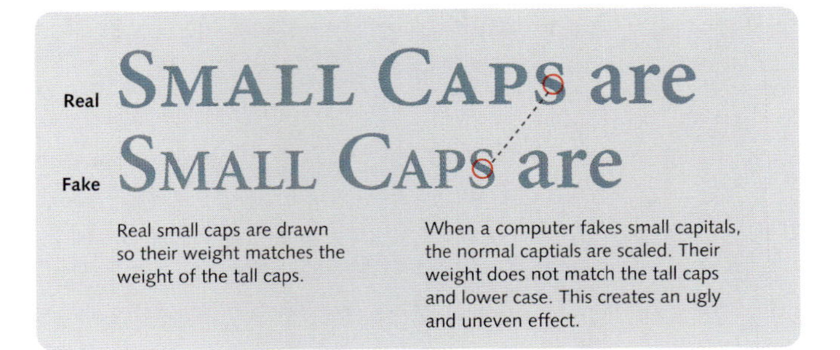

Figure 4.20 Small capitals

Although digital typography can fake small capitals, in my opinion, they look worse than true small capitals.

WEIGHT AND WIDTH

Weight refers to the thickness of a type style's stroke. Common weight styles are light, regular, bold, and heavy. Typefaces with many weight styles will have extra light or ultralight, as well as extra heavy or ultraheavy. Light is also called thin. Thicker styles can be referred to as extra bold, heavy, or black.

Width refers to the proportion of x-axis relative to the y-axis. Weight styles vary from condensed to normal width to expanded width. Condensed is also called narrow or compressed. Additional names for expanded are wide and extended. These two style variations can also be combined (Figure 4-21).

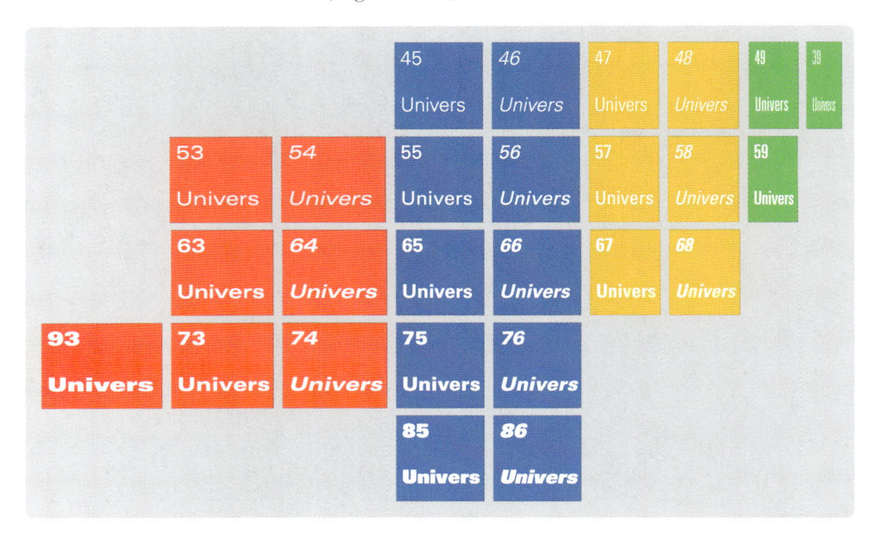

Figure 4.21 Type style weight and width example

Normally, setting body text in roman is recommended because it is most legible for long passages of text. Menus, however, do not contain long passages of text, and the text size on menus is larger than the size seen in the bodies of books and newspapers. So menu design presents more flexibility in the type styles you can choose than for headlines and body text.

Additional Styles in Typeface Families

Large typeface families have several, if not dozens of styles. In addition to styles previously mentioned, there are: old style figures, display, ligatures, swash characters, alternates, dingbats, and optical variations.

NUMBERS

Numbers come in lining and nonlining varieties. Lining figures all rest on the baseline, are the same height, and are available in almost any typeface. Old-style numbers vary in height and vertical position relative to the baseline. Some numbers rest on the baseline, on the descender line, or on the baseline but rise to the ascender line.

Lining figures are best used when setting numbers with text set in all capitals, while old-style numbers are more legible in text passages. Old-style numbers are a separate style found in serif typeface, although they are built into a few OpenType serif families. Old-style numbers are best for setting numbers in text passages, but can add distinction when used for page numbers or in headings.

Either style of numbering can have tabular or proportional spacing. Tabular spacing is used for setting numbers that need to line up for ledgers and financial tables. Proportional numbers are used when setting numbers in passages of text.

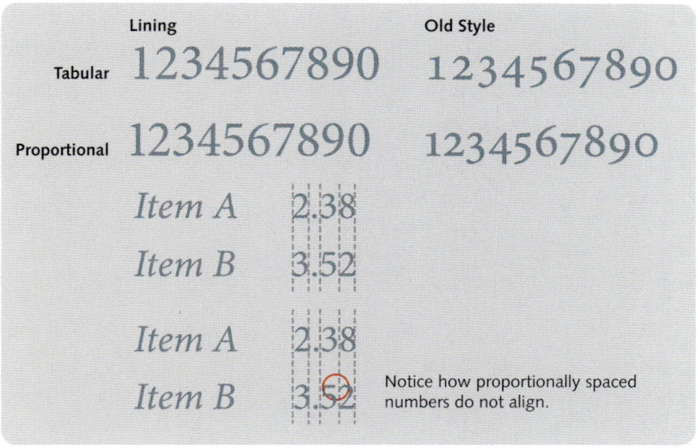

	Lining	Old Style
Tabular	1234567890	1234567890
Proportional	1234567890	1234567890

Item A 2.38
Item B 3.52

Item A 2.38
Item B 3.52

Notice how proportionally spaced numbers do not align.

Figure 4.22
Numbering styles

If you want the weight of the numbers to appears less heavy and you want a more even texture, using a slightly smaller type size can help lining numbers look better in a paragraph of text.

Several OpenType typefaces with the "Pro" designation have professional typographic features built in. One of these features is advanced control over how numbers are set. You choose a style using the fly out menu in Photoshop's Character palette.

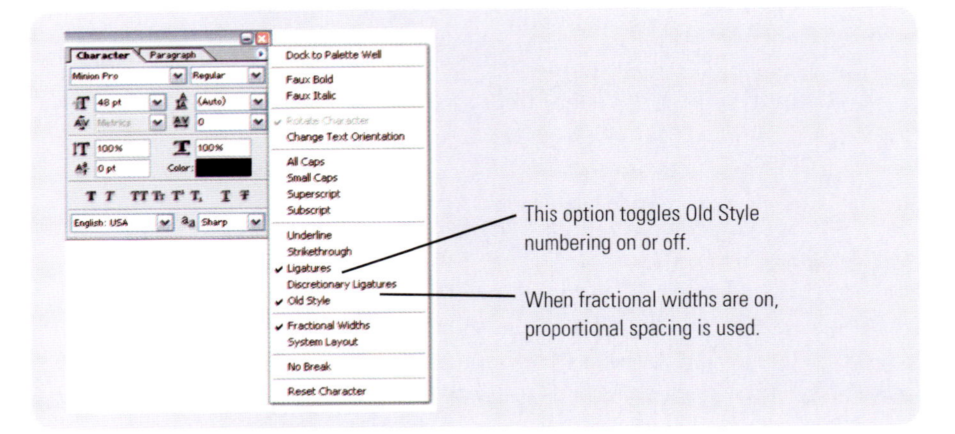

Figure 4.23 Photoshop's Character Palette and OpenType Features

Serif typefaces often have nonlining character styles, while it is rarer that a sans serif typeface has a nonlining style.

LIGATURES, SWASH CHARACTERS, AND ALTERNATES

Ligatures are two characters that connect or are spaced so closely together that they form a single character. Ligatures were originally created to compensate for awkward spacing between two letter forms. Ligatures have also been designed for decorative purposes. Swash characters and alternates are decorative alternatives for existing letter forms. Swash characters are mostly capital letters that start off a sentence or paragraph. Swash characters compliment text set in italics. Alternates are mostly designed for specific placement. Some alternates should only be used at the end or beginning of a line, but other alternates can be used inside text.

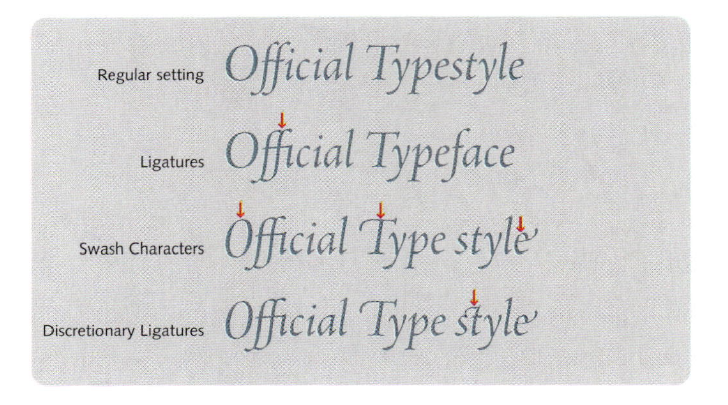

Figure 4.24 Ligatures and swash characters

DINGBATS

Dingbats, fleurons, and borders are symbols, decorative characters, and edge treatments. Dingbats can be used as informative symbols, such as bullets to punctuate a list of items, or as decorative marks, to end a story or article, for example. Fleurons are used as decorative marks in title pages, menus, and centered typography. Braces are the decorative edge treatments you often see on title pages or surrounding a small advertisement. They are created by placing eight different characters of a typeface, one for each corner and one for each side around the edges.

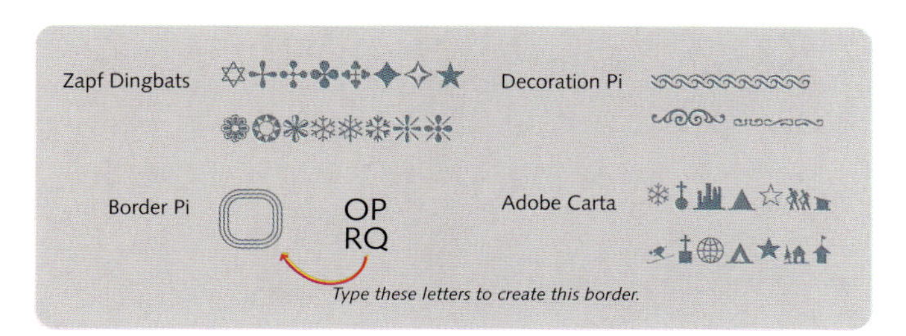

Figure 4.25 Dingbat examples

OPTICAL VARIATIONS

Optical variations were created for newspaper and book printing to reproduce text better at small sizes and to make text more compelling at large sizes. Some typefaces have designs for captions, small body text, and headlines. These designs vary the weight of the strokes and some do little tricks at the joins of strokes to "capture" more light. In Figure 4-26, three styles of Warnock Pro are shown. The display style has thinner cross strokes and should be set in a large size. The regular style is meant for body text. The caption style is subtly bolder and has a more even weight between vertical and horizontal strokes-these design elements make it easier to read at the smaller sizes.

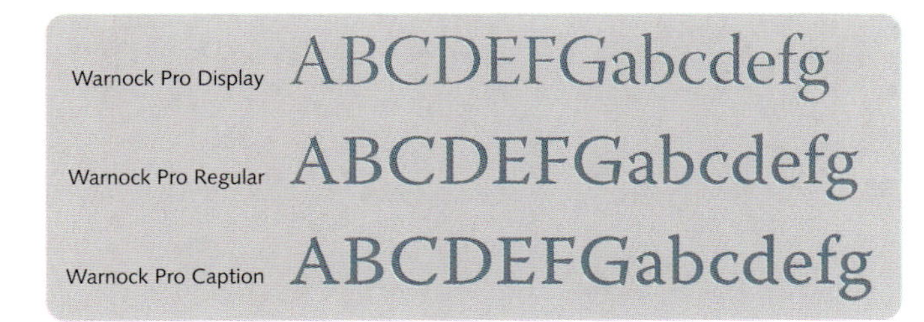

Figure 4.26 Optical variations

Punctuation and Typographic Marks

Proper punctuation and typographic marks show professionalism and craft. They also communicate and look better than the "one size fits all" marks provided on the keyboard. The two most common mistakes are not setting quotation marks properly and using a hyphen to interject a clause or show a range.

HYPHENS AND EM AND EN DASHES

Hyphens should only be used for hyphenation and compound words. Em dashes are used for interjection—like this. An en dash is a slightly narrower mark for separating two numbers in a range (e.g., 2002–2003), hyphenating open compounds (e.g., chapter index–style menu), or comparing words of equal weight (e.g., left–right alignment).

QUOTATION, TICK, AND INCH MARKS

Tick marks are what most people think of as a proper apostrophe and quotation marks. This could not be further from the truth! These two characters that share the same key and sit to the left of the Enter key are a remnant from the days when PCs had dark caves for screens and graphical user interfaces (GUIs) were just another project at Parc. At the time, developers probably never considered that people would one day use computers to create professional-looking typography and felt this one-size-fits-all approach was economical. Real quote marks are not straight, or neutered as some say, but face right or left to indicate whether they are opening or closing a quotation.

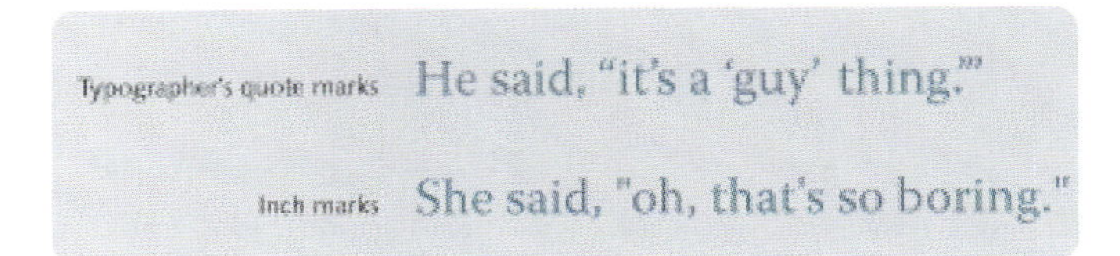

Figure 4.27 Quotation and tick marks

ADDITIONAL MARKS AND SYMBOLS

Most professionally created typefaces also include symbols for business, math, currency, and punctuation (e.g., accents and other diacritical marks used in many languages). For instance you might need the registered, trademark, or copyright symbols if you are producing DVDs of copyrighted material.

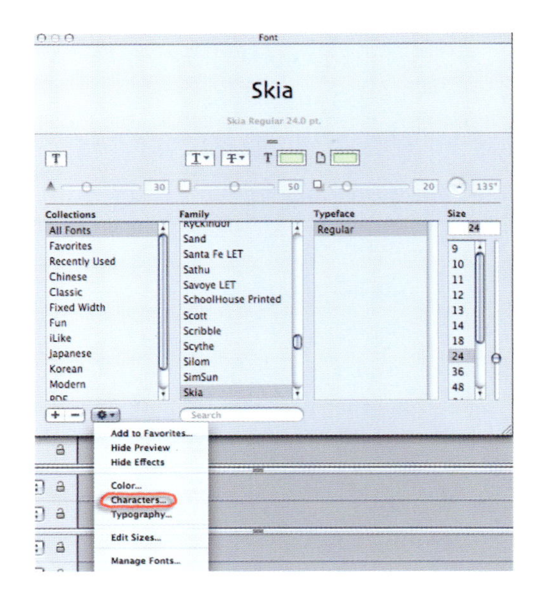

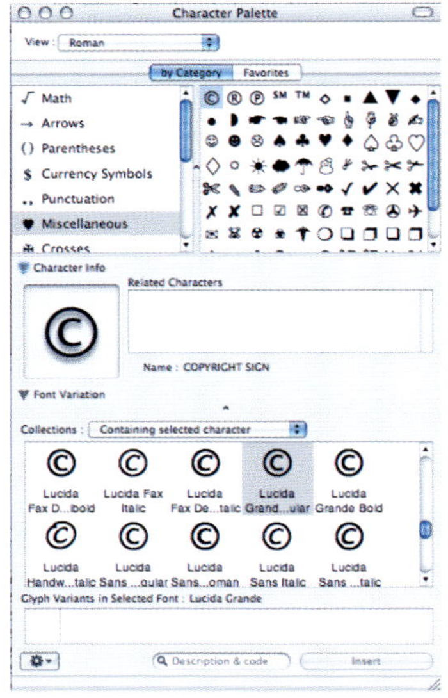

Figure 4.28 Character Map utility

ENTERING SYMBOLS

Creating professional-looking typography takes a little more effort. The main problem is that the keyboard is not set up easily to access the proper punctuation and other typographic symbols. You have a few options when it comes to adding these characters.

- Double-click the character in the Character Palette to insert it.
- Copy and Paste the character from the Character Palette.
- Memorize the keystroke combination for the desired character.

You can access the Character Palette by clicking the Action button on the Font Panel and selecting the Characters option.

Type Measurements

Besides having a classification system, a nomenclature, and a spectrum of styles, typography has a measurement system. This system mostly was based on the constraints of letterpress printing, or movable type. With this printing method, each letter of type is a single wood block or metal slug. These blocks are put together to form words, the words are spaced with letter space blocks to form lines, and strips of lead are placed between the lines to space multiple lines of text.

SIZE

The basic measurement of type is its size. With digital typography, type size is determined by the distance from the bottom of the descender to the top of the ascender.

Figure 4.29 How type is measured

Although print design measurements are based on points and picas, DVD Studio Pro measures type using pixels.

When determining text size, remember that the viewer of a DVD sees text differently than the reader of a book. The text on a printed page is probably a foot or two from the reader. The text on a DVD menu can be a foot or two from the reader if the DVD is viewed on a computer and the viewer is in front of it, but if the viewer is watching the DVD on a television or on a projected surface, the distance can be several to dozens of feet from the viewer. Given these conditions, it is important not to make your type too small because it will be illegible. Aesthetically speaking, text should not be too large because it can appear heavy handed. If you know the environment in which the DVD will be viewed, deciding on the appropriate text size is relatively easy because you can test how it looks with the medium the viewer will be using.

SPACING

All typefaces should have an em space and en space. The em space is a horizontal space that was originally determined by the width of an uppercase "M," but now it is equal to the font size. The em space is the widest continuous space available in a typeface. An en space is half the width of an em space. A normal character space is between a quarter and half of an em space. The em dash (—) and en dash (–) are determined by their corresponding spaces.

Narrow IT'S SO WIDE.
Normal IT'S SO WIDE.
Wide IT'S SO WIDE.

Figure 4.30 Examples of tracking

TRACKING

One point of confusion is the difference between tracking and kerning. Tracking is the addition or removal of uniform space between characters in a range of text. Loose or positive tracking spreads the words far apart; tight or negative tracking brings the words closer together.

LEADING

As mentioned earlier, varying widths of lead strips create the vertical space between lines of text in movable type. Because lead was used, this measurement is called leading. Leading is also referred to as interline spacing or line spacing, with leading and line spacing the two most popular. In digital typography, leading is measured as the vertical space between adjacent baselines. Leading and type size are related in fractional form when describing the two 9 point type on 12 point leading, or 9/12.

The advantage of digital typography is that a whole number does not work like a decimal number might (e.g., 13.5 pixels of leading).

Good leading guides the reader's eyes effortlessly and without fatigue. Thus, the relationship between the type size and leading is crucial to making text legible. The problem occurs when lines of text have little to no leading. Although a headline or title can be interesting with little to negative leading, stifling a paragraph with negative or zero leading causes the eye to wander vertically and get "off track." Similarly, very loose leading makes it hard for the eye to transition from one line of text to another.

Typeface Technology and Formats

When moving designs across computers or exchanging files with colleagues or clients, you need to know what typefaces are used and their file format. These typefaces should be legally installed on all machines where menu design will take place.

When to use Tracking

Many people ask, "When do I use tracking versus kerning?" I'd respond that there are no hard and fast rules, while advising that tracking is the power tool and kerning is a tool for making small adjustments.

You can apply only tracking or only kerning, or use both. Consistent optical space or even texture is the objective. Text with an even texture is easier to read because the eyes move at a constant pace and are not interrupted by jarring spaces or cramped letter forms.

I use tracking in the following instances.

- *To fit body text.* In most cases, rewriting will solve this problem, but if text cannot be rewritten, apply tracking to see if this helps. Excessive tracking may cause overly-tight or loose spacing, making text hard to read.
- *To make adjustments when there isn't time to kern.* Often, tracking produces acceptable results. Remember, you can always undo it if it doesn't look good and make small kerning adjustments.

KERNING

Kerning is the space between two letter forms. Like tracking, loose or positive kerning adds space between two letters: tight or negative kerning brings the letter forms closer together. Good kerning shows the same amount of optical space between letter forms. Kern letter forms so that the physical space is equal and legible (Figure 4-31).

When to use Kerning

- *When setting a headline or title in uppercase.* These text forms receive a lot of attention. Remember that uppercase has its roots in carved stone, and that each letter form is strong enough to stand alone. In this case, I normally do not trust tracking, so I kern the type for proper and consistent spacing.
- *When setting text for buttons.* Because viewers focus on the buttons of a DVD menu, it is important that the text look evenly spaced. More often than not, small type does not always render evenly at the coarse resolution of video.
- *When using a poorly spaced typeface.* Change the typeface if possible. But if a client has a corporate or required typeface, kerning and even tracking are the best way to deal with this problem.

Tip: In the days of lead type, a kern was the part of the letter form that extended beyond the type block

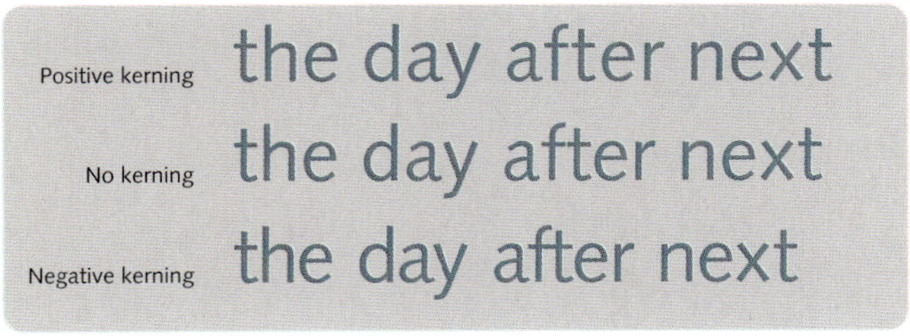

Positive kerning the day after next

No kerning the day after next

Negative kerning the day after next

Figure 4.31 Kerning examples

Postscript, TrueType, and OpenType

Before Photoshop built Adobe's second tower in San Jose, Postscript built the first. Postscript is a page description language invented at Adobe that laser printers and offset presses use to produce printed material. The letter forms in a Postscript typeface are described mathematically by this language. If you have ever converted type to outlines in Illustrator, you can see how Postscript creates form with Post-script's Bezier curves, which is much different than with the brush or pen! Postscript type is the typeface format for professional designers and does not work across platforms.

TrueType is a format developed by Apple and Microsoft and creates letter forms by quadratic, rather than Bezier, curves. Although some might argue the merits of one format over the other, I have relied on Postscript type because that is what I have always done. As long as the type is properly drawn and spaced, you should feel free to use whatever works for you.

Figure 4.32 TrueType, Postscript, and OpenType icons

OpenType was developed to solve some of this confusion. OpenType is essentially a wrapper technology that embeds Postscript or TrueType information into a single type-

Table 4-1: Type Foundries

FOUNDRY	TYPE OFFERING	FORMATS
Adobe Systems, Inc. http://www.adobe.com/type	Adobe licenses designs from other foundries but also has a collection of revival and new designs called Adobe Originals.	Postscript and OpenType
Berthold Type Foundry http://bertholdtypes.com	Berthold is an independent type foundry with an impressive collection of classical revivals.	Postscript and OpenType
Agfa Monotype http://www.monotype.com	Agfa purchased Linotype and Monotype, two of the larger type foundries. They have the largest collection of original type.	Postscript and TrueType
The Font Bureau http://www.fontbureau.com	The Font Bureau has a high-quality catalog of type from custom type development, as well as type developed for retail release.	Postscript and TrueType
Font Shop http://www.fontshop.com	The Font Shop has an eclectic mix of type and offers the Font Book, an up-to-date catalog of typeface designs from the past and the present.	Postscript and TrueType
The Foundry http://www.thefoundry.co.uk	A small type foundry that produces highly original typefaces that are more than just revival designs.	Postscript and TrueType
Emigre http://www.emigre.com	Perhaps the trendiest of the type foundries. They continue to create original type and revival designs with a unique spin.	Postscript, TrueType, and OpenType
Hoefler Type Foundry http://www.typography.com	Jonathan Hoefler and Tobias Frere-Jones have teamed together to produce type for private clients but also offer retail typefaces.	Postscript and TrueType
House Industries http://www.houseindustries.com	Another trendy foundry producing original typefaces and nostalgic revivals of period typographic styles.	Postscript and TrueType

face. It also can contain thousands of characters in a single typeface, whereas the other two formats top out in the hundreds. With larger character sets, Asian languages can "fit" within a single typeface, and Roman typefaces can combine several type families into one. OpenType with the "Pro" designation have additional characters for more advanced typography. These additional characters can be accessed from the Character palette's flyout menu in Photoshop (Figure 4.28).

TYPEFACE FOUNDRIES

Garamond is not Garamond in all cases. Adobe Garamond, Stempel Garamond, and ITC Garamond are noticeably different interpretations of the French original. By knowing how to classify and examine type, you can tell the difference between Stempel Garamond, which is a good interpretation of the original, and ITC, which is a dated interpretation.

It is often said that type is like tea—you can never have too many varieties. New type, like new tea, can be refreshing. If you are looking for the latest varieties or a specific typeface, I've listed a few type foundries in Table 4-1 to browse.

Specifying Body and Display Faces

My favorite activity is choosing type for a project. This is a great time to visit the type foundries and see what is new, or to choose a typeface that is appropriate, but that I have not used before. In specifying type, consider the following questions, activities, and guidelines.

1. Questions

- Is there a corporate typeface? If not, what typefaces seem stylistically suitable for the design? What conveys the mood and message? Do you hope your design will look old, new, rough, fresh, serene, fun?
- Does the text need to be flexible? Will links have long names? Will there be a lot of onscreen text?
- Does the typeface look legible at DVD resolution?
- What are the hierarchical relationships between text elements? How can size, color, font family, and style create hierarchy?
- Of the typefaces you have chosen, which have multiple styles?

2. Activities:

- Pick a couple each of serif, sans serif and display typefaces.
- Create studies in which you mix up to three styles from up to two typefaces.
- When settled on a system, add size, color, and the imagery to the experiment. Create storyboard animations, do quick compositions in Photoshop.
- Create three or four approaches. Print them out, look at them on screen, look at them on a television. Get the opinion of others around you.
- Pick one approach and document it.

3. **Guidelines**

- Keep your type experiments small and controlled. If each typeface is a single voice, it becomes clear that effective communication is created from fewer voices and not many.
- Avoid mixing types that share the same classification and are similar. It fails to achieve variety and creates uneven texture because of the small differences in the type styles.
- Do not fake type styles. Do not create fake bold, italic, small capitals, condensed, or extended type. It looks unprofessional and cheap and rarely does the job as well as type that is designed for the purpose.
- Apply the proper letter spacing and leading. Spacing that is overly tight or too loose creates poor texture and looks like mud on a television.
- Use proper punctuation. Careless punctuation is an obvious sign of amateur typography.
- Do not mix justification styles. Centered headlines and footers with flush left buttons is inconsistent.
- Be ready to break a rule, but do it for a good reason. Break more than two and you run the risk of committing bad typography to screen.

The Purpose of Grids

Grids help establish order to a design. Order imparts emphasis and meaning to elements in the design. Grids, when applied across a series of menus, creates consis-tency, which in turn allows the viewer to remember button placement: consistency also facilitates production because text blocks, buttons, images, and video are standardized to fit the grid.

Table 4-2: Screen sizes for NTSC and PAL video

STANDARD	SCREEN FORMAT	PIXEL ASPECT RATIO[a]	RESOLUTION
NTSC	Standard (4:3)	Computer (1)	720 x 534
		DVD-Video (0.9)	720 x 480
	Widescreen (16:9)	Computer (1)	864 x 480
		DVD-Video (1.2)	720 x 480[b]
PAL	Standard (4:3)	Computer (1)	720 x 576
		DVD-Video (1.066)	720 x 576
	Widescreen (16:9)	Computer (1)	1024 x 576
		DVD-Video (1.42)	720 x 576

a. This column lists the pixel aspect ratio in parentheses.
b. Includes a flag that instructs the player to interpret the image as anamorphic.

Screen Sizes

DVD menus, as mentioned in Chapter Two, have two sizes for both NTSC and PAL video standards. For convenience, I have listed them again in Table 4-2. The menu size and screen format is crucial in designing DVD menus because they dictate how much flexibility you have in creating a grid for the screen.

Parts of a Grid

Grids in most computer programs are Cartesian grids; the grid is constructed by a single square unit. All columns and rows are the same size. A typographic or layout grid is different. It has the following parts: margins, columns, rows, and horizontal and vertical gutters. The margin is the space between the edge of the screen and the beginning of the grid. The margin should not be smaller than the video-safe margin. Columns are the vertical sections on the screen and have width. Rows are the horizontal sections on the screen and have height. Columns are equal in width and rows are equal in height. Gutters are the spaces between adjacent columns or rows and provide padding to help legibility. These too should be consistent in width and height. The space between two adjacent columns and two adjacent rows is a field.

Items placed on the grid are not limited to one column. An object can occupy one, two, or three columns. Columns and rows that are consistent in width and height create uniformity, and the eye picks up on this internal order.

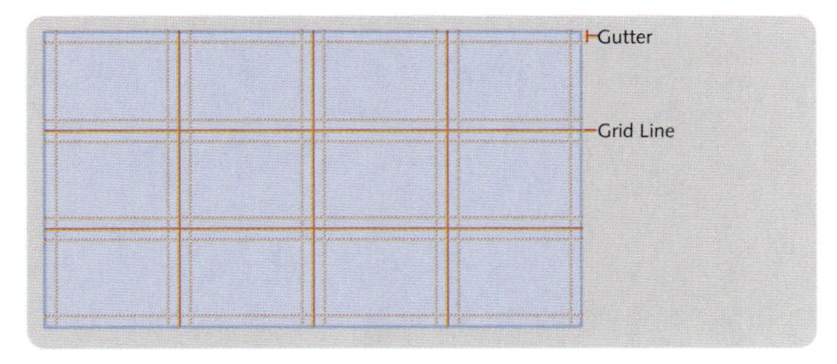

Figure 4.34 Parts of a grid

Video-Safe Margins

Title-safe and action-safe margins frame the video's visible safe zones. The title-safe margin is the inside square and is the guideline for placing text. You should not place important text outside of the inner square. The action-safe margin is a guide for im-

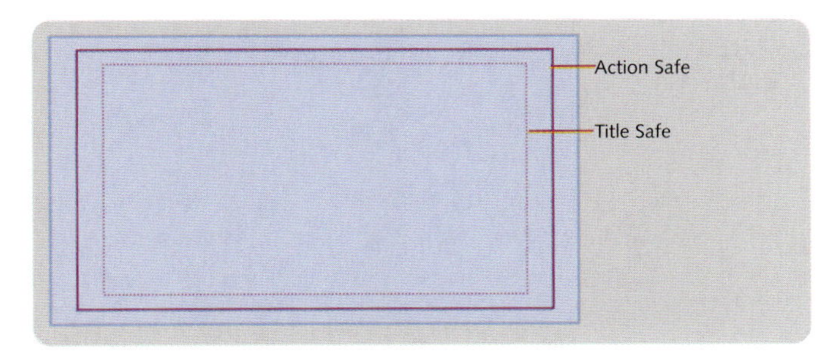

Figure 4.35 Video-Safe Margins

portant action, composition, and actors. No shots should be framed so that important elements in the shot are outside of the outer square.

Photoshop 7 cannot show safe area margins, but Photoshop CS can optionally create guides in place of the margins.

Safe zones are required because the majority of consumer televisions have over scan, which crops the outer edges of the frame, allowing the center of the picture to be enlarged. To make things worse, the amount of overscan varies across televisions, which is why the safe margins are so important. At the very least, turn on the the safe area margins to ensure that your menus will display properly. For best results, preview your video on a television monitor connected to your computer.

Creating Grids

Before you create the grid, you need to understand the content. Ask the following questions before creating a grid.

- How many buttons will be on any given screen? Will the buttons be text only, image only, or have both text and image?
- Will there be associated imagery on the menu? Will the imagery be a collage or separate elements? Does the design require placement for a logo, company name, or project title?
- What are the text needs outside of buttons? Will it be a sentence or a short paragraph?
- What is the hierarchy of all the elements on the screen? Can they be divided into groups? What will be the most visually important item to present?

One approach to creating a grid is to place the most important design element by itself on the Photoshop file and determine how the grid supports it and additional content. Ask yourself, what will be above and below it and what will be to the left and right of it? What are the spatial requirements for these elements? Create and space columns consistently. Create and space rows consistently. If everything does not fit harmoniously, resize the elements and the grid until they do. The height for gutters between rows should be the same as the leading. The width for gutters between columns should be large enough so the eye reads columns separately and easily. From this exercise, you also should have developed the size and placement of text, images, and buttons.

ESTABLISHING HIERARCHY WITH A GRID

Now that you have a grid, the process of creating hierarchy becomes easier. The grid system and the hierarchy is often created simultaneously. You rank the importance elements, group them by meaning if necessary, and then devise a grid to support these relationships. The elements that constitute the hierarchy are the title, any meaningful imagery or footage, primary buttons, secondary buttons if they are needed, and supplementary text and graphic elements.

All elements do not need to start in the same column. They can be staggered. Remember that grid uniformity ensures consistency and trains the eye. In applying the grid, it should not appear mechanical, but organic. This feeling is created by properly emphasizing each element by its placement, size, and color. The design should lead the eye through the design. Where is the opening or where does the eye begin and where does the eye end?

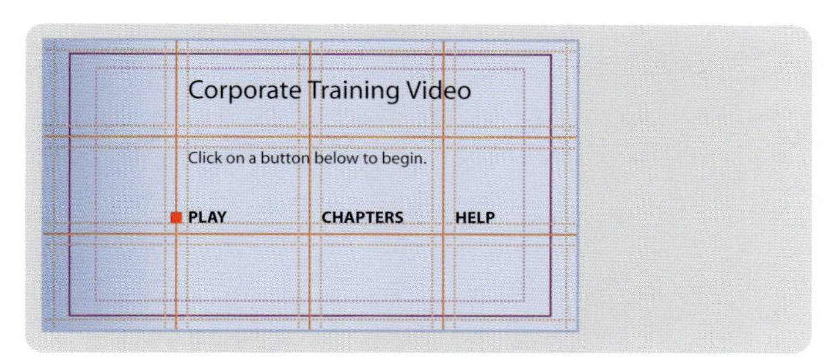

Figure 4.36 Spanning columns in a grid

Using Color

Color beautifies, but do not forget that it also creates mood and meaning. For instance, color can symbolize an idea, an event, or an entity. Think of red, white, and blue; red hot; green with envy. Do not let these or other cliches define color usage, but be aware that color has physical, political, psychological, and cultural connotations.

In communication and information design, the judicious use of color creates separation between elements, highlights important information, and communicates readiness. For instance, the sections in this book are color-coded to signal a change in subject matter.

Figure 4.37 Color in information graphics

The meaning of color can play a crucial part in user interface. Color is often used to indicate selection, activation, disablement, and whether or not something is a link. Color, however, should not be the only cue because some viewers with sight impairment cannot discern between colors. Color combined with a change in form, position, size, or other embellishment is a more effective way to communicate change.

Color Models

There are three common models for producing color: the color wheel, offset printing inks, and the color primaries of light.

SUBTRACTIVE COLOR MODELS

The color wheel and offset printing inks are both subtractive color models because combining their color primaries at full intensity theoretically creates black. In subtractive color models, adding color creates less color. A subtractive color model produces color by reflecting and absorbing color wavelengths. For instance, when you look at a color printout of yellow, the yellow is reflected and cyan and magenta are absorbed.

If you are only familiar with one of these models, it is most likely the color wheel. The color wheel is created by mixing three primary colors of red, yellow, and blue.

Mixing any two colors creates secondary colors, and the colors in between the secondary colors create tertiary colors.

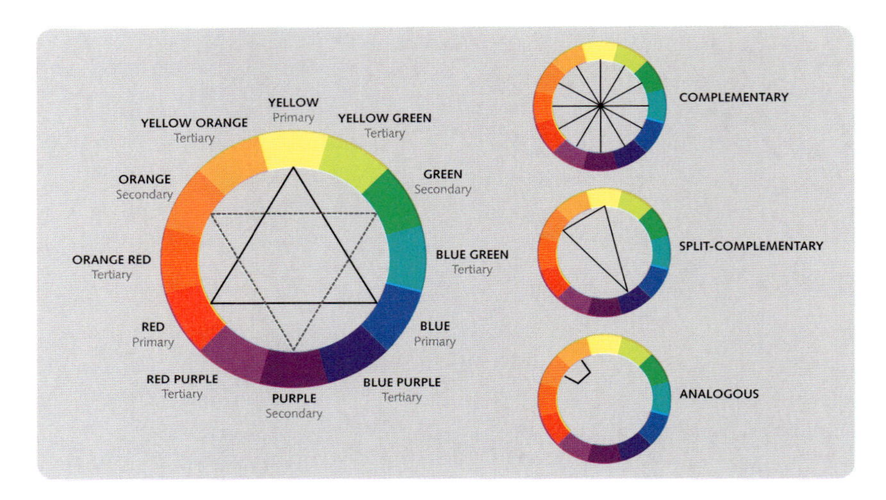

Figure 4.38 Color wheel and color relationships

RELATIONSHIPS ESTABLISHED BY THE COLOR WHEEL

The color wheel establishes fundamental color relationships. These are monochromatic, analogous, achromatic, complementary, neutral, and split complementary.

- **Monochromatic** colors share the same hue but vary in tint or shade. Tints are created by increasing a color's brightness or adding white, and shades are created by decreasing a color's brightness or adding black.
- **Analogous** colors are adjacent on the color wheel and are close in hue.
- **Achromatic** colors are shades of gray, black, and white.
- **Complementary** colors occupy opposite positions on the color wheel. Their hues are 180 degrees apart and can be thought of as two extremes. This effect helps create contrast that is rich and often symbolic.
- **Neutral** colors are formed from a single hue and varying amounts of the hue's complement.
- **Split complementary** colors are defined by the relationship between three colors: one color and the two that are adjacent to its complement. Just as its name implies, the first color splits the complement and takes the color on either side.

CMYK

Offset printing often uses CMYK (cyan, magenta, yellow, and black) to reproduce color. Each color is used for a specific plate of color. The plates are etched with halftone patterns, and when the plates combine on paper, they create tonal and color ranges.

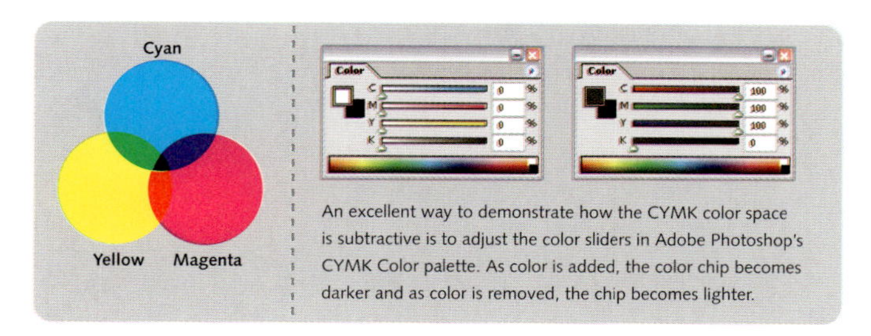

Figure 4.39 Offset printing color model

ADDITIVE COLOR MODELS

Television and computer monitors render color with red, green, and blue (RGB) light. This model is additive because when the three colors are equally combined to their full extent, they create white, which contains the full range of colors. This can be seen when white light is split with a prism or when rainbows are created by the refraction and reflection of light in water droplets.

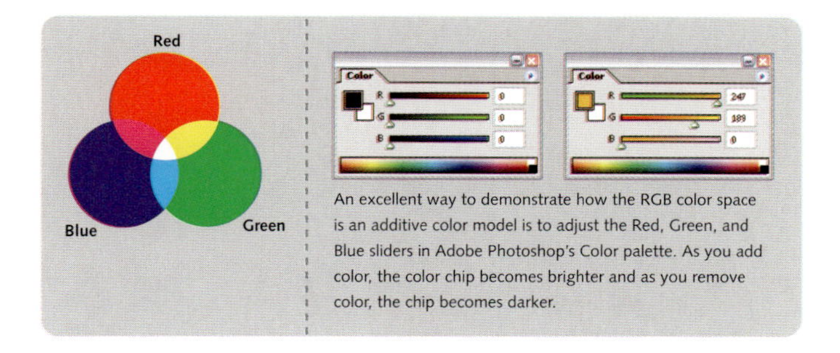

Figure 4.40 RGB color model

In designing DVD menus, you will use RGB or HSB (hue, saturation, and brightness) color models. Rather than divide white by equal parts of red, green, and blue, HSB splits color by the color's hue, saturation, and brightness. Hue, or temperature as it's sometimes called, is the shade of color from warm to cool. Saturation is the color's intensity; crimson is high saturation, whereas dull gray colors have no saturation.

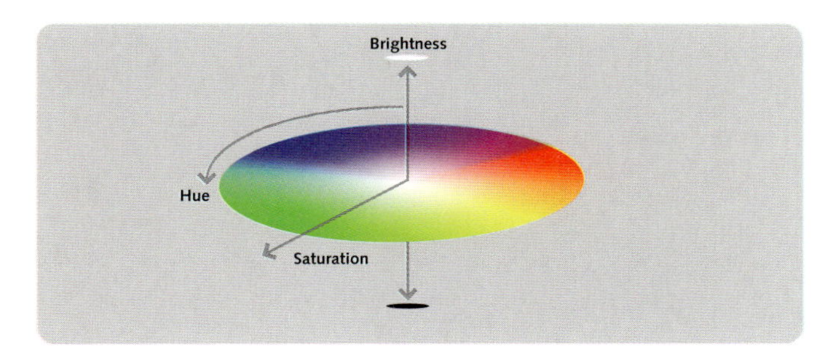

Figure 4.41 HSB color model

Brightness, as it implies, is the color's lightness or darkness. The HSB color model is an effective model for creating tints and shades of a particular color.

COLOR RESOLUTION

Color resolution is not image resolution. Image resolution is the measure of how fine or detailed an image is. Color resolution is the number of colors available to reproduce an image. The first personal computers had 1-bit black and white displays. In the late 1980s, grayscale displays became more prevalent. Grayscale monitors could reproduce 256 levels of gray when coupled with an 8-bit grayscale video card. As computer video technology improved and the first color displays were introduced, 8-bit or 256-color displays became prevalent.

Most computers today have displays that support 24-bit color, which reproduces approximately 16.7 million colors. Because each channel of color (red, green, and blue) is given 8 bits of color, 256 x 256 x 256 = 16,777,216 possible colors.

GAMUT

Gamut is the range of reproducible colors for a device. The gamut for a subtractive color model like offset printing is much smaller than that of an additive model like RGB, which is even smaller than that of the human eye.

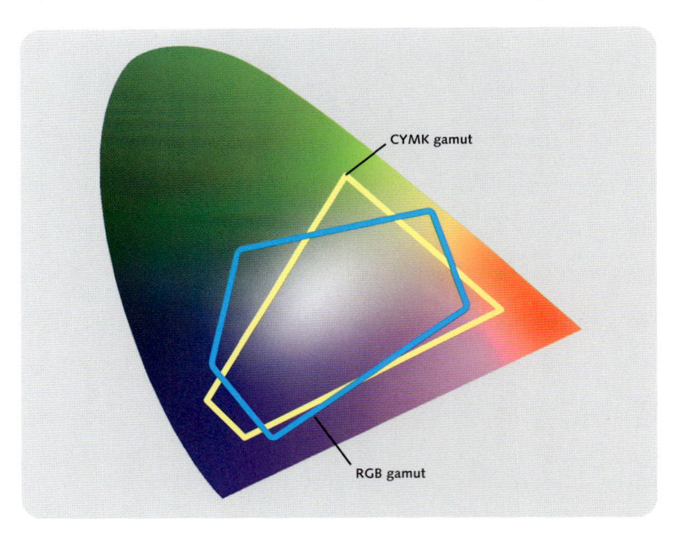

Figure 4.42 Gamuts for additive and subtractive color models

Color Sketches

When creating color sketches, consider the client's corporate identity guidelines. Think about the mood, the effect, and the message you are creating. What I find useful is creating color studies in Photoshop. I create a file with a solid white background, and I mix colors with the Color palette and put fill colors that I like onto squares, each on its own layer. I move the colors next to each other, create new ones, turn old ones off, and compare the new colors, then create a gray background and see how the colors compare to the background.

After determining how many colors are needed, I create a set of tints and shades for each color. Tints are created by adding brightness and shades by removing brightness. Document these colors by entering the RGB model for each color. Specify how each color is used. Is it the text color, background color, or highlight color?

Imagery

The subject of imagery could fill an entire book, or perhaps a dozen books, so I will cover the subject only briefly. Ask yourself the following questions when thinking about imagery.

- Medium and technique. How are the images created? Are they photographs or illustrations? Are they computer generated, like 3-D animation? Are they enhanced with filters, color processing, masking, or collage? Whatever the technique, be consistent.
- Symbolism and iconography. Do the images have any significance or meaning beyond being backgrounds? Certain techniques, such as masking and color processing, can enhance an image's symbolic power.
- Composition. Composition should be pleasing and should direct the eye to important information. Where does the eye begin, and where do you want the eye to end or focus?
- Combining type and image. How will the text and imagery work together? Will they overlap or have their own spaces on the screen? Will the imagery be in the background or occupy a space defined by the design grid?

Animation

Animation approximates motion through sequential imagery. Good animation, however, has spirit, cleverly exaggerates reality, and enhances a menu's aesthetic, communication, and entertainment value.

This chapter presents the following topics:

- The animation process.
- Animation principles.
- Common properties to animate.

The Animation Process

The animation process begins with an idea that is turned into a script or a storyboard. After the concepts presented in the storyboard are approved, animation and production begins. Test renders and animatics turn into fully rendered animations that are then imported into DVD Studio Pro and integrated with other assets to create menus.

Coming Up with an Idea

Ideas for animating motion menus differ from project to project and have to be appropriate to the material being shown. For example, it would not make sense to show something depressing with material that is meant to be inspirational. Often, the client will have some ideas, but do familiarize yourself with the content before beginning to animate because it might provide you with a host of ideas.

The process of animating a motion menu is a superset of the design process. Before anything is animated, something needs to be designed, photographed, shot on video, recorded on audio tape, or illustrated. But before any of this happens, the animation has to be scripted. I like to start by jotting down a few ideas:

Where possible, I have related the topics discussed to designing motion menus for DVDs.

A postcard of Alamo Square rotates onto screen. When it is in place, the menu title slides down from above. The buttons fade into place.

With these few ideas, I might draw a quick sketch or a couple of thumbnail sketches that begin to form a storyboard (Figure 5.1).

If you need other forms of inspiration, I would suggest looking at the title sequences that start most films. Over the last 15 years, there has been a real renaissance in film title design that has influenced most of the motion graphics seen on television, DVD menu design, and the Internet.

Figure 5.1 Ideas and thumbnail sketches

Creating Storyboards

Whereas words communicate verbally, a storyboard communicates a narrative visually. Storyboards are another development of early animated films. Directors of live-action films took notice and quickly adopted the storyboard format by hiring artists to create storyboards from their scripts. Storyboards present an idea conceptually. They indicate the camera angle, the position of characters and objects, the lighting to be used, and the action that occurs. This versatility makes them the most useful planning tool for animation.

Although DVD menus are short in length, storyboards can still help in the planning and production process because they are easy and quick to produce. Keep a supply of pencils and felt tip markers of varying thicknesses. I usually begin by sketching lightly in graphite and then adding tone with charcoal. A can of spray fixative is sug-

Figure 5.2

gested if you do not want the charcoal to smudge. Additional detail or thinner dark accents can be applied with felt markers or india ink and brush.

You can also use a drawing program such as Illustrator to create storyboards quickly. Figure 5.3 shows a system that you can use to specify movement, transition, and other visual properties in your storyboards.

These symbols and storyboard templates are available in the Animation folder. They are in Illustrator and PDF format.

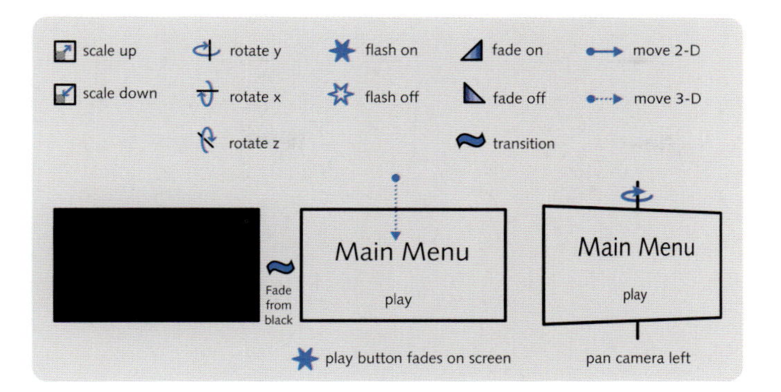

Figure 5.3 Storyboard notation

Animation Principles and Menu Design

The principles of animation were developed by Frank Thomas and Ollie Johnston (*The Illusion of Life*—Disney Animation, 1981, NYC, Hyperion) at Walt Disney in the early 1930s, and they remain a valuable set of criteria for developing and critiquing any animated work.

Figure 5.4 is an abridged version of their list that I have tailored to the design of DVD motion menus. I have taken the liberty to organize the 12 principles into three categories: variation, combination, and execution. Variation creates the difference between one frame and the next. Combination makes animations more complex by animating more than one property simultaneously. Execution is how the animation is presented and how it is received by the viewer. It is important to remember that all of these principles work together in creating effective animation.

VARIATION	COMBINATION	EXECUTION
Timing	Secondary Animation	Line of Action
Exaggeration	Anticipation	Staging
Squash and Stretch	Overlap	Craft
Ease In and Out	Follow Through	Appeal

Figure 5.4 Principles of animation

Timing

Timing, or pacing, is the speed at which the animation moves. Quick pacing implies sudden actions and behavior, whereas slow pacing implies slower movement. When a heavy weight falls off of a table, quick pacing shows the severe gravitational pull on the weight. When a feather falls of the table, slower pacing shows the floating properties of the feather.

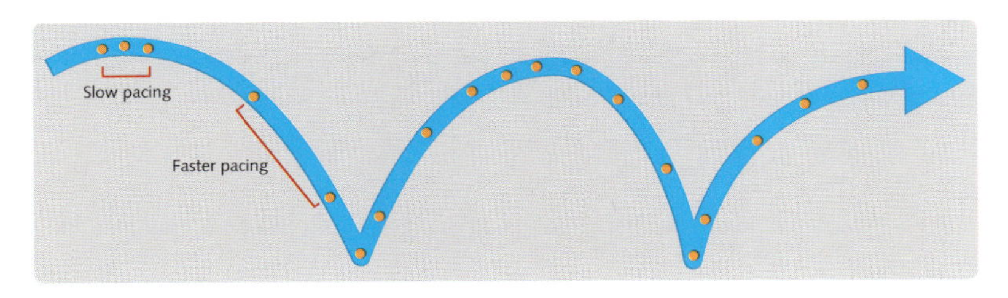

Figure 5.5 Timing of a bouncing object

KEYFRAMES AND INBETWEENS

A keyframe is an instance of any animated object at a specific time. Any animation requires at least two keyframes. The use of keyframes was developed when film studios and animation houses began creating animated films with teams of animators. Lead animators would draw the "key" poses for a character, and assistant animators would complete the sequence by drawing the frames in between. With digitally created motion graphics, you set the values for keyframes, and the computer creates the frames in between. In Figure 5.6, the red points on the path are keyframes and represent key positions in the ball's movement.

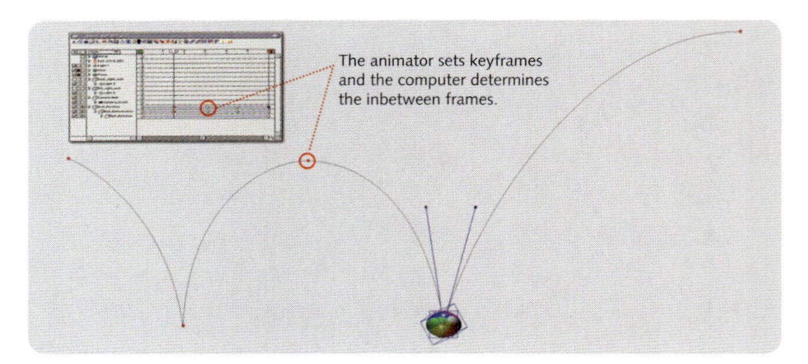

Figure 5.6 Keyframes

Exaggeration

As mentioned earlier, animation is an approximation of motion and emotions. When this approximation is pushed well beyond the bounds of reality, it becomes exaggeration, and it begins to be a parody of reality. Not only can exaggeration be funny, but it also adds emphasis. Figure 5.7 examines the difference between adding exaggeration to a bouncing ball and not applying any exaggeration.

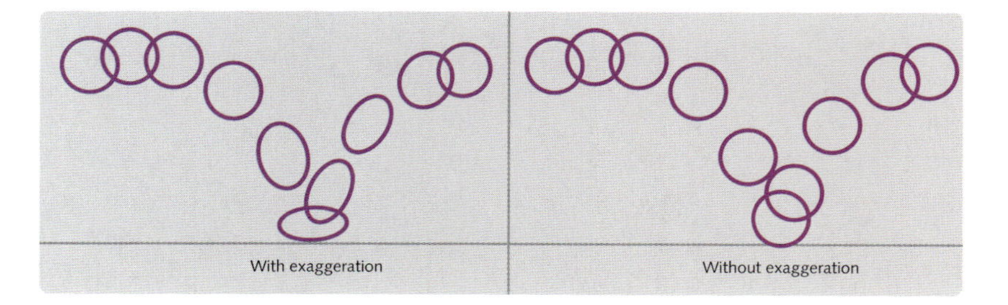

Figure 5.7 With and without exaggeration

Squash and Stretch

Squash and stretch is an animation technique that illustrates the effects of gravity and force on volume and shape. To see this principle in real life, observe the flexing of muscles, or watch a rubber ball bounce. Notice how the arm swells when the bicep is contracted and how a ball flattens and widens as it hits the ground.

Squash and stretch adds believability and interest to animation. In order for squash and stretch to be truly believable, the volume of an object is consistent even though the shape changes.

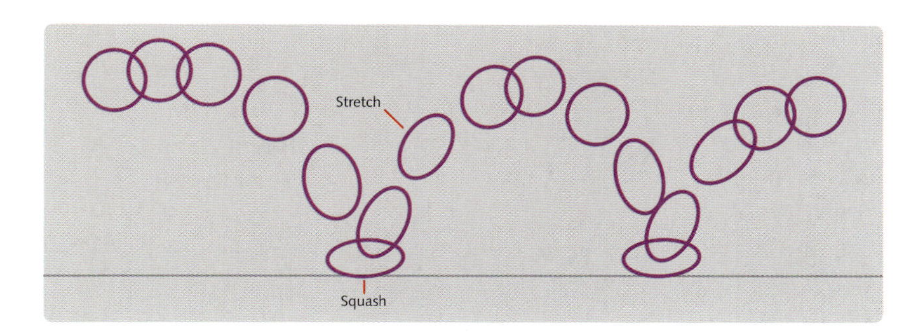

Figure 5.8 Squash and stretch

I cannot tell you which principles are appropriate to apply to your menu design, but I have listed examples of how they can be applied to headline text, buttons, or any design element in a menu. Common techniques are a rolling baseline, objects that inflate or deflate, and bouncing objects.

Ease In and Ease Out

In reality, objects in motion do not accelerate or decelerate suddenly because they resist gravity, wind, liquid, or other physical barriers. For instance, a car does not reach 25 miles per hour immediately upon ignition, nor does it stop suddenly when the brakes are pressed. A car, like most moving objects, gradually accelerates and decelerates. Ease in and ease out mimic the gradual transition between movement and stillness.

In addition, the mass of the object determines how quickly it gets into motion and stops; heavier objects take more time, and lighter objects take less time. Think about a Ping-Pong ball. Once you hit it, it zips across the table, but if you catch it in your hand, the ball immediately ceases to move. Now imagine that the ball is made of lead. It would take a great deal of force to get it up to speed. Once you caught it, your hand would recoil because the momentum of the ball is transferred to your hand.

If you are using almost any professional animation or motion graphics tool, ease in and ease out are always on by default. At times you might find you need to make small adjustments to how an object animates. If your animation package offers an editable graph view of the animation data, called a velocity graph, you can use this view to sharpen (speed up) or flatten (slow down) an ease-in or ease-out sequence.

Secondary Animation

Secondary animation is, as its name implies, secondary to the primary movement. For example, as a woman turns her head, the main movement is her head turning, but there is more going on: her hair moves, her eyes may blink, and her facial expression might change. You might not use secondary animation in your motion menus unless your design involves character animation, in which case you are probably very aware of these principles.

Anticipation

Anticipation in traditional character animation is the visual cue the animator creates to show you something is about to happen. It is a transition from one story point to another. It can be shown physically, emotionally, or both. For example, a cartoon rocket ship launches. In this example, the rocket does not go from stationary to liftoff, but ignition and exhaust are shown before it bolts off into the wild blue yonder, escaping gravity.

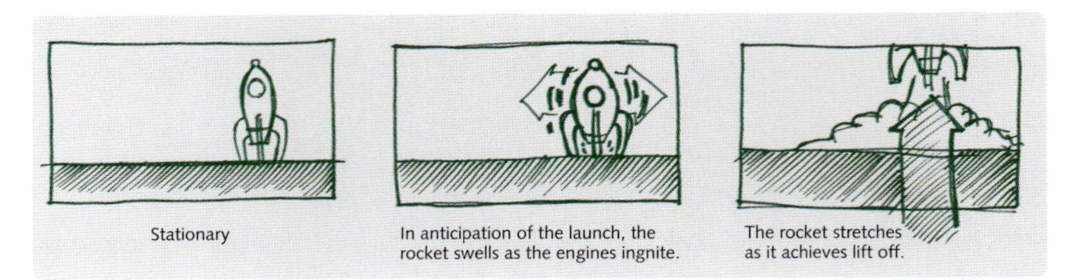

Figure 5.9 Anticipation

Anticipation can best be used when setting transitions between a menu's introductory animation and its loop point or between the end of one menu and the beginning of another.

Overlap and Follow Through

Two principles, overlap and follow through, determine how animation unfolds. For instance, when a stadium crowd performs the "wave," they do not all rise and fall at the same time—the movement between members of the crowd is delayed. This delay is the overlap. Follow through is the full range of motion that each member of the crowd completes. They do not simply stand and sit, but they bend over, raise their torso, and then raise their arms in one fluid movement.

If a piece of animation appears too jarring or abrupt, consider how overlap and follow through could be added. For example, if text slides on screen from the left, perhaps the last few letters can drag a little before catching up with the first ones.

Line of Action

The line of action is the path the animation takes in a scene. For motion menus, this can easily be defined in a storyboard sketch. When there are multiple lines of action, consider contrasting the lines to add dynamism.

MOTION PATHS

A motion path is the continuous line of movement that an object follows over time.

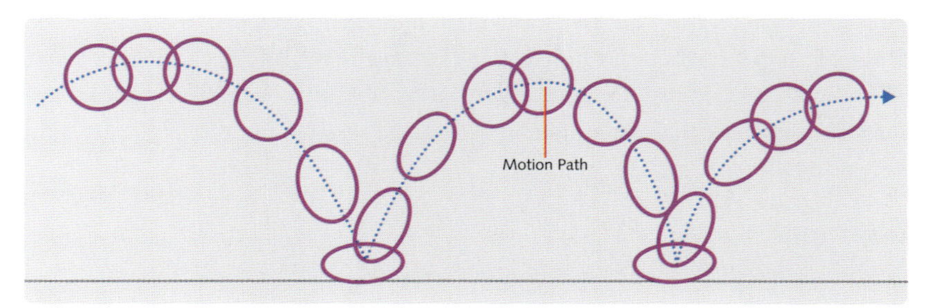

Figure 5.10 Motion path for a bouncing ball

If an object has more complicated movement, the path will not be straight, as in the case of the bouncing (Figure 5-10).

When storyboarding animation, include the motion paths on the storyboards. This will help facilitate the planning process.

Staging

Staging is the composition of the animated elements. Good staging shows animation at its best, and poor staging will weaken the animation's presentation no matter how good the animation is. Think of staging as showing the animated element's "good side." Figure 5.11 shows two examples of staging. The first frame is poorly staged—the menu's title is rotated too much, is not very legible, is too low on the screen, and appears cramped. The second frame shows the title in perspective, but it is still legible and makes better use of the space.

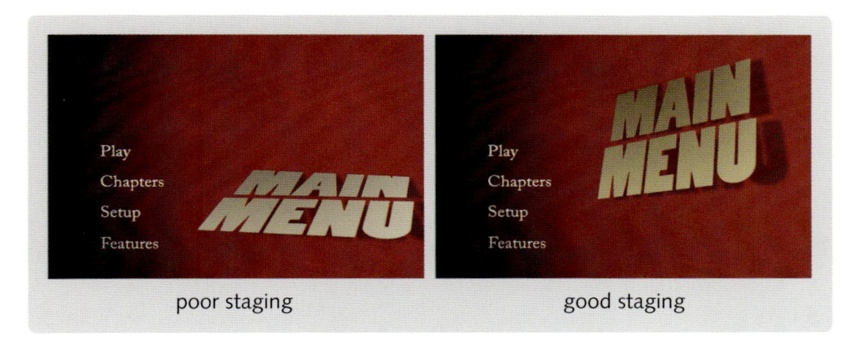

Figure 5.11 Staging

Solid Drawing or Craft

In traditional two-dimensional cell animation, solid drawing skills are stressed because well-executed drawing looks better. This is not to say the drawing has to be realistic, but it should have clearly established contrast between straight and curved lines, and the shapes drawn should be indicative of motion, gravity, and mass.

You will probably not have to draw your animation by hand, and you will likely use software to animate your motion menus. In this case, solid drawing translates to craft or production value. Good craft results from understanding design principles and having the skills to apply them in a way that is thoughtful and deliberate. For example, a skilled carpenter produces work that is seamless, smooth, and robust, whereas a weekend warrior produces work that shows its gaps, is rough, and is wobbly.

Appeal

Appeal, like delight, is an intangible quality that is measured by the viewer's satisfaction and enjoyment. Animation has appeal when the viewer finds humor or surprise. Some viewers can appreciate the complexity of motion and effects and enjoy the precision and craft of the design. Appeal is a measurement of the viewer's overall experience.

Animation Properties

In order to create animation, an object has to change in some manner. For example, it has to move, grow or shrink, change color, blow up, disappear, or melt. When any of these things occur, the object's characteristics change. These characteristics are geometric properties such as position, scale, rotation and visual properties such as opacity, color, and form.

ANCHOR POINT

When animating an object, its animation is determined by its anchor point. Like an anchor thrown in the water, an anchor point influences how an object moves. When the anchor point for an object is offset from the center, the object maintains a relative distance from the anchor point.

The anchor point is also the origin for scale and rotation. When scaling an object, it grows from the anchor point. When rotating an object, the object rotates around the anchor point.

Figure 5.12

DIMENSION

Two-dimensional animation occurs in the x (left to right) and y (top to bottom) planes. If you remember the early video game Pong, this is perhaps one of the simplest forms of two-dimensional animation. An animated object is animated in two or three dimensions.

Today, creating perspective-accurate animation has been simplified with three-dimensional animation and compositing programs such as Motion, Boris Red, and After Effects. This is achieved by simulating the characteristics of three-dimensional forms and camera properties such as depth of field and focus. Three-dimensional animation occurs in the x, y, and z planes.

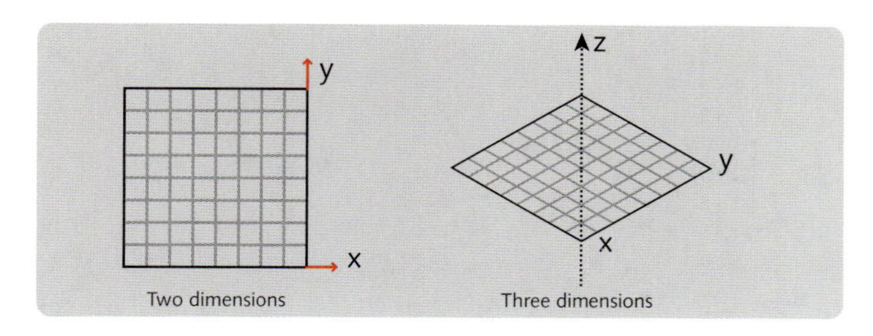

Figure 5.13 Dimension

POSITION AND DIRECTION

These are the most fundamental aspects of animation. In the simple scene of a ball bouncing, the ball's position changes from one frame to another. Its direction is a result of the animator approximating or exaggerating mass and gravity. Over time, the direction can be described as a motion path. With dimension, this path can occupy two or three dimensions.

SCALE

Animating the scale of an object over time typically indicates that the object is growing or shrinking or coming closer to or going farther away from the camera. When animating words or graphic elements, however, animating the scale of something can signify importance and hierarchical relationships. Objects can be scaled proportionally or in any combination and amount of the x, y, and z planes.

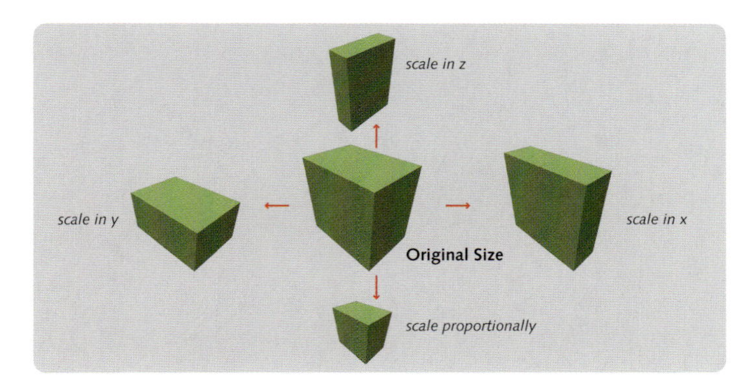

Figure 5.14 Animating scale

ROTATION

When an anchor point is at the center of an object and the object is rotated, the object spins in place. However, if the anchor point is located to the right of the object, the object will swing like a pendulum.

OPACITY

Opacity is an object's transparency. If an object is 100 percent opaque, it is solid; if it is 0 percent opaque, it is invisible. Opacity is commonly animated when creating transitions. For example, one image is layered on top of another image and revealed as it goes from transparent to opaque.

COLOR AND TEXTURE

The color and texture of an object can be animated to indicate selection, importance, hierarchy, or physical characteristics such as temperature, speed, or mood.

FORM

Animating an object's form or shape can suggest motion, speech, or a transformation in meaning. For example, the ball that bounces is flatter when it hits the ground, speech phonemes are created by animating the shape of the mouth, or an arrow can change from pointing up to pointing down to signify a change in direction.

Null Objects

A null object has all the transformation properties of a visible object but does not render. The use of null objects is a production technique that saves time, ensures consistency, and adds flexibility. The process begins by linking other objects to a null object. The linked objects then inherit properties from the null object so that as you animate the null object, the linked objects animate in the same fashion.

For example, if you want several stars on a screen to rotate at the same speed, it is faster to animate a null object and link the stars to it than to animate the stars independently. If the animation has to be changed, the null object is changed and all the stars follow suit. In addition, several null objects can be combined and linked together to create a framework for positioning complex objects or cameras. Figure 5.15 shows a top that has two null objects that assist in animating the top's position and rotation.

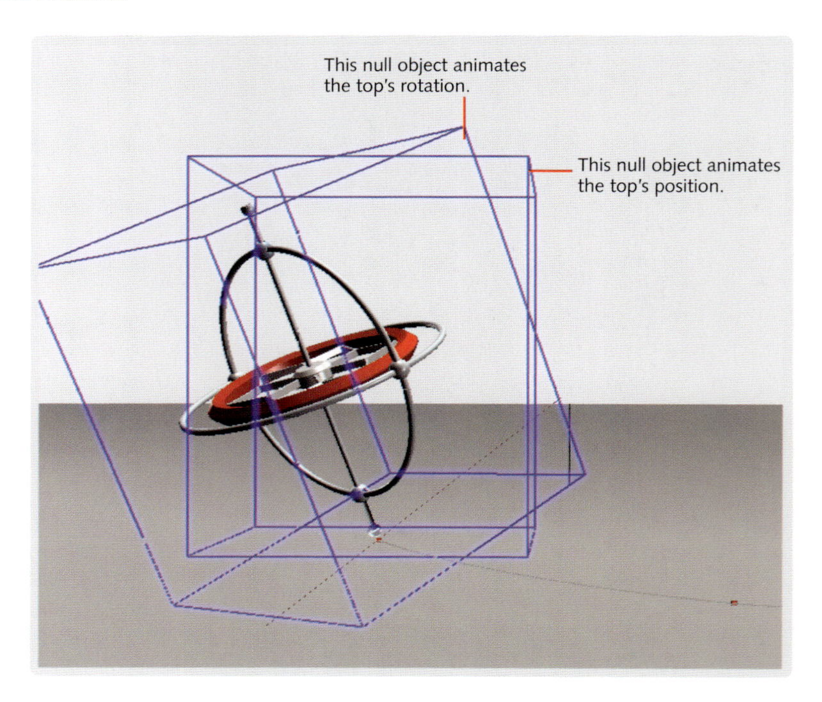

Figure 5.15 The top has two null objects: one for position and the other for rotation.

Animating the Camera

Many animation programs can now position and move a camera in three-dimensional space. In many cases, camera moves that would have been costly and require expensive camera support equipment is now achievable within an NLE or compositing application. With this facility, however, is the risk of moving the camera poorly. Whiplash zooms and pans are indicative of poor camera movement and often do more to distract and confuse than to entertain and inform.

In some cases, only the camera needs to be animated. For example, a common effect in documentaries is panning and zooming slowly into important elements of a scene. In other situations, moving the camera subtly while animating an object can create interesting effects (Figure 5.16).

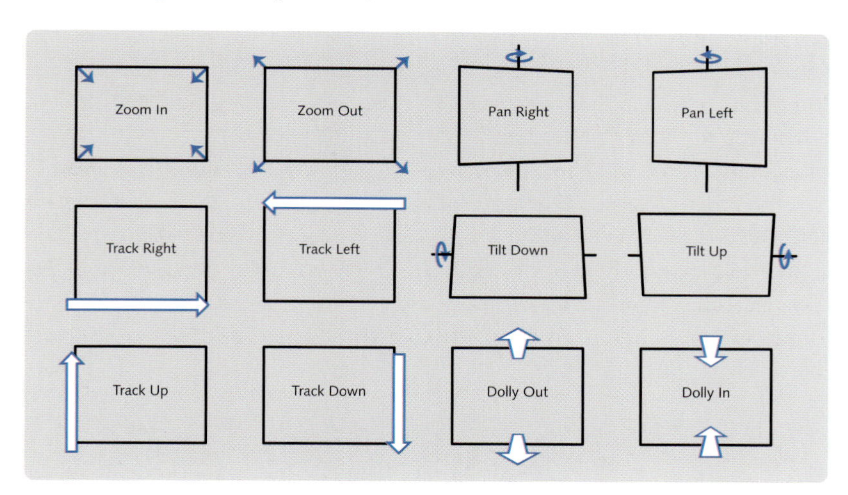

Figure 5.16 Camera movements

Pans and tilts are created when rotating the camera horizontally or vertically on a center of rotation. When the camera is rotated on a long arm that moves up and down, this is a crane movement. Zooms are created when the lens is adjusted to increase or decrease the magnification for a shot. Zooms should not be confused with a dolly move. To dolly the camera is to physically move the camera in the z plane or into or out of a shot. Tracking is moving the camera left or right or up or down. Sometimes panning is mistaken for tracking, but pans and tilts are rotating the camera, whereas tracking involves moving the camera in the x or y plane without rotation.

Transitions

Transitions are often used at edit points in a video or film sequence. Likewise in a motion menu, transitions can be used around the loop point or can be used to introduce or exit from a menu. These segments that occur before or after the menu are referred to as "intro and exit loops" or "interstitials." Whatever you call them, in most cases, these segments will employ some form of transition if they do not join together seamlessly. Common transitions are dissolves, effects, and no transition or "jump cuts" (Figure 5.17).

Figure 5.17 A linear wipe transition at a 45° angle from right to left

Final Cut Pro, Motion, and DVD Studio Pro have many transitions that can be applied.

Using DVD Studio Pro

DVD Studio Pro uses tabbed windows to organize its many authoring tasks. Each of these tabs has a name, such as the Assets tab, the Outline tab, the Menu tab, the Track tab, and so on. These tabs organize and put to use the various assets you will use to create your DVD.

As an example, the Assets tab is used to collect various types of media and hold it for use within your project. You may organize these various media into folders, such as a folder for track media and a folder for menu media. These assets are assigned to objects you define in the Outline tab, which is an outline of your DVD, its tracks, its menus, its slideshows, and so on. Think of the outline as a blueprint of your DVD. If you wanted to define your DVD as having two menus and five tracks, you would define two Menu objects and five Track objects inside the Outline tab.

Figure 6.1 DVD Studio Pro interface overview

These objects are essentially blank objects until you populate and configure them in their respective tabs. For example, the Track object requires at least a video asset from the Assets tab. Once you have assigned audio and video to the Track object, you have a track that is ready for playback; however, it likely needs a menu in order to provide the viewer of the DVD access to the track. The Menu object is also a blank object and requires you to add assets from the Assets tab in order to define the look of the menu, its buttons, and its behavior.

Assets, Outline, Menu, and Track Tabs

In this section, you'll learn about the Assets tab, the Outline tab, the Menu, and the Track tab.

Assets Tab

DVD Authoring begins with the gathering of assets required to begin assembling your project. The Assets tab uses three buttons to import, organize, and remove any asset.

Import	The Import button opens a dialog box that allows you to choose any compatible asset within the file system for inclusion into the DVD project.
New Folder	New Folder allows you to create folders to better organize the assets you will import. You may choose New Folder to create a Menu or Track folder for organizational reasons. Highlight the folder, then choose Import, and any item you import will be stored in that highlighted folder. No matter how you organize the assets in the Assets tab, their file locations on the hard drive will always remain exactly where they are located. Organizing assets in the Assets tab is a separate function from organizing your assets on your hard drive.
Remove	Remove allows you to remove any asset that is not currently in use. You will know if an asset is in use by looking at the In Use column in the Assets tab.

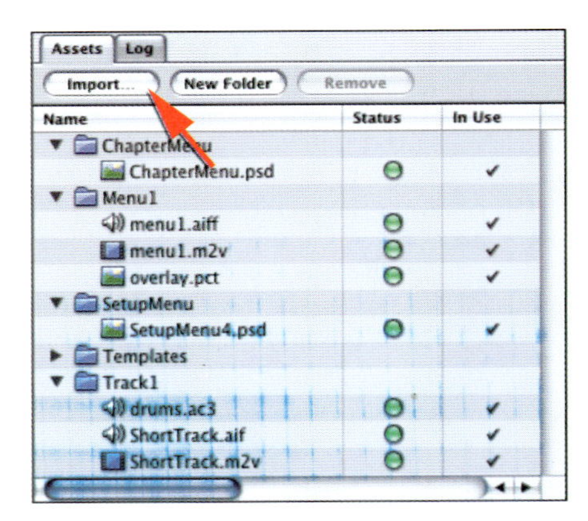

Figure 6.2
The Assets tab

Importing Assets

There are several ways to import assets into the Assets tab. The most obvious is the Import button located directly at the top of the Assets tab window. Another option is to use the File menu pull-down option File > Import > Asset. You may also use the keystroke Shift-Command-I or simply right click on an empty background in the Assets tab, then choose Import from the pop-up menu that will appear.

Creating New Folders

You may create new folders and use them to organize your assets. This does not change their location in the file system of the hard disk. Instead, this will give you a faster and easier way to locate assets within the Assets tab.

To create a new folder, simply click New Folder. If you wish to add a new folder within an existing folder, highlight that folder and then click the New Folder button. This creates a folder within the existing folder.

You can organize any asset within the Assets tab by dragging it into and out of any folder you create.

Video	Elementary MPEG2 streams MPEG1 (Half-D1) QuickTime-based Movies
Audio	AIFF 2-Channel (48000 / 96000) AC-3 Mono through 5.1 Channel DTS Audio 2.0 / 5.1 (Requires a hardware DTS decoder for playback) Wave Audio PCM Audio MPEG-1 Layer 2 Audio
Menu	Any supported still or layered image Any supported MPEG2 Any supported Audio Any supported Application project
Image	Adobe Photoshop Layered Images (Flatten Layers) PICT Images BMP Images TIFF Images QuickTime Image Format Targa Images JPG (JPEG)
Project	Motion (.motn) LiveType (.ipr)

Note: This is a table of common assets you will import and use with DVD Studio Pro.

Removing Assets

In order to remove an asset from you must first make sure the asset is not in use. To do this, make sure the items In Use status is not checked. If the item is in use, it means you have added the asset to an object, such as adding a video track to the Track object in the Outline Tab.

Default Column Views

- **Name:** The name of the file you have imported.
- **Status:** The status of the file imported.
- **Progress Bar:** The Progress Bar shows in place of the yellow, green, or red status indicator when an asset is first imported that requires encoding or parsing. This is triggered by the use of a preference setting which allows the author to encode either in the background while continuing to work with the application, or when the author uses the build function to multiplex the project to a VIDEO_TS folder or DLT tape.
- **Yellow Status Indicator:** The asset will be encoded at the time of project build. This is a preference setting. DVD Studio Pro allows for background encoding or

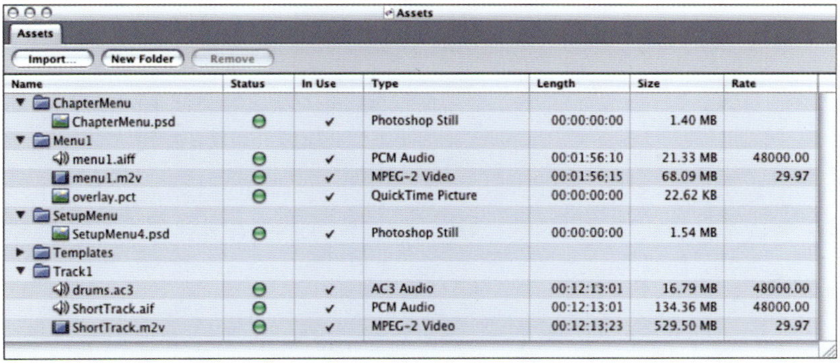

Assets

Import... | New Folder | Remove

Name	Status	In Use	Type	Length	Size	Rate
ChapterMenu						
ChapterMenu.psd		✓	Photoshop Still	00:00:00:00	1.40 MB	
Menu1						
menu1.aiff		✓	PCM Audio	00:01:56:10	21.33 MB	48000.00
menu1.m2v		✓	MPEG-2 Video	00:01:56;15	68.09 MB	29.97
overlay.pct		✓	QuickTime Picture	00:00:00:00	22.62 KB	
SetupMenu						
SetupMenu4.psd		✓	Photoshop Still	00:00:00:00	1.54 MB	
Templates						
Track1						
drums.ac3		✓	AC3 Audio	00:12:13:01	16.79 MB	48000.00
ShortTrack.aif		✓	PCM Audio	00:12:13:01	134.36 MB	48000.00
ShortTrack.m2v		✓	MPEG-2 Video	00:12:13;23	529.50 MB	29.97

Figure 6.3 Default column view

build encoding. Background encoding takes place in the background while you continue to work with the application. Build encoding is indicated by the yellow status indicator, which is shown when an asset will be encoded at the time of the project build only.

- **Green Status Indicator:** Shown if the asset has completed the encoding process. This uses the preference setting of a background encoding.
- **Red Status Indicator:** Shown if there is an error in the encoding or parsing of the asset. This uses the preference of background encoding.
- **In Use:** Any asset that has been tied to an object. In use assets show a check mark in the In Use column.
- **Type:** A brief description of the type of asset, such as PCM audio or QuickTime Picture Asset.
- **Length:** Displays the timecode value of an audio or video-based asset, such as a compressed MPEG2, AIFF, AC3, or DTS assets.
- **Size:** Displays the File Size of the asset, not the encoded size.
- **Rate:** Displays the frame rate of video-based assets or the sample rate of audio-based assets.

Parse files are created automatically as needed by DVD Studio Pro. They contain information about an imported asset, such as length and frame size. Parse files are named after the file parsed and use the extension ".par".

Additional Column Views

- **Aspect:** Shows the Aspect Ratio such as 4:3, 16:9, or 3:2 for video-based assets or Retain for still-based assets.
- **Bit Depth:** Shows the bit depth, such as 24-bit RGB.
- **Channels:** Shows the number of channels, such as 2 for stereo PCM.
- **Dimensions:** Shows the dimensions, such as 720 x 480 for MPEG2.
- **Layers:** Shows the number of layers, as such in a multilayer Adobe Photoshop-based asset.

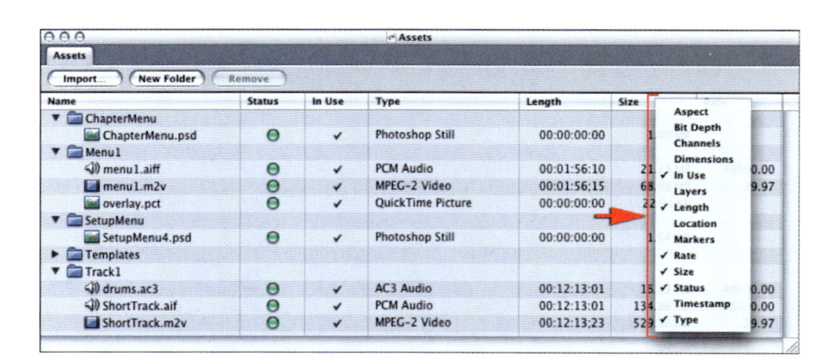

Figure 6.4 Adding additional columns

- **Location:** Shows the fully qualified location of the asset in the hard disk.
- **Markers:** Shows the number of chapter markers in an MPEG1 or MPEG2 asset.
- Timestamp: Shows the timecode value of the first frame of any video or audio-based asset.

Customizing the Column Views

You can customize the column views by clicking on the column headers and moving the column to the desired location. You can also right click on any column header to view of a list of additional column views that can be added to or subtracted from the Assets tab by checking or unchecking items listed in the column view check list.

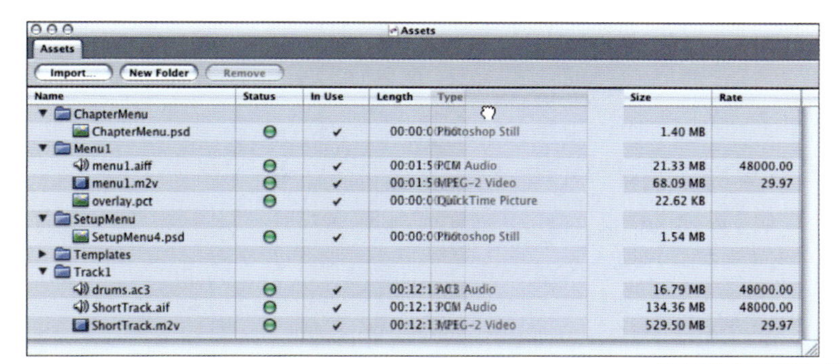

Figure 6.5 Adjusting column views

Open in Editor

Open in Editor is a function which allows you to edit any supported asset by its original content creator application.

To use Open in Editor, right click or Control-click on an asset, then choose: Open in Editor from the pop-up menu. If the asset is an Adobe Photoshop layered still image, then Adobe Photoshop will open the asset. Likewise, if the asset is an Apple Motion project, then Apple's Motion application will open with the project loaded and ready for edit.

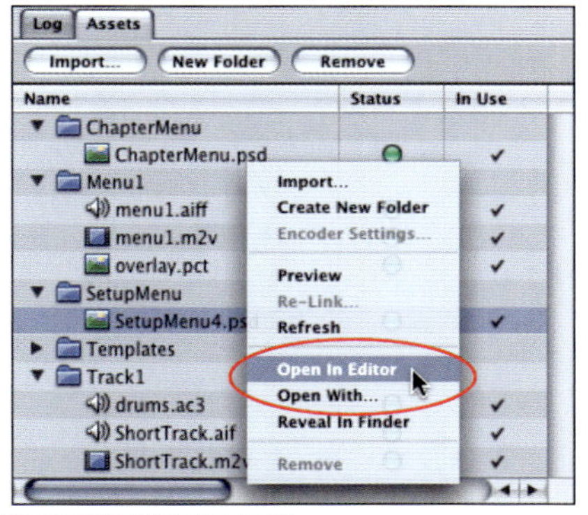

Figure 6.6 Open in Editor

If your asset opens the wrong application type, such as an Adobe Photoshop asset opening in Apple's Preview application, you may correct this by changing the file association using "Get Info", keystroke Command-I. Select the "Open with:" option and change the file type from Preview to Photoshop.

Once you have finished your edit of the image or project, simply save the image or project and return to DVD Studio Pro. The image or project will update automatically.

If your asset doesn't immediately update, right click, or Control-click for one-button mouse users, in a blank area of the Assets tab, and then choose Refresh, from the pop-up menu.

If you have modified, moved, deleted, or added a button within a menu, you should check your button placement, highlight placement, and assigned button targets.

Adobe Photoshop	Adobe Photoshop layered assets, such as those in layered or standard menus	.psd
Adobe Photoshop	Any flattened file	.jpg .tif .pct .bmp
Apple Motion	Any Motion project file	.motn
Apple LiveType	Any Live Type project file	.ipr

Table: Common menu elements and associated applications

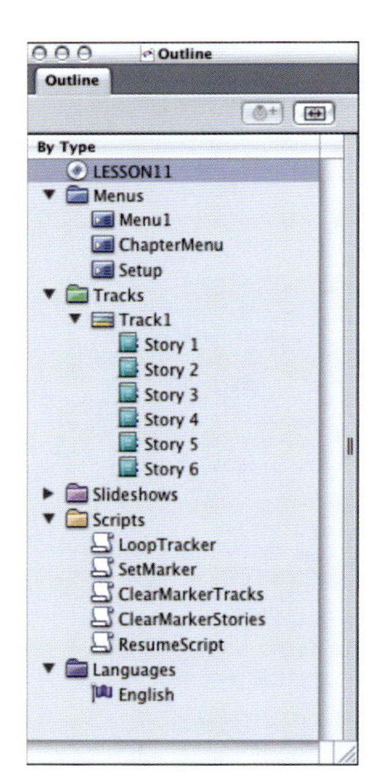

Figure 6.7
The Outline tab

The Outline Tab

The Outline tab is where you will assign your assets as objects in an outline view of the DVD you are constructing. Though the Assets tab contains the assets you will use in constructing a DVD, the Outline tab contains the logical assignments of those assets. The elementary MPEG2 video and AIFF audio, for example, come together as a track asset within the Outline view. Though these are two separate assets in the Assets tab, they unify to become a single track in the Outline tab. In addition, Track objects may hold more than one video stream, more than one audio stream, subtitles, and even subtitle images over the full-motion video. All of these assets come together in the Track object in the Outline tab.

The Outline tab is also home to other objects such as the DVD object itself, as well as ancillary Menu objects, Slideshow objects, Scripts objects, and language designations for use with multilanguage DVDs.

The Disc Object

The Disc object is the root of the DVD in its logical structure. The Disc object is configured through the use of the Property Inspector. You can open the Property Inspector at any time by clicking on the Inspector button in the toolbar, by using the command, Option-Command-I, or by using the pull-down menu option, View > Show Inspector.

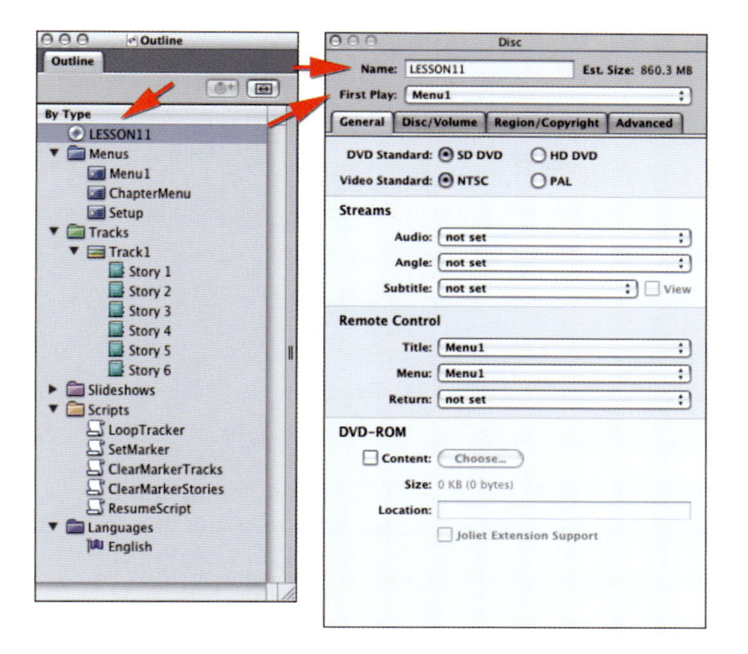

Figure 6.8 The Disc object with Property Inspector

Naming Your DVD

The Disc object's properties are separated into four tabbed sections: General, Disc/Volume, Region/Copyright, and Advanced. The first setting in the Disc property is at the top, which is the name of the disc. To change the name from Untitled to a unique name for your project, just click in the name field and change the name of the disc to the name that best suits your project name. By default, the name that you first save your project as will become the volume name unless you specifically name the volume with the name field.

Setting the First Play

The First Play is your DVD's first action. It's important to know that DVDs are always in motion. That is, they must always have something to do. DVDs are either playing a Video object or they are awaiting your commands in a menu. To start this action of play, you must first set the First Play.

First Play is set by default to the Menu 1 object in the Menus folder in the Outline tab. You may leave it set to Menu 1 or change it to another menu, track, slideshow, or script within the Outline tab.

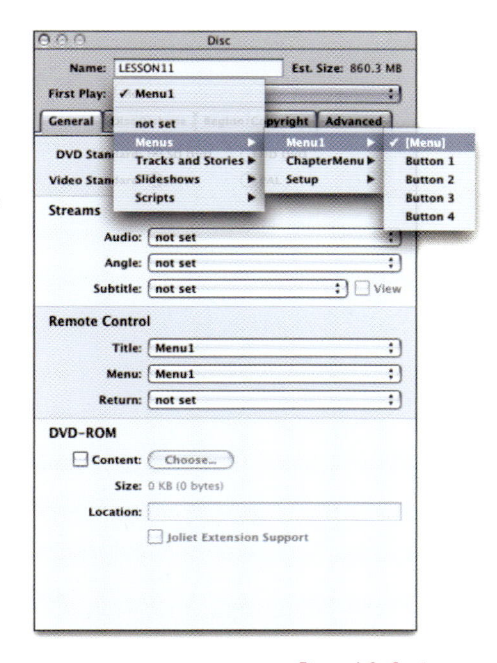

Figure 6.9 Setting the First Play

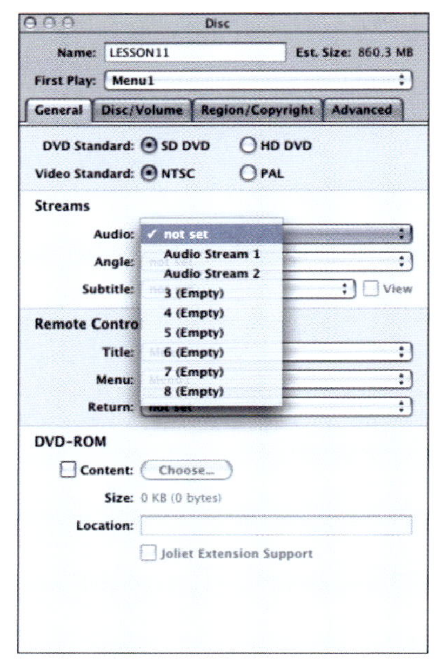

Figure 6.10 Property Inspector — setting the streams

Figure 6.11 Disc Property Inspector — general tab

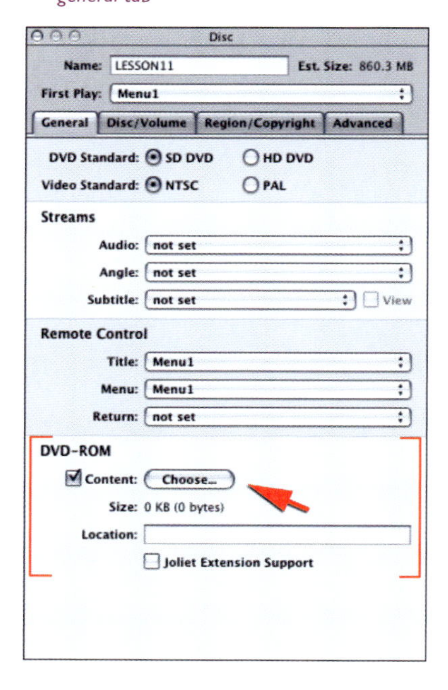

To set the First Play, simply select the First Play pop-up menu, and choose another asset. If you don't have any other items in your Outline tab, then no other selections will be available.

The General Tab

Setting the Audio, Angle, and Subtitle Streams

The Streams section of the General tab allows you to set defaults for the DVD project. If you have more than one audio, angle, or subtitle stream, then you may choose any of them as defaults by clicking on any of the three pop-up menus and choosing the intended stream. For subtitle streams, if you wish to turn them on or off in addition to selecting the subtitle stream, then you must check or uncheck the View selection box.

It is not necessary to set these streams at the Disc object level, as the DVD itself is designed to work with defaults set by the user in their hardware player. It's best to leave these selections set to the "not set" default settings.

Setting the Video Standard

You may select the Video Standard of either NTSC or PAL, however, this must be done prior to importing assets if those assets differ from your default settings.

Setting the Title, Menu, and Return Remote Control

The Remote Control settings allow you to set the Title (also known as Top Menu), the Menu, and the Return buttons on the remote control.

The Title means the primary menu. This is often the first menu the user sees, or the menu that is the host of other menus and tracks.

The Menu button is used to go to the menu that launched the item. An example is pressing the menu button while watching a specific extra feature. The expectation is to go back to the menu that you used to play that extra feature, not just going all the way back to the primary menu.

The Return button is used to go back one menu in a tree of menus. An example would be a view going from the primary menu to a secondary menu, and then from that secondary menu, wishing to return back to the menu that was used to arrive at this submenu. The remote control Return function is available on all menus, allowing you to set the prior menu as a target.

Defining the DVD-ROM Content Location

The DVD-ROM setting requires you to first set the Content selection box. Once this is done, choose the location of the content to be added to the DVD project. Here a folder must be selected. The contents of the folder, including subfolders, will be added to the root of the DVD once burned.

The Disc / Volume Tab

The Disc / Volume tab allows you to set up your project as either DVD-5, meaning a single layer on a single side, or a DVD-9 project, which is two surfaces on a single side. Most Hollywood films are distributed using DVD-9.

To select a DVD-9 size, set: 8.54GB using the 4.7GB pop-up menu selection. The number of layers will change from Single to Dual. You now have a choice of two track directions. The Track Direction setting allows for OTP (default) or PTP. OTP, Opposite Track Path, is most commonly used in DVD-Video because it minimizes the time delay between switching layers during playback.

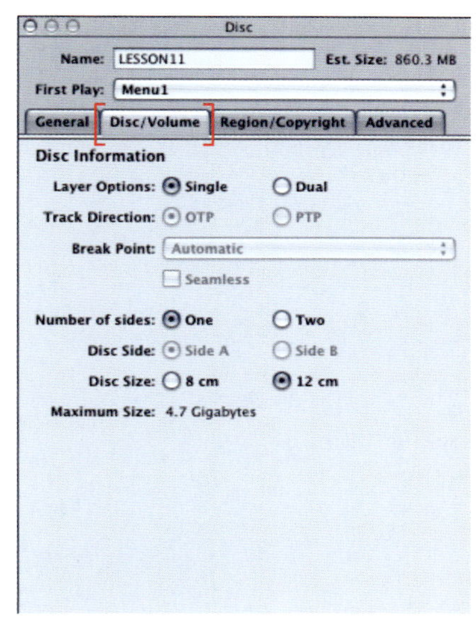

Figure 6.12 Disc Property Inspector — Disc / Volume tab

Region / Copyright Tab

You may set the Playable Region Codes here by leaving only the selections of the regions you wish to be enabled. For example, a checkmark left in the Region 1 – North America check box and no where else, means that the DVD will only play in Region 1-capable players. Items not checked are either disabled or reserved.

DVD-R media is Region ALL by design. If you wish to restrict your DVD to any specific region, you must create a DLT master, and replicate the DVD through a replication facility.

You may also choose to set copyright management functions, such as flagging your project for Content Scrambling System (CSS) or Macrovision. Replication is required for Region Coding, CSS, and Macrovision.

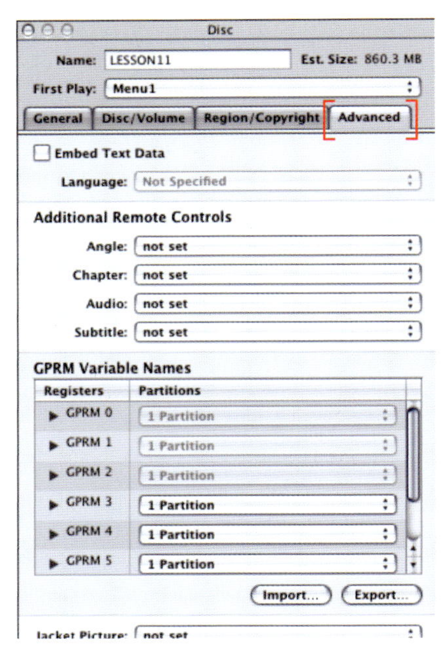

Figure 6.13 Disc Property Inspector —Advanced tab

Advanced Tab

Embed Text Data

This displays the menus, tracks, and slideshows with DVD players that support the Text Display DVD-Spec version 1.1. Most common players do not support this function.

Additional Remote Controls

You can assign more of the remote control buttons here. The purpose of this is to allow you the option to assign your own menus to spawn if the user selects the Angle, Chapter, Audio, or Subtitle buttons on the remote control. Pressing the Subtitle button on the remote for example, can be programmed to open your own Subtitle menu rather than the DVD player's built-in subtitle options during playba

GPRM Variable Names

This section allows you to name your GPRM registers. You may change the GPRM names at any time during the authoring process.

Jacket Picture

The Jacket Picture is an image that is displayed when the DVD itself has been stopped. Your player may or may not support this feature. You should look for the function in the hardware DVD player's setup function. Some carousel players use this function to display a preview of the DVDs they hold in the tray.

The Menu Object

There are two families of menus within the Outline tab. The first of these is the Standard menu. The Standard menu is the type of menu you will select to create either a still menu or a motion menu. This is defined by the assets you add to the Standard Menu object. Adding a still graphic as the background, with no motion items, drop zones, or shape objects, classifies the menu as a still menu. Adding audio, motion, or partial motion through the use of drop zones or shape objects classifies the Standard menu as a motion menu.

The second of the two classifications is the layered menu. The layered menu is a special type of menu that cannot contain any audio or motion. The layered menu derives each of its button states from a separate layer within a multilayered Photoshop image. These layered menus have some advantages and disadvantages to the viewer and the author. Because layered menus use an entire layer for each button state, you can use these states to show widely varying information as the user selects various options on a single menu. Standard menus, on the other hand, use an overlay to display states. Overlays are limited to three colors, and they cannot overlap at all. Standard menus, however, can use full or partial motion video and audio, which layered menus cannot.

Standard Menus

Standard menus may use a still image or full motion as the background. In both cases, standard menus may use audio in addition to the background choice. Standard menus also use what is known as an Overlay to designate the menu button status. Button status has three designations: Normal, Selected, and Activated.

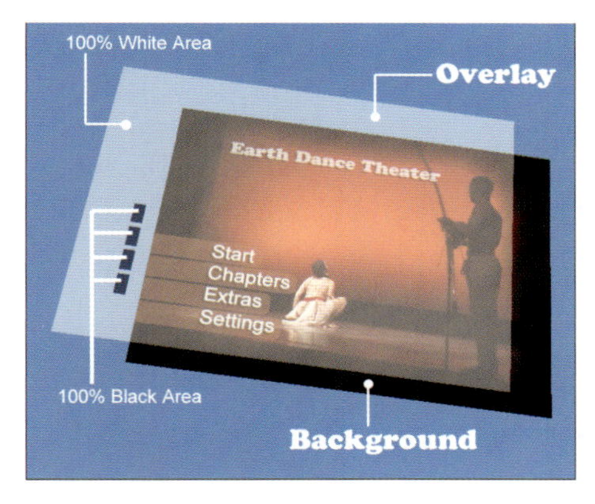

Figure 6.14 Standard menu with overlay

Layered Menus

Layered menus differ from standard menus in that they use multiple layers to provide the background element, and the three statuses of Normal, Selected, and Activated. Because each layer is used to represent a button status, the entire visual experience may change with each condition of any button on the menu, making layered menus beneficial in some circumstances. There are two penalties for this convenience, however. Layered menus cannot have any assigned audio, and layered menus are much slower-reacting than standard menus.

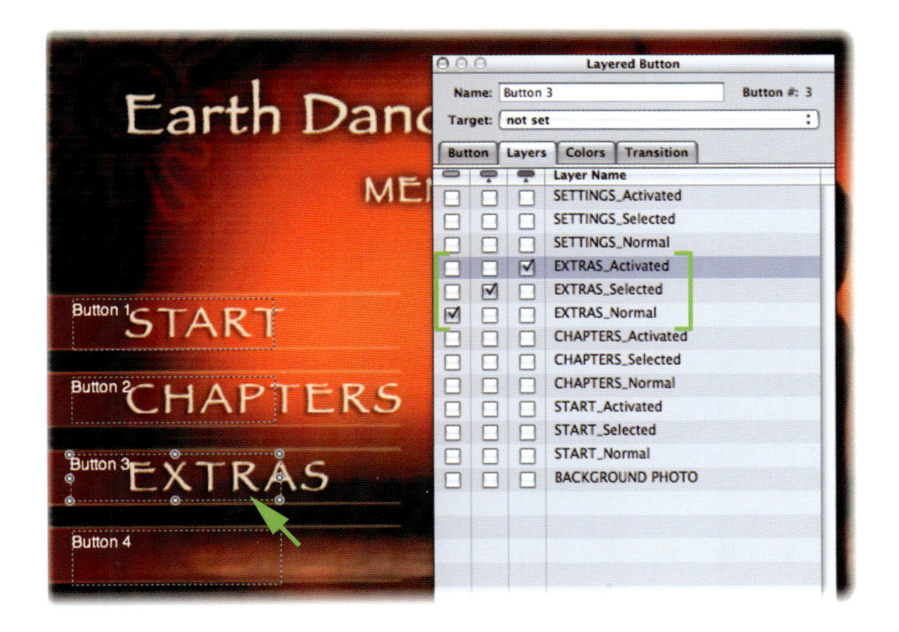

Figure 6.15 Layered menu with layer assignments

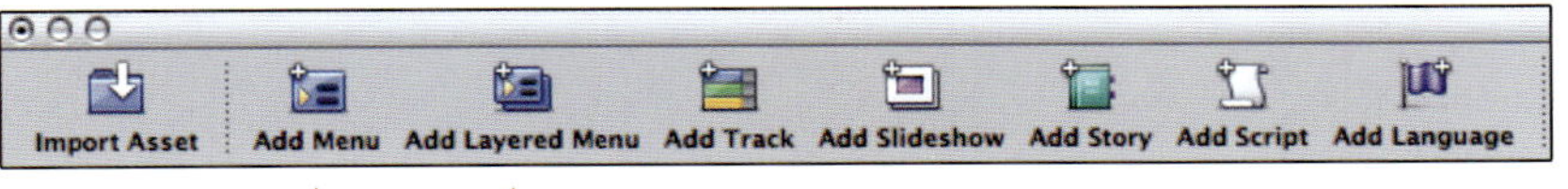

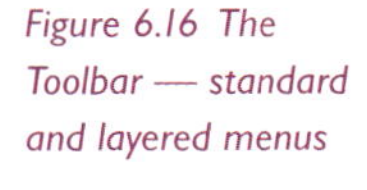

Figure 6.16 The Toolbar — standard and layered menus

Adding Menu Objects to the Outline Tab

To add a standard or layered menu to the Outline tab, choose the Add Menu option for a Standard menu, or choose the Layered menu in the Toolbar, or right click in the Outline tab and choose Add > Menu for Standard or Layered Menu from the pop-up menu that appears. If you are using a one-button mouse, you may substitute a control-click in place of a right click.

Assigning Assets to Menu Objects

You can assign an asset as the menu background by dragging the asset from the Assets tab to the Menu tab, and holding for a brief moment. When the Drop Palette appears, select Set Background to apply the current asset as the background.

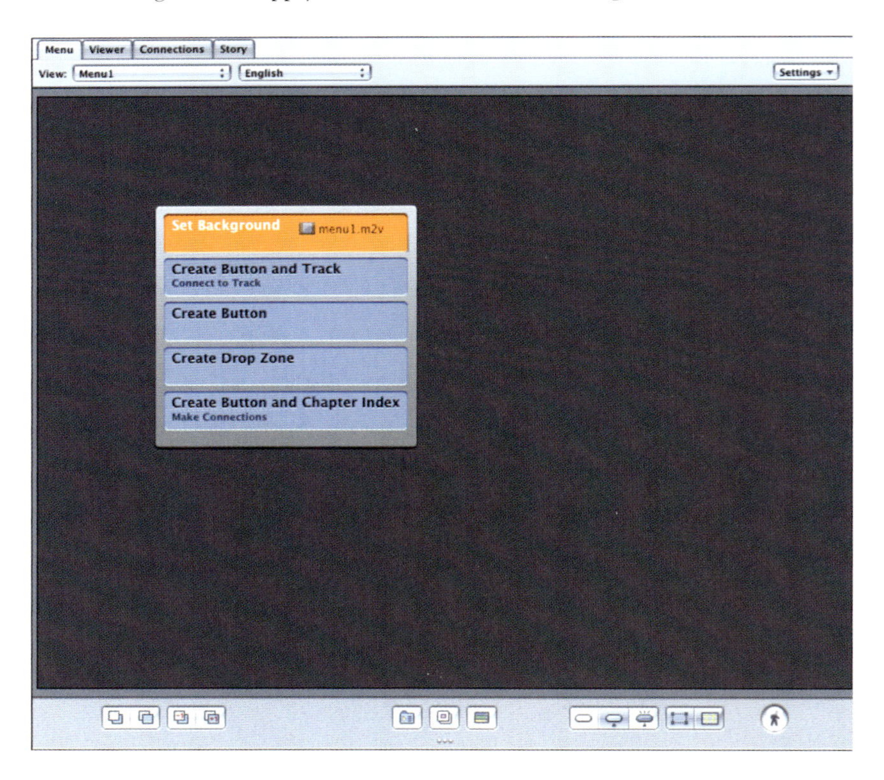

Figure 6.17 The Menu tab — Set Background

The Track Object

The Track object, unlike the Menu object, comes in a single flavor, but it does have a second component which is entirely optional. Track objects may have a subcomponent known as a story. Stories are helpful when creating a chapter menu.

Adding a Track to the Outline Tab

To add a Track to the Outline tab, click on the Add Track icon in the Toolbar or right click in an empty area of the Outline or Graphical tab, and select Add > Track.

Naming Your Track

To name your Track object, double-click or Option-Click on the Track object's name, and rename the track from its default name to a name you choose. You may also use the Property Inspector. Change the name of the Track by entering a new name in the Name field.

Setting the End Jump

Each track asset has an End Jump pop-up menu which is used to target the next asset that will play once the track is finished playing. The pop-up menu by default is not set. Click on this pop-up menu and set the target to a menu, slide show, script, or another track, chapter, or story.

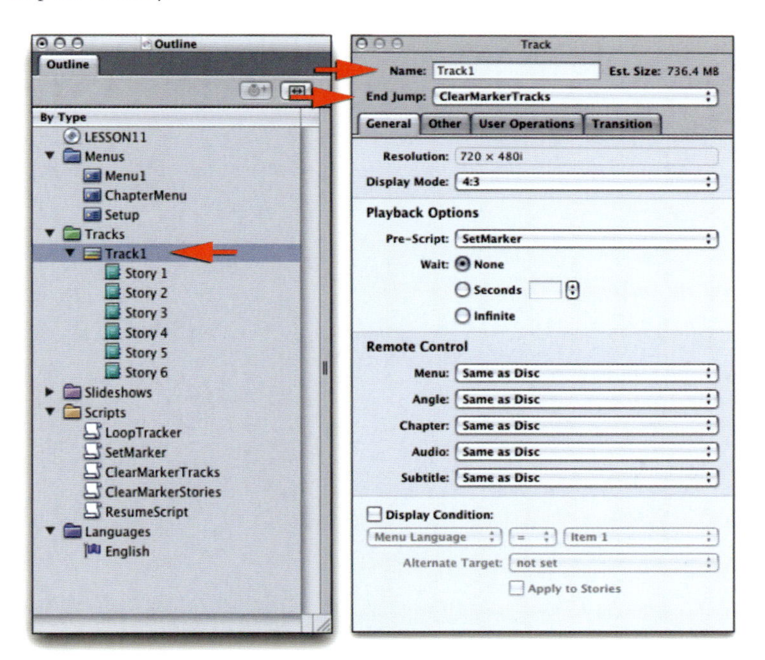

Figure 6.18 The Track object — Property Inspector

General Tab

Setting the Display Mode

Set the Display Mode using the Mode option in the General tab of the Track asset. The options are 4:3, 16:9 Pan-Scan, 16:9 Letterbox, and 16:9 Pan-Scan & Letterbox.

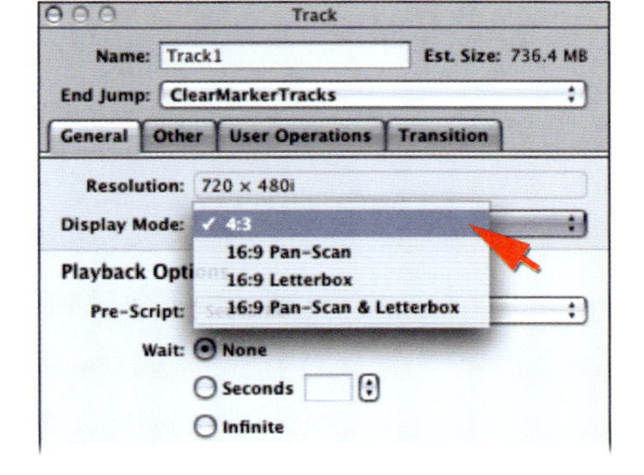

Figure 6.19 Property Inspector — the Display Mode

Playback Options

There are two playback options you can use in any track. The Pre-Script option affects what happens before the track is played, and the Wait option affects what happens after the track has completed playback. You may assign a pre-script to the track and/or set a wait variable after the track has completed playback.

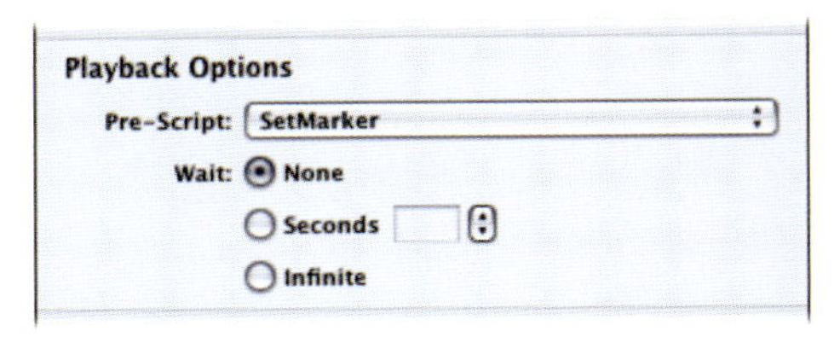

Figure 6.20 The Property Inspector — playback options

Pre-scripts are scripts that when assigned to a track's root, automatically execute. Pre-scripts are not executed when a track's chapter or story is the direct target.

The Wait variable affects the end of the track play.

None: hen the track has concluded, execute the End Jump.

Seconds: When the track has concluded, wait a specified number of seconds, then execute the End Jump.

Infinite: When the track has concluded, wait until the user presses the Play button on the remote or console before executing the End Jump.

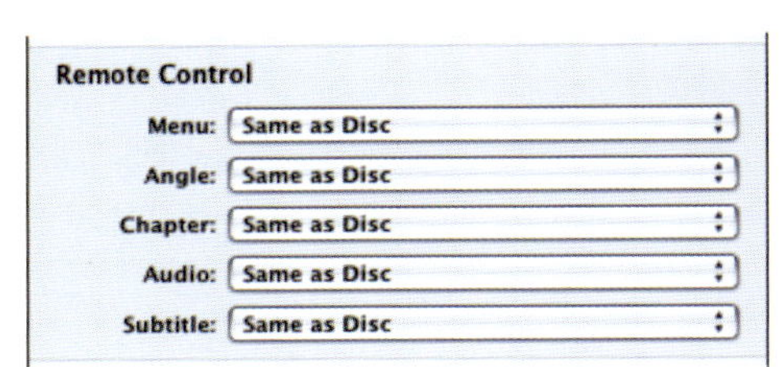

Figure 6.21 The Property Inspector — remote control

Setting the Remote Control Variables

During the track playback, any of the following remote control buttons are assignable to target any object in the Outline tab. Here are some suggested uses:

Menu	Assign to the parent menu
Angle	Leave Same as Disc, or assign to an optional Angle menu
Chapter	Leave Same as Disc, or set to a chapter menu
Audio	Leave Same as Disc, or set to a setup menu
Subtitle	Leave Same as Disc, or set to a setup menu

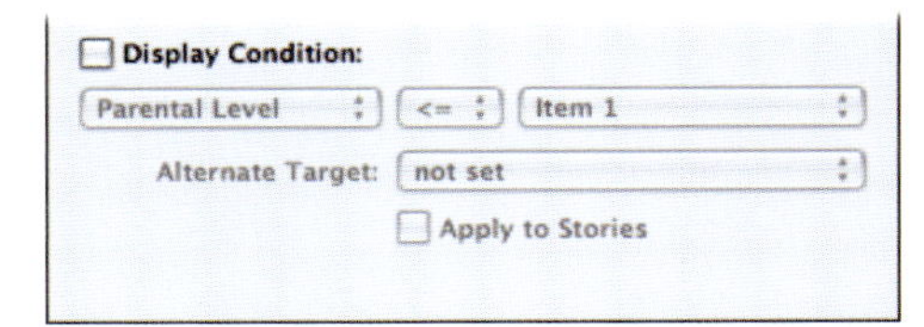

Figure 6.22 The Property Inspector — display conditions

Setting the Display Conditions

To set a Display Condition, check the Display Condition check box and choose a condition from the options. Display conditions are an efficient way to create a conditional playback of a track with an optional target if the condition is not met.

You may set a parental level, for example, that will play an alternate track or menu if the viewer's player is set to play PG-13 as a maximum level of content.

User Operations Tab

Adjusting the User Operations (UOP)

You may choose to disable any UOP in order to restrict certain remote control functions, such as disabling the ability to press STOP or PAUSE during an intro warning message.

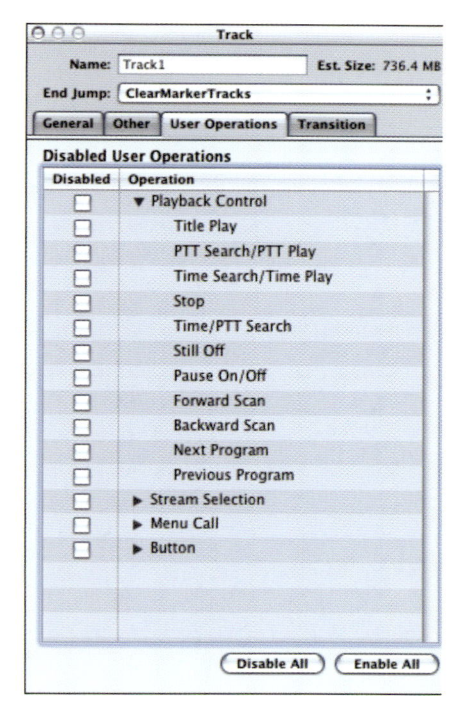

Figure 6.23 The Property Inspector — user operations

The Transition Tab

Using the Built-in Transitions

DVD Studio Pro has built-in transitions. Transitions are short, full-motion video that transitions elements of your menu into elements of your destination, such as another menu or a track. These elements are most commonly the last frame of your menu and the first frame of the target; however, the actual visual elements can be adjusted.

Because Script objects have no graphical elements, using pre-made transitions with scripts as targets will yield a blank element in the destination part of the transition. Therefore, build-in transitions with script targets should be avoided.

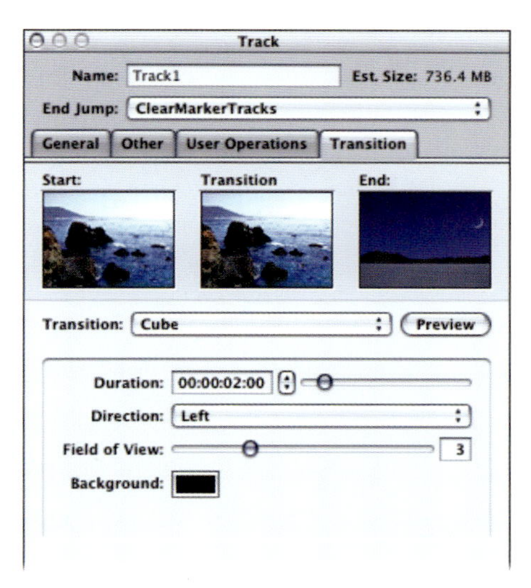

Figure 6.24 The Property Inspector — transitions

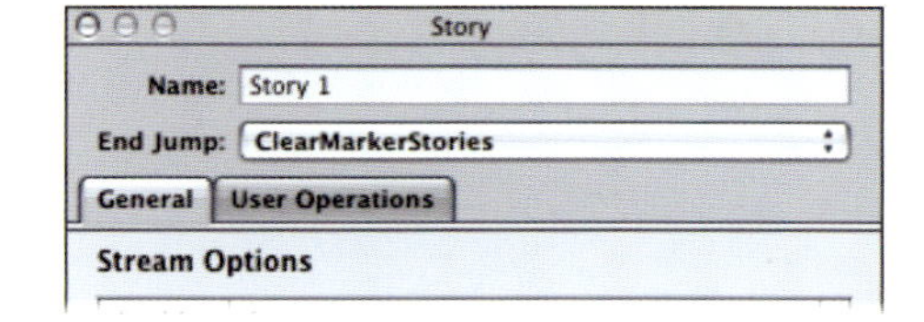

Figure 6.25 The Story object — Property Inspector

The Story Object

Stories are smaller versions of your track asset. They must be created inside of the Track object in the Outline or Graphical tab. Stories are defined using the chapter markers of a Track object.

To add a Story, select a Track object in the Outline tab or Graphical tab, and select Add Story from the Toolbar, or right click on any Track object and select Add > Story from the pop-up menu.

Naming the Story Object

To name your Story object, double-click on the Story object's name, and rename the story from its default name to a name you choose. You may also use the Property Inspector. Change the name of the story by entering a new name in the Name field.

Setting the End Jump

Just like Track objects, Stories have End Jump targets. These end jumps are unique to the story. Select the End Jump pop-up menu and choose a jump target.

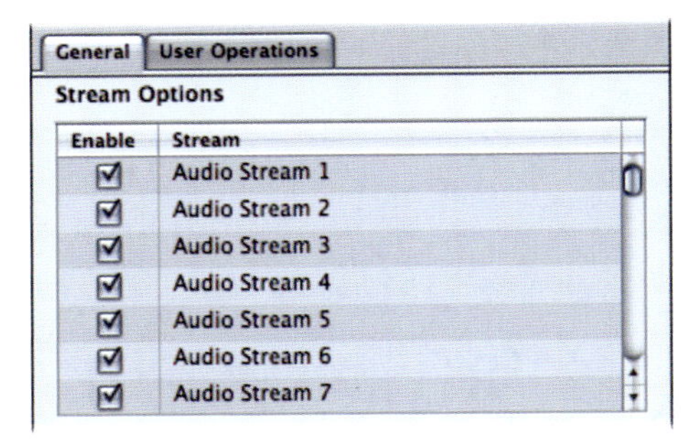

Figure 6.26 The Property Inspector — stream options

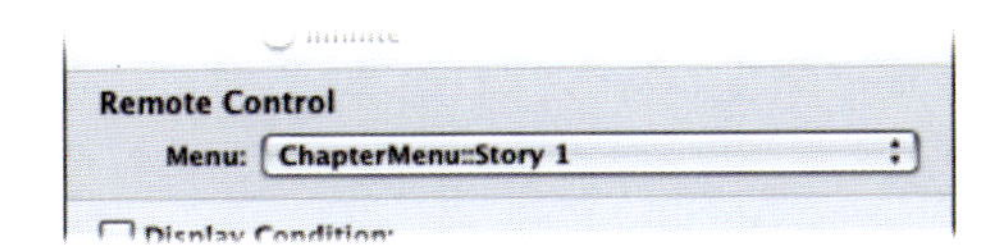

Figure 6.27 The Property Inspector — remote control

General Tab

Stream Options

You may enable or disable any audio or subtitle stream assigned to the parent track at the Story level by unselecting or re-selecting the corresponding audio or subtitle stream.

Playback Options

Playback options work exactly the same way as they do for Track objects. See the section "Playback Options" under "Track Objects."

Remote Control Options

Unlike the parent Track object, you can set a single remote control button specific to the Story object. That option is the remote control menu button. Setting the remote button to a menu that targets the story if different than the menu that targets the track as a whole can be quite useful.

Setting Display Conditions

You may set separate display conditions to the story then its parent track. See the "Track Object" section under "General Tab" and "Setting Display Conditions."

User Operations Tab

Setting the User Operations (UOP)

You may set separate User Operations from the parent track object. See the section "User Operations Tab" under "Track Object."

The Script Object

The Script object is a flexible way of authoring additional functionality into DVD Studio Pro. Scripts are based on conditions and navigation commands. An example would be that upon returning to a menu, you wish to pre-select the last button used within that menu. That is a common condition that is stored in what is known as SPRMs. SPRM (System Parameter Register Memory) stores many conditions of the DVDs in use conditions during playback of a DVD. One of these SPRMs stores the last button you selected in the last menu you used. As DVD authors you may wish to tap into that SPRM and use it to add extra functionality to your project. This is the function of the Script object.

Though there is only one Script object in the Outline tab, we think of scripts in two ways: as scripts and pre-scripts.

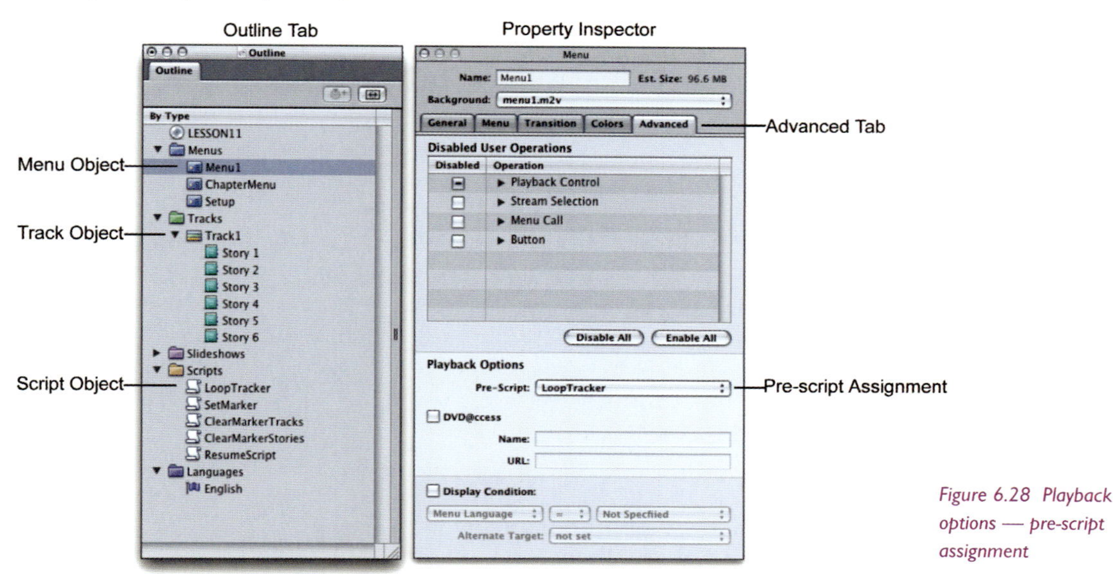

Figure 6.28 Playback options — pre-script assignment

A script is a specific target that you assign other assets to jump to directly through certain properties such as the First Play, End Jump, or Jump To targets. A pre-script is a script that is assigned to an asset itself, such as a menu or a track. When that menu or track is set as a root target, then its assigned pre-script is executed automatically. The pre-script itself as an object is never directly the target of other assets. Instead, it's assumed as sort of a preamble of the target it is associated with.

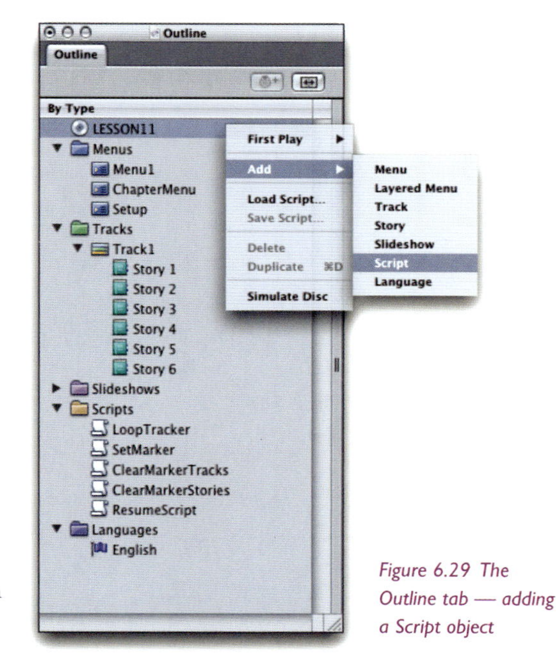

Figure 6.29 The Outline tab — adding a Script object

Adding the Script Object to the Outline Tab

To add a script, or pre-script to your project, you must first add the object to your Outline or Graphical tab. Add the Script object by selecting the script object in the Toolbar, or by right clicking in the open area of the Outline or Graphical tab and selecting Add > Script from the pop-up menu.

Adding a Pre-Script to an Asset

Setting the Menu Pre-Script

To add a pre-script to a Menu object, select the menu in the Outline or Graphical tab. Open the Menu's Property Inspector, and select the Advanced tab. Click on the pop-up menu in the Playback Options section and select a Script object.

Setting the Track / Story Pre-Script

To add a pre-script to a track or story object, select the Track or Story object in the Outline or Graphical tab, and open the track or story's property inspector. Select the General tab. Select the pop-up menu in the Playback Options section and choose a Script object.

Setting the Slideshow Pre-Script

To add a pre-script to the Slideshow object, select the Slideshow object in the Outline or Graphical tab. Open the slideshow Property Inspector. Select the Advanced tab. Select the Pre-Script pop-up menu in Playback Options section and choose Scripts > Your Script from the available scripts.

The Slideshow Object

Slideshows are a pre-packaged way of developing a slideshow directly within the application. The slide show can conform to the length of an audio track and include transitions. Slideshows are similar to Track objects.

Adding the Slideshow Object

To add the Slideshow object, click on the Add Slideshow toolbar button or right-mouse click in an open area of the Outline or Graphical tab and select Add > Slide-show from the pop-up menu.

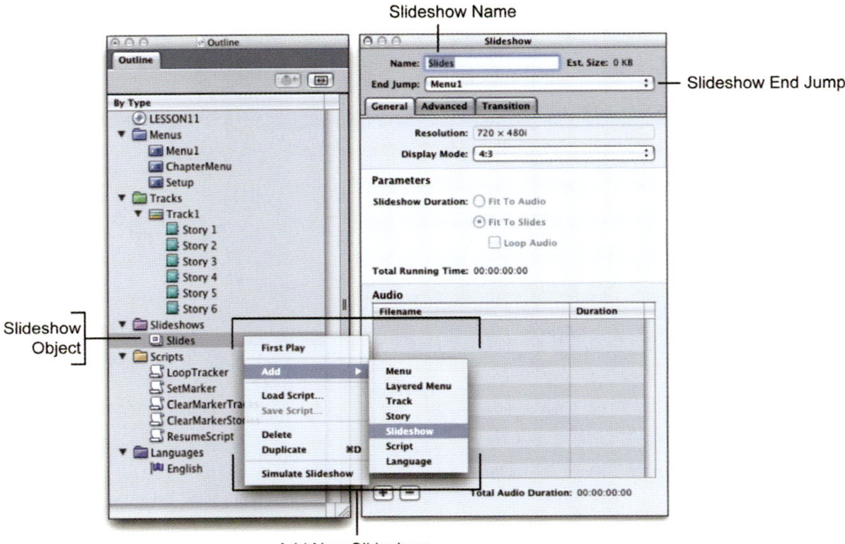

Figure 6.30 Adding slideshow to the Outline tab

Naming the Slideshow Object

To name the slideshow, double-click on the slideshow title, highlighting the name in the Outline or Graphical tab, and change the default name to a name of your choosing. You may also use the Name field in the slideshow's Property Inspector.

Setting the Slideshow End Jump

To set the slideshow End Jump, select the End Jump pop-up menu and choose the target of your choice to play after the slideshow concludes.

Adding Images to the Slideshow Tab

To add slides to the Slideshow object, open the Slideshow tab by selecting the Slideshow tab in the interface, or use the keystroke Command-7. Drag your slides from the Assets tab to the Slideshow tab.

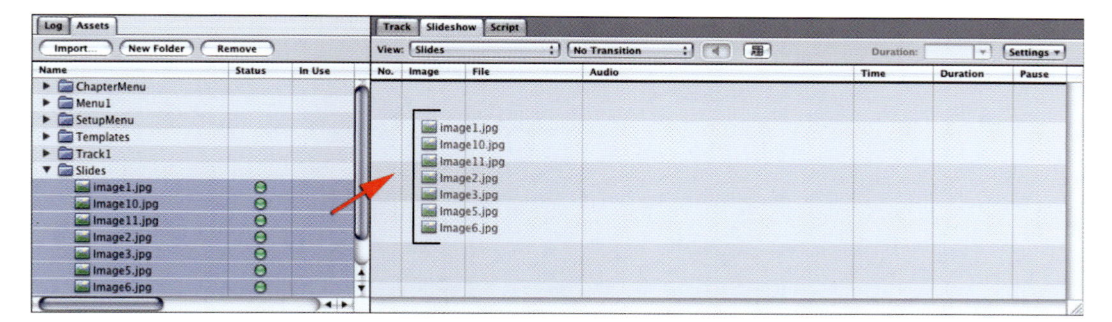

Figure 6.31 Adding slides to the Slideshow tab

General Tab

Adding Music

There are several ways to add music to your slideshow. To add music from the Assets tab, open the slideshow's Property Inspector, then choose the General tab, and drag an audio asset from the Assets tab into the Audio section of the Property Inspector.

To add music from your hard disk, select the [+] button located at the bottom-left of the General tab in the Property Inspector and choose any audio asset on your computer's hard disk.

To add audio from your iTunes library, Open the Palette either by selecting the Palette in the Toolbar, or by the keystroke Option-Command-P, then select the Audio Tab. Select your iTunes library or a playlist to display a list of available tracks. Drag the track of your choice to the Audio section of the General tab of the slideshow's Property Inspector.

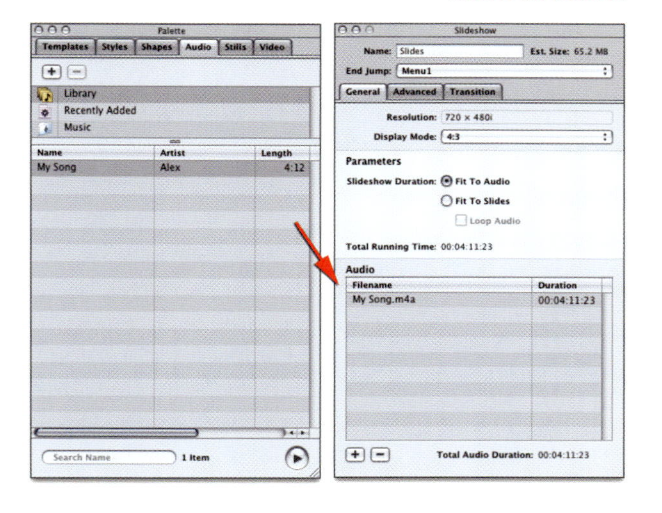

Figure 6.32 Adding music to the slideshow

Parameters

Fit To Audio

You may choose to fit the slides in the slideshow to the duration of the music you have added. To do this, select the Settings menu, then choose Fit To Audio, or select the Slideshow object in the Outline or Graphical tab and use the Fit To Audio option in the General tab of the slideshow's Property Inspector.

Fit To Slides

Fit To slides allows you to fit music to the slide duration. If the music does not match the length of the slide show, you may choose to use the Loop Audio option.

Fit To Slides is best used with loop-based soundtracks because the duration of music is based on the length and quantity of the slides, whereas Fit To Audio matches the duration of the slideshow to coincide with the soundtrack.

Advanced Tab

Playback Options

You may add a pre-script to your slideshow. Select the Pre-Script pop-up menu from the Playback Options in the Advanced tab of the slideshow Property Inspector and choose any script you have created in the Outline tab.

Remote Control

The Slideshow Remote control options are the same as the Track object.

See the section "Setting the Remote Control Variables" in the "General Tab" section under "The Track Object."

The Transition Tab

Adding Transitions

You may add a slideshow transition which sets a default transition for every slide within the slideshow by choosing a transition type in the Transition pop-up menu in Transition tab of the Slideshow object in the Property Inspector by choosing a transition in the Transition pop-up menu in the Slideshow tab itself.

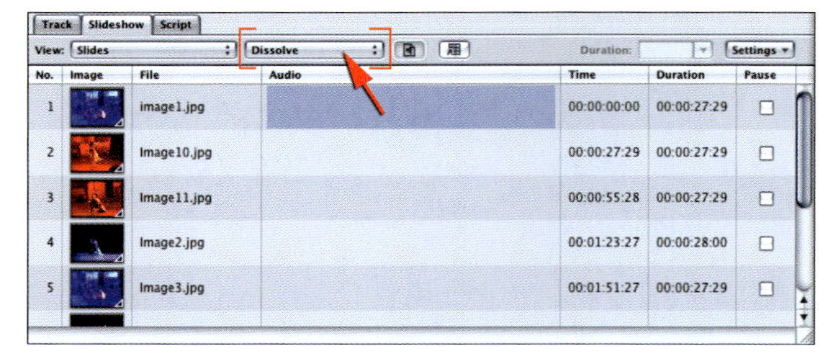

Figure 6.33 Adding music to the slideshow

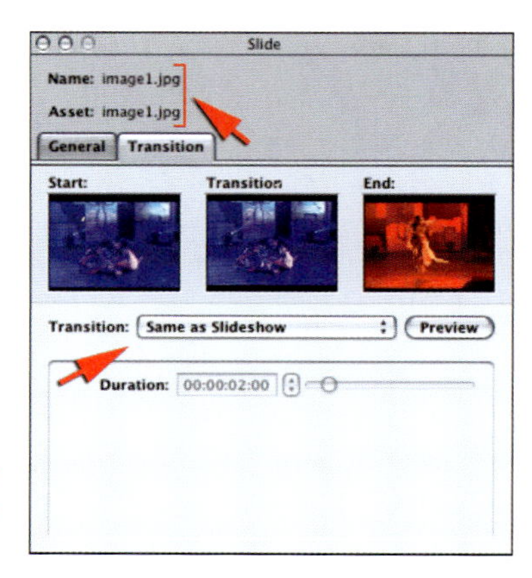

Figure 6.34 Adding music to the slideshow

You may also assign transitions independent to each slide. To do this, select a slide in a slideshow and open its Transition tab in its property inspector, and change the default transition from Same as Slideshow to its own transition.

The Languages Object

The Language object allows you to add a new menu language to your project. This setting works in conjunction with the Language pop-up menu in the Menu tab of the Menu Property Inspector of a Menu object.

Adding the Language Object to the Outline Tab

To add a new menu language to your project, first add a new language to the Outline or Graphical tab. Select Add Languages from the Toolbar, or right click in the Outline or Graphical tab. Select Add Language from the pop-up menu.

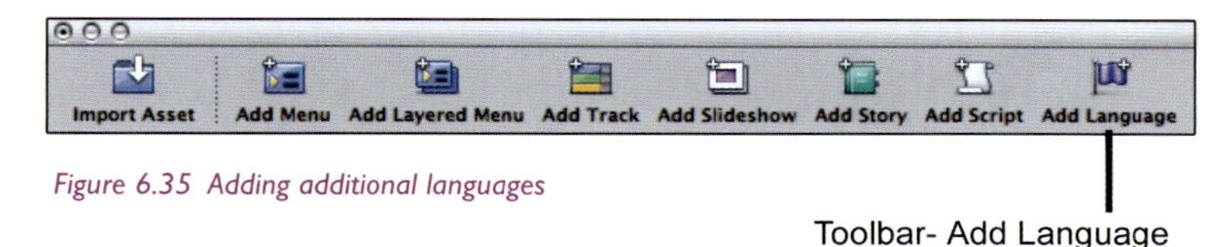

Figure 6.35 Adding additional languages

Naming Your Language

To name your language, click on the Language object in the Outline or Graphical tab, and open its Property Inspector. Select the Language Name field. Change the default language name to a language name of your choosing.

The General Tab

Setting the Language Code

To set the language code, select the default language in the Language pop-up menu, and choose a new language. It's a good idea to name the Language object the same name as the language code you have selected.

Figure 6.36 Setting the Language object language code

The Menu Tab

The Menu tab is where you will assemble your menu. No matter what kind of menu you decide to build, whether it is Standard, Layered, Still, or Motion, it all comes together in the Menu tab. The components of your menu, the settings you will create, and many objects required to build your menu all come together here.

Adjusting the View and Language

The View pop-up menu allows you to load any menu in the Outline or Graphical tab into the Menu tab for Menu editing.

The Language pop-up menu allows you to select any of the multiple languages you have created in the Outline or Graphical tab. This allows independent editing specific to each language variant you have created.

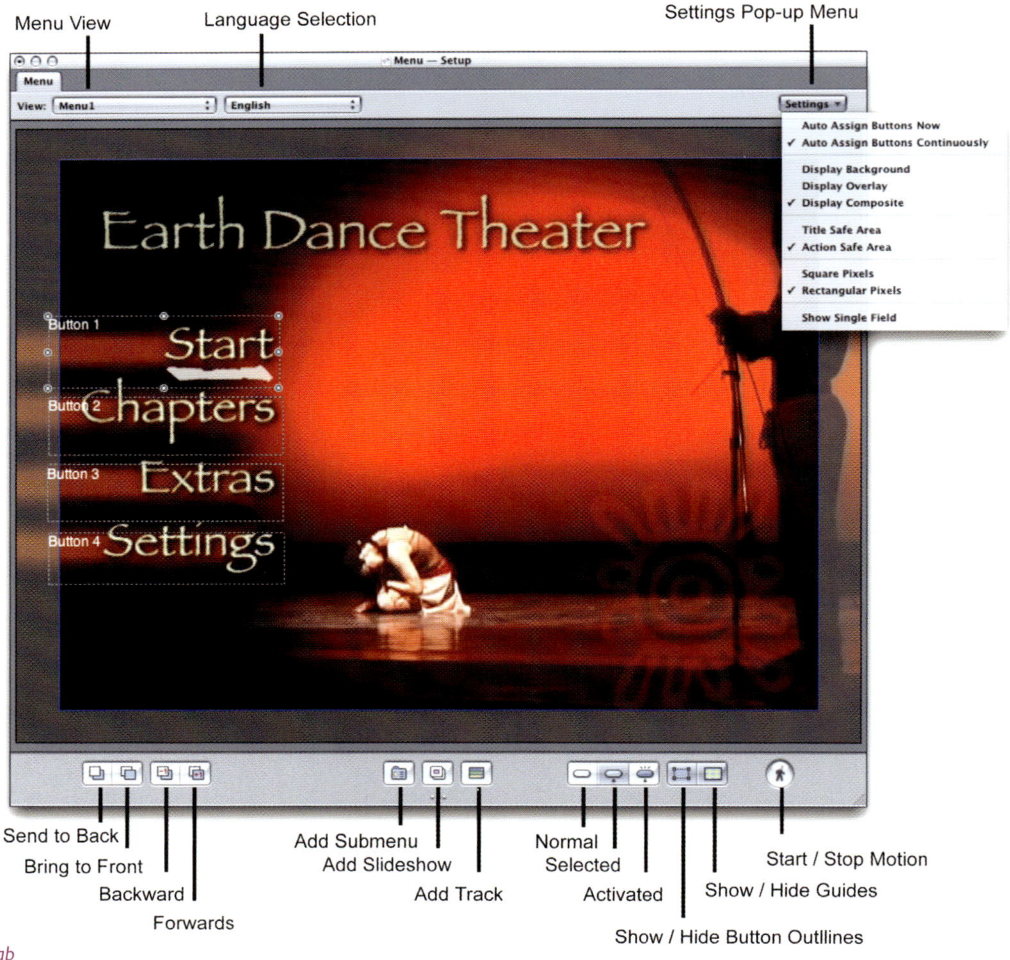

Figure 6.37
The Menu tab

The Settings Menu

Auto Assign Buttons Continuously (default)

As you create buttons on your menu, the default action is to set the remote's up, down, left, and right navigation automatically in the background while you work. Moving the menu buttons you create into alternative locations in the Menu tab during menu editing dynamically changes this up, down, left, and right button navigation if this setting is left to its default Auto Assign Buttons Continuously.

You may turn this action off by unselecting the Auto Assign Buttons Continuously in the Settings pop-up menu.

Auto Assign Buttons Now

The Auto Assign Buttons Now function is used to set the button navigation automatically, but only on demand.

Display Background

Shows the background of the menu only.

Display Overlay

Displays the Overlay of the menu only.

Display Composite

Displays both the Background and the Overlay combined.

Title-Safe Area / Action-Safe Area

Both of these items may be selected at the same time. Their purpose is to project over the menu, the title-safe, and/or action safe areas. Title-safe is the margin within which you should keep any text you want the viewer to see. Action-safe is similar to title-safe, except that it's for motion elements that you wish to remain in full view.

Square Pixels / Rectangular Pixels

The Square pixels setting allows you to see an uncorrected view of your menu, and the Rectangular Pixels setting shows you a stretched view, more inline with the view you would see on a television screen.

The Motion Toggle

The Motion Toggle allows you to quickly preview your menu with its motion and audio assets as a live preview.

Adding a Background

Your menu backgrounds may be still graphics or full motion animated backgrounds. Still images may consist of Photoshop layered images in the native PSD format, for example; .JPG, .PNG, .TIFF, and .PICT are also acceptable backgrounds. For motion backgrounds, you may use pre-encoded Elementary MPEG2 video or QuickTime-based Audio / Video assets.

Adding a Still or Motion Background

To add a still or motion background, find the asset in the Assets tab, then drag the asset into the Menu tab and hold for a brief second. A Drop Palette appears with a few options. Select the top option: Set Background.

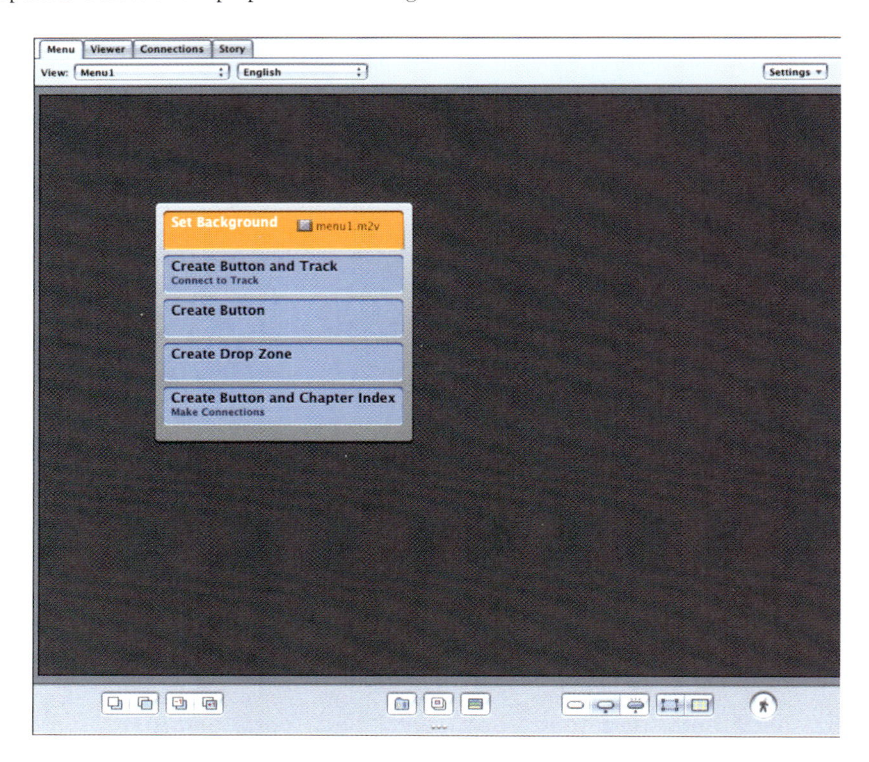

Figure 6.38 Adding a menu background

Figure 6.39 Adding an overlay to the menu

Adding Buttons

Adding an Overlay

To add an overlay, go to the Assets tab and select the overlay asset. Drag the overlay into the Menu tab and hold for a brief second. The Drop Palette will appear. Select Set Overlay.

Using Simple Highlights

To set up a simple highlight, you must first have the overlay added to your menu. Click on the menu background in the Menu tab, and open the menu's Property Inspector. Select the Colors tab. Adjust the Normal, Selected, and Activated color and opacity settings to your liking.

Adjusting the Overlay Color States

Using grayscale as an example, the highlight color is always 100% black, whereas the transparent area is always 100% white. To adjust the highlight color, you will only choose the color of the three button states.

In order to properly see all three states, you'll need to create at least one button. Click and hold any area of the background menu, then drag the mouse diagonally downward or upward. You will see a bounding box defined that spans from the area you first clicked and held, and spans to the position you now hold the mouse in. In order to set up your buttons using overlays, you will need to draw these boxes over the general area of the key-color you have set up in your overlay.

This bounding box you have created is a Button object. Select this box so that it is the active object in the menu. Like other objects, the Button object has a Property Inspector. Open the Property Inspector, and click on the Colors tab.

Figure 6.40 Creating buttons in the Menu tab

Setting the Normal State

Select the Normal state, and choose a color and opacity. If the opacity is set to 0, then you see nothing, no matter which color you select. Opacity ranges from 0 to 15, where 0 is fully transparent, and 15 is absolutely solid.

Setting the Selected and Activated States

Select the Selected or Activated color pop-up menu and choose a color, then an opacity setting. To see the results of your changes in the Menu tab select either the Show Button Selected State toggle button, for the selected state, or the Show Button Activated State for the activated state.

Using Advanced Highlights

Advanced Highlights differ from Simple Highlights in that they use one of two types of overlay. Rather than using only 100% white and black, they use four colors and come in two variants: Chroma and Grayscale.

CHROMA

The Chroma overlay uses four key-colors, which are all 100%. They are white, which serves as the background transparency, and black, red, and blue, which serve as key-colors that allow you to create multicolor buttons.

GRAYSCALE

The Grayscale overlay used variants in the black color to define its three-color key for buttons in addition to using 100% white as the background key. These black variants are 100% black, 66% black, and 33% black.

Because there is no single key-color as with simple highlights, you now have the option of defining which key-color will be used for any of the colors in the button, up to three colors in addition to the transparency color.

Using Color Sets

Color Sets allow you to define up to three unique sets of highlight states. Each button can be set to use one of these three sets, allowing you to further enhance the menu.

By default, you are always working in Set 1. You define Set 2 and Set 3 by selecting the appropriate set number and setting your color states as you did with the default Set 1.

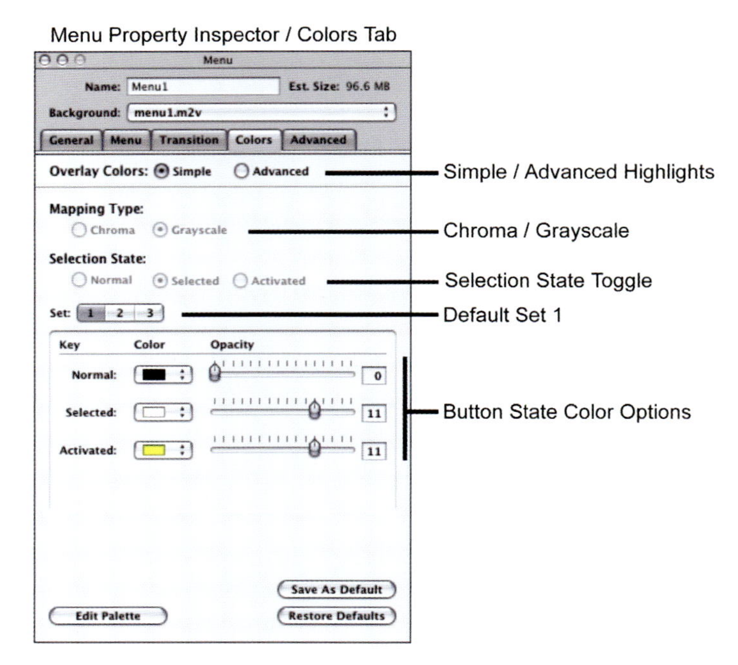

Figure 6.41 Menu Property Inspector — Colors tab

Button Properties

Button properties allow you to set up the Button object in quite a few ways. By selecting the Button object, then opening the Button's Property Inspector, you'll find four tabs designed to help you configure your button's style, navigation, associated streams, and functions, as well as the overlays and highlights, and transitions if there are to be any. The most basic functions, however, are the name of the button and its target.

Naming the Button Object

Select the button in the Menu tab, and then open the Button's Property Inspector. The default names of the buttons are Button 1, Button 2, and so forth, as this is their navigational order. To the right of Button 1 for example, the button's true assigned number is shown.

Assigning the Button Target

Select the button Target property, and use the pop-up menu to select any menu, track, story, script, or other target.

The Style Tab

The Asset pop-up menu allows you to assign any asset to the bounding box that is your button. This can be a still image or a full motion video from a still image or a QuickTime movie.

The Motion check box allows selecting motion or no motion from a full motion asset. Unchecking this box when selecting a full motion asset allows you to pick any single frame from the motion asset and use that as the image for the button background.

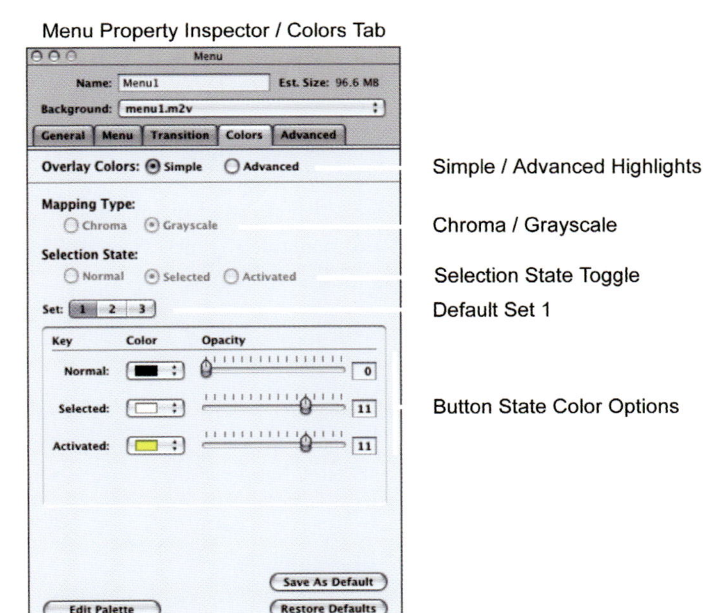

Figure 6.42 Button 1 — Property Inspector

The Shape pop-up menu allows you to add a Shape object to your button. Shape objects have their own highlights and allow you to dress up the appearance of your buttons by giving the buttons borders or other shapes. The still or full motion asset you select will be behind the shape you add to your button.

You may add a drop shadow to your Shape object by selecting the Shadow check box.

Because Shape objects have their own highlights, you may choose the Shape highlight for the shape object's selected state. This selected state comes from one of the three sets of highlights. The default is set 1, but you may choose another. The opacity of the Shape object highlight is defined by that set's selected state opacity setting. Changing this opacity setting of the Shape object highlight also changes the opacity setting of that set's opacity. They are not unique to each other.

The Text area allows you to add text to the button and to position that text as well. If you like, the text can be included in the button; thus it has a highlight too, or it can remain as separate text not affected by the highlight.

The Advanced Tab

The Advanced tab allows you to set manually the navigation of the buttons. In addition, buttons can also directly associate a particular video angle, audio, or subtitle stream.

NAVIGATION

Use the Up, Down, Left, and Right navigation pop-up menus to choose other button targets within the menu. The purpose of these targets are not tracks, but instead, other buttons, as this section determines how the remote control's up, down, left, and right buttons will behave. A quicker way to do this is to use the Menu tab's Settings pop-up menu to assign button navigation, then return to the Advanced tab on a button-by-button basis, and fine-tune your button navigation to your liking.

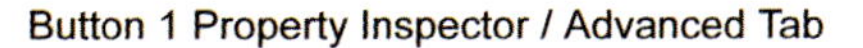

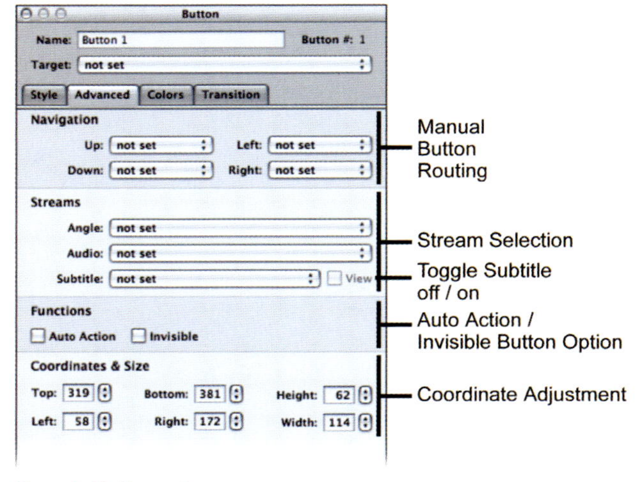

Figure 6.43 Button 1 — Advanced tab

STREAMS

To assign a stream to a button, simply select from any available stream. Streams are defined in the Track tab.

Functions

AUTO ACTION

Auto Action is a bypass for the activated state. Instead, the selection state is carried out immediately when Auto Action is checked.

INVISIBLE

Invisible allows you to create a button which is hidden from view. Though this button may be defined over an overlay designated key-color, it will not show through to the viewer.

COORDINATES

The coordinates are on a button-by-button basis. Select a button in the Menu tab, and its coordinates are revealed. This can be used to fine-tune button placement.

Colors Tab

The Colors tab is used to define the overlay, such as simple or advanced overlays, Chroma or Grayscale, and color sets.

Transition Tab

The Transition tab when used with a button property is defined specifically to the button, and not the Menu as a whole. This allows a more refined transition on a button-by-button basis.

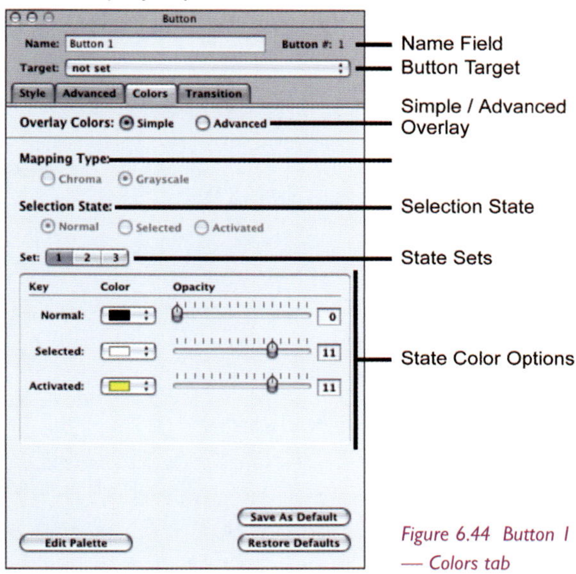

Figure 6.44 Button 1 — Colors tab

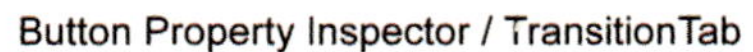

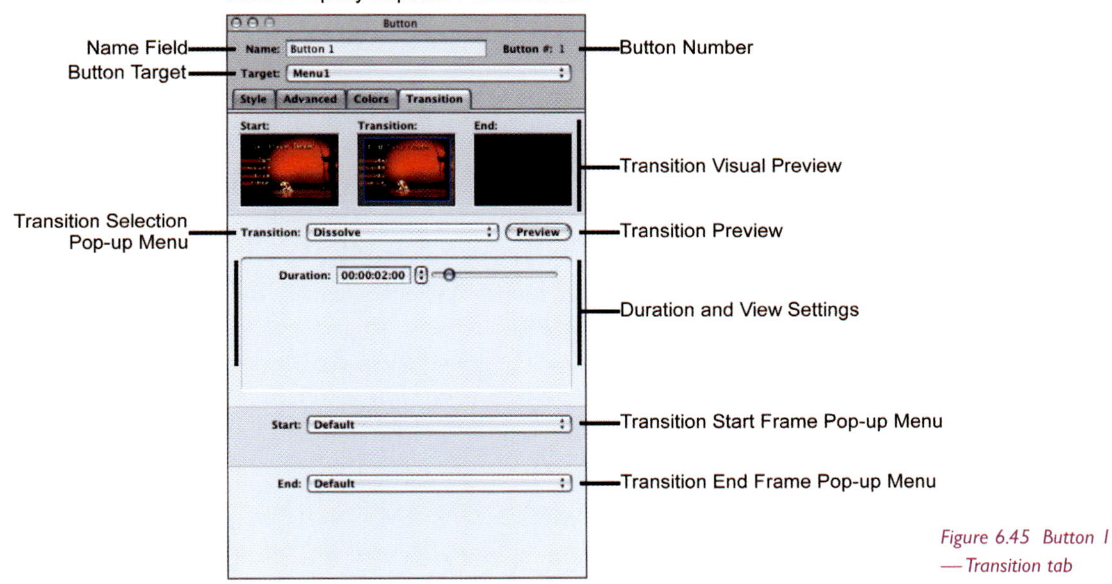

Figure 6.45 Button 1 — Transition tab

Working with Drop Zones

Drop Zones can help you composite a DVD menu directly in DVD Studio Pro. Drop Zones are objects that allow you to add images or video into a special defined zone, which is then rendered into the menu at the time of the build. This can help you design a template-based approach to DVD authoring.

A Drop Zone may be as simple as a single still image, or more complex, consisting of a multilayered Photoshop asset.

Importing Drop Zones

Drop Zones are imported in two ways.

Single Layer	Select Import in the Assets tab. Select any single layer image you wish to use as a Drop Zone.
Multi-Layer	Open the Palette window. Select the Shapes tab. Select the Custom button. Select Import. Select your multilayered Shape object.

Positioning your Drop Zone

Single Layer	From the Assets tab, drag your Drop Zone onto the menu and hold for a brief moment. When the drop palette appears, select Create Drop Zone. Once the Drop Zone has been created, you may drag it to any location on the menu.
Multi-Layer	Open the Palette. Select the Shapes tab. Select the Custom button. Drag the Shape object to the menu, and hold for a brief moment. When the Drop Palette appears, choose Create Drop Zone, Set Shape, and release the mouse button. Move the Drop Zone to any area of the screen. Open the Property Inspector for the Drop Zone, and use the Rotation button to rotate the Drop Zone on the menu.

Working with Shape Objects

Shape objects are multilayer objects just like Drop Zones with the addition of a fourth layer, which is the highlight layer. Because Shape objects are designed to be used for buttons, they make use of a highlight layer that allows the Shape object the use of its own built-in overlay. This built-in overlay is the highlight layer.

Importing Shape Objects

Open the Palette, and then select the Shapes tab. Select the Custom button, and then choose Import at the bottom. Locate your Shape object from the file system, and choose Import.

Adding Stills and Animations to Shape Objects

To add any still or animation to a Shape object, first add the Shape object to the menu by dragging the Shape over the menu and holding for a brief moment; when the Drop Palette appears select Create Button, Set Shape.

Position the Shape object to any location you like, then using the Assets tab select any still or animated item, and drag it on top of the Shape object, holding for a brief moment until the Drop Palette appears. Select Set Asset if this is a still or animated item.

Linking Shapes to Tracks or Menus

Because Shape objects are really buttons, you may also use direct linking features built into DVD Studio Pro to set the animation of the shape as well as its target in a single option.

Drag a Shape object to the menu and hold for a brief moment until the Drop Palette appears. Select Create Button Set Shape. Next, drag a Track object from the Outline tab to the Shape Object and hold for a brief moment until the Drop Palette appears. Select Set Asset Connect to Track. The Shape object is a button with its name already set as the Track name, and its target is the Track asset in the Outline tab.

Click on the button to select it and open its Property Inspector. You have all the familiar tabs to customize the button further.

Working with Text

You may add text directly to the menu using the built-in text features. This text is treated as an object and can be positioned anywhere in the menu. It is limited in formatting capability.

Adding Text

To add text to your menu, double-click in an empty area of the menu. A cursor will appear, allowing you to type text directly on the menu.

Formatting Text

Highlight the text you wish to format. Using the top pull-down menus, choose Format > Show Fonts

The Track Tab

The Track tab defines track elements such as audio, video, and subtitles. Each of these elements goes beyond a single asset, making use of what is known as streams of audio and subtitles, and angles for video.

Adjusting the Track View

Adjust the view of the audio and video elements by pulling or shrinking the scroll bar at the bottom of the Track tab.

Assigning an MPEG2 Asset to V1

Drag an MPEG2 asset from the Assets tab into the V1 section of the Track tab. You're adjoining audio asset may import automatically.

Adding Chapters

Adjust the play head in the Track tab, and determine the location of the chapter. Press M to mark the chapter location.

Importing Chapter Markers

To import chapter markers, you must have a prepared list of timecode, and corresponding chapter names. This list should be saved as a pure text file.

00:03:00:01	chapter 1
00:12:00:05	chapter 2
00:14:02:10	chapter 3

Right click in the marker area, and choose Import Marker List. A file browser will open. Choose the text file you have created in the format above, and select Choose from the Choose Marker File window. The list of chapters, including the names, is added to the track and designated as the purple markers.

Assigning an Audio Asset to A1

If your adjoining audio asset didn't import automatically at the time you imported your video asset, drag the audio asset from the Assets Tab into the A1 section of the Track tab. This creates the default Audio Stream.

Setting the Language Code

Choose a language code by selecting the language pop-up menu in the A1 section of the Track tab. For English, choose C – F > English. The language code is set to "EN" for English.

Adding Subtitles to the S1 Stream

Adding subtitles to your project can be done either directly within the application, or by importing ready-made subtitles from external applications including a common text editor.

TXT	A plain text file
STL	The Spruce Technologies format
SON	The Sonic bitmap-based format
SCR	The Daiken-Comtec Laboratories Scenarist bitmap-based format

Adding a Subtitle Using the Track Tab

Open the Track tab and position the playhead indicator at the beginning of any area where you wish text to appear over your video. Right click in the background and choose Add Subtitle at Playhead.

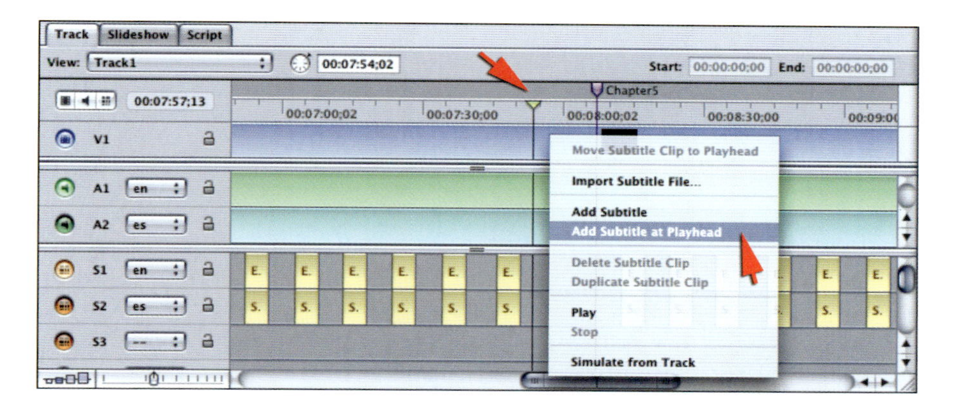

Figure 6.46 Adding a subtitle at the playhead

A cursor appears over the video in the Track tab. You may type directly over the video or use the Property Inspector text field to enter your text.

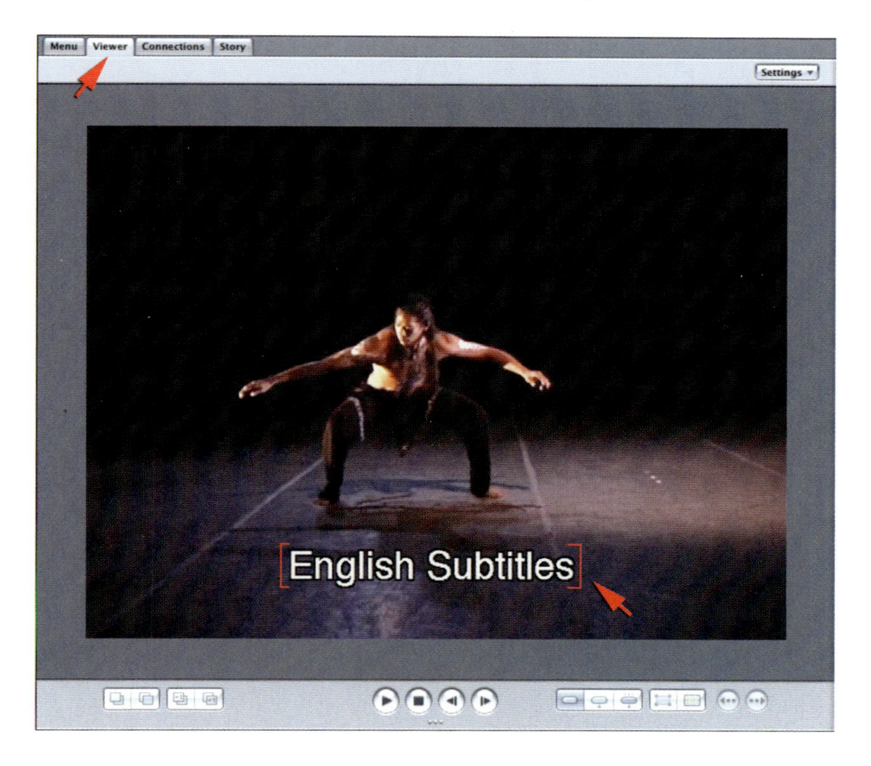

Figure 6.47 Typing subtitles over video

Importing Subtitles through a Text File

When importing from a file, the timecode is defined in the file, rather than through the Track tab and playhead location.

To import your subtitles, choose a subtitle stream target, then right click in the open area and choose Import Subtitle File.

subtitles.txt

```
00:01:33:19 , 00:01:35:01 ,It was impressive...
00:01:36:01 , 00:01:40:01 ,The guys were hot too!
00:01:41:23 , 00:01:45:09 ,laughing and embarrassed
00:01:46:14 , 00:01:51:03 ,You know they were..
```

Figure 6.48 Text File with subtitles

Your subtitles are added to the project, where you can make changes if needed just by double-clicking on each of the subtitles and editing them directly in the Viewer tab or the Property Inspector.

Assigning a Language to Your Subtitle

Select the Stream Language Selection Menu, and choose your subtitle's language for the list of languages. This inserts a two-letter language code in the subtitle stream. Viewers will see the language choices you create here when using the DVD player's Subtitle button.

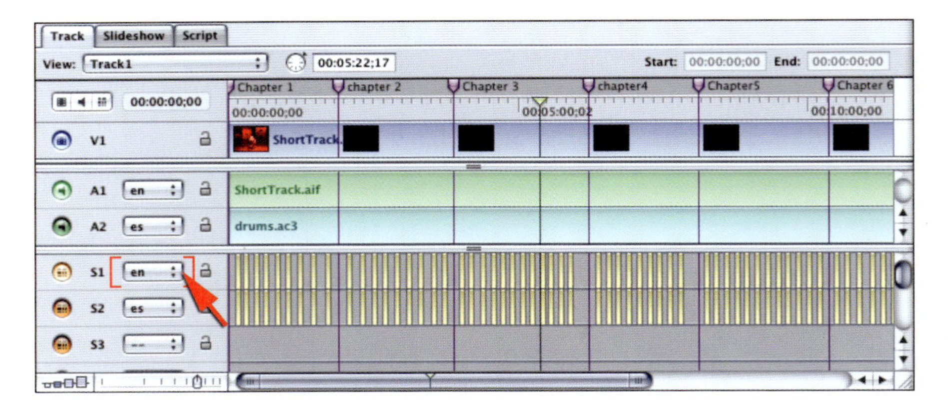

Figure 6.49 Setting the subtitle language code

Preparing Still Menus

The Workflow

Still menus are menus that contain a background image and an overlay.

The background may contain several flattened layers, designed within Adobe's Photoshop application, while the overlay will be either a simple overlay or an advanced overlay.

A simple overlay is a black-and-white image on a single layer; an advanced overlay uses either four gray tones, or four color tones, such as white, blue, red, and black. It is the job of the overlay to map through the use of colors the exact shape and placement of a highlight.

A highlight is the status color defined by a button. A button highlight in the normal state may be programmed to be the color blue, for example. When this same button is in the selected state, you may change the color from blue to red. And at the very moment the button is chosen, it can change to a third color very briefly, known as the activated state.

Working with Adobe Photoshop

When creating a still menu, you will define the aspect ratio, such as 4:3 or 16:9, and the television standard, such as NTSC or PAL.

You will also need to adjust for pixel aspect ratio differences of the computer and its image editor, and the television.

Photoshop Setup for NTSC or PAL

To begin creating a menu with Adobe Photoshop, first decide on the dimension you will be working with. The table below shows the various dimensions for popular formats.

Television Standard	Aspect Ratio	Dimension	Pixel Aspect Ratio	Dimension	Pixel Aspect Ratio
NTSC	4:3	720 x 534	1.0	720 x 480	.9
	16:9	864 x 480	1.0	720 x 480	1.2
PAL	4:3	768 x 576	1.0	720 x 576	1.066
	16:9	1024 x 576	1.0	720 x 576	1.42

For NTSC 4:3 television, for example, you'll create a 720 x 534 menu with a 1.0 pixel aspect ratio. Once your menu is finished, you'll convert that menu to 720 x 480 with a .9 pixel aspect ratio.

You can follow along by simply opening the finished PSD file of this lesson, located here: Chapter 7/Tutorial 1/L1_1_4X3_Menu.psd.

Figure 7.1 Photoshop — new document

Step 1

Open Photoshop, then using the top pull—down menus, choose: File > New.

Set the width and height to match the dimensions for your television standard type. For NTSC 4:3 television, you'll use 720 x 534 to begin. Set the Resolution to 72 pixels per inch, set the Color Mode to RGB Color, and leave the background transparent.

If you are using Photoshop CS, choose the Advanced option, and set the Color Profile setting to "Don't Color Manage this Document." Set the Pixel Aspect Ratio setting to "Square," then select OK.

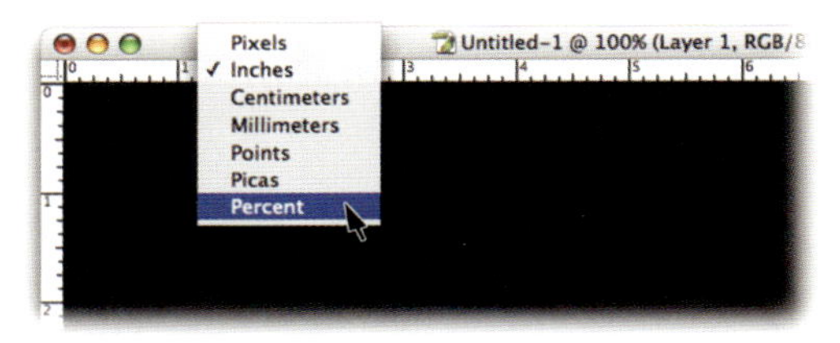

Figure 7.2 Photoshop — Ruler View — Percent

Action / Title Safe Guides

You'll need to add guides to your menu in order to avoid adding text or graphics that are outside the viewing area of a standard television.

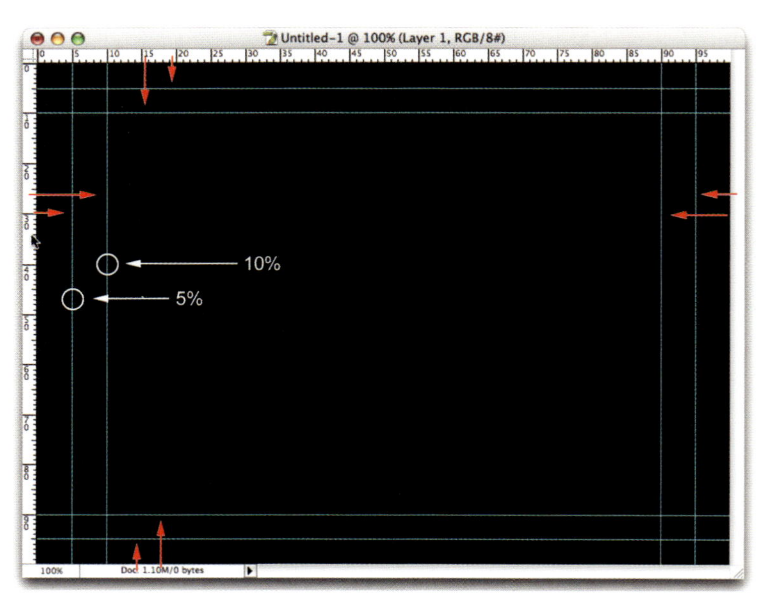

Figure 7.3 Photoshop — setting guides

If you do not see the ruler around the margins of your menu, use the pull down menu and choose View > Rulers, or use the keystroke Command-R. Once the rulers are in view, right-click or control click on the ruler to open the ruler's display options. From the pop up menu, choose Percent.

Step 2

To create a guide, position the mouse within the ruler, then click, hold, and drag into the image. You'll see that you pull guides from within the rulers.

Set your guides to 5% and 10% on all four sides of your menu.

The guides set to 5% are your action-safe area, and the guides placed at 10% are the title-safe area. Make sure all text stays within the title-safe area, and all images that you wish to remain within complete view stay within the action-safe area. The background itself should consume the entire screen.

The Background

The background of your menu may be one or more layers within the same Photoshop image. Use Adobe Photoshop to open the L1_2_4x3_Menu.psd file located in the Tutorial 1 folder.

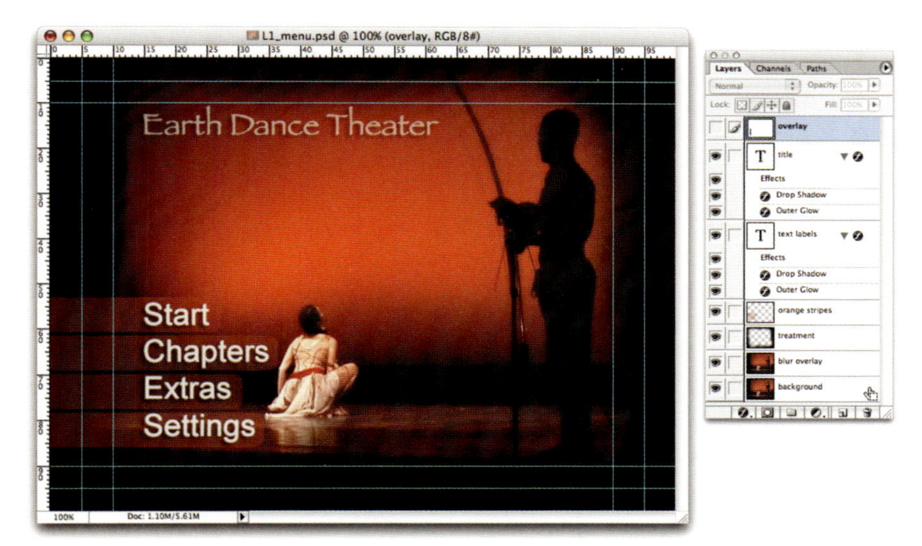

Figure 7.4 Photoshop — background layers

DVD Studio Pro is not currently compatible with the effects layers you might employ in your Photoshop artwork. To solve this problem, you will need to flatten any layer effects you have assigned to any Photoshop layers, such as layer modes, shadows, and so on.

To add layer effects to your Adobe Photoshop art, select the desired layer in the Layer palette, and then right-click, or Control-click that layer. The Layer

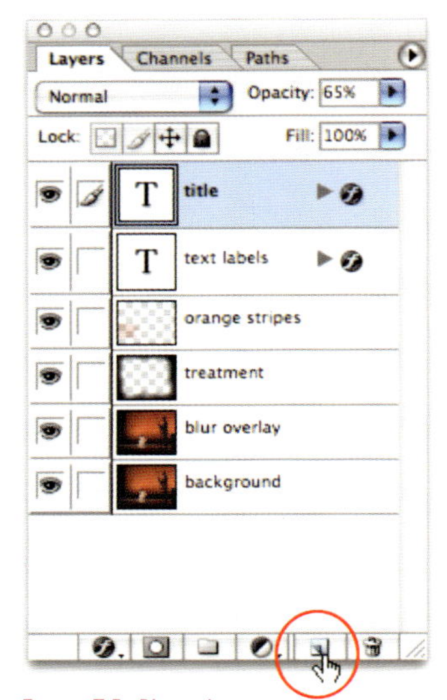

Figure 7.5 Photoshop — Effects layer

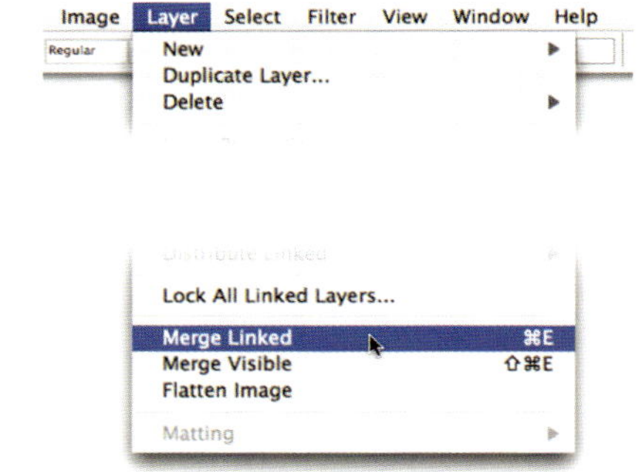

Figure 7.7 Photoshop — Merge Linked

Style palette opens. You may choose layer effects such as Drop Shadow, Color Overlay, and many others, as well as fine-tune each of varying properties of these effects.

Step 3

Choose the Title Layer in the Layers palette, and then select the Create New Layer button at the bottom of the palette.

This adds a new layer within the Layers palette. You will merge this new layer with the title layer. This will preserve the layered effects by rasterizing them into a single layer that DVD Studio Pro can understand.

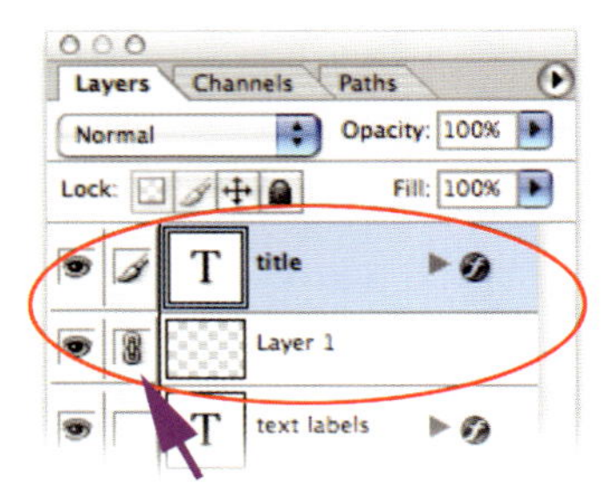

Figure 7.6 Photoshop — Linked layer

Step 4

Position the new layer under the title layer. Select the title layer, and then click in the box just to the right of the eye icon in the Layer 1 layer. You will see a chain link appear.

Step 5

Using the pull down menus, select Layer > Merge Linked.

Notice the title layer no longer has the "T" icon in the layer thumbnail. This is because this is no longer a text layer. It is nothing more than an ordinary image now with no associated effects. The effects that were part of that text layer are now rasterized into the image itself.

In the Tutorial 1 folder, open the L1_3_4x3_Menu.psd document to see a finished version of this menu.

Creating an Overlay Layer

When you are making a selection in a DVD's menu, you are using a subpicture overlay to do so. In the menu example below, note the rectangular shape that defines the currently selected button within this DVD's menu. The currently selected menu item is titled Start.

That rectangle is one of two colors in the subpicture overlay map. This particular map type is known as a simple overlay, meaning it has just two colors, which are white and black.

The Overlay layer is above the background. The white area in this simple overlay will become transparent in the menu, and the black areas are used to define the selection states of the buttons they will represent.

To create a simple overlay, follow these steps:

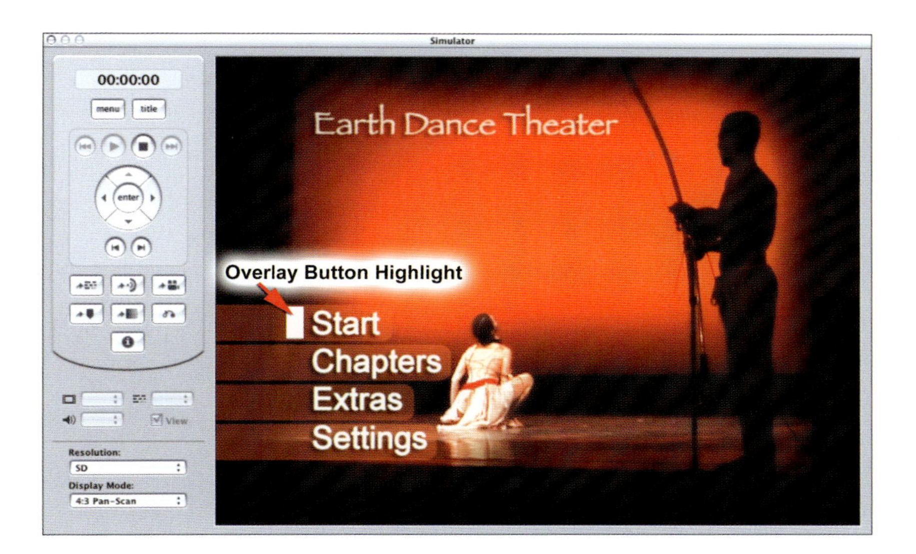

Figure 7.8 DVD Studio Pro — the simulator

Step 1

Open the L1_3_4x3_Menu.psd image in Photoshop. In the Layers palette, select the top layer, which is "title," then select the Create New Layer button at the bottom of the palette.

This creates a new layer above the previously selected layer, thus adding a new layer, Layer 1, to the top of the Layer palette.

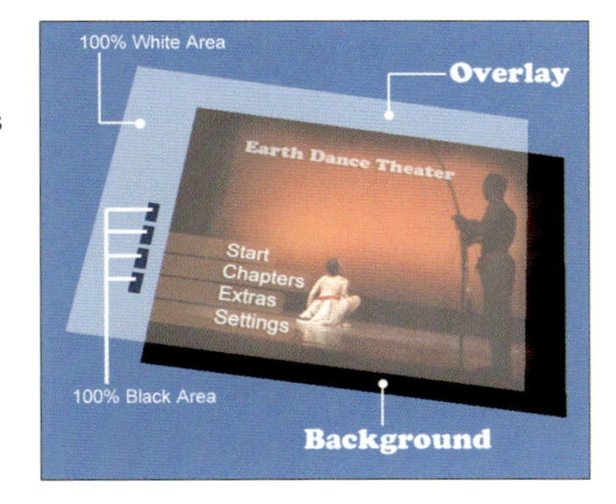

Figure 7.9 Simple overlay

Step 2

Rename the new layer to Overlay, as this will help you later in DVD Studio Pro. Next, select the Paint Bucket in the toolbox, and then set the foreground color to white.

Figure 7.10 Adobe Photoshop — new layer

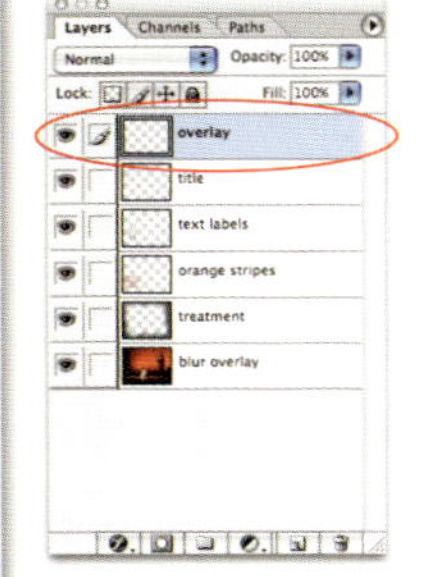

Figure 7.11 Adobe Photoshop — creating the overlay

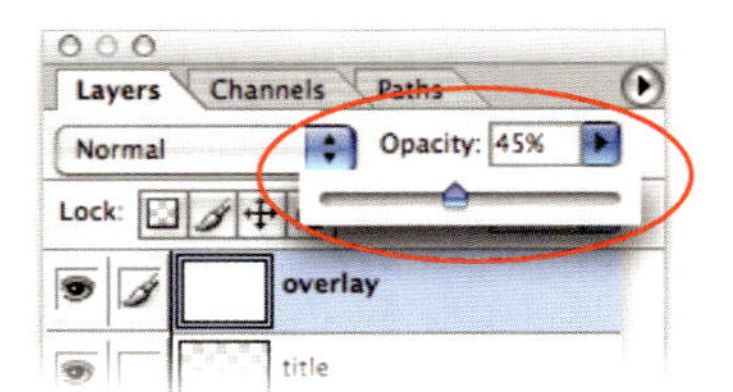

Figure 7.12 Setting the opacity

Step 3

With the Paint Bucket and the overlay layer selected, paint the layer white.

Step 4

Using the Opacity setting in the Layers palette, set the overlay layer to an opacity of 50%, give or take a little.

This will make the overlay layer semitransparent, which will help you define the black areas you will create next.

Step 5

Change the foreground color to black, and then select the rectangular marquee tool from the toolbox. Create four rectangles with the marquee tool just left of the button names.

Figure 7.13 Mapping buttons in the overlay

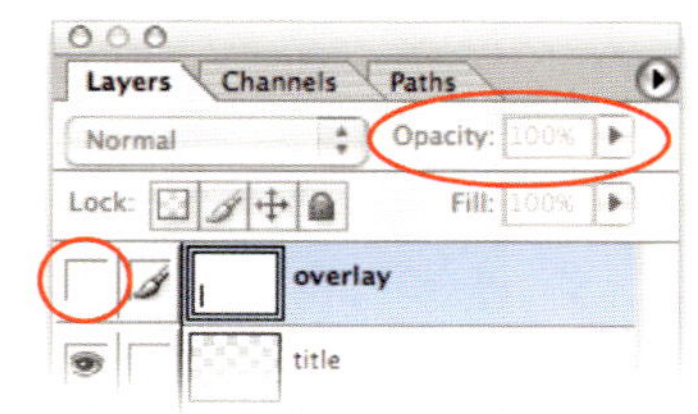

Figure 7.14 Turn off visibility

Step 6

Select the Paint Bucket from the toolbox, and paint the four rectangles black.

Step 7

Change the overlay layer opacity back to 100% and save your menu.

You now have a mostly white area, with just four small rectangles off to the left. It's very helpful to turn the overlay layer visibility off, so you are able to visually recognize the menu later.

Pixel Aspect Ratio

Your computer and the image editing application use a square pixel aspect ratio, while your NTSC television uses a rectangular pixel aspect ratio. As a result of this, uncorrected images created on your computer will look stretched from top to bottom as these images are displayed on the taller, rectangular pixels of the television.

The correct dimensions for menu art prior to importing into DVD Studio Pro depends on the television standard, and whether the menu is being designed for 4:3 or 16:9 aspect ratios.

In the example above, a square pixel aspect ratio image created at 720 x 480 would appear stretched on a 4:3 aspect ratio NTSC television.

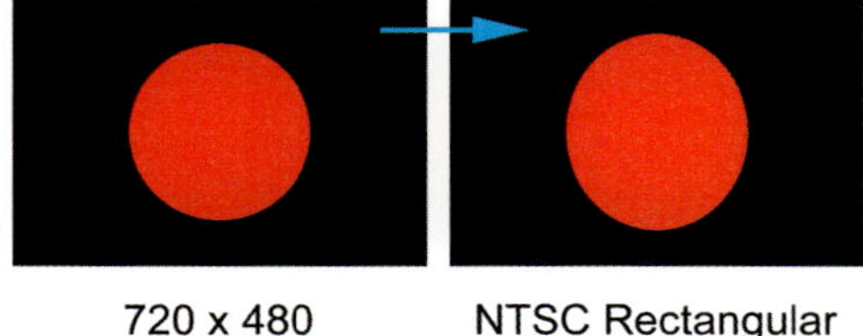

Figure 7.15 Square versus rectangular pixel aspect ratio

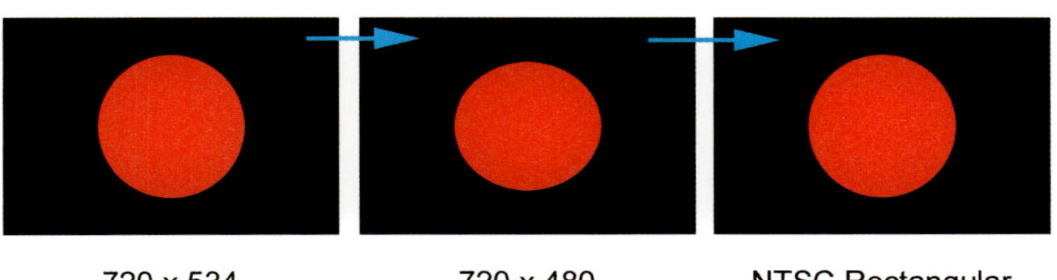

Figure 7.16 Compensating differences of square versus rectangular pixel aspect ratio

To solve this problem, start with 720 x 534 pixels for the menu design. When finished with the menu, you will resize from 534 to 480 pixels, which will result in a crushed-looking image on your computer display. However, when displayed on the NTSC television the stretching effect will bring the image back to normal appearance.

Television Standard	Aspect Ratio	Starting Dimension	Pixel Aspect Ratio	Corrected Dimension	Pixel Aspect Ratio
NTSC	4:3	720 x 534	1.0	720 x 480	.9
	16:9	864 x 480	1.0	720 x 480	1.2
PAL	4:3	768 x 576	1.0	720 x 576	1.066
	16:9	1024 x 576	1.0	720 x 576	1.42

The chart above describes which starting dimensions you will begin creating your menu in, and what corrected dimension you need to reduce to in order to compensate for the differences between computer image editing software and television viewing.

To correct your menu's size in Adobe Photoshop follow this last step.

Step 8

Open the L1_4_4x3_menu.psd in Adobe Photoshop. Using the pull down menu, select Image > Image Size.

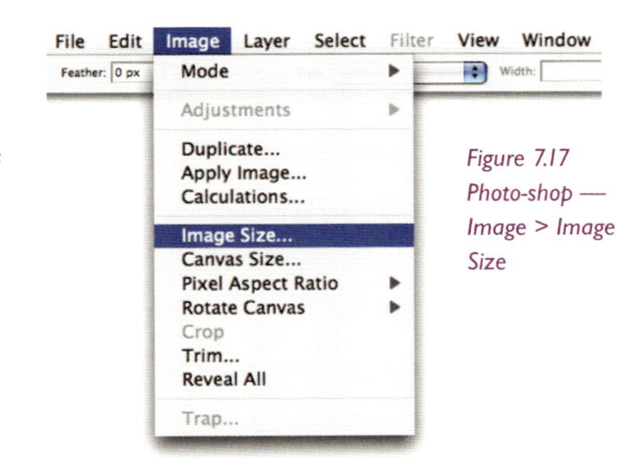

Figure 7.17 Photo-shop — Image > Image Size

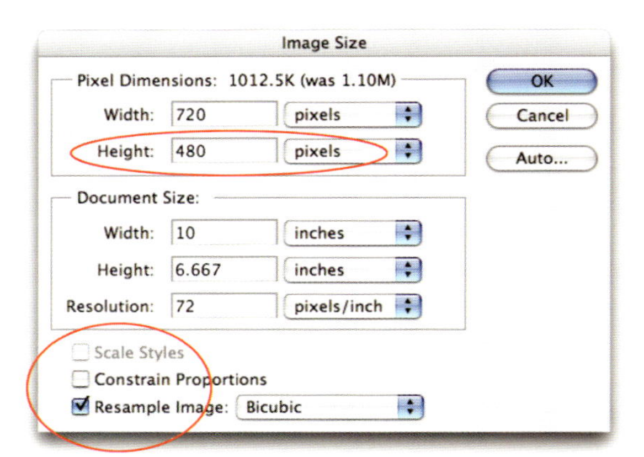

Figure 7.18 Photoshop — changing the image size

Change the Height field from 534 to 480 after you remove the option to Constrain Proportions.

By removing the Constrain Proportions option, you force Photoshop to crush the image from 534 pixels down to 480 pixels, without affecting the width of the menu at all.

Select OK, and then save the menu. The menu now appears in Photoshop to have a crushed appearance. However, once this menu appears on a television it will become stretched just enough to compensate back to its original appearance.

Working with Photoshop Still Menus Inside DVD Studio Pro

In this section you will:

- Import your Photoshop-based still menu
- Add the Photoshop menu to the Menu Object in the Outline tab
- Assign Background layers
- Assign an Overlay layer

Copy the Tutorial 2 folder from the Chapter 7 folder in the DVD to the desktop or another location of your choice. There are two items here, the Lesson 2 DVD Studio Pro project file and the Lesson 1 4x3 menu.

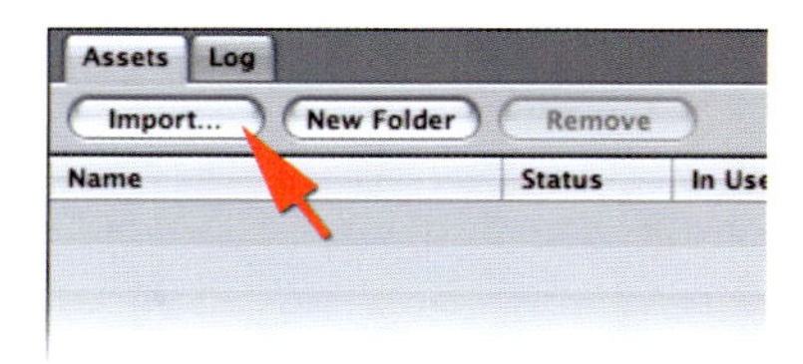

Figure 7.19 Importing assets into the Assets tab

Importing a Menu Asset

Step 1

Launch the DVD project by double-clicking on the project icon. Locate the Assets tab, and select the Import button.

Locate the L1_4_4x3_Menu.psd asset, and then choose Import.

Adding the Menu Asset to the Menu Object

Step 2

Select the Menu 1 object in the Outline tab, and then open the Menu tab if it is not already open.

Drag the L1_4_4x3_Menu.psd asset onto the Menu background and hold until the Drop Palette menu opens.

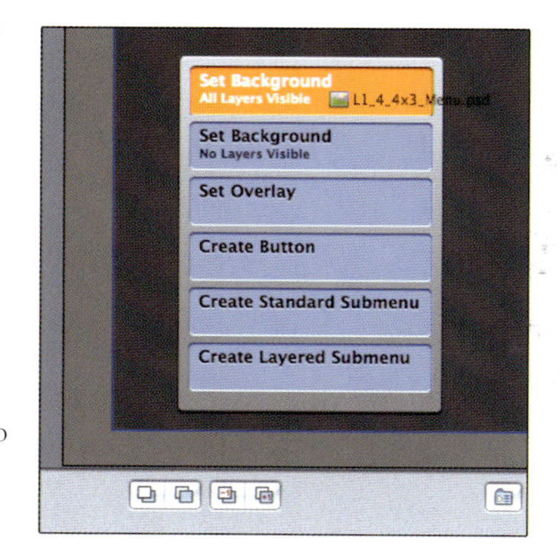

Figure 7.20 Setting the background

Select the Set Background: All Layers Visible option, and then release the mouse. The Menu background will load all the layers from the menu asset created earlier. At this point, all that is visible is the overlay layer, with its white background and four black rectangles.

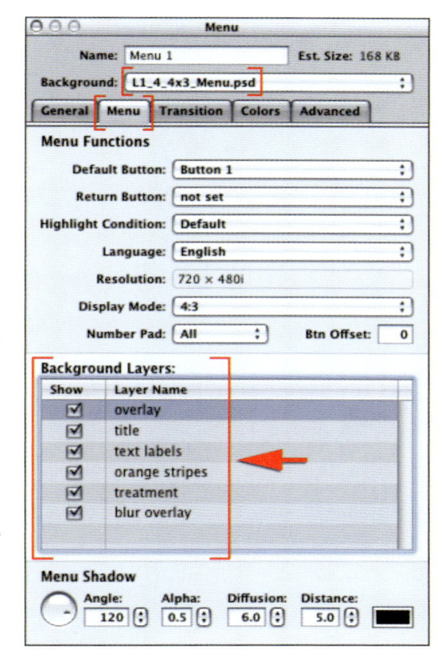

Figure 7.21 Menu tab — background layers

Assigning the Background Layers

Step 3

Click on the Menu 1 object in the Outline tab, and open the Property Inspector if it's not already open. You can open the Property Inspector for any object by first selecting the object and then using the keystroke Command-Option-I.

Open the Menu tab of the inspector and notice the Background Layers area is already populated.

By dragging the menu asset on the background of the Menu and choosing Set Background: All Layers Visible you have already assigned a menu background with all the layers defined as the background layers.

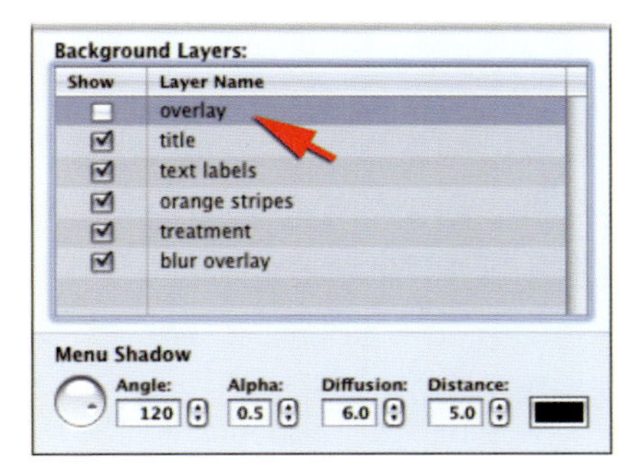

Figure 7.22 Menu Tab — adjusting the Show Property

The overlay layer is the only layer that should not be defined as a background layer, so unselect the Overlay layer from the checked boxes in the Background Layers section.

Assigning the Overlay

Step 4

Now open the General tab, and then select the Overlay File field pop-up menu near the middle of the inspector and choose the L1_4_4x3_menu.psd file as the overlay file. Because the menu asset contains the Overlay layer already, you are choosing the same file as the holder of the Overlay layer.

Select the Overlay File field and choose the background PSD, which

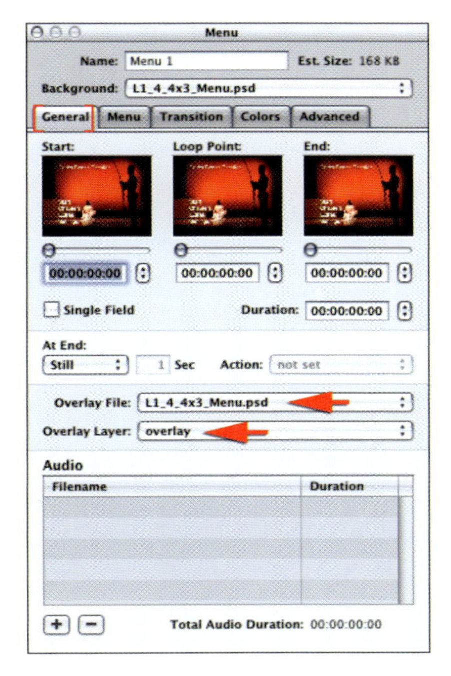

Figure 7.23 General tab — selecting the Overlay layer

contains the Overlay layer as one of its many layers. In the Overlay Layer field just below, select the layer that will serve as the Overlay layer. In this case, that layer happens to be named Overlay. You now have a Menu with defined background layers and a defined overlay. Your next step is to define your menu buttons within the Menu tab.

You now have a menu with defined background layers and a defined overlay. Your next step is to define your menu buttons within the Menu tab.

Defining the Menu Buttons

In this section you will use the Overlay layer to define button highlights and set up basic navigation within a single menu.

Step 1

Open the Lesson 3 project file. Within that project you will notice that the Assets tab has a single asset, called Menu 1.psd. This Menu 1 asset has been assigned to the Menu 1 menu object in the Outline tab.

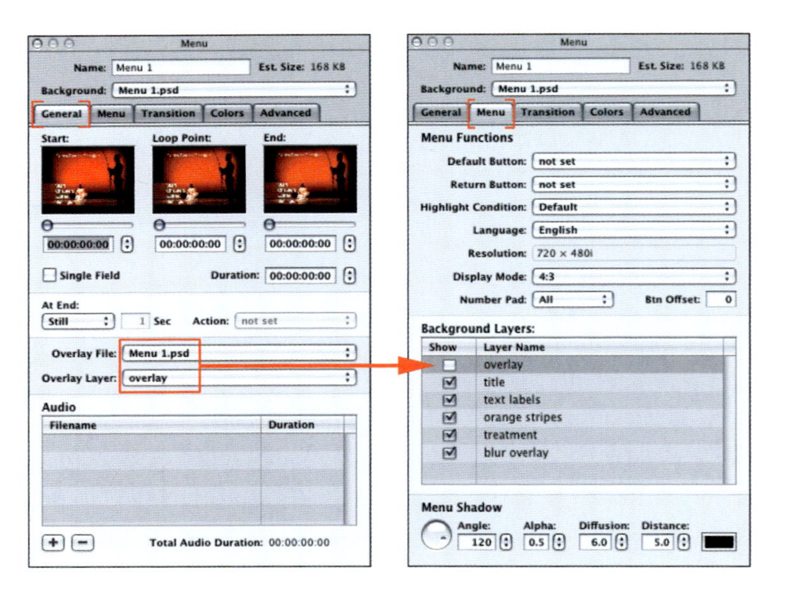

Figure 7.24 Selecting the Overlay layer

Figure 7.25 Activating the Show Property for the Overlay layer

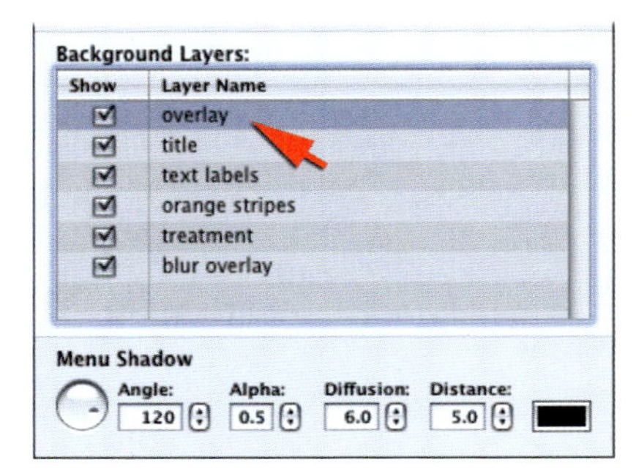

Step 2

Click on the Menu 1 object in the Outline tab and open its Property Inspector. Open the General tab, if not already opened, and notice the Overlay Layer field is set to Overlay, which is a layer in the Menu 1.psd. So the Overlay File field tells DVD Studio Pro which file has the Overlay, and the Overlay Layer field tells DVD Studio Pro which layer within that same file is the layer that will be used as the Menu's Overlay.

Step 3

In the background layers area of the Menu tab, temporarily activate the Overlay layer by checking the Show box next to the layer name. This turns on the Overlay layer so you can clearly see where the button outlines need to be created.

Figure 7.26 Drawing the button outline in the Menu tab

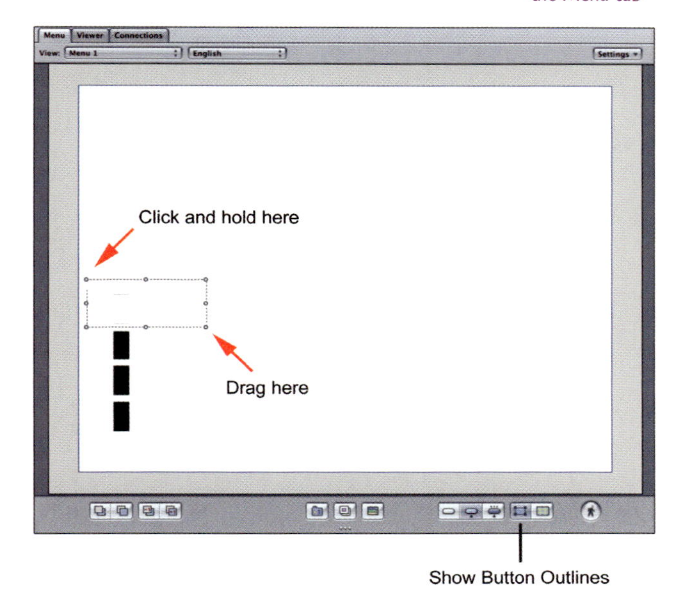

Step 4

Open the Menu tab if it isn't opened already. Click on the Show Button Outline, making sure it is selected. Using the mouse, click and hold the upper-left-hand side of the first rectangle in the menu, and then drag diagonally to the lower-right-hand side. This creates an outline around the rectangle. This outline is the button itself, and now its own Property Inspector.

Do the same for the other three rectangles.

Step 5

When you have all four button outlines created, click on the Menu 1 object in the Outline tab, and then uncheck the show box from the Overlay layer in the General tab of the Menu 1 Object Property Inspector.

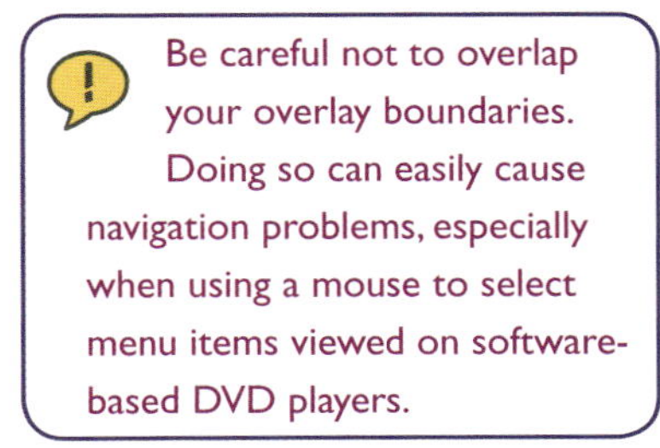

Your menu will look something like this, showing four buttons now, each labeled Button 1 through 4 in the order in which you created

Figure 7.27 Defined button outlines

them, starting from the first button created at the top labeled Button 1 and on down to the last labeled Button 4.

Notice the Settings pop up menu at the upper-right-hand side of the Menu tab; this is where you will choose your button navigation auto settings.

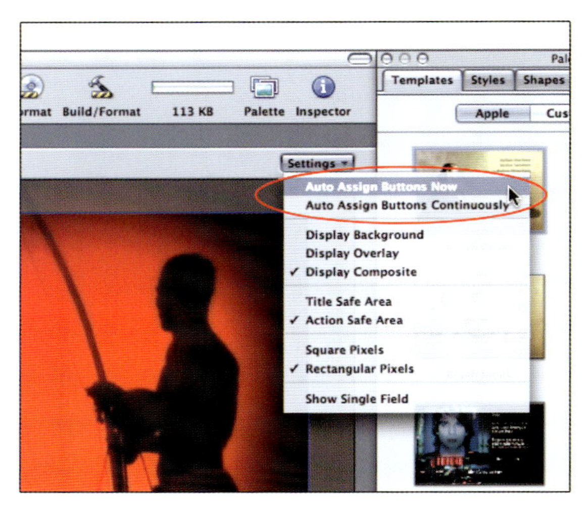

Figure 7.28 Menu Settings — button navigation

Menu Button Navigation

Perhaps the best way to understand button navigation is simply to see it in action.

Step 6

Open the Menu tab, and select the Settings pop up menu.

Select Auto Assign Buttons Now.

Step 7

Now click on the Simulator button in the Toolbar to simulate this small project. Once the simulator opens, use your keyboard's Up, Down, Left, and Right cursor keys to change the current selected menu item.

Figure 7.29 The simulator — DVD Studio Pro 4

What you are seeing is basic menu navigation created automatically for you. DVD Studio Pro took the position of each of the four button outlines and made a guess as to how best to set the up, down, left, and right navigation settings for each of the button outlines in your menu.

Exit the simulation.

Step 8

Click on the Button 1 button outline in the Menu tab. Open its Property Inspector and select the Advanced tab.

Figure 7.30 Button Property — navigation fields

The navigation section shows the exact up, down, left, and right settings for this particular button. Each button will have four settings, one for each of the four directions. You may alter these if you wish, or even set them entirely manually.

The Button Property

In this section, you'll learn about the following:

- Setting the button target.
- Adjusting the button overlay highlights.
- Adding transitions using the built-in transitions.

SETTING THE BUTTON TARGET

Each button outline has its own set of properties that you will set and edit within the Property Inspector. Perhaps the most important of these properties is the Target property, which allows you to set a target for your button. A target may be as simple as another track or menu or more complex objects such as script objects or even chapter points.

To set the button target follow these steps.

Step 1

Click on the button outline in the Menu tab.

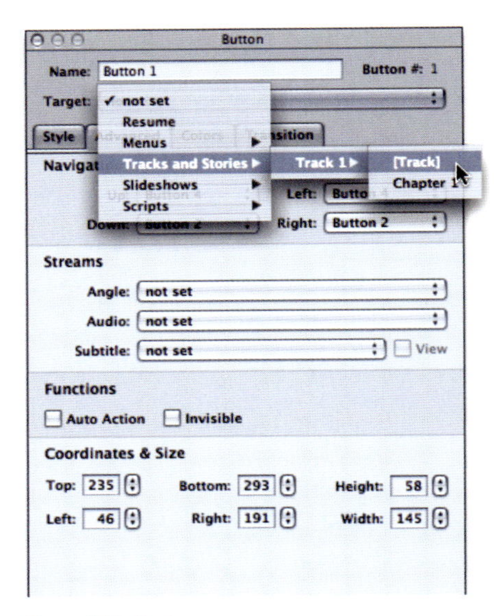

Figure 7.31 Setting

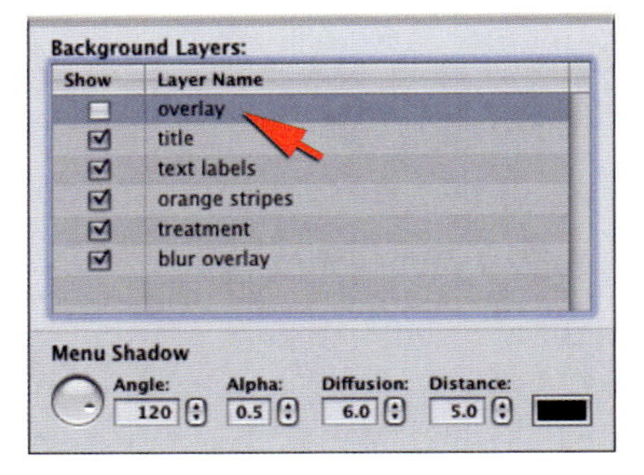

Figure 7.32 Button property — the Colors tab

Step 2

Open the button's Property Inspector, and then use the Target pop up menu to choose from any of the available targets.

You'll notice that the available targets are grouped together in a logical way. Tracks are grouped with their story or stories, as well as chapters, while menus are grouped with their individual menu buttons, allowing you to target another menu button in another menu.

ADJUSTING THE OVERLAY PROPERTIES

To adjust the overlay, you may use the Color tab of the menu itself, or use the Style tab or Colors tab of the button's own property.

Setting the Overlay Map Type

Setting the overlay map type requires forethought, as this is a product of the asset you will create before you reach this stage of selection. For a two-color simple overlay, you will use the Simple Overlay map type. However, if you have specifically created a four-color Overlay map with the use of either grayscale or chroma, then you would use the advanced overlay settings.

The black-and-white overlay used in this section is of the Simple type, and so you will leave the default Simple selection as the chosen Overlay Colors.

USING SELECTION STATES

You can store up to three different sets of color states. The default set is always Set 1.

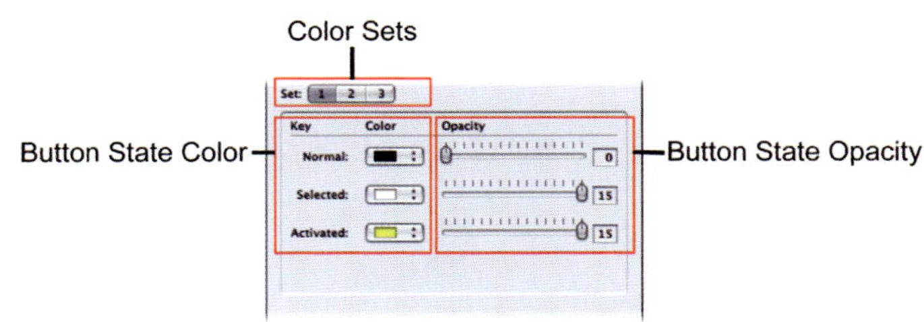

Figure 7.35 Button states and color sets

Each set is composed of three buttons states: Normal, Selected, and Activated. Each of these three states may be assigned a unique color, and that color may only have 1 of 16 opacity levels.

There are three selection states each button will use.

Highlight Button States — Simple Overlay

Normal	Color displayed of all non—selected buttons
Selected	Color displayed of current selected button
Activated	Color displayed after the user presses play or enter

MODIFYING THE SELECTED STATE PROPERTY

Figure 7.33 Button overlay — selected state

Step 1

Open the menu in the Menu tab. At the bottom, select the Show Selected State button.

Step 2

Select any one of the four button outlines. Open the button's Property Inspector. Slide the Selected slider from left to right, and notice that the color of the selected state goes from dimmer to brighter as you do so. This slider represents the opacity of the color. Select the color pop—up menu and choose another color in the quick color palette.

Adding Transitions

You can add a transition to the menu, which then affects each button in the same way, or you may choose a unique transition on a button-by-button basis.

Open the Lesson 4 project file in Tutorial 4 in the Chapter 7 folder in the DVD-ROM to follow this lesson.

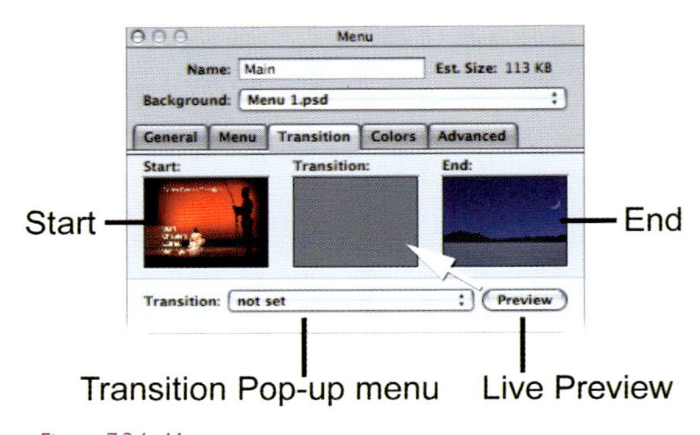

Figure 7.34 Menu Property — the Transitions tab

ADDING MENU TRANSITIONS

Step 1

Open the Menu tab, and make sure you are viewing the menu called Main.

Step 2

Open the Property Inspector for this menu, and click on the Transition tab.

Step 3

Select the Transition pop up menu and choose the Motion Dissolve transition from the menu.

Step 4

Select the Preview button and the center transition box. You will see a dissolve transition between the Start menu and the generic soft blue sky with the moon image.

Step 5

Click on the Chapters button outline in the Menu tab.

Figure 7.35 Transitions — start, transition, and end property

This is the Chapters button property. Select the Transition tab, and notice that the End preview changed from the blue sky with the moon image to the chapter button's target, which is the Chapters menu.

Notice the Transitions pop up menu. It no longer shows the selection is Motion Dissolve. Instead it simply says, Same as Menu. This is because setting the menu transition sets a parent transition for all buttons within the menu. You may override this by simply selecting any button and setting the transition once again, at the button level. Doing so changes the transition for that button only.

Additional Adjustments

You have learned that DVD Studio Pro uses native Photoshop multilayered assets as its still menu background and overlay. Even more powerful is the ability to further edit those multilayered images even after you have imported them into DVD Studio Pro.

In this section, you will learn how to use the Open in Editor function to re-edit your menu graphics directly in Adobe Photoshop and have that result instantly updated in your menu. In addition, DVD Studio Pro will allow you to quickly turn on and off layers of the Photoshop-based menu directly within DVD Studio Pro.

Using Open in Editor

To open the Menu 1.psd asset in Photoshop for further editing, follow these steps:

It's always a good idea to copy the project folder to your desktop, and use those copied files with these lessons. This will leave the DVD drive free for other use.

Step 1

Right-click on the Menu 1.psd asset in the Asset tab and select Open in Editor from the pop up menu options. If the file does not open with Adobe Photoshop, you'll need to set the asset file association to open with Photoshop.

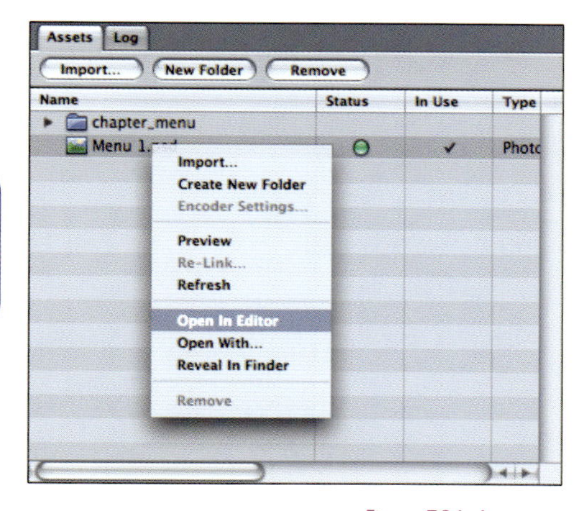

Figure 7.36 Assets Tab — Open In Editor function

To set up the Photoshop files with the .PSD extensions to automatically open with Photoshop, select the Photoshop file and use the keystroke Command-I, or right-click, or Control-click the asset and then choose Get Info. Change the Open with field to Adobe Photoshop, and then close the Apple Info palette.

Figure 7.37 Menu 1 opened in Adobe Photoshop with layers

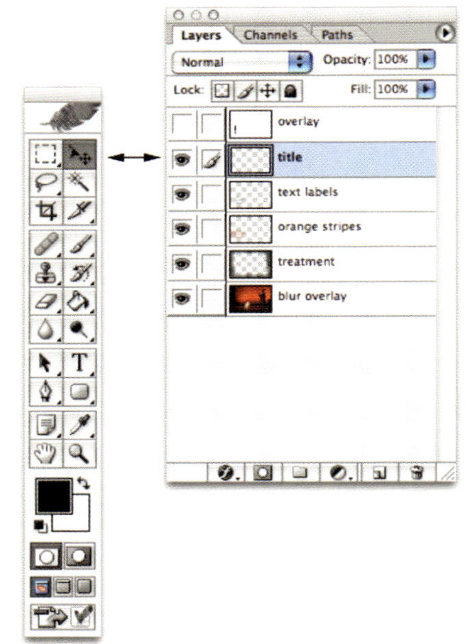

Figure 7.38 Photoshop — the toolbox and Layer palette

Step 2

Adobe Photoshop will open automatically, and you will have access to all the original layers you used to create this menu.

Step 3

Select the Title layer from the Layers palette within Photoshop, then select the Move tool from the toolbox or use the keystroke V.

Figure 7.39 Photoshop — Adjusting the title layer position

Step 4

Reposition the title text from its upper-left-hand location to the bottom-right-hand area.

Step 5

Now, save the Photoshop image and exit the application.

Step 6

Return to DVD Studio Pro.

You will notice that the title text has been updated, no longer in the upper-left-hand corner; it now resides in the lower-right-hand corner.

Use the same steps to return the title text back to its original location.

Adding, Subtracting, Hiding, and Revealing Layers

In the same way you modify layers using the Open in Editor function, you may also add layers or subtract layers entirely inside Adobe Photoshop.

Step 1

Use the Open in Editor on the Menu 1.psd asset within the Assets tab.

Step 2

Once the menu has loaded inside Adobe Photoshop, highlight the title layer, and then drag it to the trash can at the bottom right of the Layer palette.

Step 3

Save the Adobe Photoshop image, and without quitting Photoshop, switch back to DVD Studio Pro.

Step 4

Adjust the background layers and Overlay layer setting in the Menu tab of the Main menu Property Inspector.

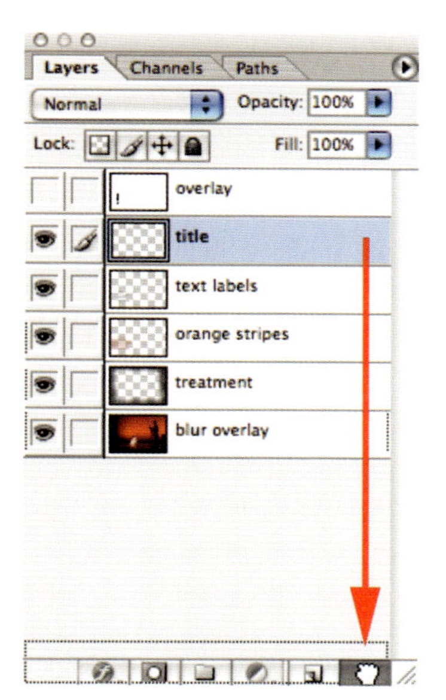

Figure 7.40 Deleting a layer

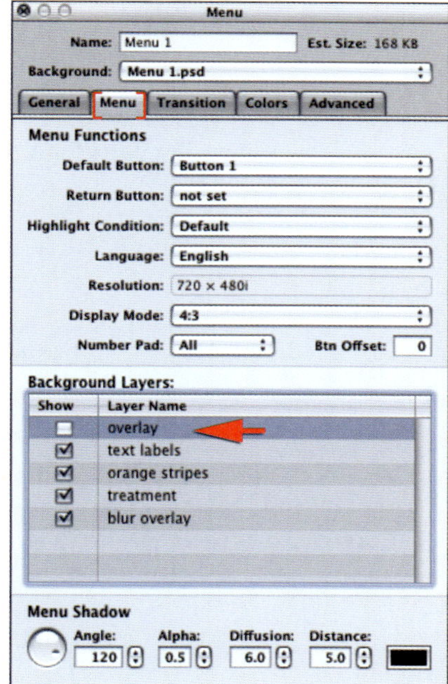

Figure 7.41 Menu property — adjusting the Show Layer properties

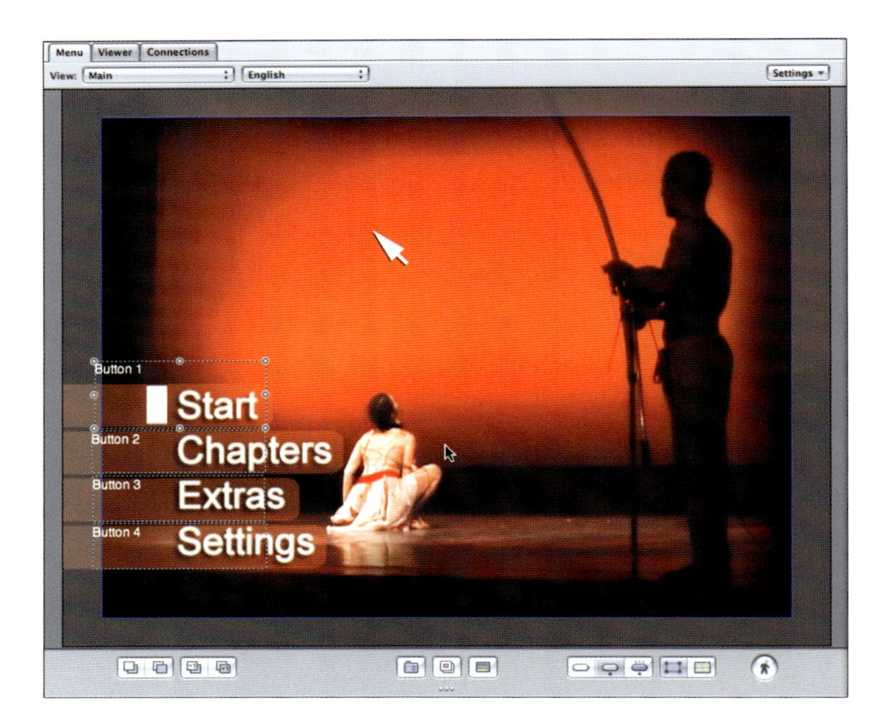

Figure 7.42 The Menu tab

Step 5

Go back to the Menu tab, and notice that the title Earth Dance Theater is no longer there. You have removed the layer from Adobe Photoshop, and the results of that removal are now reflected within the Menu.

In the same manner, you may add layers to this existing menu using the Open in Editor function.

You may also hide and reveal layers that exist within the Background Layers property.

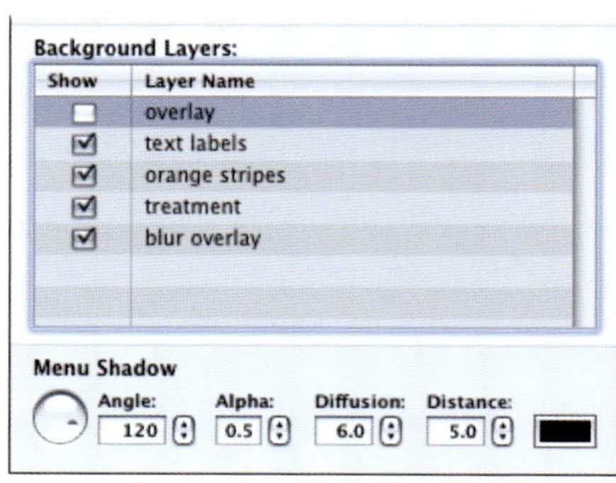

Figure 7.43 The Menu tab — Background Layers property

Step 1

Open the Menu tab to view the Main menu.

Step 2

Open the Menu tab of the menu's Property Inspector.

Step 3

Select and deselect the Show property while watching the effect it has on the menu in the Menu tab. You are hiding and revealing layers without actually deleting them in Adobe Photoshop.

Previewing Your Menu

You can preview your menu with the built-in project simulator. The simulator is a powerful way to test your DVD, its menus, tracks, and transitions before you actually commit to building or burning a DVD.

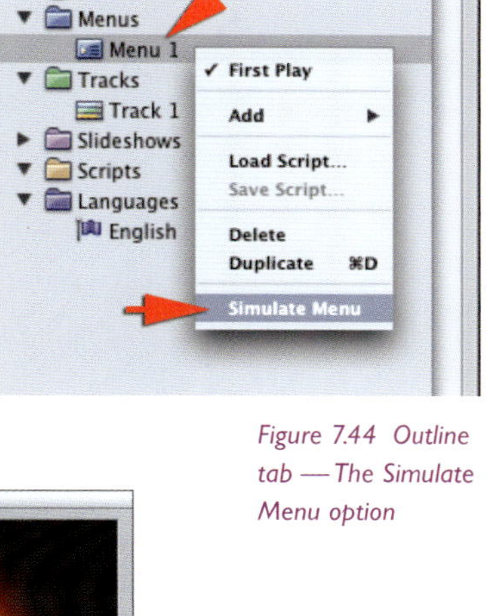

Figure 7.44 Outline tab — The Simulate Menu option

Using the Simulator to Preview Your Menu

Step 1

Open the Outline tab, and then right-click on the Main menu and choose Simulate from the Options menu.

Step 2

Use the side remote only and select the Up, Down, Left, and Right arrows to simulate button navigation within this menu.

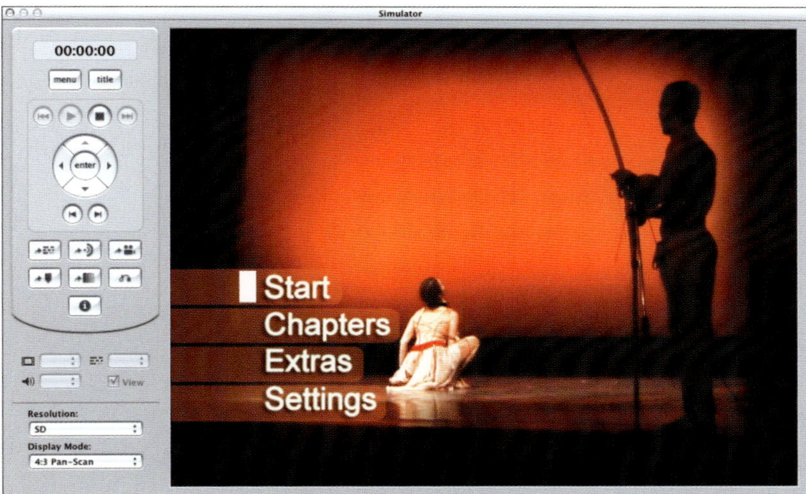

Figure 7.45 The simulator — DVD Studio Pro 4

You may right-click on any menu, and gain access to the Simulate function specifically for that menu.

Step 3

Select the Chapters button and then press the Enter button. This will simulate the Motion Dissolve transition you added earlier.

A Glimpse of the SPRM and GPRM Registers in Preview Mode

The simulator is also the doorway into the inner workings of the DVD. DVDs interact with the setting the viewer has already made on the DVD player hardware. These settings are the menu's default menu language, subtitle preferences, and many other settings.

In fact, just moving up and down a menu selecting buttons changes the settings of

DVD player hardware. These settings are stored in tiny register memories that are only 16 bits per register.

You can see these registers in action when you simulate your project by selecting the "I" for Information button on the simulator's remote keypad.

Figure 7.46 The simulator — register information

While the Start button is selected, look at the top right at Item Properties. There you will see the name of the menu, whether a pre-script has been assigned, and time-out settings, the current button name, and its jump target.

The section at the bottom right is a simulated glimpse of the SPRM and GPRM register values. If you do not see these registers and values, place a check mark in the SPRM and GPRM check boxes located at the bottom left of the information panel.

System Parameter Register Memory (SPRMs) are a reflection of the settings programmed into the DVD player hardware and the current status of certain conditions within the DVD's current session. An example of this would be the current menu button selected. That determines the value placed in the SPRM 8 register. Other SPRM registers maintain the use of which audio stream is in use, and what language the DVD player menus are set up as, and so on.

Look at SPRM 8 in the list of SPRMs. The description says SPRM 8 is the highlight button. Just right of the description is the current value of SPRM 8, and if the Start button remains selected that value with read 1024.

Using the remote keypad, select the Chapters button.

Look at SPRM 8 again. SPRM 8 now holds a value of 2048.

Look at the Item Properties on the top right-hand side again. Notice the button name is now Button 2, and the jump target has changed to Chapter::Button 1.

These setting will help you later on to create more advanced DVD menus and navigation functions.

Preparing Layered Menus

Layered menus are unique in that they do not require the use of either a simple or advanced overlay map. Instead, each button state is defined by its own separate layer within a multilayered Adobe Photoshop asset. This allows the author to present a higher degree of graphic detail in the representation of button states, including an entirely new screen appearance for the Normal, Selected, and Activated button states. The use of overlay maps differs sharply as overlays are restricted to the appearance of 2-bit shapes as defined in a single overlay layer with a limit of up to three colors.

There are distinct disadvantages to the layered menu approach. Layered menus cannot use animation or audio, and they are inherently slow to load each of the three states of Normal, Selected, and Activated. As the viewer navigates Up, Down, Left, and Right within the menu, each state loads much more slowly than the still menu that uses the standard overlay method of menu design.

The Workflow

- Define the type of television standard your audience will use
- Create the background graphics
- Define the number of buttons you will need
- Define the style of each state of each button you will need
- Name your layers after their button name and state
- Import your menu into DVD Studio Pro
- Define a layered menu object
- Import your layered menu asset into your layered Menu object
- Set the background layers
- Define buttons within DVD Studio Pro
- Assign button states to Photoshop layers
- Create button navigation
- Assign button targets
- Assign transitions
- Test your menu

NTSC or PAL

As with all menu design, you first need to decide on your menu parameters, such as

NTSC or PAL, a 16:9 wide-screen aspect ratio or a standard television aspect ratio of 4:3. For NTSC 4:3 you will begin with 720 x 534.

Use the chart below to create the proper size menu for your television standard.

Television Standard	Aspect Ratio	Start Dimension	Pixel Aspect Ratio	Final Dimension	Pixel Aspect Ratio
NTSC	4:3	720 x 534	1.0	720 x 480	.9
	16:9	864 x 480	1.0	720 x 480	1.2
PAL	4:3	768 x 576	1.0	720 x 576	1.066
	16:9	1024 x 576	1.0	720 x 576	1.42

Action-Safe and Title-Safe Regions

Use Adobe Photoshop to open the Start.psd graphic from the Chapter8/Tutorial 6 folder in the DVD-ROM.

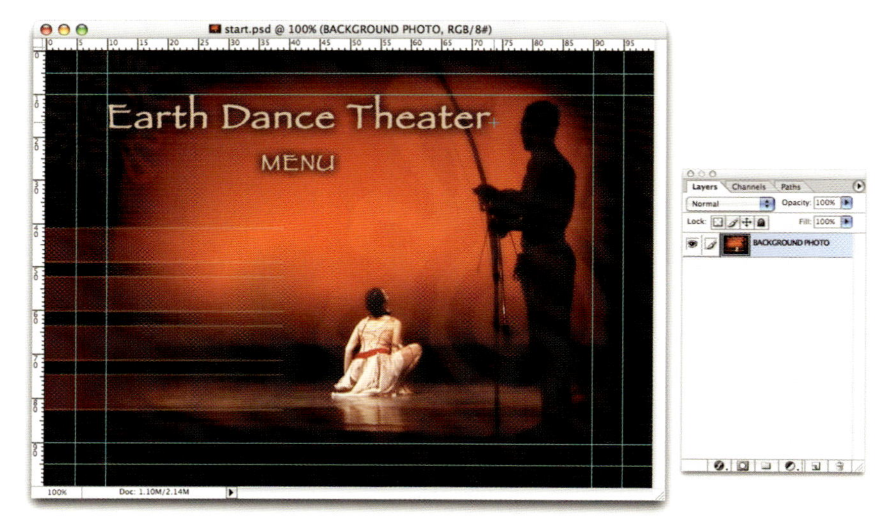

Figure 8.1 Adobe Photoshop — background layer

Here you see a single background layer, and guides that have been added at 5%, 10%, 90%, and 95% from left to right, and top to bottom. This creates two borders; one exists at 5%, while the other is at 10% all around my background.

The 5% inner board represents the action-safe region, whereas the outer 10% area represents the title-safe region.

Creating a Layered Menu

A Layered menu with a single button which uses three layers for each of its three states will have at least four layers:

- Button 1 – Activated State
- Button 1 – Selected State
- Button 1 – Normal State
- Background layer

Notice the order of the layers above. The activated state is on top, followed by the selected state, the normal state, and background layer. This is an ideal layer stacking order for a layered menu.

The Background Layer

Step 1

Open the start.psd asset in Adobe Photoshop.

In this section you will see a single layer background with the guides already added for you. Notice that the background is a single layer. This is not a requirement, but it does make this type of menu a little easier to work with.

Step 2

Set the foreground color to white, and then select the Horizontal Text Tool in the Toolbar, or use the keystroke "T". Use the Papyrus font size 48 pt and type the word

Figure 8.2 Add the Start Text layer

"Start" in the first defined rectangle in the menu. This creates a new text layer within the Layer palette.

Step 3

Select the text layer in the Layer palette. At the bottom of the Layer palette, select the Layer Style button > Blending Options. Select the Drop Shadow style from the list of styles on the left side, and then choose OK.

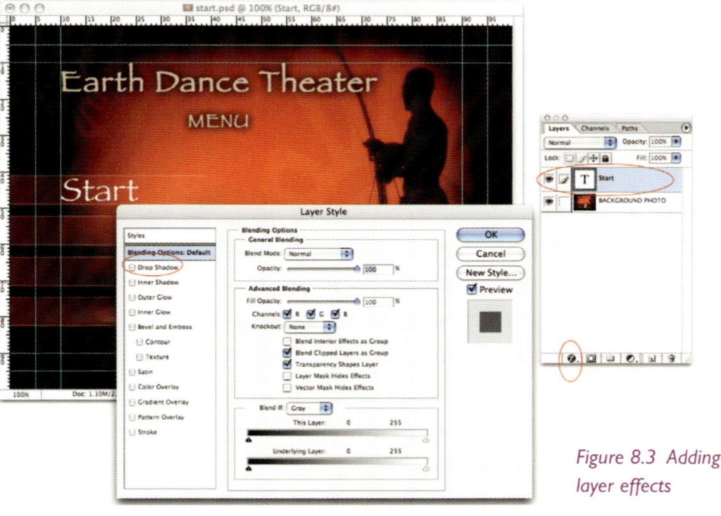

Figure 8.3 Adding layer effects

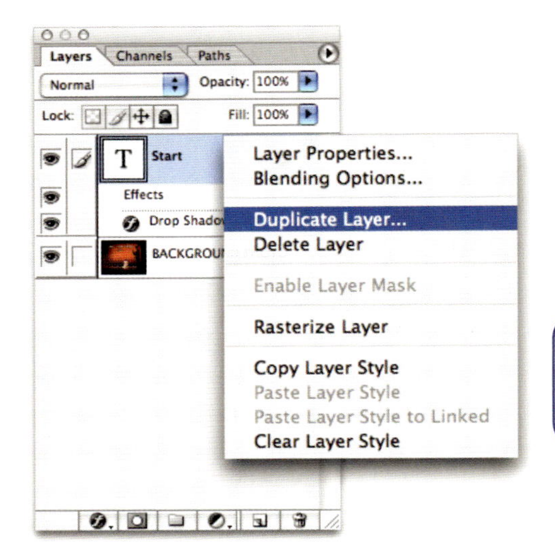

Figure 8.4 Duplicating layer effects

You have now added a drop shadow to the Start text in the menu.

Step 4

Duplicate the text layer twice, so you are left with three identical text layers.

You can duplicate layers easily by right-clicking, or Control-clicking on the layer in the layer palette, or selecting Duplicate Layer… from the Options menu.

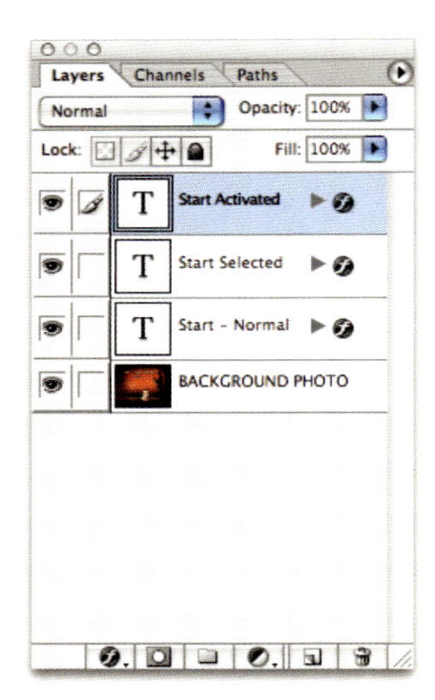

Figure 8.5 Start Normal, Selected, and Activated layers

Step 5

Start renaming these layers from the top down. Double-click on the layer names to edit the layer names.

Name the top text layer, Start Activated; the middle, Start Selected; and the bottom text layer, Start Normal.

At this stage, each of these text layers is visually identical. Each layer is white text with a shadow. You will change the text color to red in the Selected state and black in the Activated state. You will also remove the shadow in the Activated state to give the illusion that the text button has moved closer down to the menu to simulate a real button being pressed down.

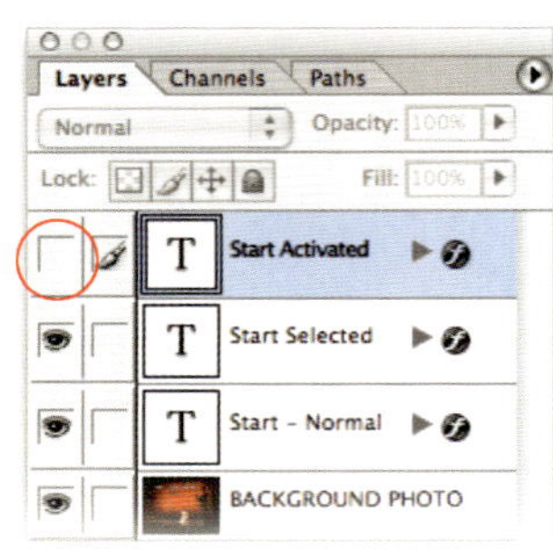

Figure 8.6 Unselecting the view in the Layer palette

Step 6

Go back to the Layer palette, and turn on the view of the top layer by clicking once on the eye, removing it from the box. You will no longer visually see the layer in the canvas.

Right-click on the Start Selected layer and choose Blending Options to launch the Layer Style palette.

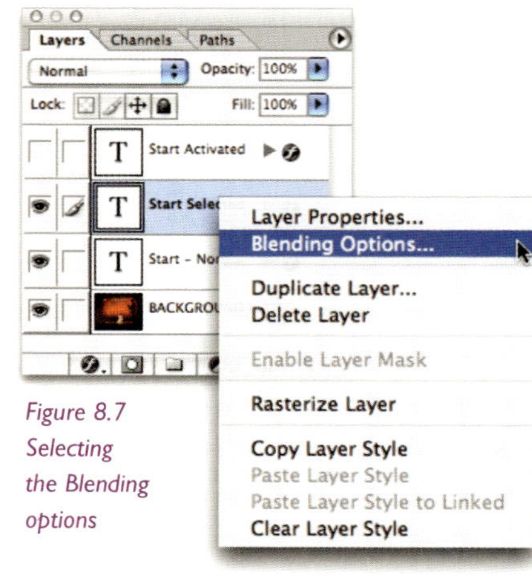

Figure 8.7 Selecting the Blending options

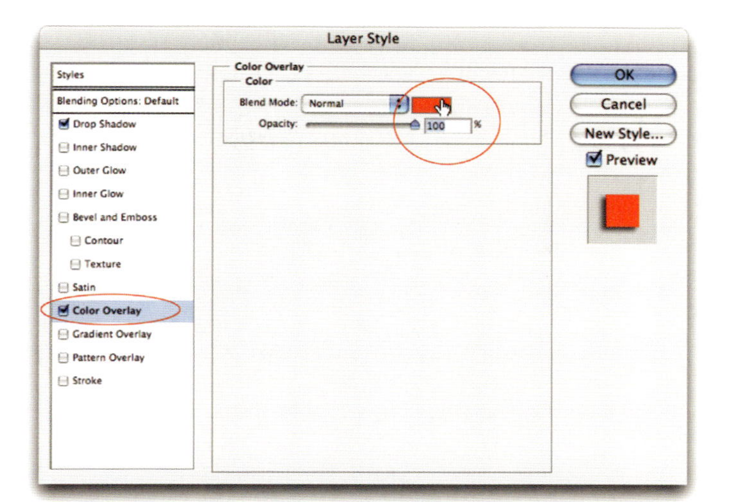

Figure 8.8 Layer Style palette

Choose the Color Overlay style, and then click on the overlay color chip to open the color picker.

Figure 8.9 Using the color picker

Move the color picker over the menu graphic, and the arrow cursor will become an eye dropper. Select the brightest orange color on the menu with the eye dropper tool.

Click OK.

Step 7

Now test your work thus far. Toggle the Start Selected layer on and off by repeatedly selecting the view check box. Notice how the text toggles from orange to white. This is part of the desired effect you are going to create in DVD Studio Pro. By turning off the Start Selected layer you expose the Start Normal layer.

You have one more layer to finish, which is the Start Activated layer.

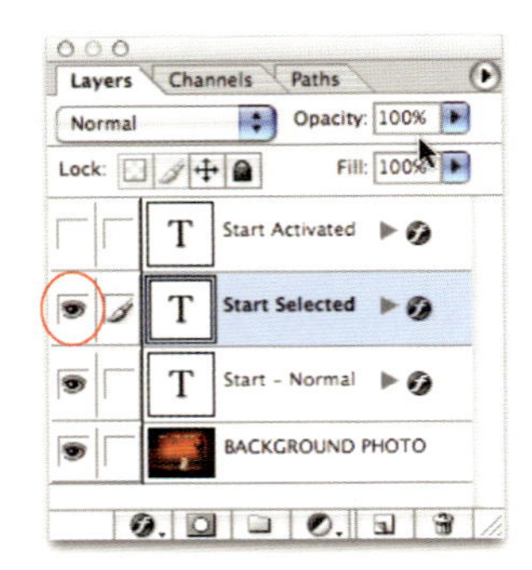

Figure 8.10 Toggling the View property

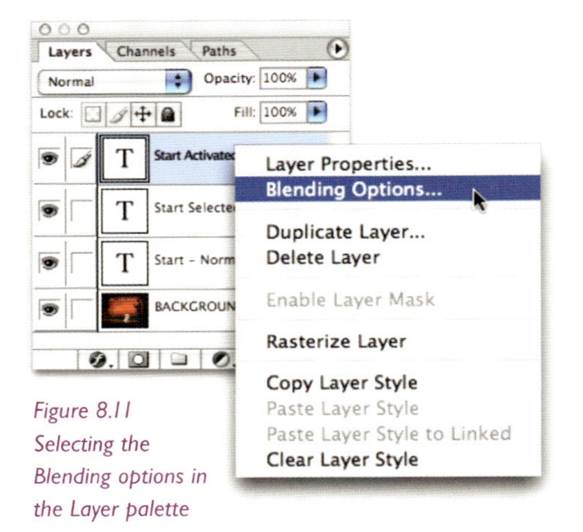

Figure 8.11 Selecting the Blending options in the Layer palette

Step 8

You will change the color of the white text in the Start Activated layer from white to black. You will also remove the shadow effect from this layer.

Right-click on the Start Activated layer, and choose Blending Options.

Step 9

Uncheck Drop Shadow and change the color overlay from white to a mid-gray color.

Select OK.

There are three distinct variants of the same button now. The Normal state will be white, while the Selected state will be orange, and the Activated state will be the mid-gray color.

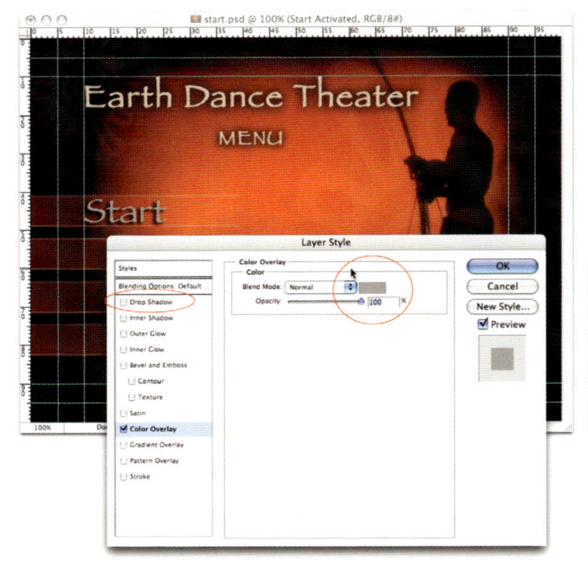

Figure 8.12 Adjusting the drop shadow in the Layer Style palette

Preparing for DVD Studio Pro Import

Each of your text layers has style effects applied that are not recognized by DVD Studio Pro. These effects include the color overlays and the shadow effects. You will need to rasterize each layer prior to importing the menu into DVD Studio Pro. Once a layer is rasterized, it cannot be reversed. To solve this problem, save a copy of your menu prior to rasterizing it.

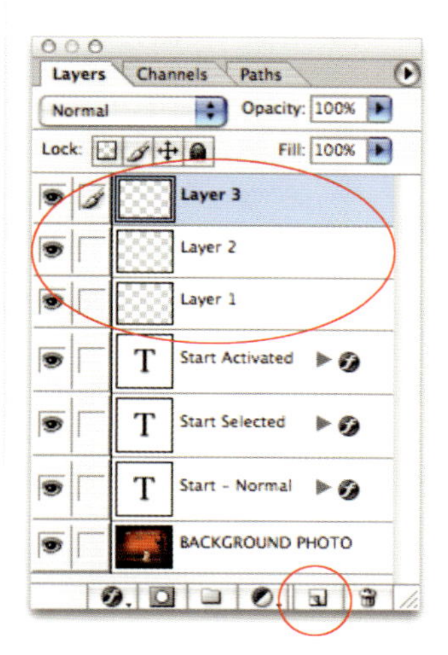

Figure 8.13 Adding blank layers in the Layer palette

Step 1

Add a blank layer under each text layer. To do this, locate the Add New Layer button located at the bottom of the layer palette, and then press it three times.

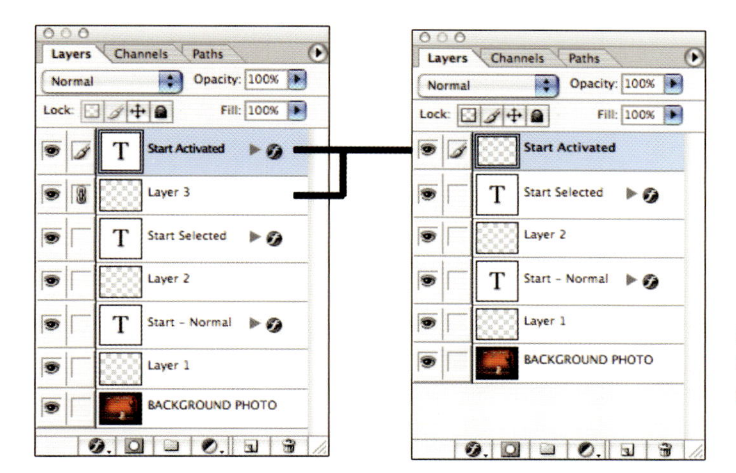

Figure 8.14 Merging layers in the Layer palette

Step 2

Arrange one empty layer under each of the three text layers.

Select the top text layer and then add a link to the empty layer below it. Use the keystroke Command-E to merge the linked layer into the text layer. The text layer and the linked empty layer become one single rasterized layer with all the effects merged into that single layer.

Now merge each of the remaining two text layers with their respective empty layers, which will result in three separate rasterized layers that represent each possible state of a single button.

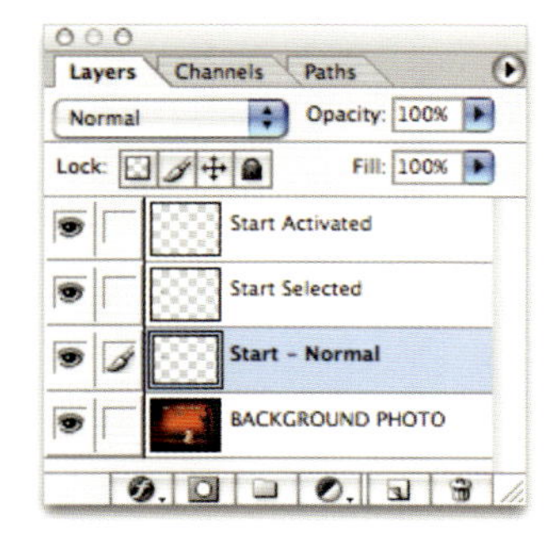

Figure 8.15 Start Button — rasterized Normal, Selected, and Activated states

Resizing the Menu Asset

Before you import a menu asset into DVD Studio Pro, you ought to resize it to the proper dimensions. This menu started as 720 x 534 with a 1.0 pixel aspect ratio. Now that you are finished with editing this menu, it's time to resize it to 720 x 480 with a .9 pixel aspect ratio.

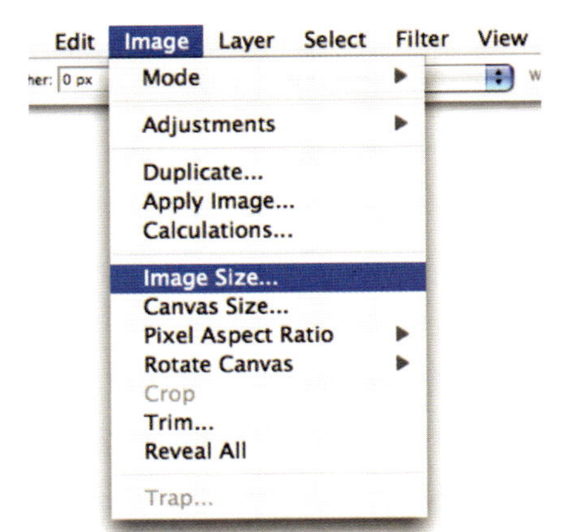

Figure 8.16 Opening the Image Size palette

Step 1

Using the top menus, choose Image > Image Size.

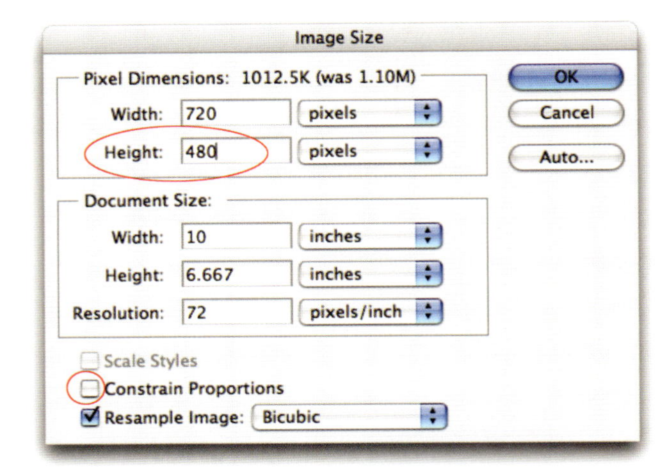

Figure 8.17 Adjusting the image height

Step 2

Uncheck the Constrain Proportions check box if selected.

Change the Height field from 534 to 480, and then select OK.

Save your menu, and exit Photoshop.

Working with Layered Menus in DVD Studio Pro

In this section you will

- Import a layered menu asset into DVD Studio Pro
- Create a layered Menu object in the Assets tab
- Define the background layer
- Configure button states using layers rather than an overlay
- Assign a button target
- Assign a transition

Copy the Lesson 7 folder to your hard disk, the open the Lesson 7 folder and double-click on the DVD Studio Pro project file labeled Lesson7.

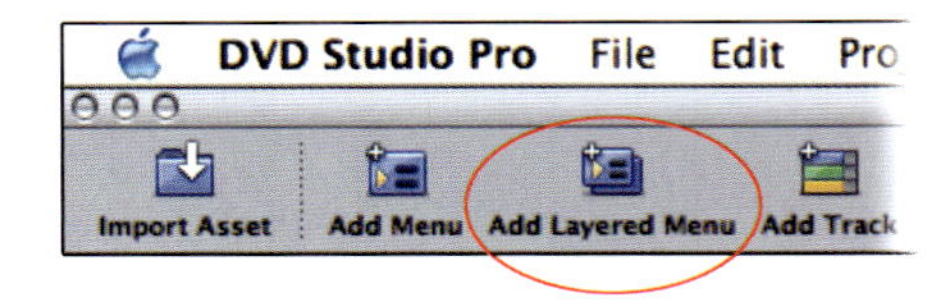

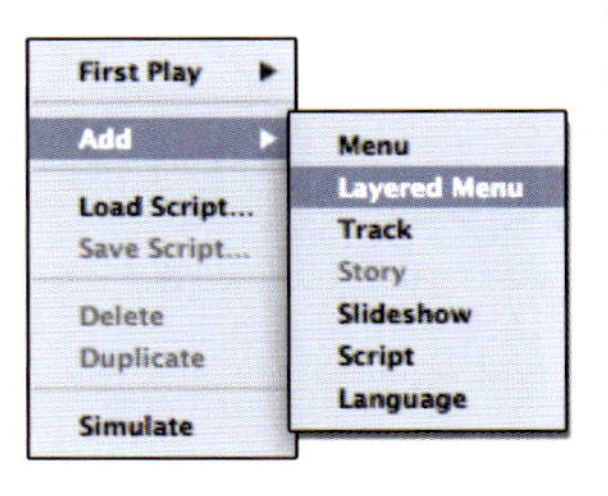

Figure 8.18 Adding a Layered Menu object in the Outline tab

Adding a Layered Menu to the Outline Tab

Step 1

Right-click in an empty area of the Outline tab and select Add >

Layered Menu, or use the Toolbar button Add Layered Menu to add a layered Menu object to the DVD project.

Step 2

This action will add the Menu 2 object, which has a slightly different appearance then the Menu 1 object. Both menus are represented by the blue menu icon. However, the Menu 2 object is two blue menus stacked one on top of the other, whereas still menus are just shown as a single blue icon.

Figure 8.19 Menu 2 — The layered Menu object

Importing the Layered Menu

Step 1

Click on the Import button in the Toolbar or in the Assets tab, and locate the LayerMenu.psd file, and then select Import.

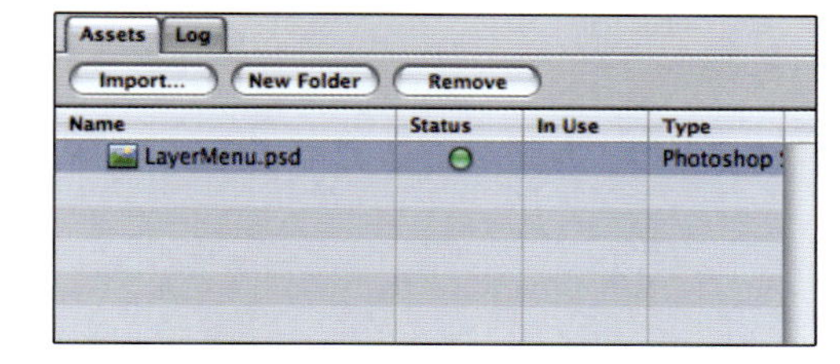

Figure 8.20 The assets tab — Layered Menu asset

Setting the Background Layer

Step 1

Drag the LayeredMenu.psd file to the Menu tab, and hover for a moment until the Options palette opens. Then choose Set Background: No Layers Visible.

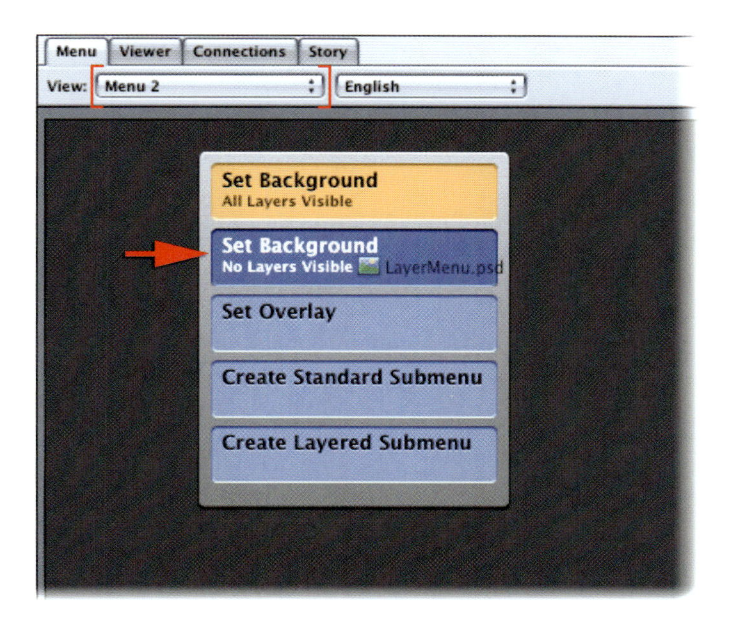

Figure 8.21 Adding the Layered menu to the Menu 2 background

Step 2

Open the Layered Menu Property Inspector. In the General tab, look at the Background section and note that the LayeredMenu.psd file has been assigned as the background. All the layers are currently off.

Scroll down to the last layer, and put a check mark in the Show box. You will notice the same background layer you were working with before is now the background of this layered menu. Make sure all the other layers have no check marks in their show boxes.

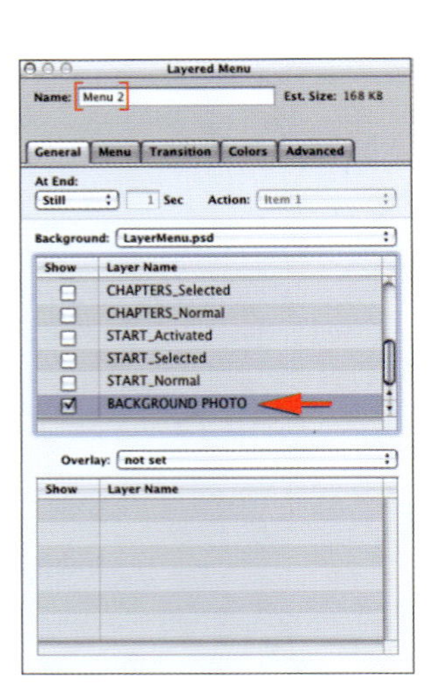

Figure 8.22 Adjusting the Show Layer property

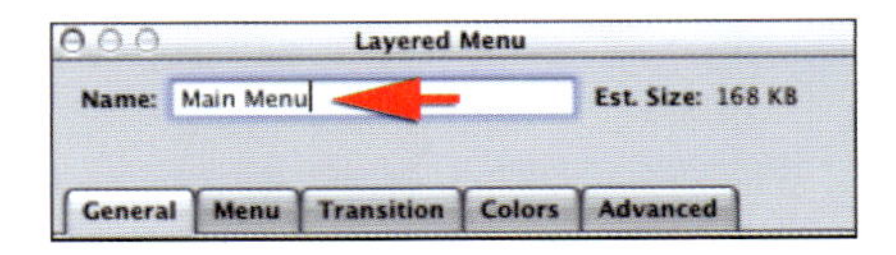

Figure 8.23 Naming the Menu 2 object

Naming the Layered Menu

To name your layered menu, you will use the Property Inspector.

Step 1

Click the mouse button in the Name field, and then delete the name Menu 2. Type the name "Main Menu" and then press Return.

Creating Buttons within the Layered Menu

Creating buttons within the layered menu is much different than button creation in the still menu because there is no overlay. Instead the button states of Normal, Selected, and Activated are each tied to a separate layer within the Adobe Photoshop multilayered asset.

Show	Button Name	Layer Number	Layer Name
	Settings	Layer 13	SETTINGS_Activated
		Layer 12	SETTINGS_Selected
		Layer 11	SETTINGS_Normal
	Extras	Layer 10	EXTRAS_Activated
		Layer 9	EXTRAS_Selected
		Layer 8	EXTRAS_Normal
	Chapters	Layer 7	CHAPTERS_Activated
		Layer 6	CHAPTERS_Selected
		Layer 5	CHAPTERS_Normal
	Start	Layer 4	START_Activated
		Layer 3	START_Selected
		Layer 2	START_Normal
ON		Layer 1	BACKGROUND

Look at the chart above, and notice that the Start button has Layers 2, 3, and 4 as part of its group. The single Start button will make use of three layers from within the 13 layers of this Photoshop asset. Likewise, the Chapters button also makes use of three of the 13 layers, and so on.

You will assign one layer for every possible button state of the combined four buttons. Since there are three buttons states, and there are four buttons, you will need 12 layers to accommodate all the possible states.

Before you begin, you must create the four buttons in the Menu tab.

Figure 8.24 Adjusting the Button Display property in the Menu tab

Step 1

Select the Show Normal State, and the Show Button Outline buttons in the Menu tab Toolbar located at the bottom of the Menu tab.

Figure 8.25 Adding buttons to the menu

Step 2

Using the mouse, draw four button outlines in the four designated areas. Make sure you start from the top, and work downward, so that button 1 is on top and button 4 is on the bottom.

Assigning Layers to Button States

Once your four buttons are created, you must assign a Normal, Selected, and Activated layer to each of the four buttons. This is done through a special property in the Button Property Inspector.

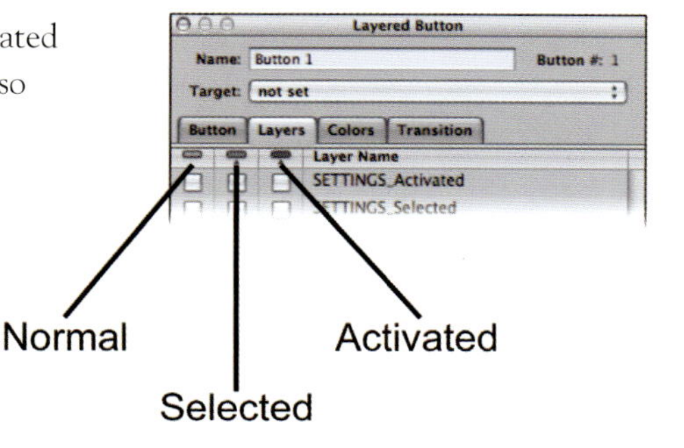

Figure 8.26 Normal, Selected, and Activated button state property selection

Step 1

Select Button 1 in the menu. Open the Property Inspector for Button 1, and then open the Layers tab. This is a unique tab only available to buttons in layered menus. At the top of the layers, you see three icons. These are the check box headers, and they represent Normal, Selected, and Activated states. The check boxes cascade downward in these three columns.

Figure 8.27 Start button — defining button state property

Step 2

Follow the Normal State column down to where it intersects with the Start_Normal layer, and check that box. You are indicating that this layer is the Start button's normal state.

Now follow the Selected State column down to where it intersects with the Start_Selected layer, and check that box. This layer is now the designated selected state of the Start button.

Follow the Activated State column down to where the Start_Activated layer intersects and then check that box. That is now the Start button's designated activated layer.

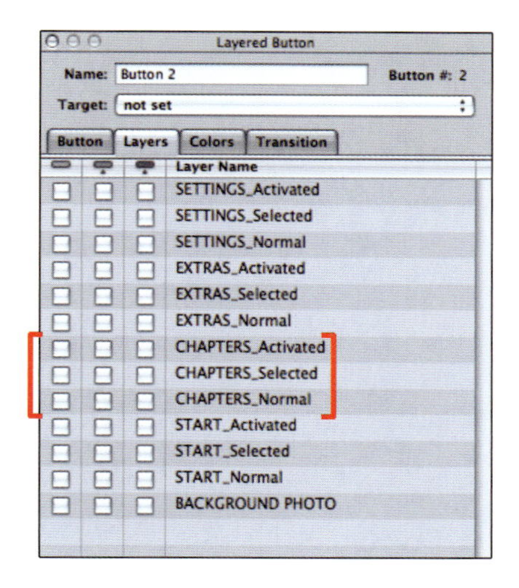

Figure 8.28 Chapters button — button states

Step 3

Click on the Button 2 outline now. Notice that the checked boxes disappear. This is the Property Inspector for an entirely new button, and no layers have been assigned to this button, so there are no checked boxes.

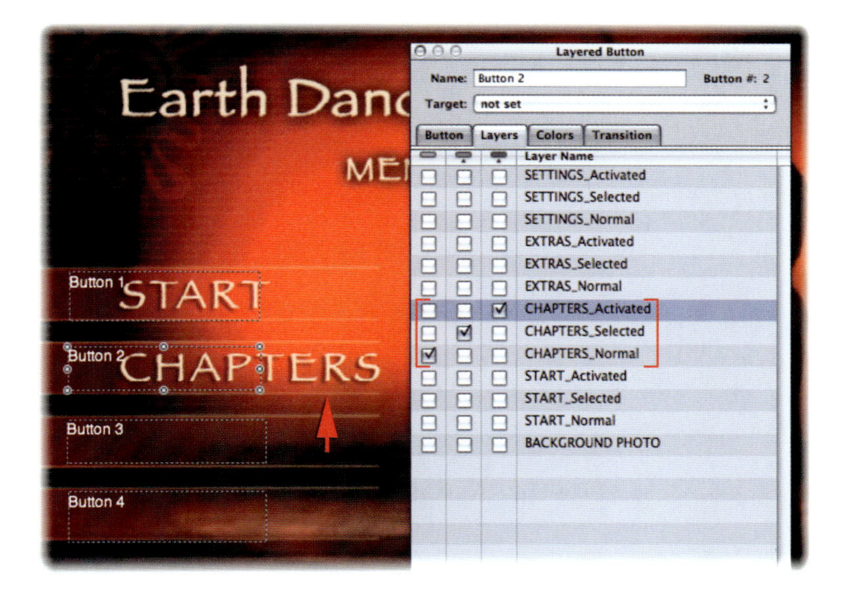

Figure 8.29 Chapters buttons — defining button state properties

Step 4

As before, follow the Normal column down to where the Chapters_Normal layer is, and then check that box to assign that layer to the normal state of the Chapters button. Likewise, do the same for the Selected and Activated states.

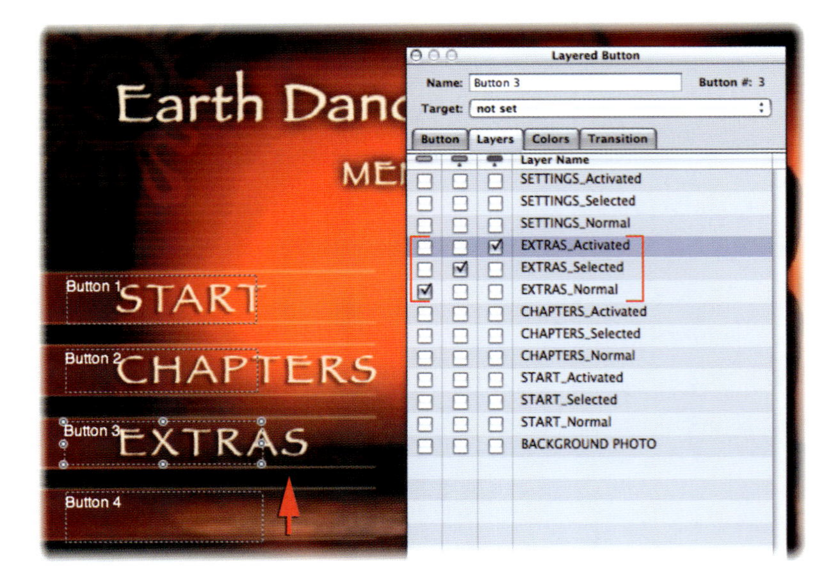

Figure 8.30 Extras button — defining button state properties

Step 5

Select Button 3, and then check the corresponding Normal, Selected, and Activated check boxes to the Extras_Normal, Extras_Selected, and Extras_Activated layers.

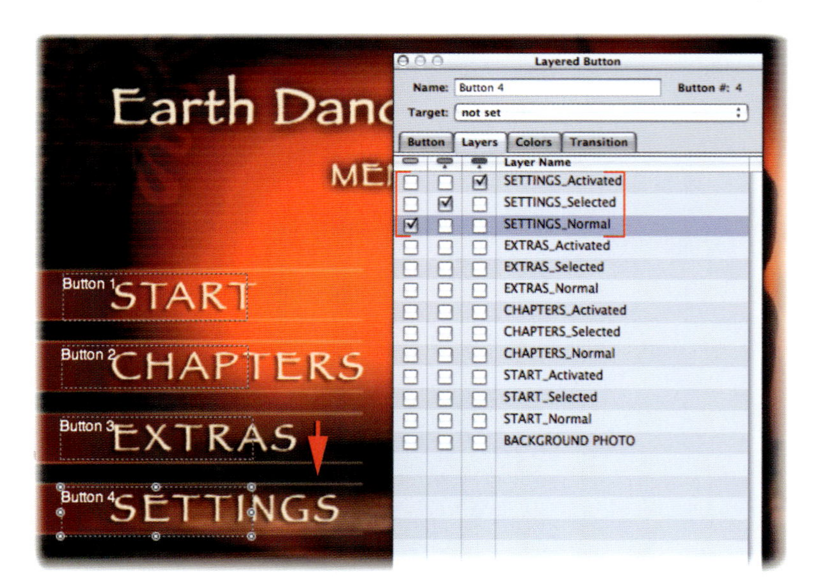

Figure 8.31 Settings button — defining the button states

Step 6

For your last button, select Button 4, and then check the corresponding Normal, Selected, and Activated check boxes to the Settings_Normal, Settings_Selected, and Settings_Activated layers.

Setting the Button Navigation

Your menu navigation is by default set to assign button navigation continuously as you create and arrange your menu buttons.

You may adjust this setting by opening the Menu tab's Settings drop-down menu and removing the check mark on the Auto Assign Buttons Continuously setting. When this is done, each time you finish creating and arranging buttons in a menu you must remember to assign the navigation.

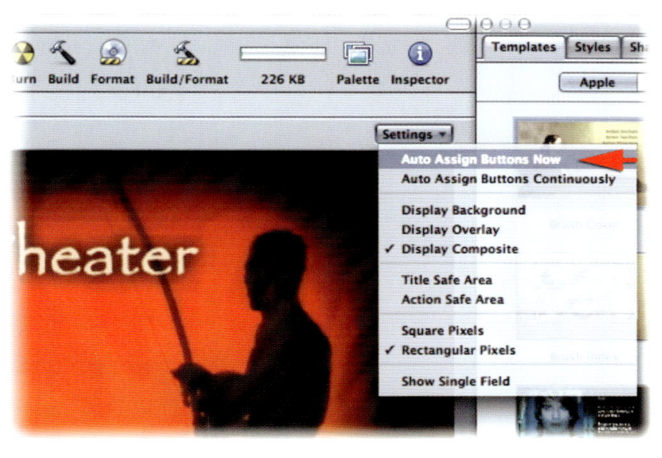

Figure 8.32 Menu settings — auto assign button navigation

To automatically assign button navigation select the Auto Assign Buttons Now setting. This will assign the Up, Down, Left, and Right button navigation automatically.

Simulating the Menu

You can simulate the behavior of the button navigation to test the various states of the buttons and their assigned layers.

Figure 8.33 Simulating the menu

Step 1

To simulate the buttons, move the mouse over the menu, and then right-click. A tiny menu with a single option to Simulate will open. Choose Simulate to load this menu into the simulator.

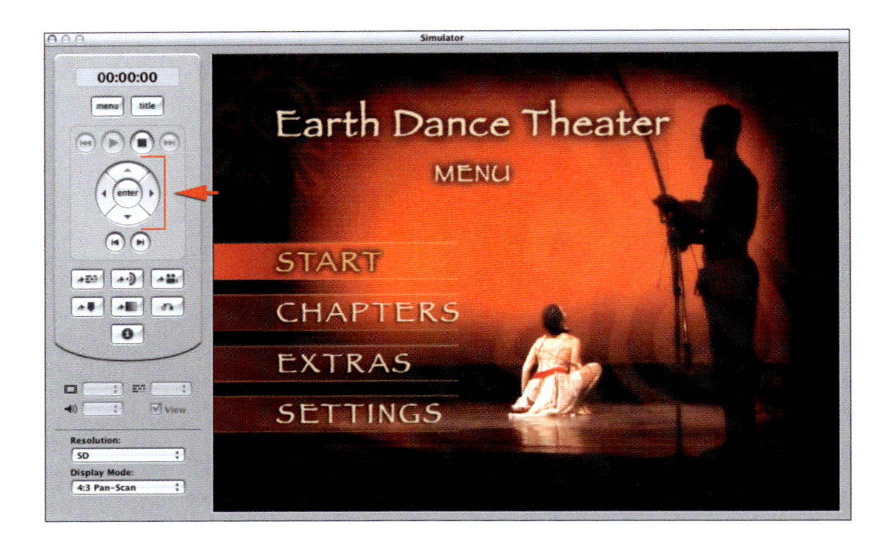

Figure 8.34 The simulator — DVD Studio Pro 4

Step 2

Once the simulator has opened, you will need to use the simulator remote or the cursor keys on your keyboard to accurately simulate navigation. Do not use your mouse to hover over buttons as a test of the menu's navigation.

Press the Up, Down, Left, and Right simulator remote buttons and watch the button states change from Normal to Selected.

Press Return on any of the buttons to see the state change from Selected to Activated.

Notice the vibrant shifts in button colors, shadows, and surrounding colors as you switch from button to button. None of these effects are possible with highlight overlays used in still menus.

Preparing Motion Menus

Motion menus are menus that carry full-motion backgrounds. These menus can use audio and a loop point for continuous play.

The Workflow

- Preparing a video clip in Final Cut Pro
- Importing Video into Motion
- Adding Animation and Button text
- Saving your Motion project
- Compressing Motion projects for DVD Studio Pro
- Preparing the overlay
- Importing assets into DVD Studio Pro
- Assigning Background Motion, Audio, and Overlay
- Setting the Loop Point
- Setting up menu buttons and targets
- Scripting the Loop Point
- Testing your menu

Working with Final Cut Pro and Motion

Motion menus can make use of full-motion backgrounds and animated text. Final Cut Pro is an excellent nonlinear editor used to acquire footage and edit in a nondestructive way.

Menus may involve animated text over full motion video. For this reason, Final Cut Pro makes a great application to acquire background footage, whereas Apple's Motion application provides an excellent way to add text and effects on top of the full-motion element.

You will use both applications in addition to DVD Studio Pro and Adobe Photoshop to create a motion menu.

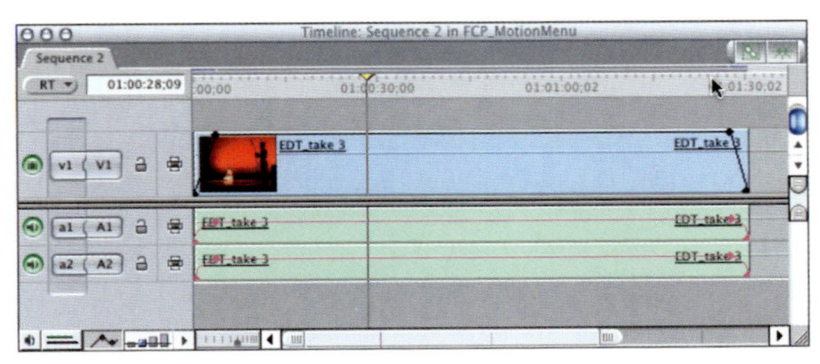

Figure 9.1 Final Cut Pro — timeline

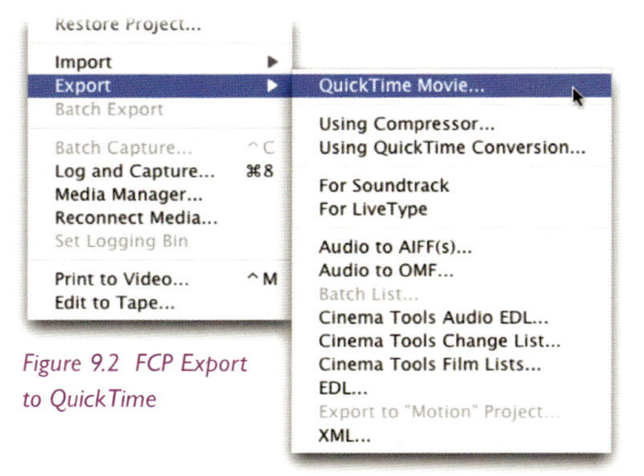

Figure 9.2 FCP Export to QuickTime

Step 1

Assemble your timeline in Final Cut Pro.

Step 2

Once your background video is complete, select the sequence file in the bin, and use the pull-down menus to export the video into a self-contained video that you will use with Motion.

Using the pull-down menus, choose File > Export > QuickTime Movie.

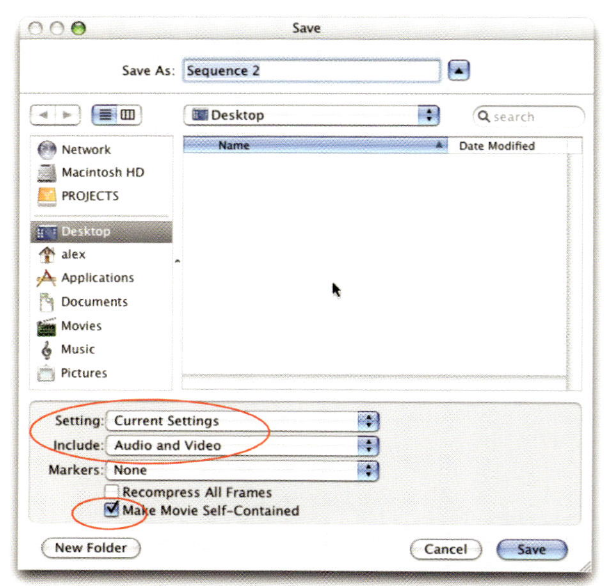

Figure 9.3 FCP — Exporting a self-contained movie

Step 3

When exporting your menu, keep the settings set to Current Settings, include Audio and Video, and mark the sequence as Self-Contained. This way, the entire sequence has no dependencies with Final Cut Pro. This is required if you plan on working on the menu from any workstation other than the originator of the sequence materials.

The output of this action is a single QuickTime file with your audio and video in the native resolution and quality of the timeline.

Preparing Video with Motion

The background video created in Final Cut Pro is the foundation of the motion menu. Once you have this primary asset, you're ready to begin compositing text, animation, and effects using Motion.

Creating a Timeline for the Motion Menu

Launch Motion to begin.

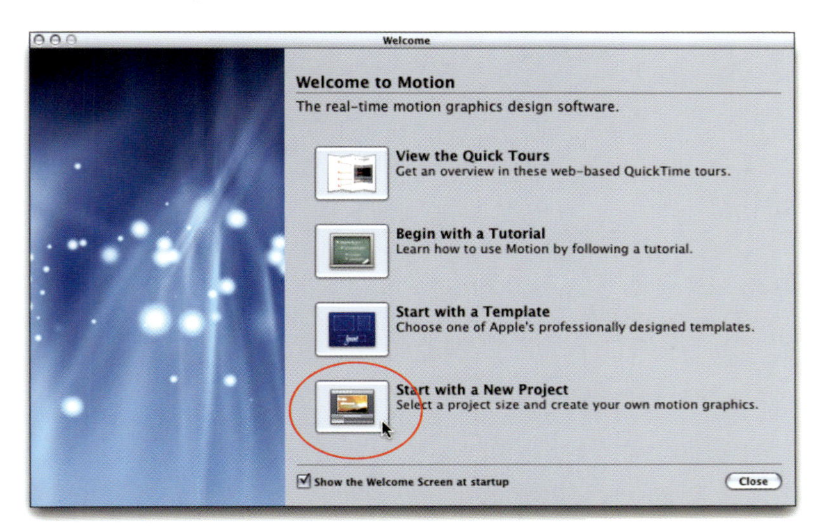

Figure 9.4 Motion — new project

Step 1

Choose the Start with a New Project option.

My default is NTSC DV with a 10-second project duration. No matter what your default duration is, it will likely need to be changed to match the length of the sequence exported from Final Cut Pro.

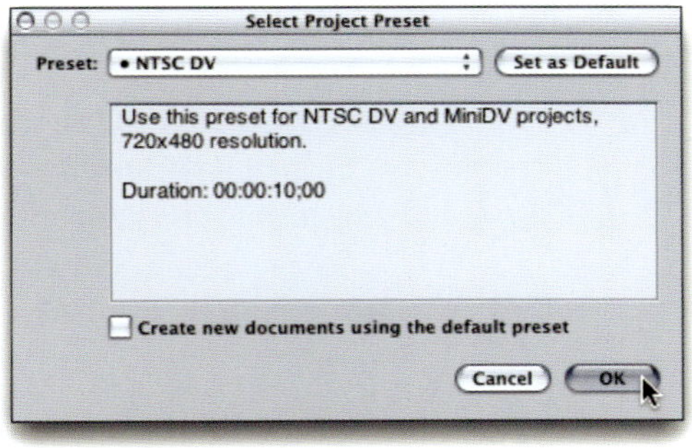

Figure 9.5 Motion — selecting a project preset

Step 2

Accept the default duration.

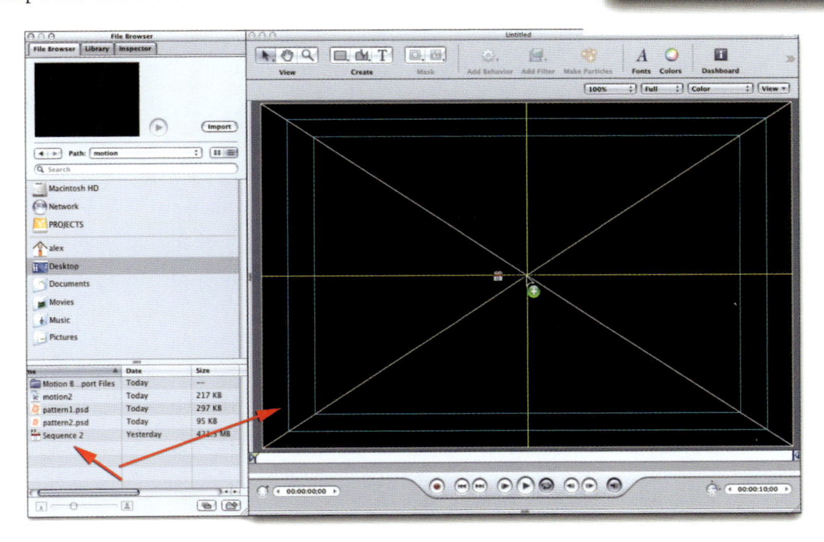

Figure 9.6 Adding FCP movie to motion background

Step 3

Use the File Browser to locate your Final Cut Pro exported sequence. Drag and hold the sequence over the Motion canvas until you have it centered.

Step 4

Click on the sequence clip in the File Browser, and the preview at the top will tell you the duration of the clip in timecode.

Figure 9.7 Setting the project duration

Stopwatch
Project Duration Field

Step 5

Click on the stopwatch on the lower-right-hand side of the canvas window to toggle the Project Duration Field from frames to timecode. Now enter the timecode value of the sequence as shown in the File Browser. Your project is now the exact duration of the primary background clip.

Designing a Motion Menu with a Loop Point

Motion menus are simply menus with motion within them. Think of any Hollywood DVD you have rented. Many of them have full motion in the background, and many of these sophisticated menus have a clever animated sequence before the buttons become available for selection. In DVD Studio Pro terms, this function of displaying the selections after the menu has played some sort of an intro is called the Loop Point.

The Loop Point is a secondary start point where the loop of the menu begins when the menu plays again after the initial playback.

Open the DVD-ROM, and copy the Chapter 9>Motion folder to your desktop. Once copied, double-click on the Motion2 project icon to launch a sample motion menu.

Tip: If Motion reports that Sequence 2 is missing, a prompt window will appear, offering to search for the asset. Select the Search button, and then locate Sequence 2, which is located in the Motion folder inside the Chapter 9 folder. Once found, select the Sequence 2 asset, and then choose Open on the lower-right-hand side of the file browser window.

Figure 9.8 Motion — the Toolbar — timing

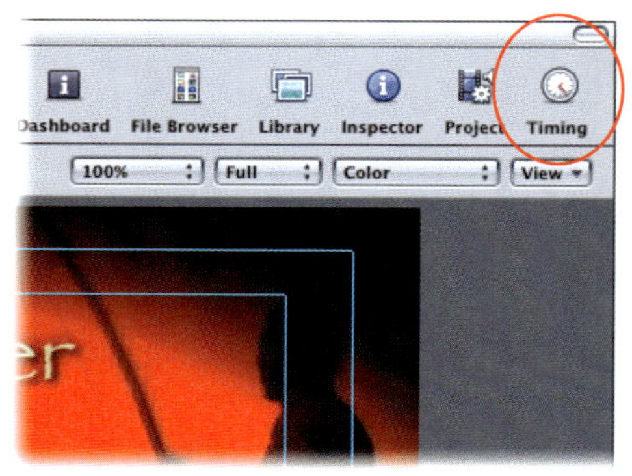

Press Play to watch the sample menu play. Notice it takes a few seconds for the buttons to animate into full view.

At the start of the menu, you see nothing but black. The title of the menu fades in, followed by the text buttons, which takes just past 15 seconds. After that, you see the continued full motion of the dancer in the background. If the viewer of the DVD does not make any selection in the menu, it will repeat itself.

Where the menu begins, its second play is governed by this Loop Point. Rather than watching the opening animation all over again, that section can be skipped. The Loop Point is the new beginning of the menu after it has been played once already.

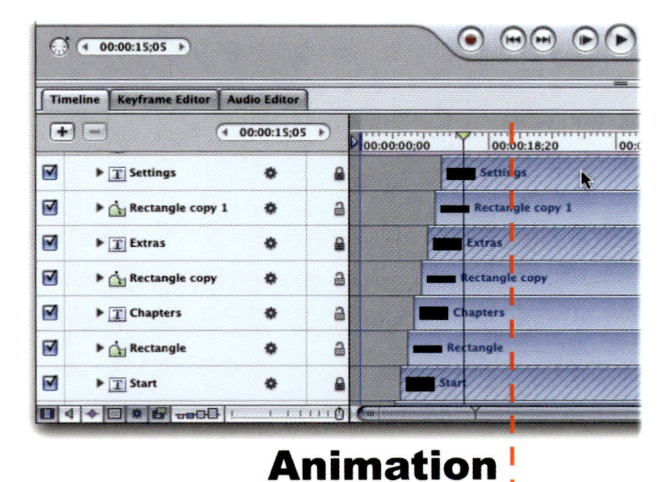

Figure 9.9 Defining the Loop Point

Examine the timeline of this menu in Motion by opening the layered timeline area. To do this, press the Timing button in the Toolbar.

The timeline gives you a better view as to why the text was hidden for the first 15 seconds of the motion menu. The text layers do not start at the beginning of the timeline. When these text layers start, at later timecodes, they do so with fade-in effects applied. Just before 16 seconds of the timeline have elapsed, the text held in the text layers starts to play and becomes completely visible. This point in the timeline will be used later in DVD Studio Pro as the designated Loop Point of this full motion menu.

Audio Considerations for the Loop Point

When designing a menu with a Loop Point, it is important to understand the impact of the Loop Point on the audio you may wish to have in this menu. The best audio is audio that has a natural reoccurring beat without vocals.

At the end of the looping menu, it will start over, skipping the beginning of the menu and beginning at the Loop Point. If the audio is repeating audio, such as when using musical loops, then there will be less of an audible disturbance when the viewer watches and listens to the loop within the menu.

Some soundtracks lend themselves better to looping menus. A continuous loop, with a person speaking, for example, is an excellent choice for a looping menu's soundtrack. The shorter the musical loop is, the more points you have to interrupt the music without it sounding as if it has been interrupted. This is especially true if the music naturally has low-volume points that you can use at your Loop Point.

Creating an Overlay for Your Motion Menu

Motion menus use an overlay almost the same way a standard menu uses an overlay. Before you can begin to create an overlay for a motion menu, you'll need to know where to add your button highlights in relation to the motion items in the animated menu.

Step 1

The Loop Point is where the menu text becomes stationary, so place the playhead after the Loop Point in Motion's timeline, then using the pull-down menu, choose File > Export.

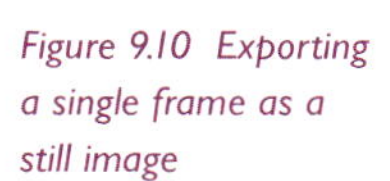

Figure 9.10 Exporting a single frame as a still image

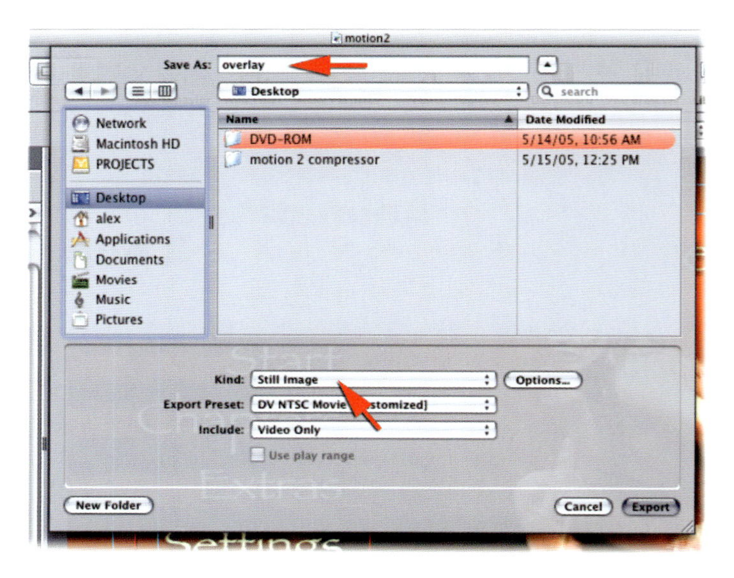

Figure 9.11 Setting the Export options

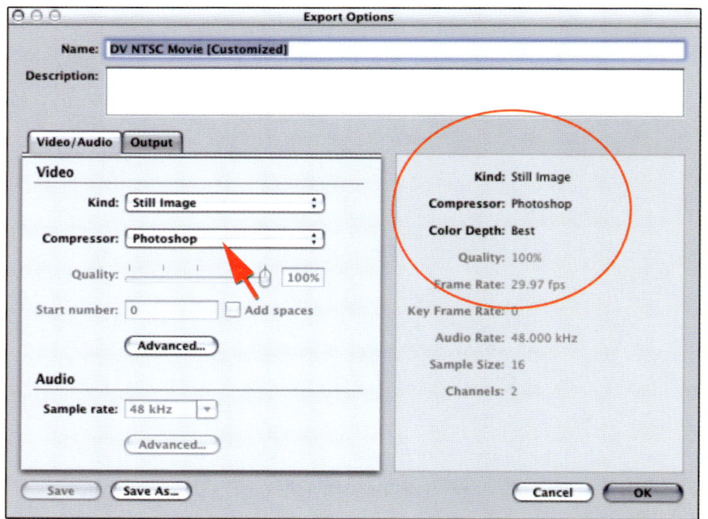

Step 2

In the Save As field, type in any name you like. In the Kind field, choose Still Image, and then select the Options button.

Step 3

Inside the Options, set the Compressor to Photoshop, and then select OK. This will bring you back to the original window. Press Export to save this frame as a Photoshop image.

Step 4

Open the PSD document you just created with Adobe Photoshop.

The objective is to create a layer above this layer that is now the background. This new layer will be the overlay for the animation, and you will destroy the background you see now. It is only used as a guide to help you determine where best to place the highlights you will use in the overlay.

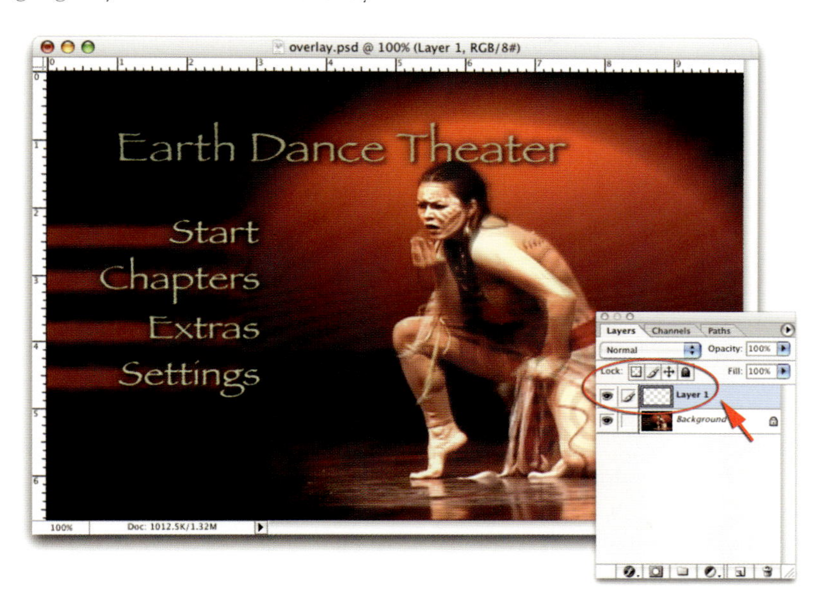

Figure 9.12 Adding a layer to the Layer palette

Step 5

Using the pull-down menus, select Layer > New > Layer. This will leave you with a new layer over the background. Open the Layers palette in Photoshop to see this new layer.

Step 6

Paint the entire new layer white by selecting the Paint Bucket from the toolbox, then choosing the color white from the Swatches palette.

Step 7

Now select the Rectangular Marquee tool from the toolbox, and then choose black from the Swatches palette.

Step 8

Set the opacity of the new layer to 50%.

Figure 9.13 Defining the overlay

Step 9

Draw four rectangles under the four text items in the menu. Paint each one black with the Paint Bucket tool.

Step 10

Using the Layers palette change the opacity back to 100% for the new layer. You should see nothing but a solid white-filled screen with four underlines. The text items are no longer visible.

Figure 9.14 Deleting the background layer

Step 11

Now delete the original background layer by dragging it to the Layer palette trash can.

Step 12

Using the pull-down menus, choose File > Save As. A Save As window will open. Change the Format field from Photoshop to PICT File, and remove the Alpha Channels check box.

Step 13

A PICT File options window will appear. Choose the OK button, accepting the default parameters.

You've just created an overlay that is ready for importing into DVD Studio Pro.

Encoding Your Menu for Use with DVD Studio Pro

There are two ways to encode a menu for use with DVD Studio Pro:

1. Encode the assets prior to bringing them into DVD Studio Pro.
2. Allow DVD Studio Pro to encode them for you.

Encoding Your Menu Prior to Import

Open the Compressor application located in the Applications folder, and then locate the Motion2 project icon located in the Chapter 9 > Motion folder.

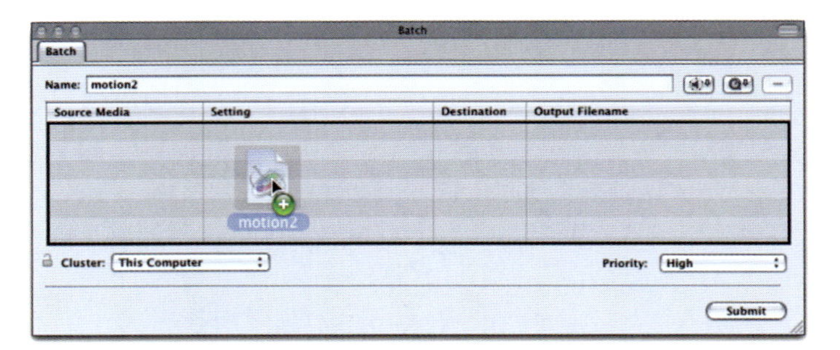

Figure 9.15 Exporting the Motion timeline

Step 1

Drag the Motion2 icon into the Compressor window.

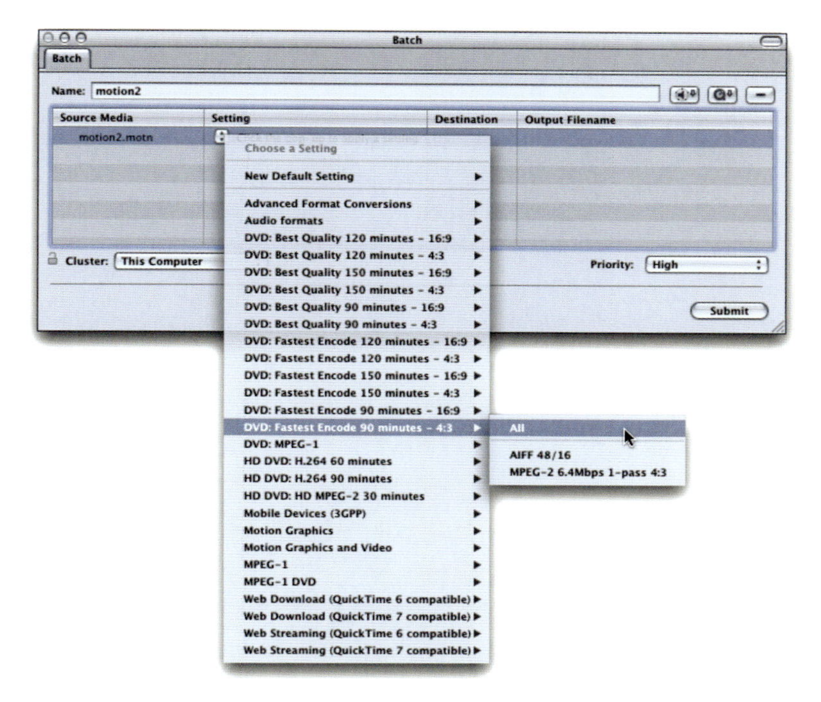

Figure 9.16 Selecting the compression type and quality

Step 2

Click on the Settings button, and then select the DVD Fastest Encode 90 Minutes — 4:3 / All.

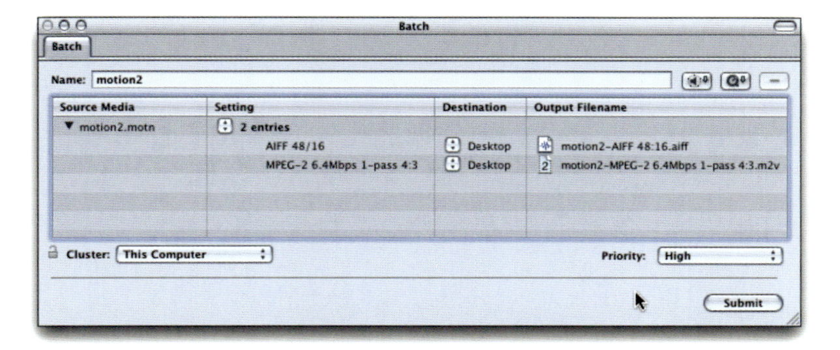

Figure 9.17 Setting the compression file save destination

Step 3

Click on the Destination button and choose your desktop as the location.

Click Submit, and Compressor will encode the motion project into an elementary MPEG2 asset and an AIFF or AC3 audio asset ready to import into DVD Studio Pro.

Importing Motion Projects Directly into DVD Studio Pro

As mentioned earlier, you may choose to allow DVD Studio Pro to encode the menu for you. To accomplish this, simply import the Motion2 asset directly into DVD Studio Pro.

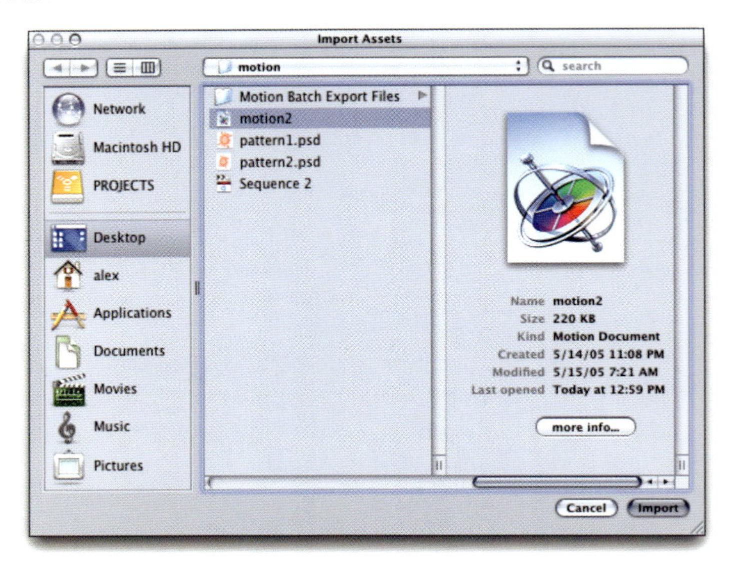

Figure 9.18 Importing a Motion project into DVD Studio Pro

If you are building your menu entirely within Motion, there are benefits inherent in allowing DVD Studio Pro to encode your menu.

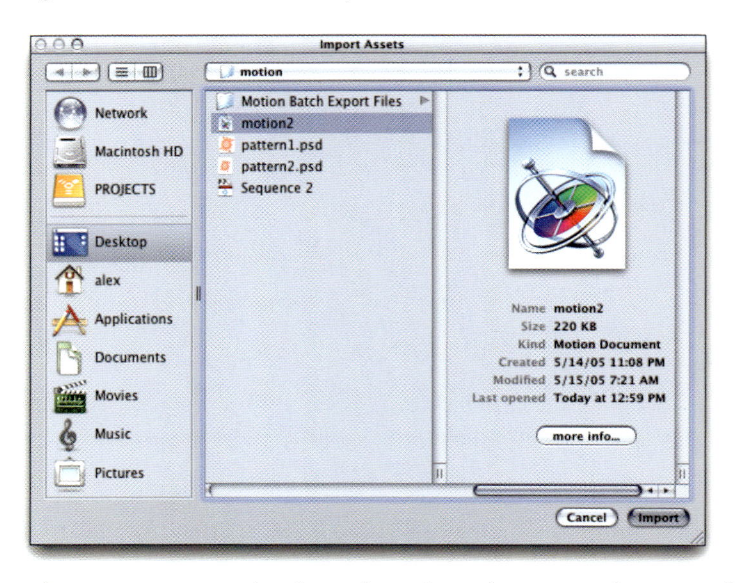

Figure 9.19 Using the Open In Editor function with the Motion project

Once the motion menu is already in place, if you choose to make any modifications, you may right-click on the Motion Project file in the Assets tab, then select

Open In Editor. Motion will relaunch, and any modifications you make will be reflected back in DVD Studio Pro once you save them in Motion.

Working with Motion Menus in DVD Studio Pro

You've just learned a little background on the concepts of motion menus. Now it's time to build one. Copy the Chapter 9 folder in the DVD-ROM to the hard disk, and then open it.

Double-click on the Lesson1 DVD Studio Pro project icon to launch the project into DVD Studio Pro. The project is formatted in DVD Studio Pro 4 because of features specific to version 4. If you are not using version 4, don't panic. Just read through this section anyway, as you are about to build this yourself. This is merely a preview.

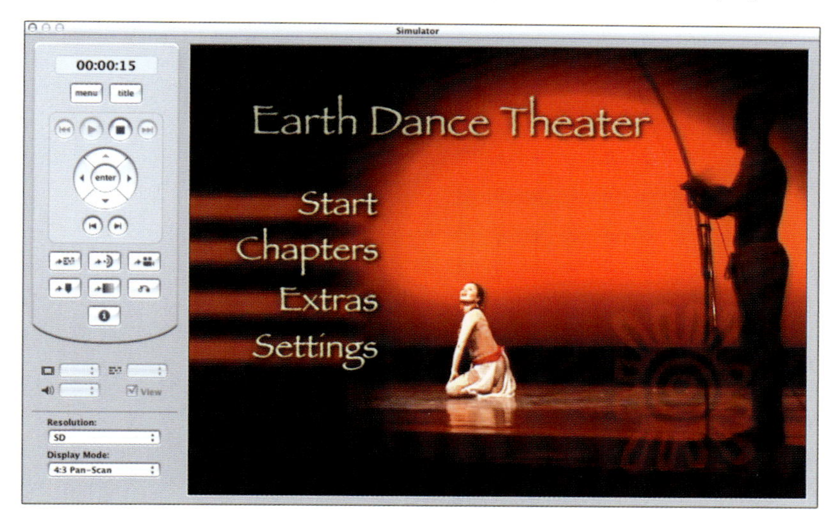

Figure 9.20 Simulating the motion menu

As soon as the project has finished loading, start the simulator and watch the motion menu in action. Immediately you will notice that the text buttons are not available. They take about 15 seconds to fully appear, at which time the Start text becomes underlined and ready for user selection.

The menu is about two minutes long. Just let it fully play, and watch it auto-repeat itself. Take notice that when the menu repeats itself, it doesn't fully repeat everything you saw the first time. It's missing the first 18 seconds of play where the buttons animated into the motion menu. That part has been skipped. This skipping is called the Loop Point.

Use the simulator's remote control and press the enter key in the middle of the four cursor arrows to make a track selection. You will select a sample text track play, and when it is finished it will return back to this motion menu. Again, notice that the beginning 18 seconds of the menu are skipped.

Now select Enter again to play the sample track, and this time press the Title button on the simulated remote control. You will go back to the menu, and again, you will skip that first 18 seconds.

Now, exit the simulation, and then exit DVD Studio Pro. You're going to build this exact sample yourself next.

Step 1

Make sure you have a copy of the Chapter 9 folder on your desktop. Then launch the DVD Studio Pro application.

Step 2

Your first task is to import all the items needed to make the simple demo you just watched. Click on the Import icon in the Toolbar.

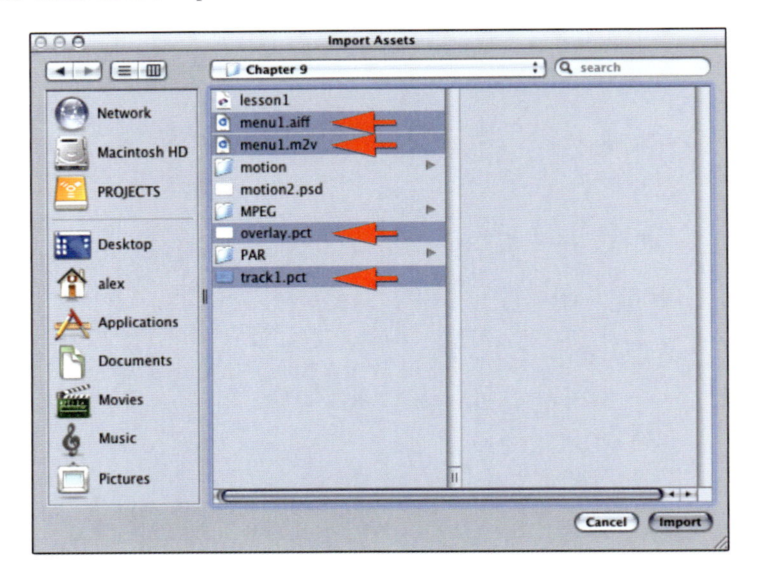

Figure 9.21 Importing assets into the DVD Studio Pro Assets tab

Step 3

Hold down the Apple or Command key then click on each of the four following items in the Chapter 9 folder:

1. Menu 1.aiff
2. Menu 1.m2v
3. Overlay.pct
4. Track1.pct

Once all are highlighted, select the Import button to import all four assets into the Assets tab in DVD Studio Pro.

Step 4

Open the Outline tab, and click on the default Menu 1 object in the Outline tab. Open the Property Inspector and leave it open from now on. In the Menu 1 Property Inspector, click in the Name field and change the name of the menu from Menu 1 to MyBigMenu.

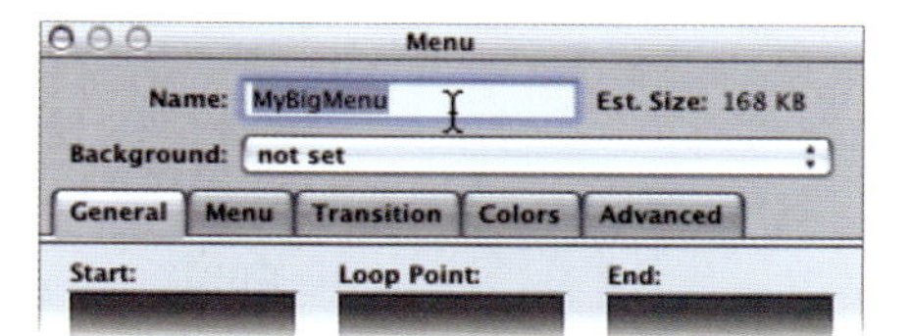

Figure 9.22 Naming the motion menu

Step 5

From the Assets tab, drag the menu1.m2v asset over to the Menu tab and hold until the Drop palette appears. Choose the Set Background option. This action sets this full-motion two-minute clip as the background of the menu.

Look at the Inspector-General tab of your menu object. In the audio section, notice that the menu1.aif audio asset has already been added to the menu's audio field. This happens automatically when the name of the video and audio asset match in name with the exception of the .m2v and .aif.

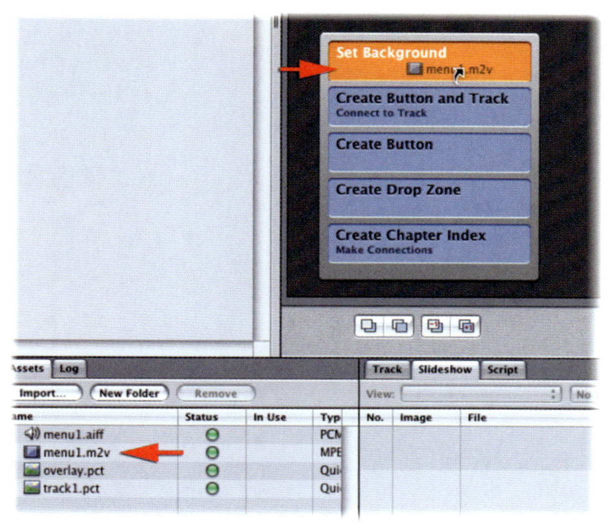

Figure 9.23 Setting the Motion menu background

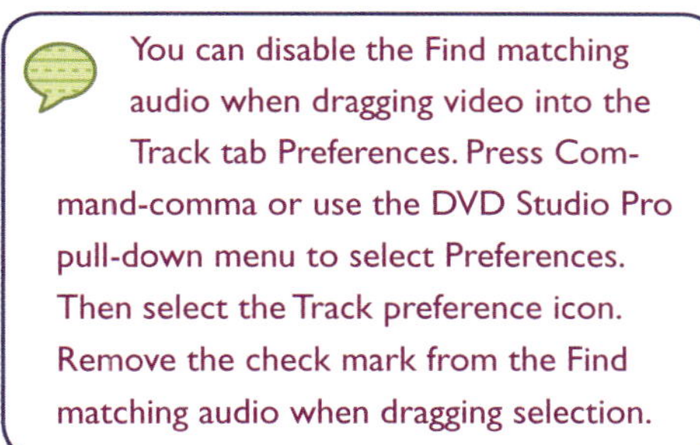

You can disable the Find matching audio when dragging video into the Track tab Preferences. Press Command-comma or use the DVD Studio Pro pull-down menu to select Preferences. Then select the Track preference icon. Remove the check mark from the Find matching audio when dragging selection.

Step 6

From the Assets tab, drag the overlay.pct file over to the Menu tab, and hold until the Drop palette appears, and then choose Set Overlay. These are the underline highlights for the four buttons you saw in the preview.

Note: The Menu tab view will not show any apparent changes when the overlay.pct file is dropped onto the Menu tab. However,

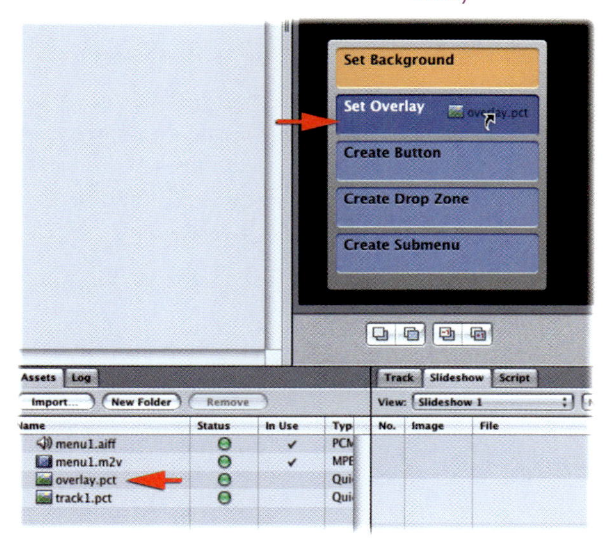

Figure 9.24 Setting the Motion menu overlay

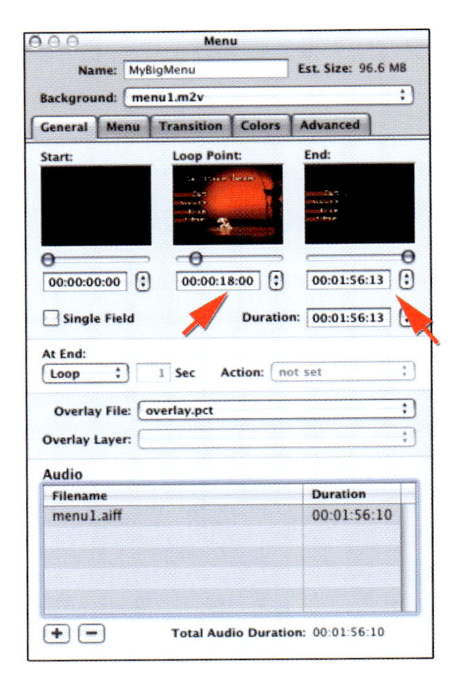

Figure 9.25 Setting the Loop Point and menu play duration

the General tab as shown in the Inspector will reflect the file, overlay.pct, in the Overlay File field.

Step 7

Using the General tab of the menu's property inspector, set the Loop Point field to 18 seconds and the end field to its maximum timecode. You can quickly adjust the end field timecode by positioning the slider above the end field timecode. Position the slider all the way to the right to set the maximum timecode.

Figure 9.26 Drawing button outlines for the Motion menu

Step 8

Make sure the Show buttons Selected State is in the On position. In the menu draw a button outline around the Start text in the menu background. Extend this outline enough to expose the highlight under the word. Do the same for the other three background text items.

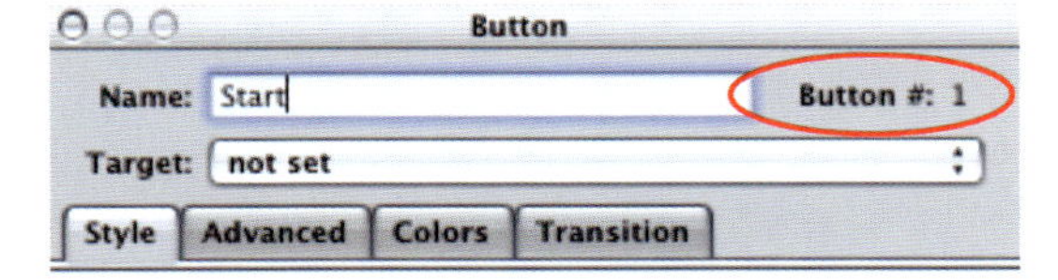

Figure 9.27 Changing the Button Name property

Step 9

Select the button outline of the first button, which is the Start button, and look to the Property Inspector. In the Name field, change the default name of Button1 to Start. Do the same for the other three buttons, naming them after their text names of Chapters, Extras, and Settings.

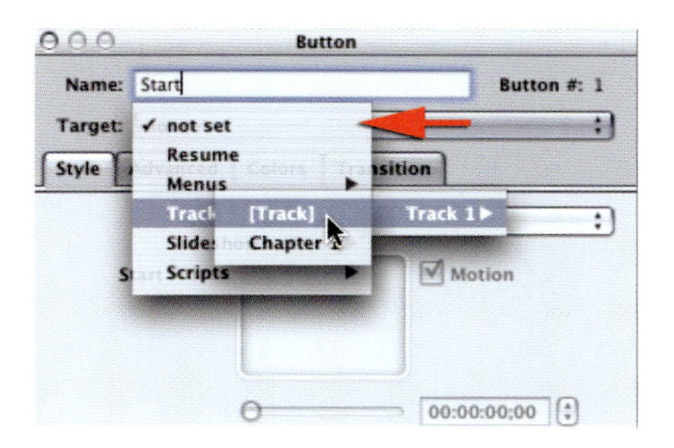

Figure 9.28 Setting the button target

Step 10

Select the Start button outline in the menu, and again look to the Button Property Inspector. Click on the Target field and navigate to the Track > Track 1 > [Track] item and select that. Set the three other outline buttons exactly the same way to the very same track.

Step 11

Click on the background of the menu so that none of the outlines are selected. Now go back to the Property Inspector, and click on the Colors tab.

Set the Normal option to the color black, with an opacity of 0.

Set the Selected option to the color white, with an opacity of 10.

Set the Activated option to the color yellow, with an opacity of 10.

Figure 9.29 Adjusting the button highlight color properties

Step 12

Select the Track tab, so that you can see its empty contents. Take the track1.pct asset from the Assets tab and drag it into the V1 section of the Track tab and drop it there.

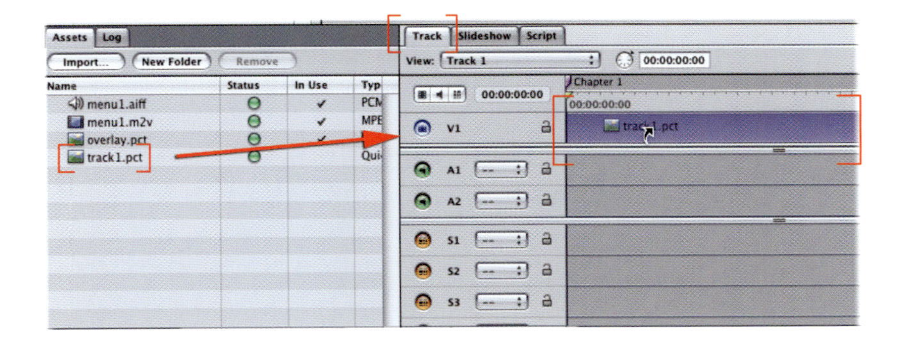

Figure 9.30 Adding a simple video element to the Track object

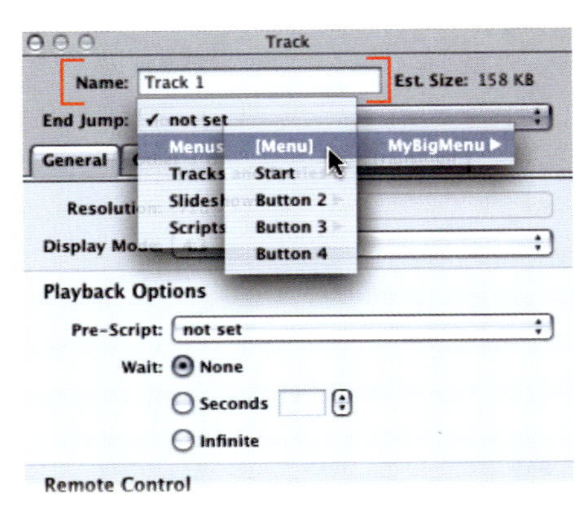

Figure 9.31 Setting the End Jump target for the Track object

Step 13

Select the Track 1 object in the Outline tab, and then refer to its Property Inspector. Click on the End Jump drop-down menu and select Menus > MyBigMenu > [Menu]. When this track is finished playing, it will now return to the menu you have created.

Now it's time to simulate the menu.

Click on the simulator, and if all went well with your lesson you should be watching a menu with full motion in the background. You hear the music, and at about 18 seconds of playback, the underline highlight appears under the Start button. This is your Loop Point.

Let this menu play all the way through to the end, and watch it repeat itself. This will take about two minutes. Once the menu has completely finished playing, you will see that it repeats itself, but this time it starts from the Loop Point you set at 18 seconds.

While the menu is playing its second time, select any of the buttons by selecting the Enter button on the simulator's remote control. This will play the simulated track you have added to the Track tab.

When the track is finished playing, it returns to the menu and starts playing the entire menu all over again. You see the text items animate for the first 15 seconds again as well. The Loop Point has not helped you this time, but it will if you allow the menu to play for the full two minutes again.

You saw in the menu I built that the menu played the Loop Point only once, and there was no way to play that Loop Point again after it already had played once. That is what you are going to learn next. This requires a little script that you will attach to the Menu object.

Scripting the Loop Point

Add a script by clicking on the Add Script icon in the toolbar. Keep the default name of the script, which is Script 1. Then open the Script tab, which is usually by the Track tab.

There is one command by default in any new script you create. Click on the command on the number 1 line called Nop, and then look at the Property Inspector. The Property Inspector becomes a Script Command Editor. This editor works in a visual way.

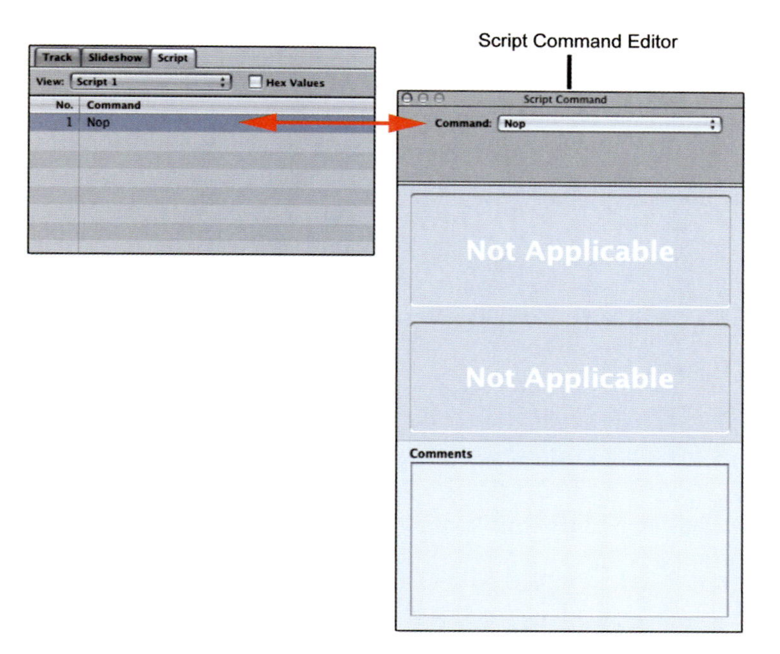

Figure 9.32 Default Script Command property

Click on the Command pull-down menu and change the command from Nop to Set GPRM.

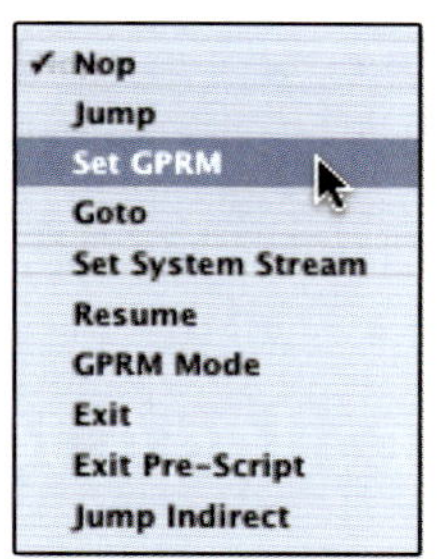

Figure 9.33 Script command — SetGPRM

Once the command Nop is replaced with the Command Set GPRM, you'll notice quite a few changes have taken place both in the script and in the script editor. Two more sections now exist in the Script Command Editor.

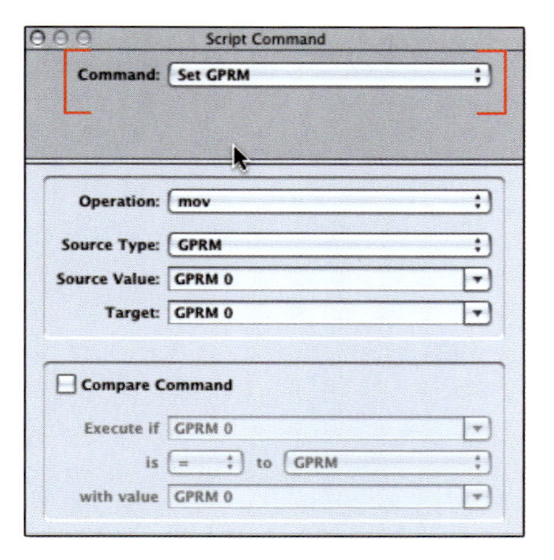

Figure 9.34 Script Command property

Figure 9.35 Set GPRM command operation

Look at the first operation, which is where it says "mov". Change the mov command to the Add command.

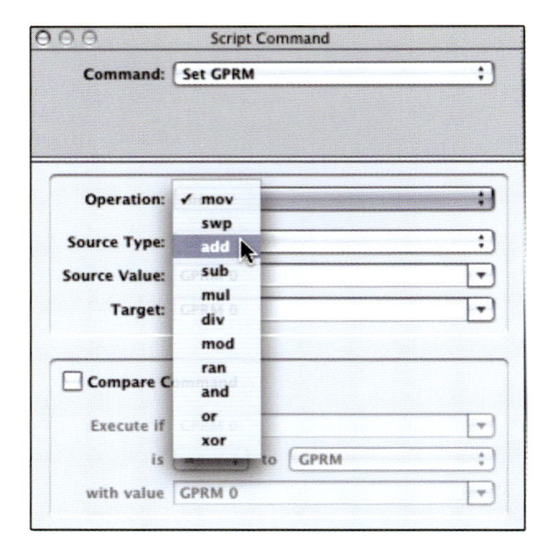

Figure 9.36 Set GPRM command operation source type

Now change the Source Type from GPRM to Immediate.

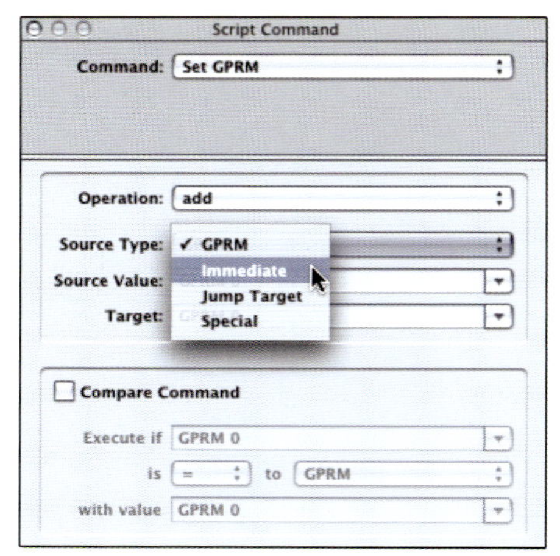

Figure 9.37 Set GPRM command operation source type value

In the Source Value field, type in the number "1", and leave the Target field set to GPRM 0 as it is now.

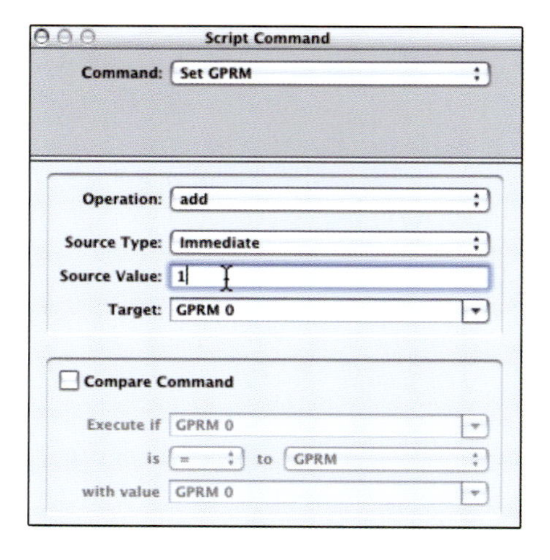

Now take a look at the Script tab again, and you'll see that you have changed the command from its original command of Nop to a short line of code that reads "add GPRM 0, 1".

Click on the Add New Command button to add the next line of code to this small script. Notice that another line of code appears in the Script tab, and just as before, the basic command of Nop is inserted. This is how all new commands start, as you can now see. It is up to you to modify the new commands you insert into the commands you would like to have.

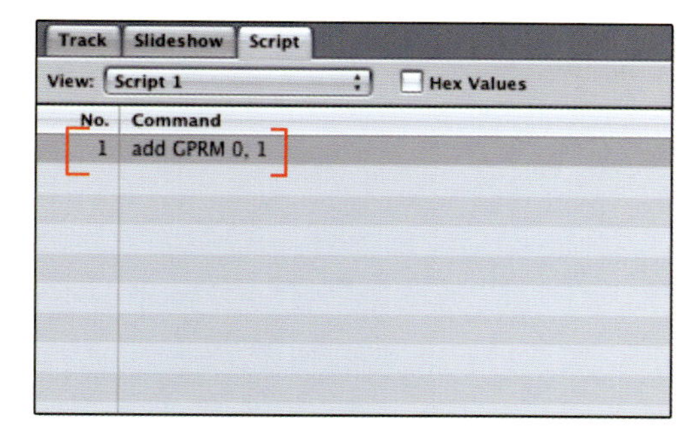

Figure 9.38 Finish command line 1

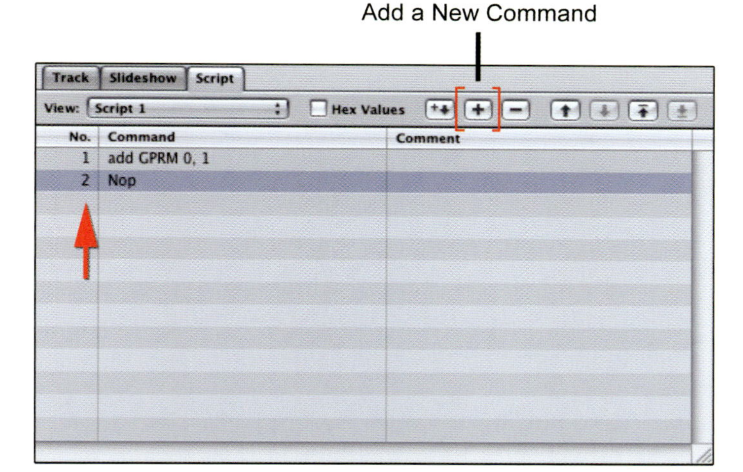

Figure 9.39 Adding a new default command to the script

Highlight the Nop command in the Script tab, then in the inspector, click the Nop command pull-down and select Jump.

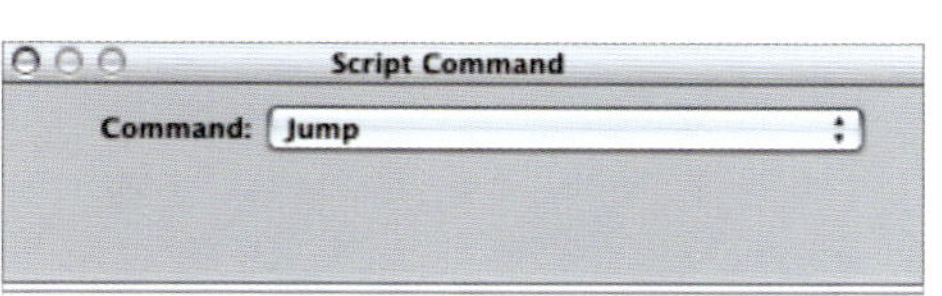

Figure 9.40 Setting the Jump command

Set the Jump To target by using the Jump To pull-down menu and choosing Menus > MyBigMenu > [Menu].

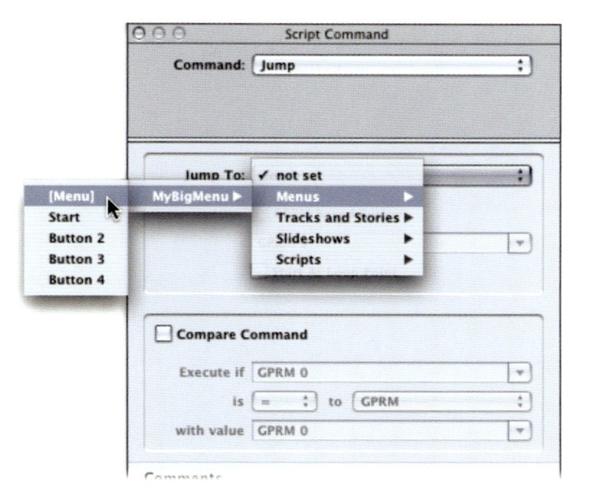

Figure 9.41 Setting the Jump To target

Next check the Start At Loop Point check box.

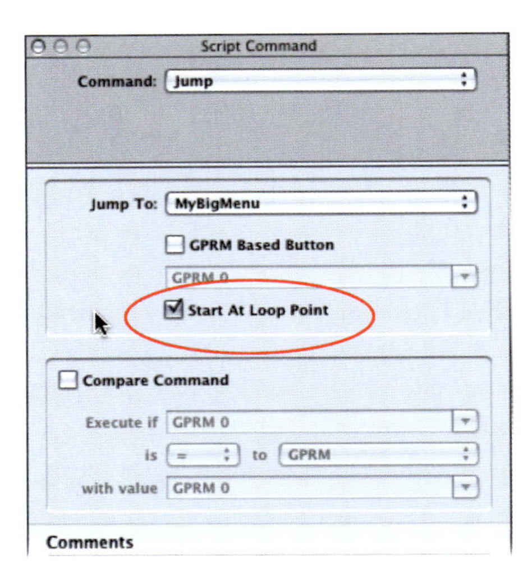

Figure 9.42 Targeting the menu Loop Point

Now check the Compare Command check box. This opens the options under the compare section. Click on the "is" field, changing = (equal) to >= (greater than or equal to). To the right of that, it says GPRM, which you need to change to Immediate. This allows you to type in a value in the field labeled "with value" below. Type the number "2" in the "with value" field.

This is what your script now should look like. You have one more simple line to go, and then I'll explain all about this script.

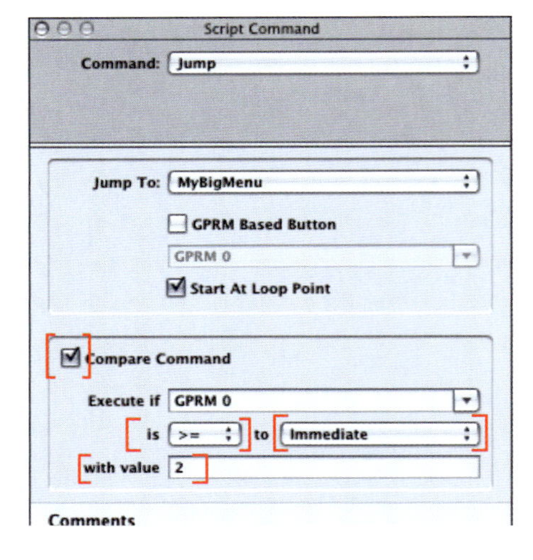

Figure 9.43 Defining the command as conditional with the compare option

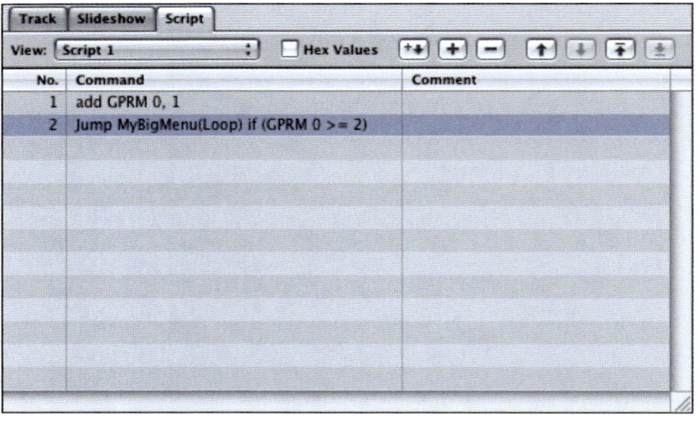

Figure 9.44 Script Editor

Click on the Add Command button again to add the third and final command, which again will default to Nop in line 3.

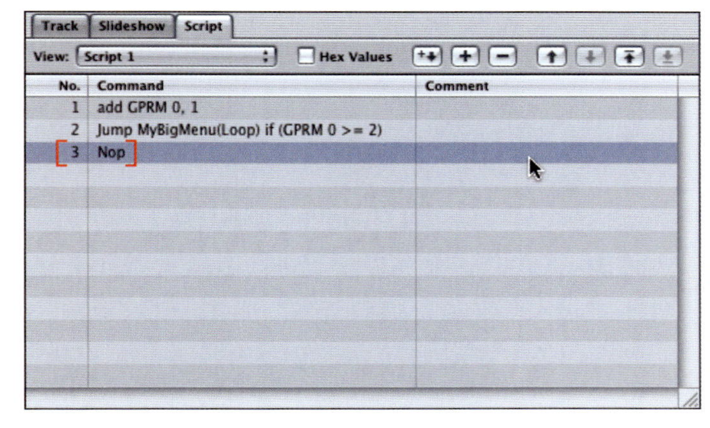

Figure 9.45 Script Editor — new default command

Just as before, click on the Nop command in the Script Command Editor and change it to Jump, then in the Jump To field, select the same menu, leaving everything else blank.

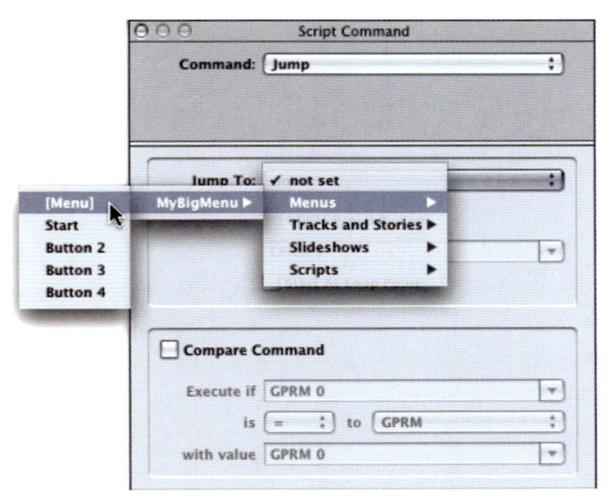

Figure 9.46 Command — Jump with menu target

Your script should like this. If it does, you are done. What does the script mean? Well, remember that you want the motion menu to play from the start only the first time it is played. Each time the viewer goes back to this menu, you would like to spare them watching the intro section of the menu a second, a third, and so on time. This script accomplishes exactly that.

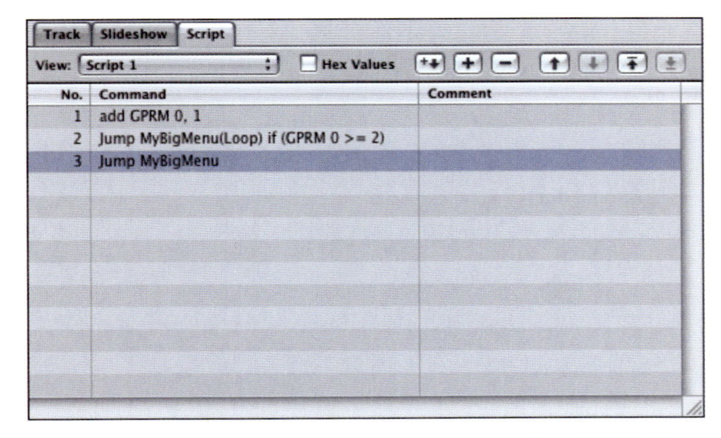

Figure 9.47 Script Editor

Let's go over each line, one at a time, to make sense of this. In line 1, you see the "add GPRM 0, 1" script. GPRM (General Purpose Register Memory) is likely the most unknown item in this line. This is a user-defined memory that your DVD player makes available to DVD authors. There are 16 of these; however, DVD Studio Pro itself uses eight of them to handle all the chores of authoring it does on your behalf, leaving you with eight blank registers to use any way you see fit. These eight blank registers are labeled GPRM 0 through GPRM 7, totaling eight user-defined registers.

You are using GPRM 0 to count how many times the motion menu has played. If it plays more than a certain amount of times, then you will prevent the intro section, which is the section that starts the menu and extends to the beginning of the Loop Point, from playing ever again.

1. add GPRM 0, 1

This is really a counter. Each time the menu is played this script adds the value of 1 to the register GPRM 0. Therefore GPRM 0 is equal to 1 the first time this script is played. The second time this script is played the value of GPRM 0 is 2, and so on and so on.

Let's look at line 2 now.

2. Jump MyBigMenu(Loop) if (GPRM 0 >= 2)

Jump of course means to go to another place, in this case, the motion menu. Which menu you jump to is the Jump To target, and in this case that target is MyBigMenu. The (Loop) designation following the menu target is the specific location within the menu where the target is directed. The motion menu's loop point is 18 seconds into the menu, so this line of script is going to jump 18 seconds into the motion menu.

There is a condition to this action, however, and that is what the "if" part of this line of script is telling you. Remember line 1, where you are counting how many times this menu has played. The if condition extends the command to say that in order to jump 18 seconds into the motion menu, the following condition must be met. The condition is that GPRM 0 must be equal to a value of 2 or more.

These lines of code are executed in the order of their line numbers. Since line 1 immediately starts by adding a value of 1 to GPRM 0, you know that the first time this script is executed the value in GPRM 0 is going to be equal to 1. The condition in line 2 will not be met because the condition must equal 2 or more to be met. If the condition is not met, then the third line of code is executed, because line 2 is ignored, having not been met.

3. Jump MyBigMenu

Line 3 tells the DVD to play the same menu, but not to start at the loop point. This is because this must be the first time the menu has been played.

The next time this script is executed, the value of GPRM 0 will equal a value of 2. After that, each time the script is executed, the value of GPRM 0 increases by a value of 1, and thus the condition in line 2 will always be met after this script is run just once. Therefore, the Loop Point will always be the target after the menu has played a single time.

Now, you might be asking yourself, how does this script execute each time the menu is viewed? The answer is a function of the menu called pre-script. A pre-script is any script that is assigned to a menu as a pre-script. Each time the menu is accessed by the viewer, its pre-script commands are first executed before the menu is actually displayed.

Assigning a Pre-Script

To assign this script as a pre-script, click on Menu in the Outline tab, then in the inspector choose the Advanced tab. In the Playback Option section of the Advanced tab, you will see the Pre-Script option. This is a regular pulldown menu. Now, choose the script you just created, thus assigning it as this menu's pre-script.

Now simulate the project again. Once the menu begins, the intro will play for 18 seconds, then the Start button will show its underlined highlight. Choose the Start button and watch the sample track play for 5 seconds. When it is done, you will return to the menu, this time skipping the first 18 seconds, and going straight to the beginning of the Loop Point.

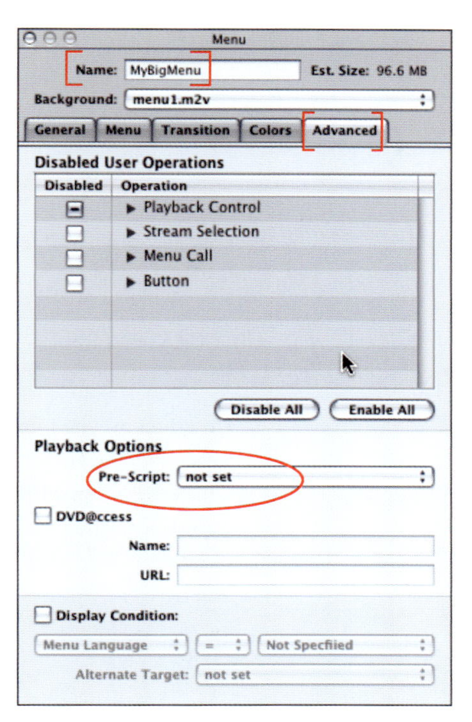

Figure 9.48 Menu playback option — pre-script

Chapter Menus and Navigation

In this section you'll learn how to set up a chapter menu. Chapter menus are sometimes called submenus. Chapter menus are really no different from other menus, with just a few exceptions that have to do mostly with navigation.

As the term chapter menu implies, these menus are designed to play a chapter of the timeline. Most Hollywood DVDs feature a chapter menu that starts by playing the chapter of choice and then continues to play all the way through to the end of the DVD. DVD Studio Pro is actually much more flexible than what you have likely seen in those Hollywood DVDs.

In this chapter, you'll not only create a chapter menu, you'll create a sophisticated navigation system to go with it. As sophisticated as this navigation will be, no scripting will be required at all.

In this section you will learn to accomplish the following:

- Create a thumbnail preview of each chapter point
- Enhance your thumbnails with Shape objects
- Use the Story object to enhance navigation
- Program the remote control's top menu function
- Program the remote control's menu key
- Program the remote control's return key

Project Overview

Before we begin, open the DVD-ROM that came with this book. Find the Chapter 10 folder and copy the entire Lesson 10 folder to your Macintosh desktop.

Notice the two DVD Studio Pro project files labeled Lesson 10 and Lesson 10_Finished. Just as their names imply, one is a starter project you will work with now, and the other is the end result that you are after.

Double-click on the Lesson 10 project icon to get started.

Once this project has fully loaded, you'll see that this is a partially finished DVD project. It is based on all the things you have learned thus far. Look at the Outline tab, and get familiar with all that has already been done for you.

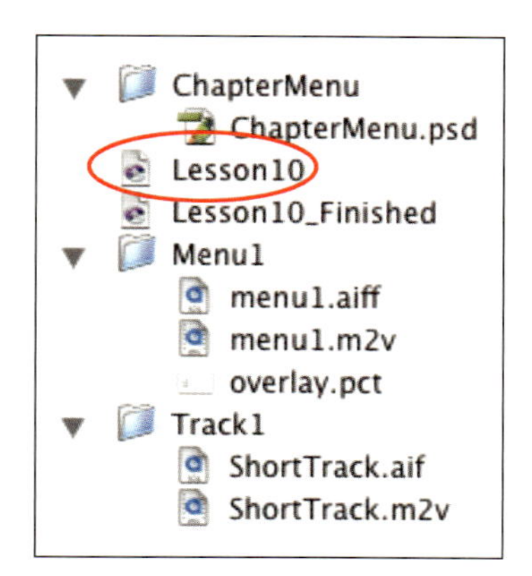

Figure 10.1 OSX folder — list view

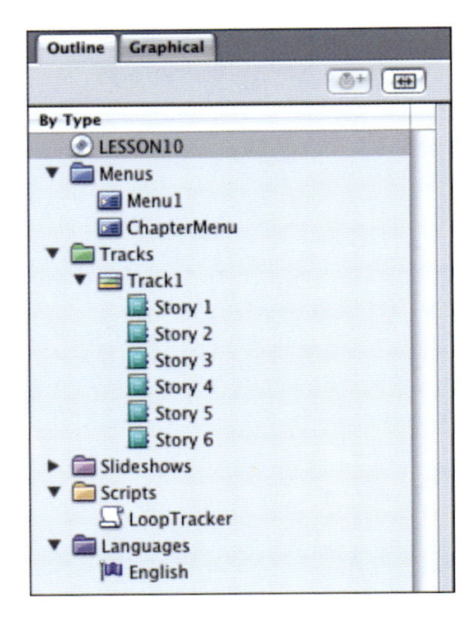

Figure 10.2 Outline tab

In the Menus folder, you see two menu objects labeled Menu1 and ChapterMenu. Menu1 is the Motion menu you just learned about in the prior chapter. The ChapterMenu object is completely blank. You will add all the assets and functions that will make that menu a functional chapter menu.

Open the Script tab and examine the script that is in place already. This is the same script you just learned to create in the prior chapter. Select the Menu1 object in the Outline tab, and then look at the Property Inspector. Select the Advanced tab of the inspector, and you'll notice that the script called LoopTracker has been assigned to Menu1 as a pre-script, just as in the prior lesson.

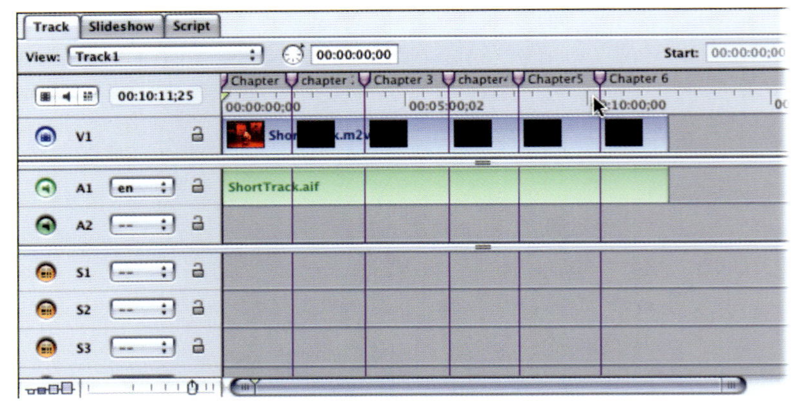

Figure 10.3 Track tab

Open the Track tab, and you'll notice a new asset as been added from the prior lesson. This is a 12-minute track with six chapter points already added for you.

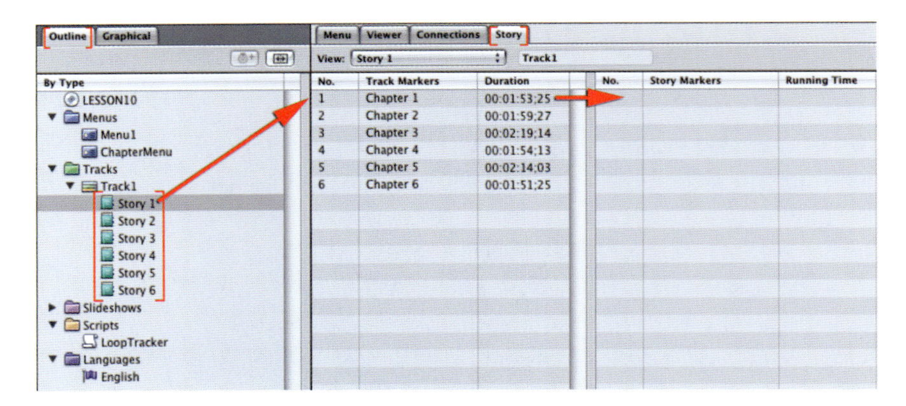

Figure 10.4 Outline tab with the Story tab

Now, look back at the Outline tab, specifically at the Tracks folder. Expand Track1 to reveal the Story objects that are associated with Track1. You will learn to create these in just a minute, but for now, notice that I have made six Story objects for you.

The Story objects are configured through a tab I have not yet discussed. This is the Story tab. Arrange your Story tab so that you see it the way I show it in Figure 10.4.

These are the main areas you will work with for this lesson.

Creating Stories

What is the Story object, and why are you learning it?

Chapter menus point to chapters within the total track. A Story object is a container that can hold one or more chapters. Think of stories as you would think of a photocopy of a chapter in a book. You still have the book, but the photocopy is a copy of one chapter. You might catch the train in the morning and read that one chapter, leaving the entire book at home. The photocopy is its own asset, separate from the book, but still a part of the book at the same time. After all, it is a 100 percent replica of one of the chapters.

The Story object is like this but with an exception: The Story object doesn't actually copy a chapter from the track. It does not increase the size of the DVD at all. It is simply a container which is used to reference a chapter from within the track. It is its own object, and as such it can be linked to, just like a track. And just like a track, it has its own End Jump.

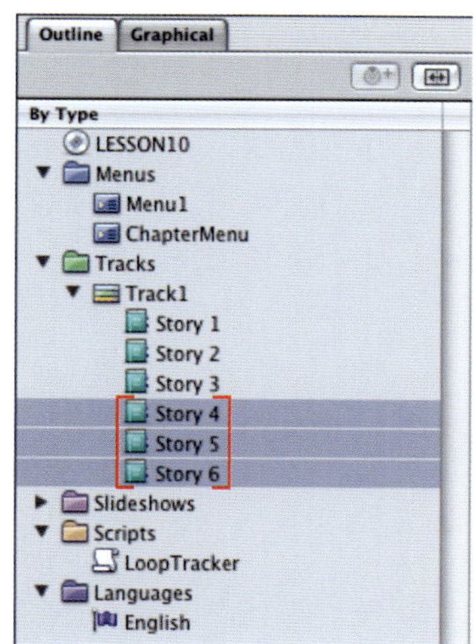

Figure 10.5 Deleting Stories

Why use a Story object?

You will use the Story object to gain the benefits of the separate functionality the Story object has from its older brother, the Track object. Specifically, consider the situation of this DVD. You have a main menu which links to the track asset. You also have a chapter menu, which links to chapters within that same track asset. The question is, when the viewer of your DVD uses your chapter menu to watch a chapter of your film, and that chapter concludes playing, which menu should the viewer be returned to, the main menu or the chapter menu?

Since the user chose to play the chapter from the chapter menu, it would be quite nice if the user was returned to that chapter menu once the chapter finished playing. That is the functionality you gain from using the Story object.

Step 1

First, I would like you to delete Stories 4, 5, and 6. I want you to actually create and then populate the stories with assigned chapters so that you actually do the steps needed to create stories on your own later. Delete Stories 4, 5, and 6.

Step 2

Now, highlight the Track1 object, then use the Toolbar to add a Story object to the Outline tab. When you click on Add Story, you will see Story 4 is added to the Track1 object.

Click Add Story twice more, and Stories 5 and 6 will be added to the Track1 object in the Outline tab once again. Stories are objects associated with a particular Track object. There is a limitation implied here. That is, stories cannot contain chapters from other tracks. Stories can only contain chapters from the single track they are associated with.

Assigning Chapters to the Story Object

Step 1

Open the Story tab so that you see both the Outline tab and the Story tab at the same time. Select the Story 1 object, then use the Story tab and drag the Chapter 1 line into the Story Markers section on the right side.

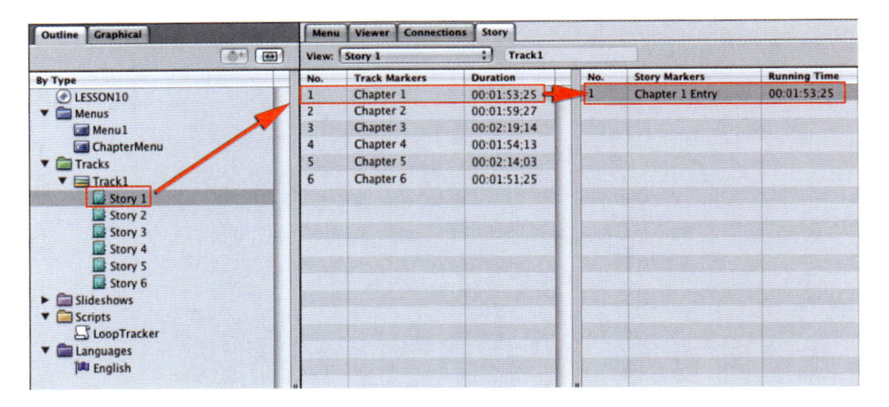

Figure 10.6 Story 1 — Defining a story work flow

The center column is merely showing you all the available chapters you may use with this Story object. The only assigned chapter in this story is Chapter 1 Entry, which is shown in the right-side window.

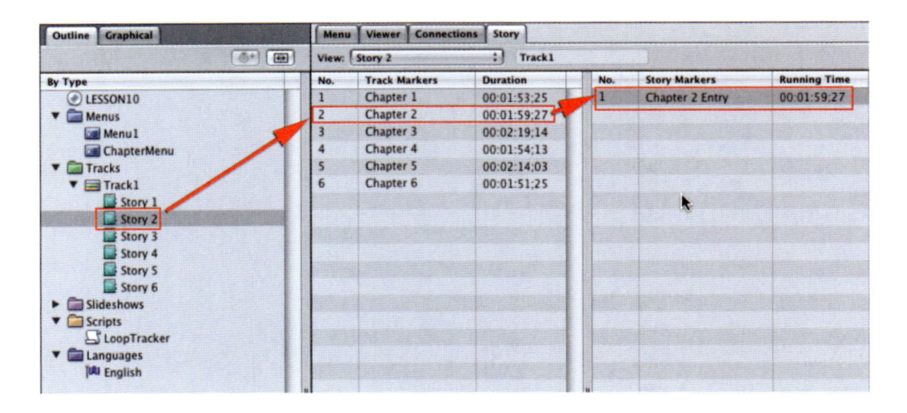

Figure 10.7 Defining Story 2

Story 1 is now a container for Chapter 1. You want to leave Story 1 alone now, as it is finished.

Step 2

Click on Story 2 in the Outline tab, and watch what happens to the right-side window now. It is empty, because Story 1 and Story 2 are completely different objects with completely different chapter assignments.

While Story 2 is still selected, drag the Chapter 2 line into the Story Markers section on the right-side window.

Step 3

Now do the same for the remaining four stories, adding Chapter 3 to Story 3, and Chapter 4 to Story 4, and so on until you have each story populated with its corresponding chapter number.

Creating the Chapter Menu

Chapter menus may be like any of the menus you have already created, which are still menus, motion menus, or layered menus. You will create a chapter menu using a still asset as a background, then adding preview thumbnails of each chapter as motion boxes.

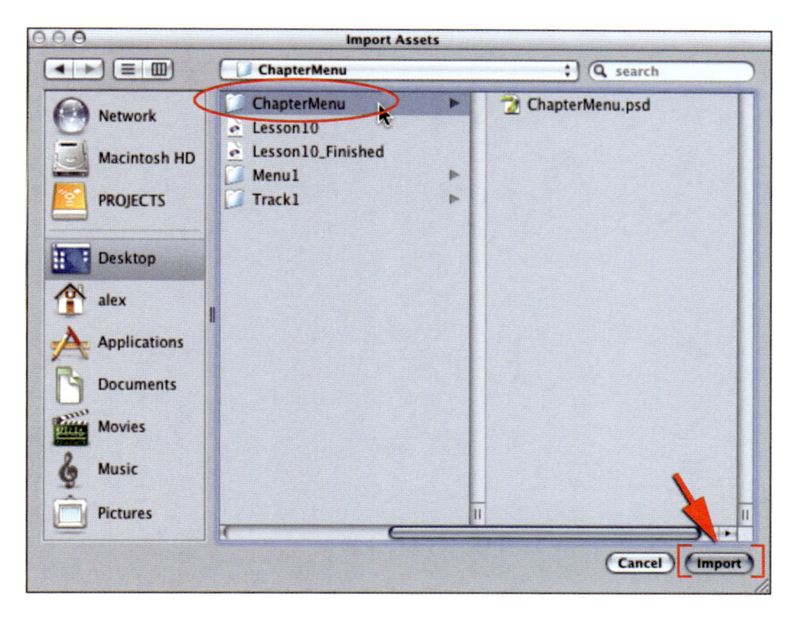

Figure 10.8 Importing the chapter menu background

Step 1

Import the ChapterMenu folder from the copied Lesson 10 folder on your Macintosh desktop. This will add a folder called ChapterMenu, which contains a background you will use as the background for the chapter menu.

Adding a Background to the Chapter Menu

Step 2

Select the ChapterMenu object in the Outline tab, and then open the Menu tab as well. You are going to add the background you just imported to the ChapterMenu background.

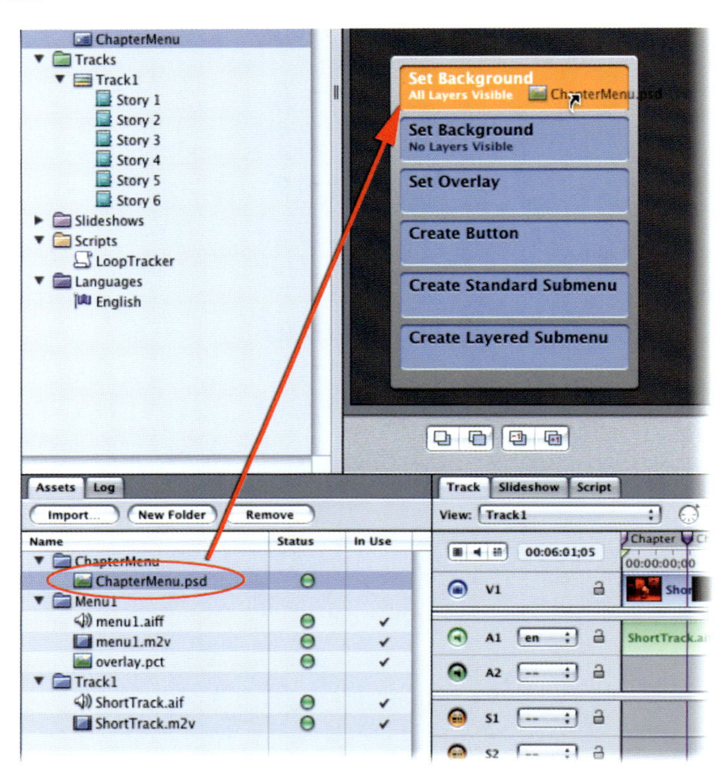

Figure 10.9 Assigning the menu background with the Drop Palette

Step 3

Drag the ChapterMenu.psd from the Assets tab to the background of ChapterMenu in the Menu tab, hovering for a moment until the Drop Palette opens. Select Set Background All Layers Visible.

Creating a Thumbnail Preview Button

Step 4

Drag the Story 1 object to the ChapterMenu background and hover for a moment until the drop palette appears. Choose "Create Button - Connect to Story". This single action has two functions. First, this will create an animated thumbnail button complete with a preview video that is representative of the contents of the Story 1 object. In this case, that would be Chapter 1.

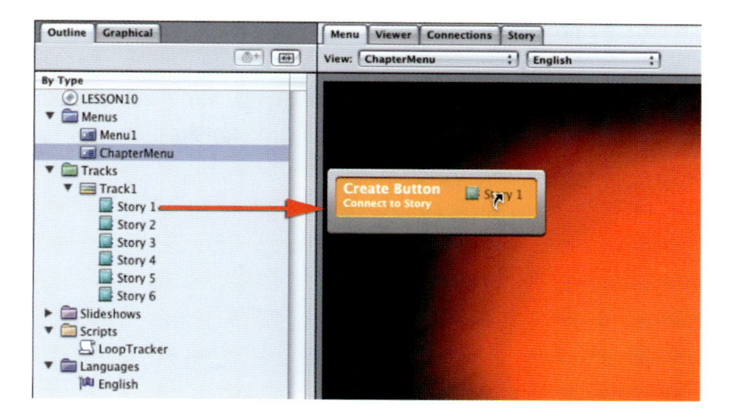

Figure 10.10 Create a button — link to Story

The second action taken is what the subheading, "Connect to Story," means. The button you have just created already has its Jump To target automatically assigned to the Story object in the Outline tab. There is no need to set this button's Jump To target.

Adjusting the Start Frame in the Preview Button

Step 5

Open the inspector for the animated button you just created in the menu. You will see a preview of the animated button as a still frame in the inspector. It should appear to be black. This is because all my chapters start from a fade from black. You can adjust what frame the thumbnails start with by adjusting the Start Frame parameter.

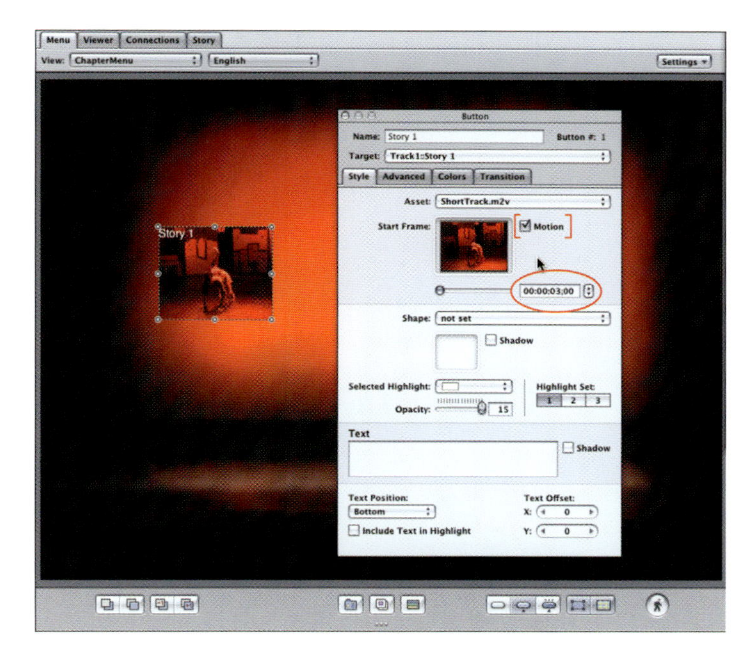

Figure 10.11 Adjusting the Motion button property

Notice the Motion check box is currently checked. Now under that, click on the up part of the up/down timecode field, adjusting it to about 00;00;03;00 (3 seconds). The first thumbnail now has a full frame of video rather than the empty black box. It does, however, look a little plain.

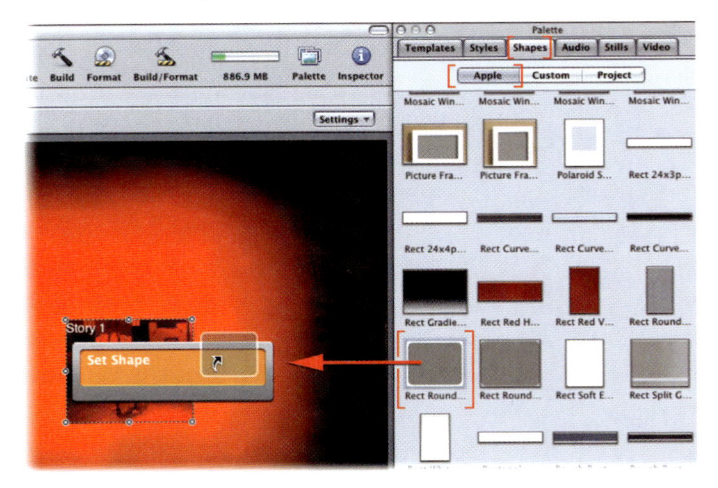

Figure 10.12 Setting the Motion button shape

Step 6

Apply a Shape object to the thumbnail button. To do this, open the Palette, then from the available tabs choose Shapes, then the sub-tab Apple. Scroll down until you find the Rect Round Window BorderHighlight shape. Drag that Shape object on top of the thumbnail preview button and hover for a moment. A drop palette appears. Choose Set Shape.

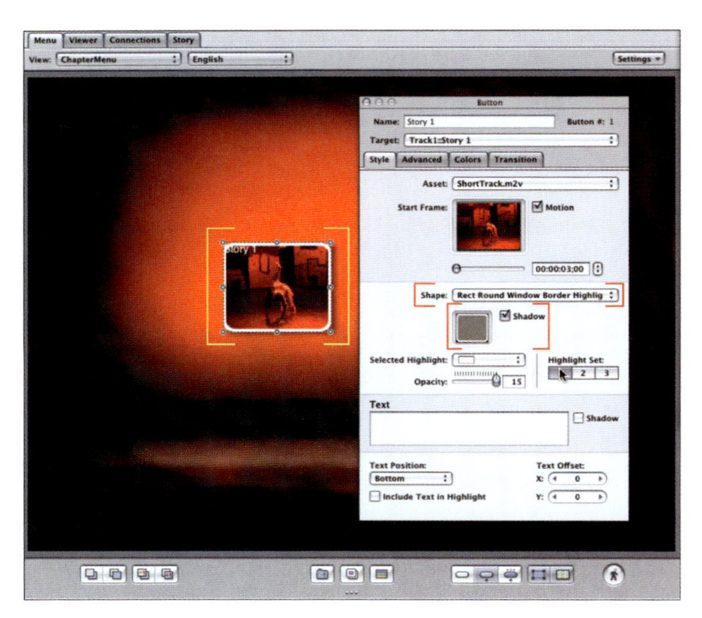

Figure 10.13 Adding a shadow to the button shape

Place the mouse pointer over the Shape object, and then let it remain motionless for a moment. The complete name of the shape will hover over the shape, making it much easier to determine the shape's full name.

Step 7

Once the shape is applied, you see a white boarder around the thumbnail button. Go back to the inspector, and take a look at the Shape field. It now states which Shape object is associated with this button. Just under that, place a check mark in the check box for Shadow. A shadow appears under the thumbnail button.

Setting the Default Button Style

Step 1

Right-click on the button with your added Shape object and shadow effects applied, and then choose Set as Default Button Style.

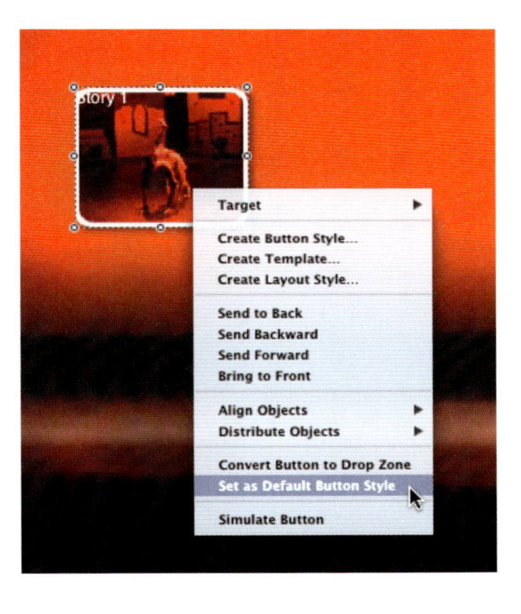

Figure 10.14 Setting the Button property as the default button style

Step 2

Go back to the Outline tab and drag the Story 2 object onto the menu and release it. Now select this new thumbnail box, and you will notice that the Shape object and shadow you applied to the first button have automatically been applied to this second button. This is because you made those characteristics the default button style.

Step 3

Go to the inspector for the Story 2 button, and adjust the Start Frame 3 additional sections from the current position of 00:01:53;25 by clicking on the up arrow in the timecode field six times.

Step 4

Drag the Story 3 object onto the menu and release it. Notice it too has the same style as the prior two buttons. Adjust its Start Frame an additional three seconds as well.

Aligning Buttons on the Menu

Step 1

Hold down the Shift key and select the three thumbnail buttons you have added to the menu thus far. Each of them will turn white, which is their selected state overlay highlight color.

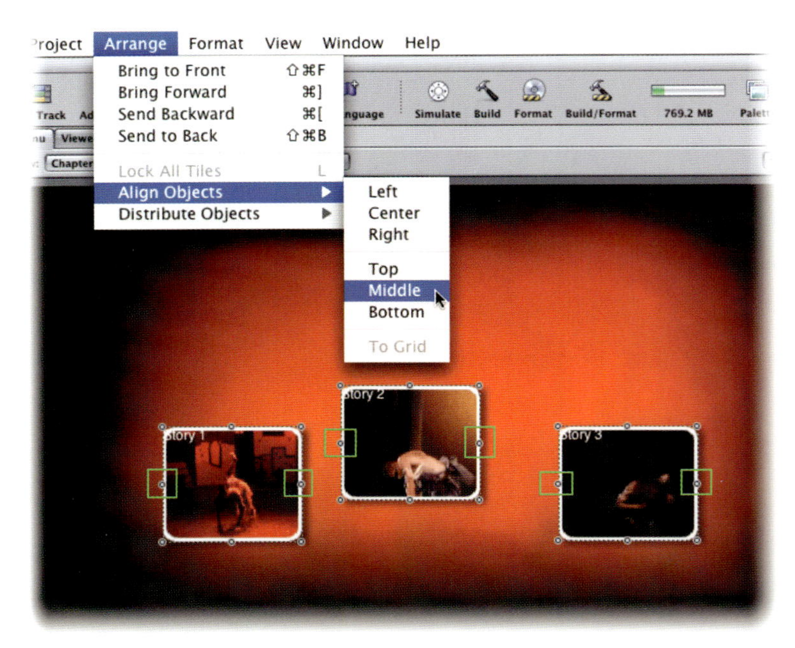

Figure 10.15 Aligning the buttons by middle

Step 2

Using the pull-down menus at the top, select Arrange > Align Objects > Middle.

Step 3

Now that the center points are all aligned, use the pull-down menu again to distribute the objects evenly away from each other. Using the pull-down menu, select Arrange > Distribute Objects > Horizontally.

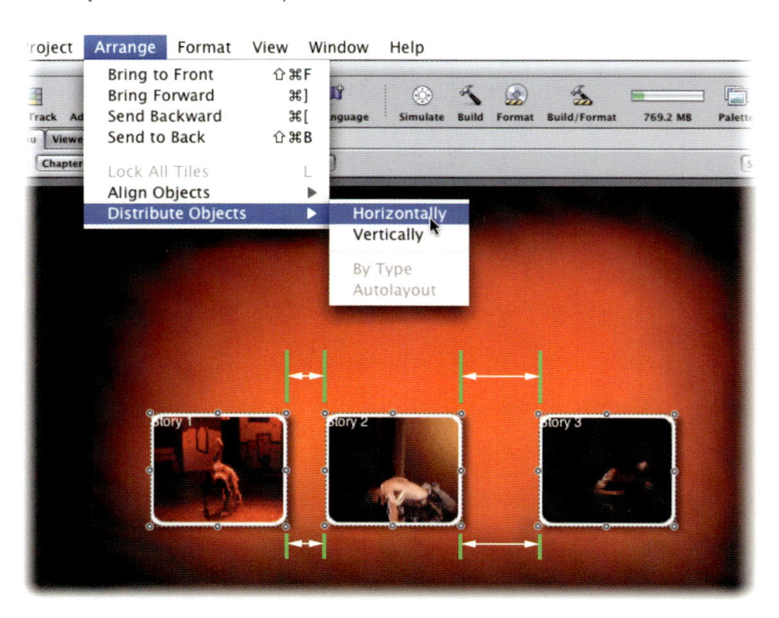

Figure 10.16 Distributing buttons horizontally even

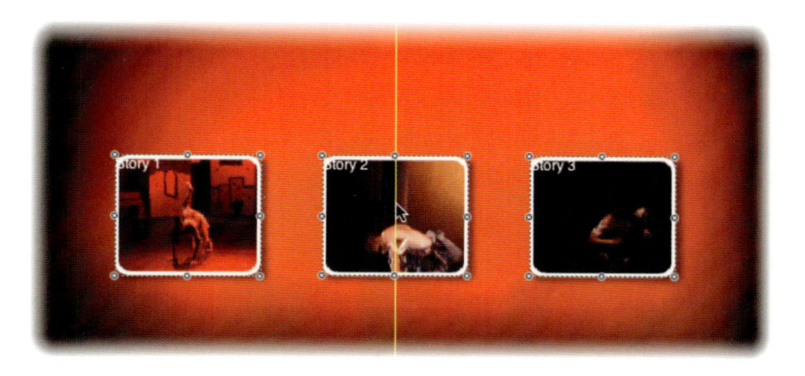

Figure 10.17 Adjusting the group center

Step 4

While all three thumbnail buttons remain selected, click and hold the Center object and drag it slightly left or right until you see the yellow center guide appear, then release the mouse. You now have three centered objects, evenly spaced apart.

You can adjust the Dynamic Guide behavior in the preferences. Open the Preferences, and then choose Alignment. You may toggle the Dynamic Guides on and off, as well as Dynamic Guides for object center, and object edges.

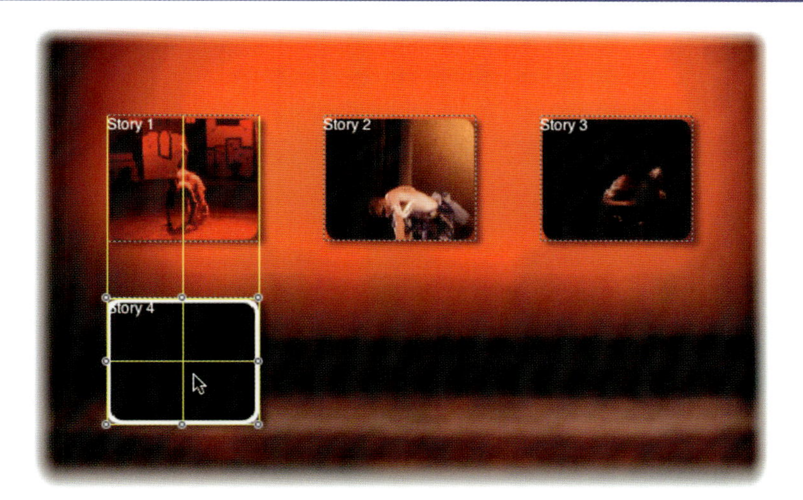

Figure 10.18 Using the dynamic alignment guides to align buttons

Step 5

You can use these centered objects as guides to add the remaining three Story objects to the menu.

Drag the Story 4 object on to the menu and release it. Now drag this thumbnail button under the first button until you see the alignment markers appear telling you that the button is aligned on all three points.

Remember to adjust the Start Frame of the thumbnail ahead three seconds so you see a solid frame in the thumbnail preview.

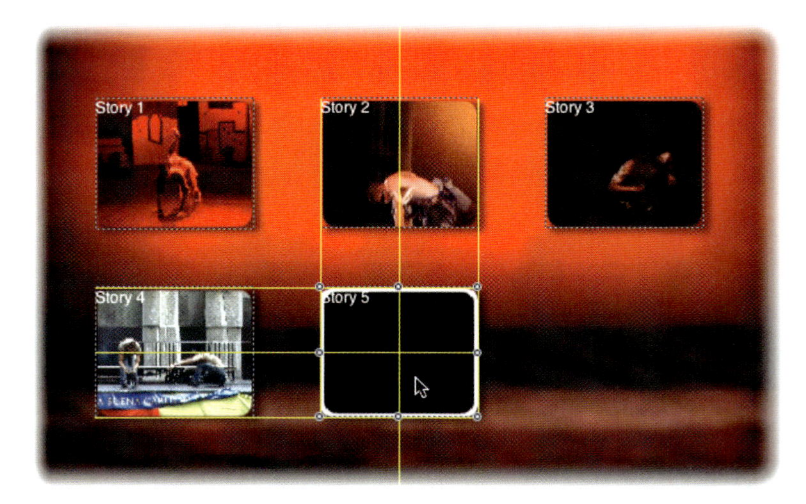

Figure 10.19 Dynamic guides vertical and horizontal

Step 6

Drag the Story 5 object into menu and release it. Then move it into position using both the thumbnail object above and to the left as guides. When you have it matched with both left and top objects you will see the automatic guides show you all six points aligned.

Again, remember to adjust the Start Frame of the thumbnail ahead three seconds.

Step 7

Step 7 is exactly the same as Step 6.

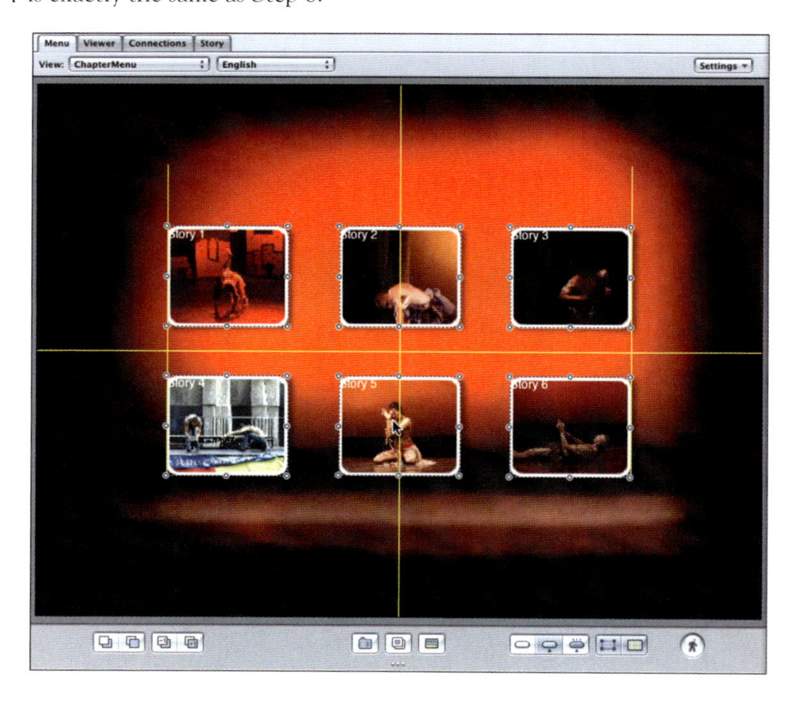

Figure 10.20 Group all center

Step 8

Once you have all six thumbnail buttons on the menu, hold down the Shift key and select all six of them so that all of them are highlighted in white. Position them until you see the yellow automatic guides showing you that the horizontal and vertical are centered.

Make sure yours look as mine do. The objects should be more in the center and away from the edges.

Keeping Your Assets Title- and Action-Safe

Step 9

Turn on the action- and title-safe guides to make sure you are within the limits of the television viewing area.

Figure 10.21 Turning on action-safe and title-safe guides

Use the Settings pop-up menu and check off Title-Safe Area and Action-Safe Area. If you kept your thumbnails close together, you should be well within the guides.

Adding Text to Buttons

Step 1

Select the Story 1 thumbnail button, and then go to the inspector. Notice at the bottom there is a Text field; type in the name "Creation". By default, you will see a 24-point Helvetica font. This is slightly too large for this menu.

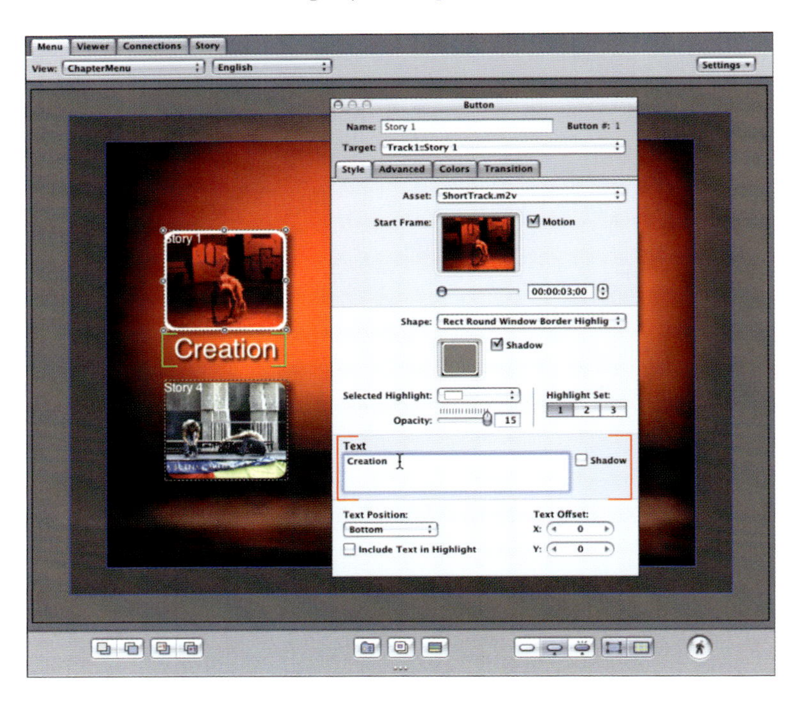

Figure 10.22 The button text field

Step 2

Use the pulldown menu at the top and choose Format > Font > Show Fonts.

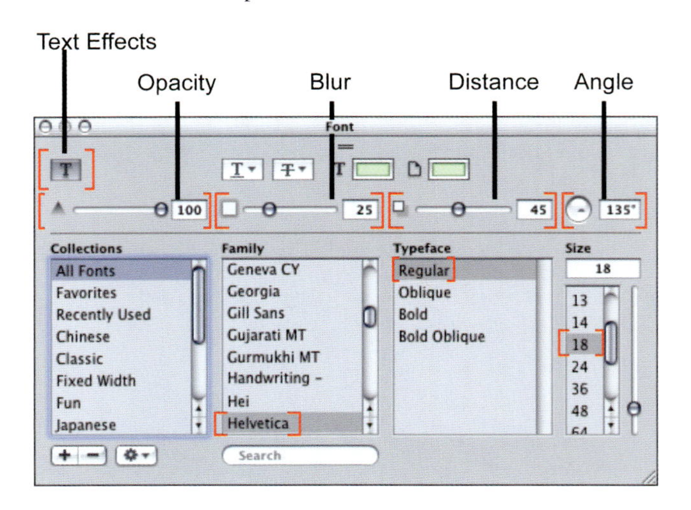

Figure 10.23 Text properties

Step 3

Highlight the Creation text at the bottom of the button, then in the floating font panel change the size from 24 to 18 points. Select the Text Effects button, then adjust the Opacity to 100, the Blur to 25, the Distance to 45, and leave the Angle to the default 135 degrees.

If you would like to reset your preferences back to the default, you can. Close the DVD Studio Pro application, and then go to your home directory / Library / Preferences. Locate the com.apple.dvdstudiopro.plist file and drag it to the trash can. When you restart DVD Studio Pro, the preferences will be factory default.

Step 4

Add the following names with the same effect to the remaining five thumbnail buttons.

Story 2 — Thunderstomp
Story 3 — The Gift
Story 4 — Offering
Story 5 — The Naming
Story 6 — Ancestor's Dream

Notice that the second time you add text to a button, the text is again defaulting to 24 points. Adjust it again to 18 points. When you select the Text Effects in the Font Panel, the prior settings remain and are applied, saving you time.

Your menu should look like this now.

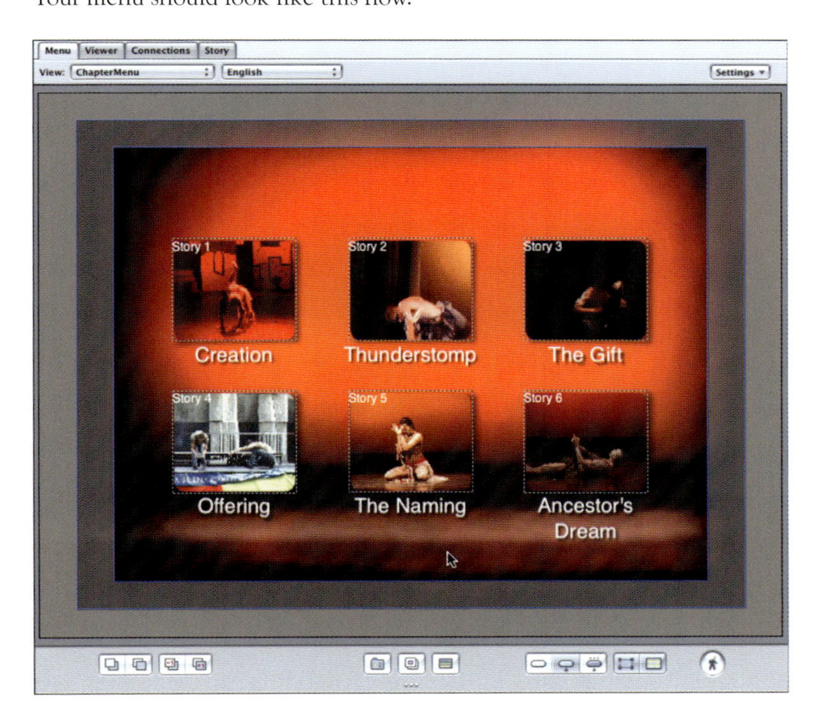

Figure 10.24 Chapter menu

Adding Text to the Menu

Step 1

Double-click the empty area above the thumbnail previews. A cursor blinks, allowing you to type text directly onto the menu's background. Add the text "Earth Dance Theater".

Figure 10.25 Menu text

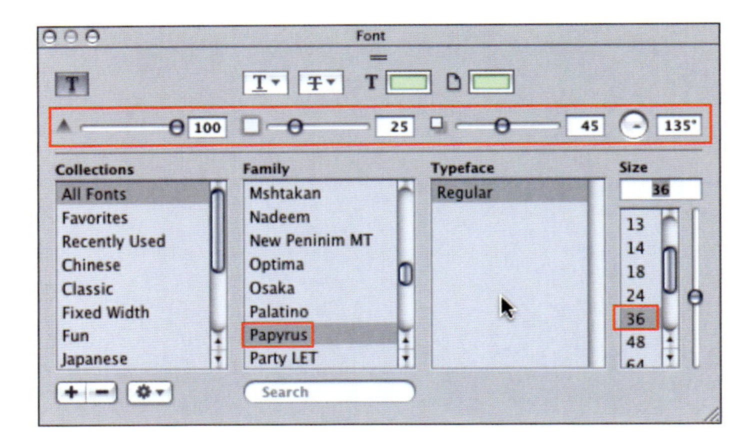

Figure 10.26 Choosing font family, typeface, and size

Step 2

Change the font from Helvetica to Papyrus, with a point size of 36. Again select the Text Effects option, which adds the same effects to the title as the buttons you have just finished adding.

Figure 10.27 Chapter menu text headline

Step 3

Adjust the text so that it is to the left but does not cross into the title-safe area of the top and left sides of the menu.

Because this is a chapter menu, you will want to have a method for allowing the viewer to return to the menu which leads to this menu.

Figure 10.28 Adding shapes from the Shapes palette

Step 4

Drag the small white triangle Shape object to the lower-left-hand corner of the chapter menu.

Step 5

Using the Palette, open the Shapes tab, then select the Apple sub-tab, and find the small white triangle facing left.

Step 6

Select the Shape object in the menu you have just added. This is actually now a button. Use the inspector; add the text word "Back" to the text field. Under that, you will see the Text Position field. Change this from Bottom, to Right. This places the word Back to the right of the shape object you have added.

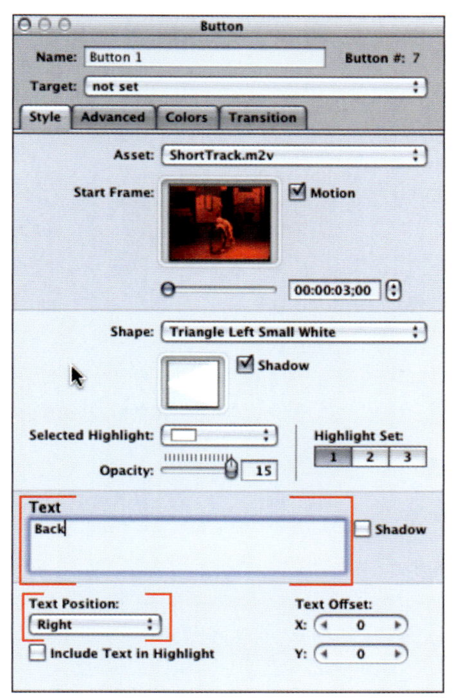

Figure 10.29 Adding and setting the text position

Step 7

Open the floating font panel again by using the pull-down menu Format, then selecting Font > Show Fonts. Adjust the text to match the other text, setting it for Helvetica with a point size of 18. Add the Text Effects option again.

Figure 10.30 Chapter menu

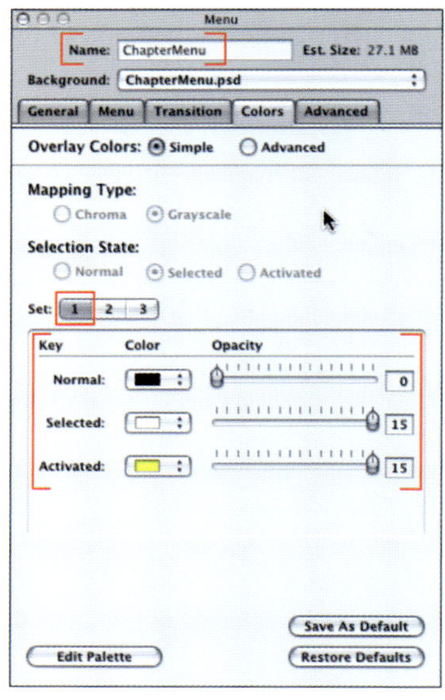

Figure 10.31 Chapter menu Property Inspector — Colors tab

Your menu should now look as mine does here. Save your work.

Adjusting the Highlight Properties

Click on the background of the menu without selecting any of the items on the menu itself. In the inspector, choose the Colors tab, as shown in 10-31.

The Normal state is at level 0 opacity, color black, meaning you see nothing in the Normal state. The Selected state is set to level 15 opacity, color white.

Click on any of the thumbnail preview boxes in the menu and notice it turns white all around the preview box. This is that Shape object's Selected highlight overlay state.

If you do not see the selected overlay state, click on the Menu tab's Show Button Selected State or use the keystroke —W to accomplish the same.

Click on the menu background again.

The Activated state is set to level 15 opacity, color yellow.

The best way to see these settings is to see them in action by simulating the menu.

Figure 10.32 Simulating the chapter menu

Right-click the menu's background, and choose the Simulate Menu option from the pop-up menu that appears. Each thumbnail button has a border around it; however, you only see one highlighted in white at a time. That is because only one button can be in the selected state. All the other buttons are in the normal state, which is set to color black with a level 0 opacity, so they appear to be invisible for now.

The selected state highlight is white, and if you click on it, it will become yellow briefly, then begin to play the story that it points to.

Quit the simulation.

Setting the Button Navigation

On the Menu tab, click on the Settings pulldown menu. There are two functions that address assigning the navigation of your buttons within the menu. By default, this is set to Auto Assign Buttons Continuously.

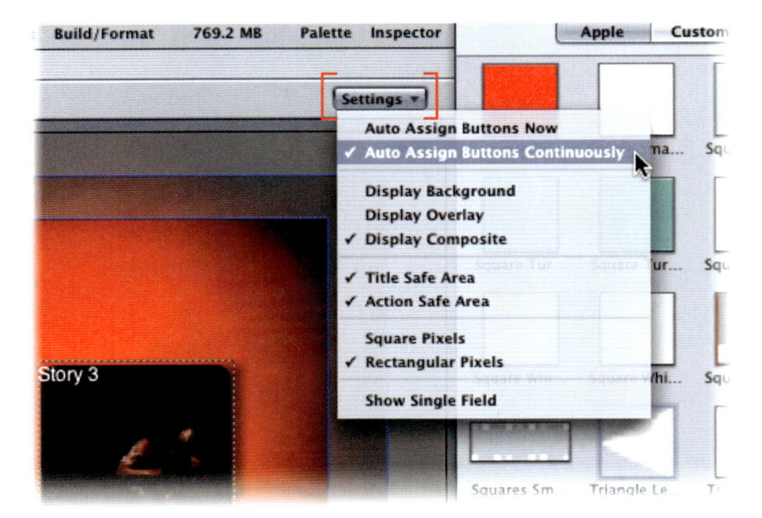

Figure 10.33 Menu settings — Auto Assign Buttons Continuously

Select the Story 4 thumbnail button in the menu, and then select the Advanced tab in the inspector. This is the continuous navigation at work on your behalf. Remember that you added the Back button long after you created the thumbnail preview buttons. Yet in the navigation section here, if you look at Story 4, you see that the up target is Story 1, and the Down target is Button 1. Button 1 is really Button 7, and the

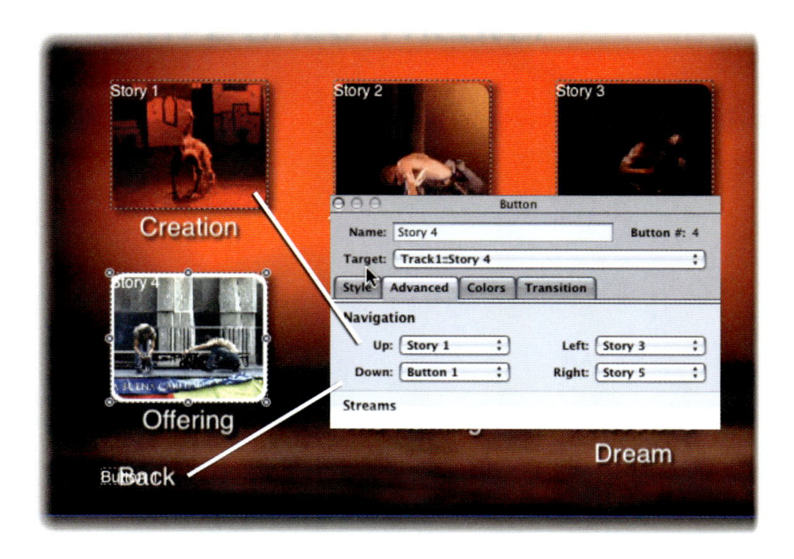

Figure 10.34 Button navigation

Back button. It is called Button 1 by name only, because no other button held the name "Button x" when it was created, so it assumed Button 1 as its name.

Click on the "Back" button you created earlier, and then go to the inspector. Notice at the top, the Name field is Button 1, but if you look to the right side, you see the actual button number, which is Button 7, since this was the seventh button to be created.

Notice the Navigation section in the Advanced tab. The Up assignment is Story 4, the story you just looked at.

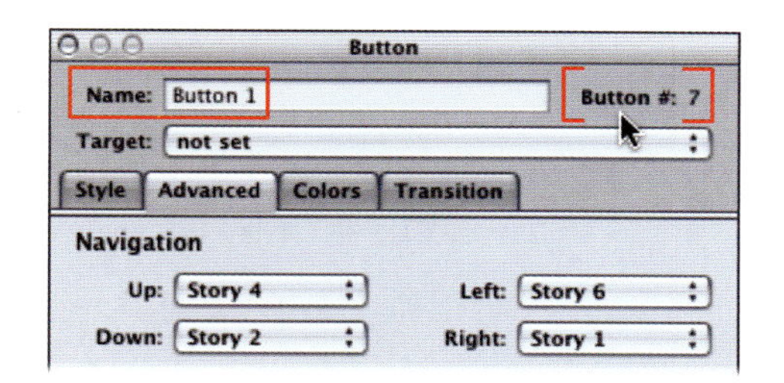

Figure 10.35 Button name versus Actual Button Number

Setting Button Targets

When you first added these Story objects to the menu, you used a function called Create Button, Connect to Story. This means that the Jump To target was automatically created for each of the six thumbnail buttons you have created.

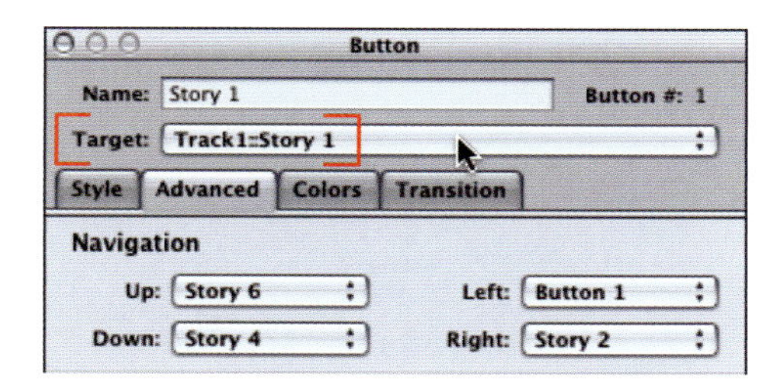

Figure 10.36 Button 1 — Setting the target

Step 1

Click on the first thumbnail button you created, which is labeled Story 1. Notice the Name field is already filled in with the name of the object used to create the thumbnail.

Below that, the Target field is already set to Track1::Story 1. There is no need to set this target, as it is already done for you as part of the interactive drag and drop of the Story object to the menu.

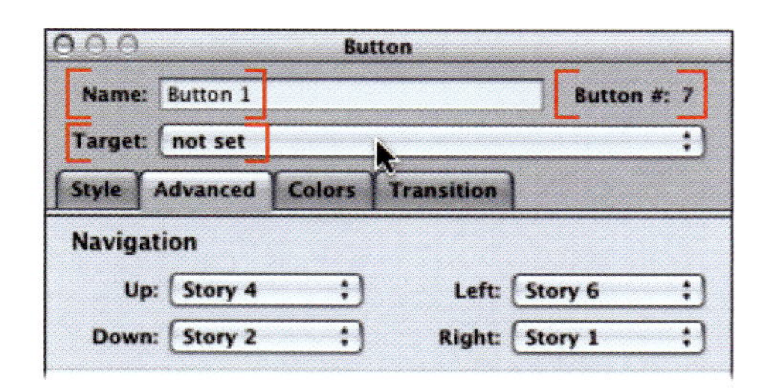

Figure 10.37 Button 7 — Setting the target

Step 2

Click on the Back button in the menu. This is not a thumbnail preview and was not created with the drag and drop function as the other six buttons were. It is still in its default state.

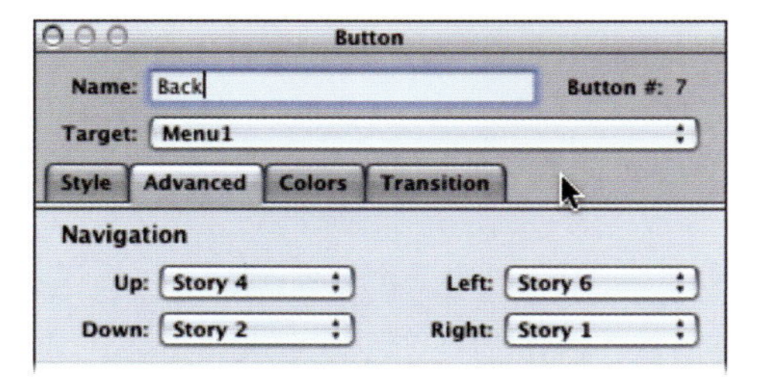

Figure 10.38 Button 7

Step 3

Using the inspector, change the name of the Back button from Button 1 to Back, and then set the target to Menu1 by clicking on the Target pop-up menu and choosing Menus > Menu1 > [Menu].

Step 4

Switch to Menu1 by switching the View option in the upper-left-hand side of the Menu tab to Menu1.

Figure 10.39 Changing the Menu tab view

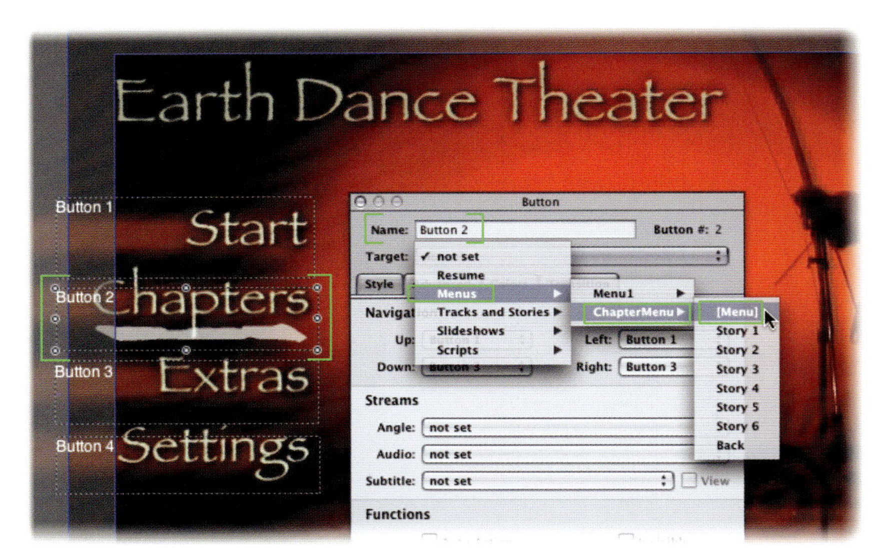

Figure 10.40 Setting the Chapters button target

Step 5

Select the Chapters button outline, then in the inspector set the button target to the Chapter menu you have created by choosing the Target pop-up menu, and choosing Menus > ChapterMenu > [Menu].

Step 6

Now return to the chapter menu by changing the View property back to ChapterMenu.

Figure 10.41 Changing the button view

Setting the Track and Story End Jump

You have set the button targets, and now it is time to set the End Jump. The End Jump is what happens when the target has finished playing.

The purpose of the Story the way you are using it in this chapter menu is to give the viewer an option to play just a chapter at a time, and then return to the chapter menu when the chapter has concluded playing.

Click on the Track asset in the Outline tab, and then look at the inspector. The End Jump field is set to Menu1, meaning when track1 and all of its chapters are finished playing, Menu1 is the next destination the viewer will see.

Click on the Story 1 object and notice the End Jump field is populated with "Same as Track." That means that when the story is finished playing, it will do exactly what the track's End Jump is set to do.

Change the End Jump from Same as Track to ChapterMenu::Story 1 by selecting the End Jump field and choosing Menus > ChapterMenu > Story 1.

Now Track1, and Story 1, have unique End Jump settings. When Track1 is finished playing, it will return to Menu1. When the viewer uses the chapter menu to play chapter 1, it will return to the chapter menu, and button 1, called Story 1, will highlight again, taking the viewer to the exact place the user was when the user made the selection.

Figure 10.42 Setting the Story End Jump property

Now click on Story 2 in the Outline tab, and notice the End Jump says Same as Track. By default, all the Stories are going to hold the "Same as Track" End Jump property.

Change each Story End Jump field to its associated menu and button.

Story 2 End Jump — ChapterMenu::Story 2
Story 3 End Jump — ChapterMenu::Story 3
Story 4 End Jump — ChapterMenu::Story 4
Story 5 End Jump — ChapterMenu::Story 5
Story 6 End Jump — ChapterMenu::Story 6

Defining the Remote Control's Menu Function

Now that each story will return back to the originating chapter menu, you will need to program the remote control's menu function.

Select the Story 1 object in the Outline tab, and look at the General tab of the inspector. Near the bottom you will see a single Remote Control setting with a field for the Menu key. It is set by default to Same as Track.

Select the Track1 object in the Outline tab, and look at the General tab of the inspector. You will see there are many remote control fields here; however, the Menu field is populated with Same as Disc by default.

Select the Disc object in the Outline tab, and look at the General tab of the inspector. Notice the Remote Control fields. These are Title, Menu, and Return.

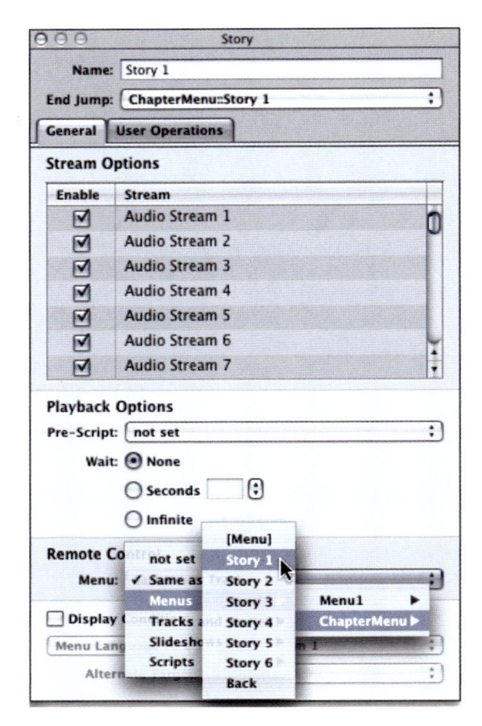

Figure 10.43 Story property — setting the Menu key

Title means Top Menu. It is the highest menu in your DVD. Because this DVD has two menus, the Menu1 object and the ChapterMenu object, there is an implied hierarchical flow. The Menu1 object is used to gain access to the ChapterMenu object. Therefore, the chapter menu is a submenu, and the Menu1 object is its parent. The Remote Control field of Title therefore is correctly set as Menu1.

The Remote Control Menu field is also set as Menu1, and this is correct only part of the time the user is viewing the DVD. When the user is watching any target launched from the Menu1 object, then this is correctly set. However, the Story objects are launched from the chapter menu, and so during that time this field needs a new setting.

Select the Story 1 object from the Outline tab, and look again at the General tab, then the Remote Control field. It is set as Same as Track. The track is set to Same as Disc. You can override that setting while the Story is playing by setting this Menu field to target the ChapterMenu object, and specifically, the Story 1 button in the ChapterMenu object.

Click on the Menu field pop-up menu, and choose Menus > ChapterMenu > Story 1.

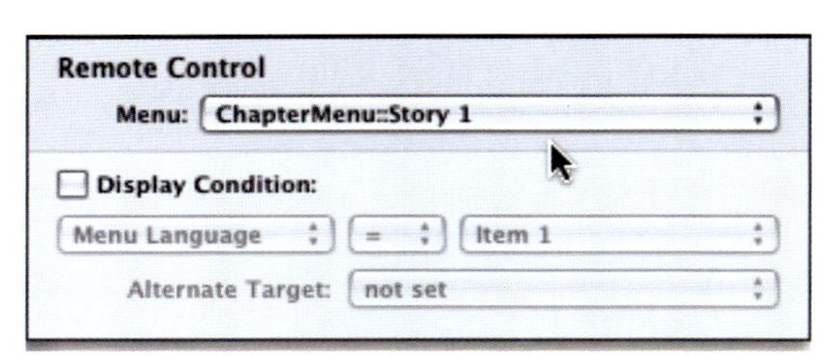

Figure 10.44 Story — Remote Control property

Your Menu field should look as mine does.

Now select the Story 2 object in the Outline tab. Notice that the Remote Control field is also set as Same as Track.

Adjust Stories 2 through 6 in the same manner as you did the first story, but set to their respective buttons in the Chapter menu.

Story 2 Remote Control — ChapterMenu::Story 2
Story 3 Remote Control — ChapterMenu::Story 3
Story 4 Remote Control — ChapterMenu::Story 4
Story 5 Remote Control — ChapterMenu::Story 5
Story 6 Remote Control — ChapterMenu::Story 6

With these settings, if the viewer uses the chapter menu to play Chapter 4 and hits the Menu button on the remote control, the viewer will be taken back to the chapter menu, and that specific button used to launch that specific chapter will again be highlighted. This is true of all six chapters.

Setting the Remote's Return Function

The Return button on the remote, as far as DVD Studio Pro is concerned, functions as a hierarchical Return to Parent menu feature. The Menu1 object is really the parent of the chapter menu since the chapter menu cannot be accessed without the Menu1 object.

The purpose of the return function here is that when the user is in the chapter menu, they may wish to return to the menu that led them to this chapter menu quickly. By pressing the Return button on the remote, the user can be sent back to the parent Menu1 object.

Click on the background of the chapter menu, so that nothing on this menu is selected.

In the inspector, choose the Menu tab this time, and look at the various fields under the header of Menu Functions.

Figure 10.45 Chapter menu — Return Button property

Set the Return Button field to Menu1::Button 2.

When the view is in the chapter menu, hitting the Return button on the remote control now will send the user to Menu1, which then automatically highlights Button 2, which is the button that led to the chapter menu.

Save your work.

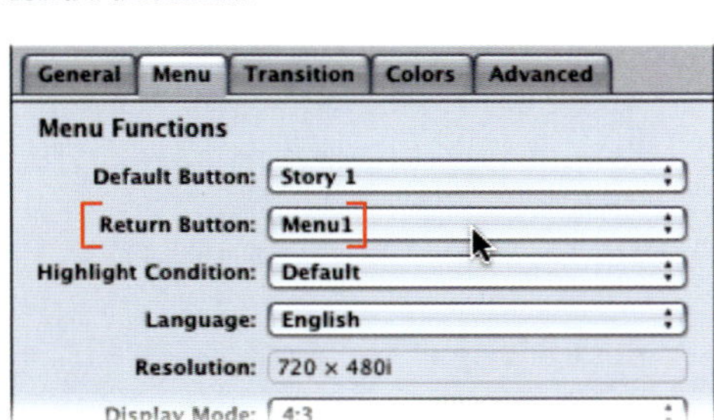

Figure 10.46 Return Button Field

Simulate Your Chapter Menu

Now launch the Simulator to test the functionality you have just created. Once the Simulation starts, watch the animated menu until the buttons become available to choose. Select the Chapters button.

Each of the chapters in this sample is about 2 minutes long. Pick one of them from the chapter menu. While the chapter is playing, hit the simulated Remote Menu button. You will be taken back to the chapter menu.

Once in the chapter menu, hit the simulation's Return button. You will be taken back to the starting menu, and the intro section, that being the first 18 seconds of that menu which are skipped, as you learned in the prior chapter.

Press the Start button, which plays the track asset. While the track is playing, hit the simulated Menu key. You are taken back to the starting menu.

The chapter menu and the starting menu both have their own settings. Go back to the chapter menu in the simulation, and select the Back button. You are taken back to the starting menu.

The Setup Menu

The Setup menu is where the viewer can go to choose which audio and subtitle stream they would like to listen to and/or read as they watch your film.

In this chapter you will learn several small scripting techniques and how to switch varying audio and subtitle streams while maintaining the ability to resume play.

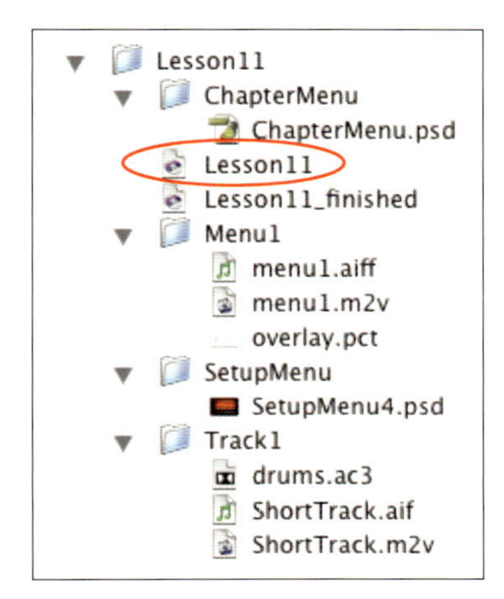

Figure 11.1 OSX file folder — Lesson 11

Creating the Setup Menu

Before you get started, you will need to copy the Chapter 11 folder from the DVD-ROM to your desktop.

Notice that there are two DVD Studio Pro projects just as in the prior chapter. You may open and examine the Lesson11_finished project to get a better idea about what you will be working on.

To get started with this chapter, please double-click on the Lesson11 DVD Studio Pro project file.

This should look very familiar to you. This is almost where you left off on the last chapter. I have added a few items in preparation for this chapter for you.

In the Outline tab, I have added the beginning of a Setup menu. Click on the Setup menu object in the Outline tab, and examine the menu for a minute. It offers two main areas. The first offers two audio options, those being English and Spanish. Because my short demo track is really a dance video, there is no actual verbal dialog, so I have instead used two very different audio tracks as a substitute for English and Spanish. This will become clear shortly.

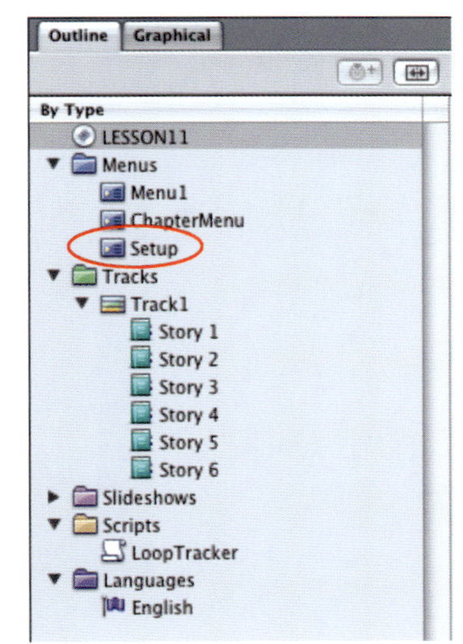

Figure 11.2 Outline tab — Setup menu

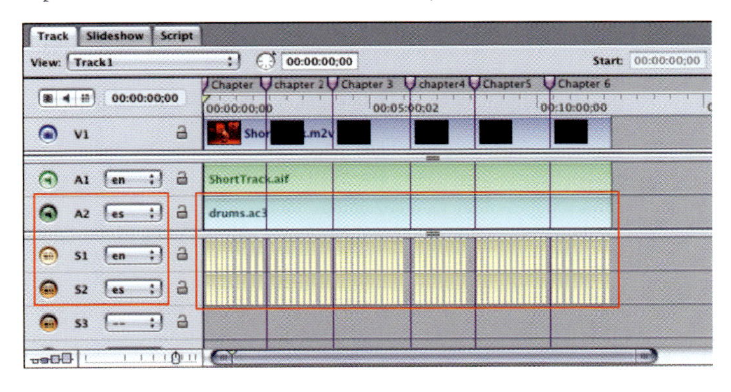

Figure 11.3 Track tab — audio and subtitle streams

Examine the track now, and notice the difference from the last project. In Lesson 10, you had a single V1 asset and a single A1 asset. In this project, you have A1 and A2, which means you have two different audio streams for the same video track.

Below the two audio tracks, you will see two subtitle tracks, marked as S1 and S2. These are our subtitle streams. You will program the Setup menu to allow the viewer to pick and choose between each of the two audio and each of the two subtitle streams you see here in this track.

Figure 11.4 Menu tab —View field

Using the Menu tab, change the view property to Setup to open the Setup menu. Examine this menu, as it is not like any other menu in the DVD you are building. Rather than pointing to assets such as other menus, tracks, or stories, this menu will change audio and subtitle streams, and it will use a small array of tiny scripts to make sure of a sophisticated resume function.

You will be working with this menu and the button properties of each of the seven buttons within this menu. Open the Property Inspector and leave it open throughout these lessons.

Defining Audio and Subtitle Buttons

Your first task is to set the English and Spanish buttons to play the A1 audio stream and the A2 audio stream contained in the Track tab. To do this, start by clicking on the English button outline in Setup menu, then open the Advanced tab of the inspector.

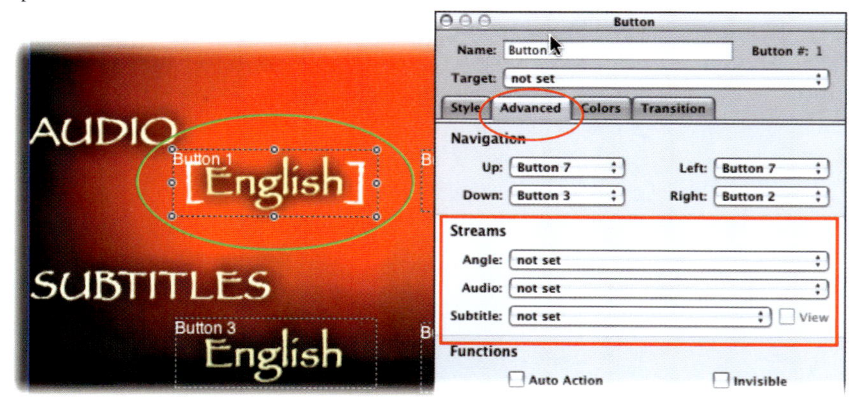

Figure 11.5 Button property —Advanced tab — Streams

Setting the Audio Stream

The Advanced tab has options for setting the streams within the DVD. Streams are broken down into three sections: Angle, Audio, and Subtitle. You will be working only with the Audio and the Subtitle streams.

Step 1

Make sure you have the English Audio button outline selected, then under the streams section in the Advanced tab of this button's property, change the Audio field so that it reads Audio Stream 1.

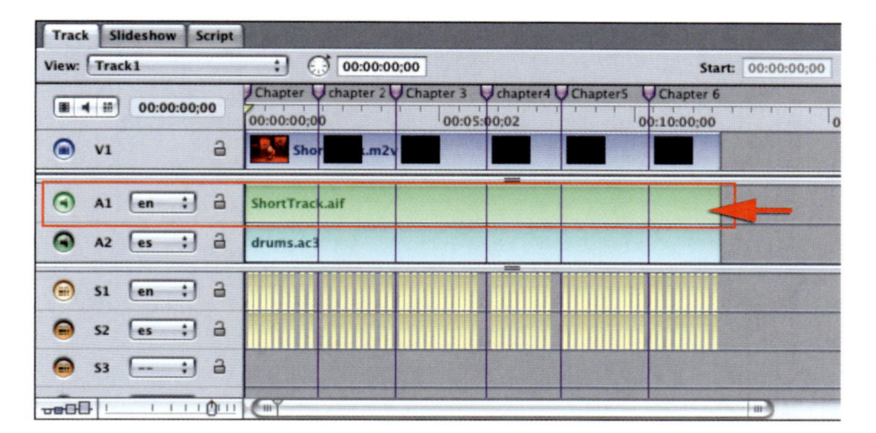

Figure 11.6 Track tab — Audio Stream 1

Figure 11.7 English audio button 1

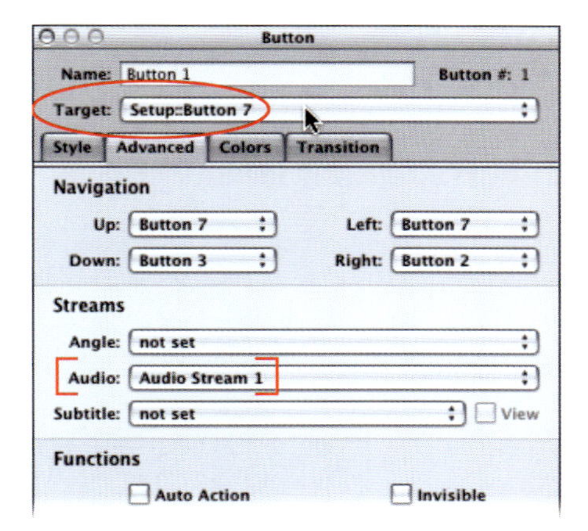

Take a look at the Track tab now. The section that says A1 is the Audio Stream 1 you have just selected. This is your English audio stream. Notice just to the right of the A1 designation there is a selection with a two-letter code, which reads "en"which stands for English. You can set this code to any language you choose. Your DVD player reads these codes and will allow the viewer to change the audio stream while the DVD is playing your film. When the viewer selects Audio on their remote control, the available audio streams will be represented as you created them and designated them here in this section of the Track tab.

You will now set the target of this button to the Setup menu itself. The reason for doing this is that the user remains in setup until the user decides they are finished.

Step 2

Set the target of the English audio button to Setup, Button 7. This is the Back button. This way, the user acknowledges that the DVD accepted their choice because they move from one button highlight to another within the same menu.

Now set the Spanish button in the Setup menu to Audio Stream 2, where the Spanish audio track has been inserted into the Track tab.

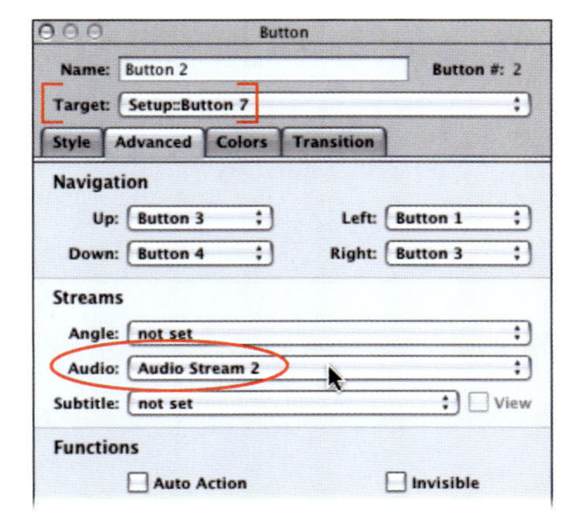

Figure 11.8 Spanish audio button 2

Step 3

Select the Spanish outline under the Audio heading in the Setup menu, and then change the button target to Setup, Button 7, the same as you did with the prior button. This time set the Audio field in the Streams section of the Advanced tab to Audio Stream 2.

You have now made two buttons, each capable of changing the audio stream. Button 1, your English audio button, now will set A1 as the audio stream, and Button 2, the Spanish audio button, sets A2 as the audio stream.

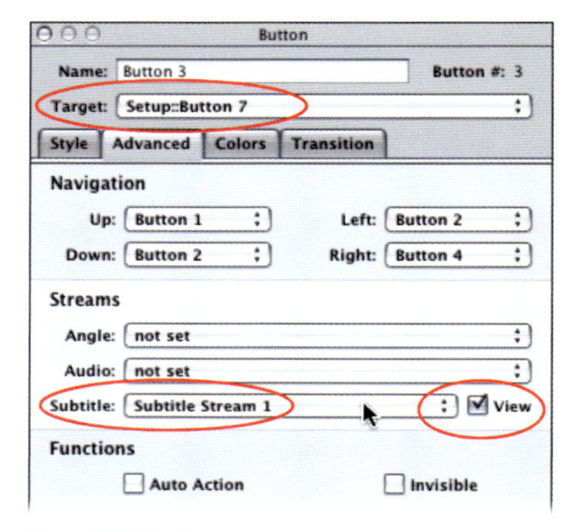

Figure 11.9 English subtitle button 3

Setting the Subtitle Stream

Step 1

Select the English button under the Subtitles heading. This is Button 3. As before, use the Advanced tab and go to the Streams section. Now set the Subtitle field to Subtitle Stream 1, and mark the View check box.

Set the button target to the menu Setup, Button 7, so that the viewer remains in this menu after making this selection.

You have now done two things with the first subtitle. You have selected a subtitle, and in addition you have turned it to the "on" position, meaning that after the viewer selects this button, Subtitle Stream 1 will be selected and viewable. The viewer now sees the subtitle text over the playing video.

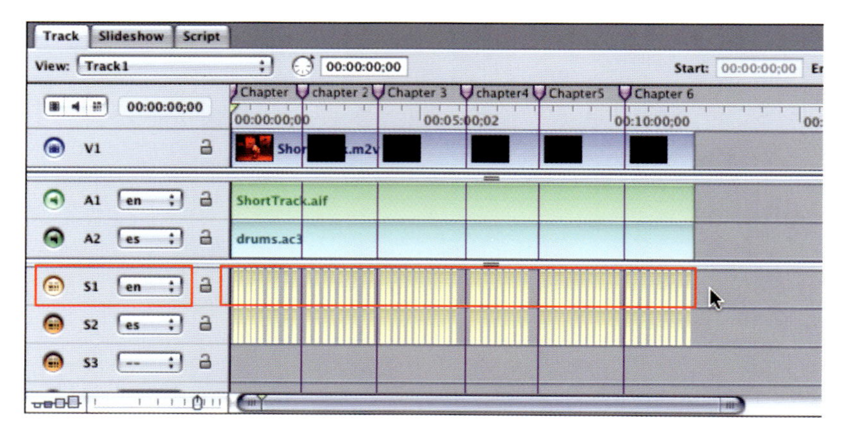

Figure 11.10 Subtitle settings — language code

Take a look at the Track tab again. The Subtitle Stream 1 you just selected is the S1 track you see here in the Track tab. The "en" code just right of the S1 designation is the language code. This is something you set. I have this one set to English. This way when the viewer chooses the Subtitle button on their remote control, they will see an option to watch English subtitles.

The subtitle stream below this, as designated by the S2 and "es" designations, is the Spanish subtitles.

Step 2

Select the Spanish outline in the Menu tab now. This is Button 4. Use the inspector to set the button target to the menu Setup, Button 7, and then change the Subtitle field to Subtitle Stream 2 and check the View check box to force the subtitle view to the "on" position so the viewer sees the subtitles.

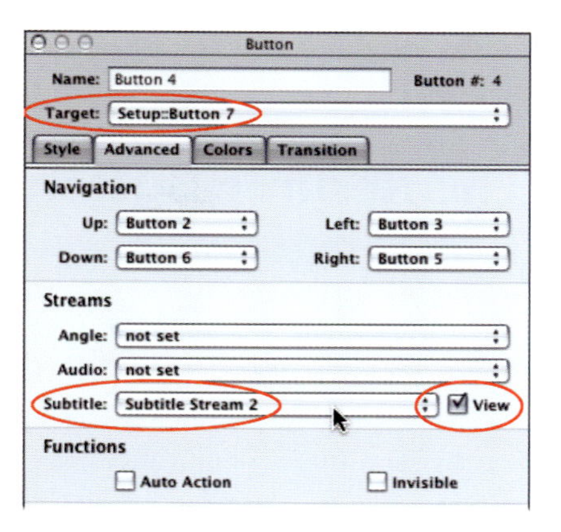

Figure 11.11 Spanish subtitle button 4

Turning the Subtitle Stream Off

Select the Off outline under the same heading of Subtitles. This is Button 5, and will serve as a method of turning off subtitles. Go to the inspector and change the target of this button to Setup, Button 7, which is this very menu again.

Under the heading of Streams, change the Subtitle field to Subtitle Stream 1, and then leave the View check box empty. You are essentially choosing the default stream and turning it off from the view of the watcher.

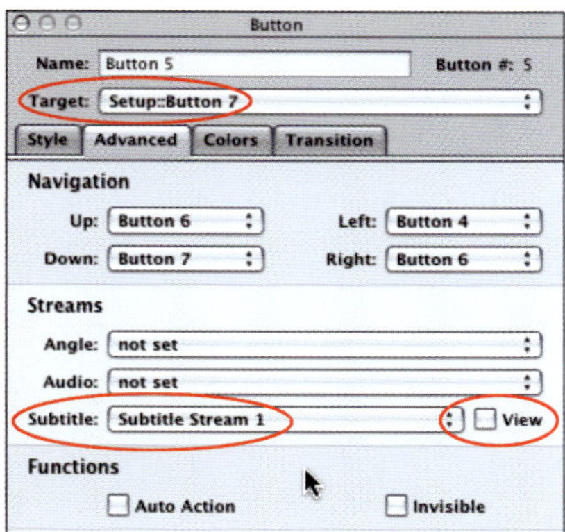

Figure 11.12 Subtitles off button 5

Returning to the Prior Menu

You now need to program the Back button, which is Button 7, to return to the menu that delivered the viewer to the Setup menu. There are two items to be aware of in this situation. The user will likely use the Back button, so you will use this button to target Menu1, which is the parent menu in this hierarchy of menus.

You also have the option of setting the Return button on the remote control. You're going to do both.

Step 1

Select the Back outline in the Setup menu. This is Button 7. Change the Target field in the inspector to Menu1. This button now will take the viewer back to Menu1.

Step 2

Select the background of the Setup menu, making sure no button outlines are currently selected. Select the Menu tab in the inspector, and then set the Return Button field to Menu1. When

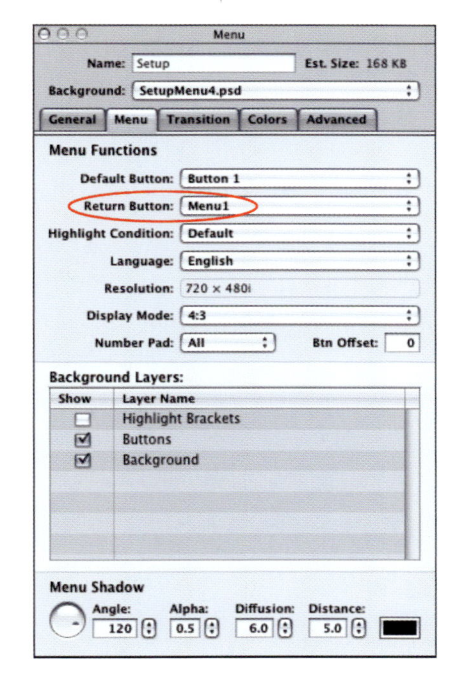

Figure 11.13 Setup menu property — Remote Return key

the viewer presses the Return button on the remote control while in the Setup menu, they will immediately return to Menu1 now.

The Resume Button

I skipped over Button 6 in these lessons because Button 6 is the Resume button. The Resume button deserves half of this chapter unto itself because it can be a complicated button to program depending how you would like it to function.

What is the Resume button?

To put it simply, the Resume button gives the viewer the ability to return to an exact place within your film after the viewer has interrupted your film by prematurely exiting it. Say, for example, that you are watching a film, and 15 minutes into this film you press the Menu button on the remote control. Perhaps you decided after 15 minutes of watching the film that you would like to change the audio or the subtitle, and thus you interrupted the play of the film to make the settings change.

The resume function, once selected, will return you back to that track you were watching, to the exact point at which you exited when pressing the menu or top menu as well. There is just one "gotcha" with this button. If the viewer of the DVD selects the Resume button in the Setup menu when there has been no interruption of any of the tracks you have, then there is no place to return to. As a result, the user may become confused as to why nothing happens when pressing resume.

A sophisticated Resume button should know if the user has interrupted a track in play or not. That way, if the user presses resume and there is nothing to return to, another action can take place so that the user is aware that the button on your Setup menu actually does work, and that it isn't an oversight of some kind.

The rest of this chapter is designed to teach you how to use scripting to create a conditions-based resume function in the Setup menu. You will learn to use registers as markers that will signal the resume function to the status of the track. That status is whether the track has finished playing or has been interrupted. If such a task scares you, there is a simple way out.

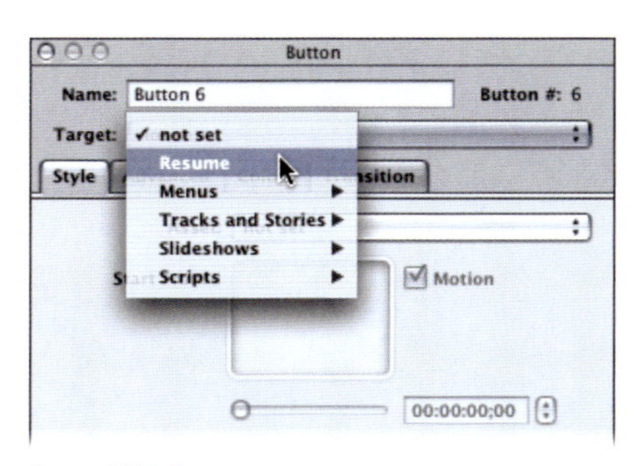

Figure 11.14 Resume button 6 — simple resume

Basic Resume

Select the Resume outline in the Setup menu. This is Button 6. Using the inspector, set the Target field to Resume.

If no track has been interrupted, then this will take no action. The viewer will simply stay in the Setup menu and ponder why nothing has happened. If, on the other hand, a track has been interrupted mid-play, then this resume function will return the user back to the point at which the viewer left the track.

Setting a Script-Based Resume Action

So you have decided to go further and build the perfect resume function. Congratulations!

There are four basic scripts you will learn to create and assign in order to create a script-based resume function:

- SetMarker (GPRM 1)
- ClearMarkerTracks (GPRM 1)
- ClearMarkerStories (GPRM 1, GPRM 2, and SPRM 8)
- ResumeScript (GPRM 1)

SetMarker is a simple script that you will use to flag a track prior to playing that track. It is essentially a value placed on a track. When a track is told to play, a value in a register will be set. When the resume function is selected, your script will first check to see whether that value exists. If it does, it knows a track had been in play, and it will resume play. If the value does not exist, then rather than attempting to resume, it will send the viewer back to Menu1. This way, if there is nothing to resume, the user goes back to the menu to make a selection.

ClearMarkerTracks and ClearMarkerStories are each scripts that remove the flag value you set using the SetMarker script before a track is played. These scripts are going to be assigned to the End Jump of each track and Story in the Outline tab. When a track or Story has finished playing it is no longer eligible for the resume function, so you will then remove the flag value.

ResumeScript is your custom-made resume script. This script checks for the existence of the SetMarker. If the SetMarker value is there, then a track must have been interrupted mid-play, because when all tracks finish playing, your ClearMarker scripts remove the marked value. So the resume script is quite simple. Check for the value, and if it exists, resume any interrupted play. If the value does not exist, there is nothing to resume, therefore go to Menu1 so that the viewer may make a selection.

The SetMarker Script

Add a script to the Outline tab, and then change the name of this script to SetMarker. Open the Script tab, and select the default command Nop. You are now ready to modify this command using the Script Command Editor, which is the inspector.

Change the Command field from Nop to Set GPRM.

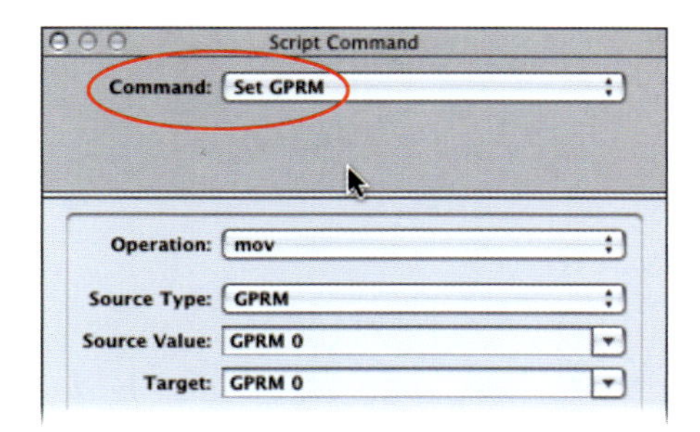

Figure 11.15 Script command — set GPRM

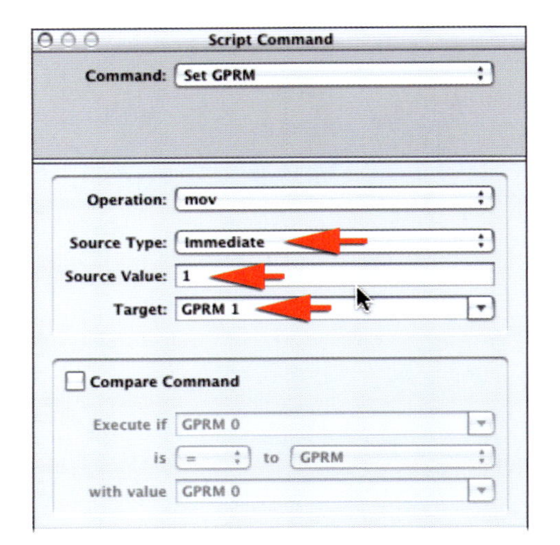

Figure 11.16 Script command — set GPRM

Change the Source Type from GPRM to Immediate.

Change the Source Value from 0 to 1.

Change the Target from GPRM 0 to GPRM 1.

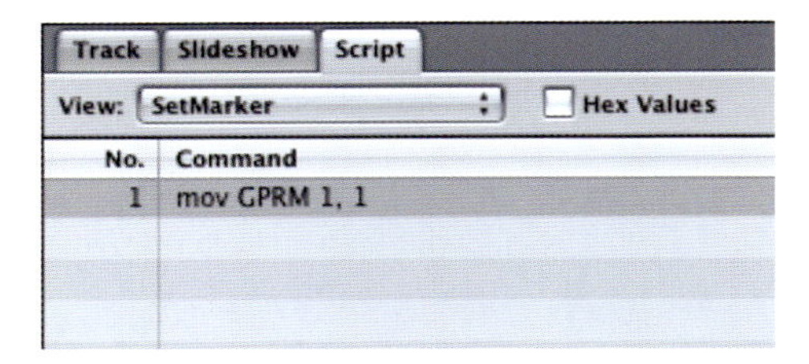

Figure 11.17 SetMarker script

Look at the Script tab to check your completed script. It is a very simple single-line script that now needs to be assigned to each Track and Story object in the Outline tab.

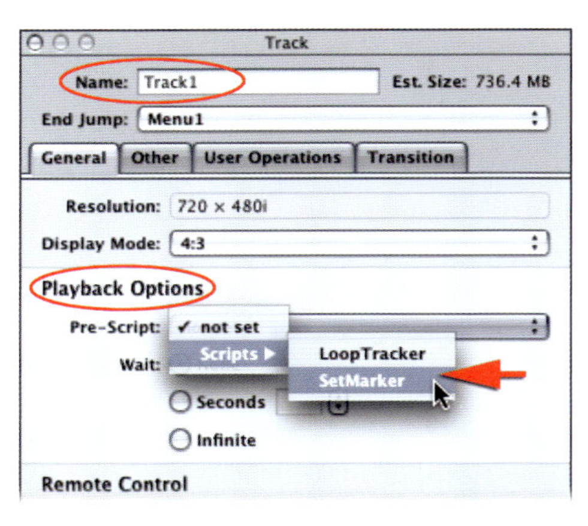

Figure 11.18 Track 1 — Pre-script — SetMarker script

Using the Outline tab, select the Track1 object, then the General tab of the Track1 inspector to assign the SetMarker script as the Track1 pre-script.

Now select each of the six Story objects one at a time. Use the General tab in each one to assign the SetMarker script as each of their pre-scripts.

Now each time a Track or Story is played, the GPRM 1 register will be given a value of 1. If at any time the track or story is interrupted, the GPRM 1 register will still hold the same value of 1.

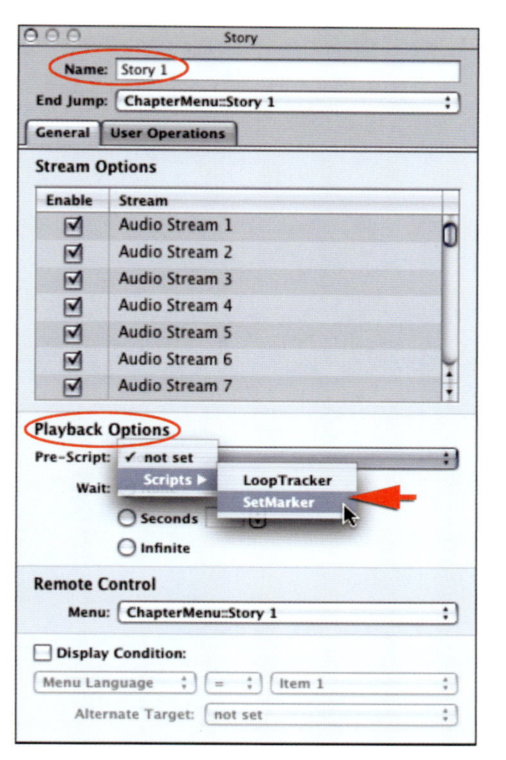

Figure 11.19 Story playback options — Pre-Script > SetMarker script

The ClearMarkerTracks Script

Now that the track and stories have use of GPRM 1 to hold a value of 1 when they are in use, you have to undo that when the track or story has finished playing fully. When a track or story is finished playing, it executes its End Jump field. You will use this function to remove the value from the GPRM 1 register.

Select the Track1 object in the Outline tab, and look at the inspector's End Jump target. It is currently set to Menu1. If you replace this End Jump with a script, you will also need to replace that jump to location so that two tasks are performed:

1. The register GPRM 1 which has the value of 1 must be cleared.

2. The End Jump we take away from the track's End Jump must be replaced in the script.

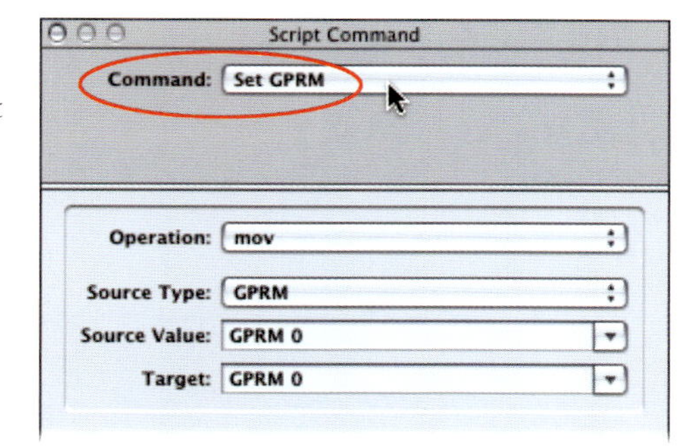

Figure 11.20 Script command — Set GPRM

Add another script object to the Outline tab by selecting the Add Script button in the toolbar, and then change the name of this script to ClearMarkerTracks.

Open the Script tab, and then select the Nop command. Use the Script Command Editor, changing the Command Nop into Set GPRM.

Change the Source Type from GPRM" to Immediate. Leave the Source Value set to the default value of 0. Change the Target from GPRM 0 to GPRM 1.

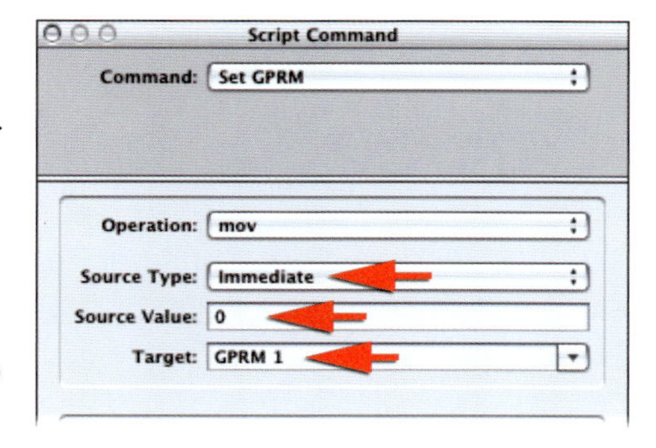

Figure 11.21 Script command — assigning a zero value to GPRM 1

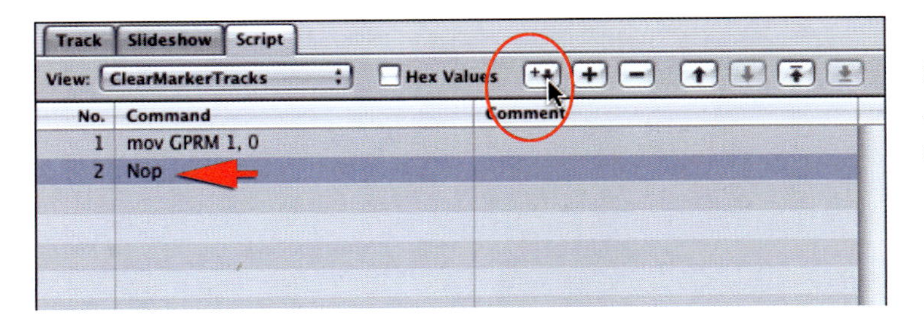

Figure 11.22 Adding additional script commands

Go back to the Script tab, and then select the plus sign/Down Arrow button to add a second command to the script.

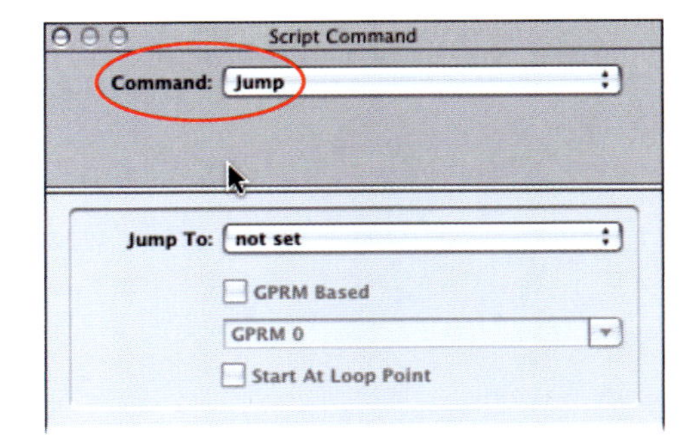

Figure 11.23 Script command — Jump

Select the Nop command and then use the Script Command Editor to change the command from Nop to Jump. Notice the Jump To setting beneath the command: Jump now exists.

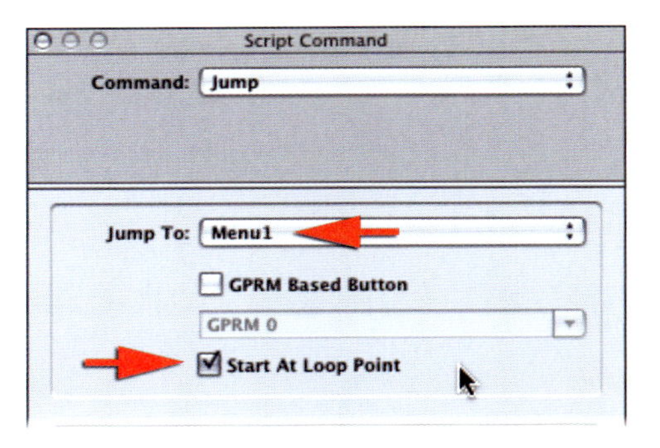

Figure 11.24 Script command — Jump to Loop-Point in Motion menu

Set the Jump To: field to Menu1, and then check the Start At Loop Point check box.

Figure 11.25 Script — ClearMarkerTracks

Your script is finished. In line 1, mov GPRM 1, 0 sets the value of the register GPRM 1 to "0". Essentially that means we have cleared any value held in this register. It is completely clear.

In line 2, you jump directly from this script to the Menu1 asset, and then specifically to that menu's Loop Point, which is 18 seconds beyond its start as described in prior chapters.

Select the Track1 object in the Outline tab, and then use the inspector to assign this script ClearMarkerTracks to the Track1 End Jump target.

The ClearMarkerStories Script

Now the Track has a script designed to clear the register GPRM 1 of its value when it is finished playing. Unlike the Track1 object, you have six Story objects, and each one is designed to return back to the chapter menu and highlight the specific button that sent the viewer to that particular story.

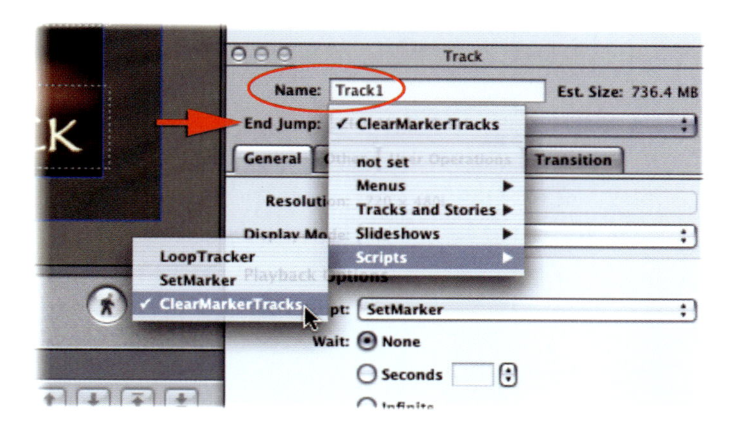

Figure 11.26 Track End Jump — Script: ClearMarkerScript

You need a script that goes a little beyond the ClearMarkerTrack script you just learned to create. Go to the Outline tab, and select the Story 1 object. Look at the End Jump setting in the inspector. It is set to return to ChapterMenu, Story 1.

Select the Story 2 object in the Outline tab and again, look at the End Jump in the inspector. The End Jump is set to ChapterMenu, Story 2. Each story is designed to go back to the chapter menu and specifically back to the button that launched that particular story.

You don't want to create six scripts, one for each story, to clear the register value in GPRM 1, and then replace each of these End Jumps, do you? I thought not. So you need a slightly more sophisticated script that each of the six stories can use to clear the register and then return back to the proper button that played that particular story.

Go to the Menu tab, and change the view to ChapterMenu. In the chapter menu, select the first story in the upper-left-hand corner. This is labeled Story 1. Story 1 is really Button 1. To see this for yourself, look at the inspector while Story 1 is selected in the Menu tab. Notice the target of this button. It is set to Track1, Story 1.

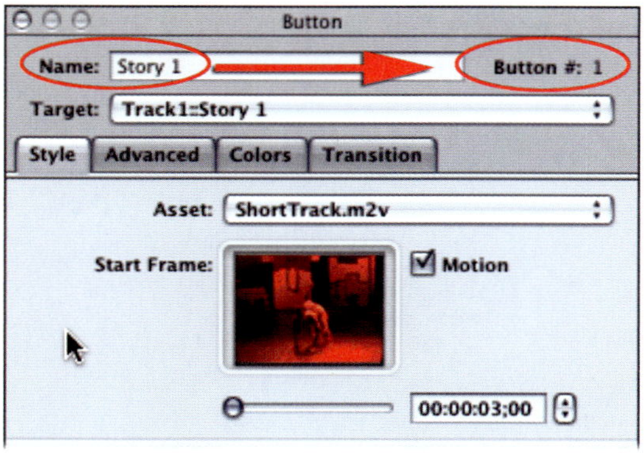

Figure 11.27 Button number and name

Click on Story 2, and look at these same settings. You will see Story 2 is really Button 2, and Story 2 is set to play Track1, Story 2. The rest do exactly the same thing all the way up to Story 6, which is really Button 6 and is set to play Track1, Story 6.

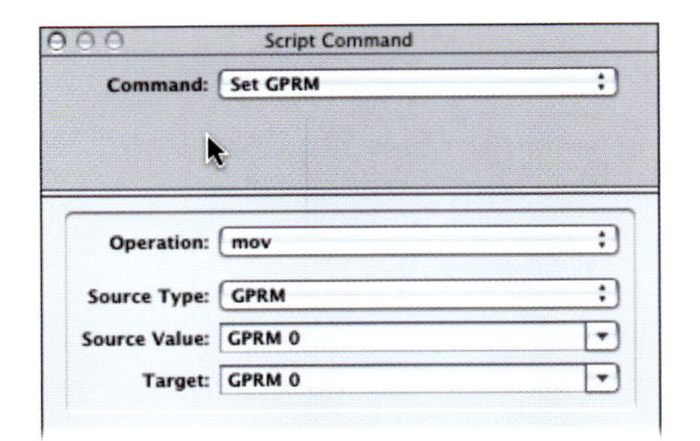

Figure 11.28 Script command — Set GPRM

Using the Toolbar, add another script object to the Outline tab, and then rename this new script Clear-MarkerStories.

Go to the Script tab, and then select the Nop command. Now, using the Script Command Editor, change Nop to Set GPRM.

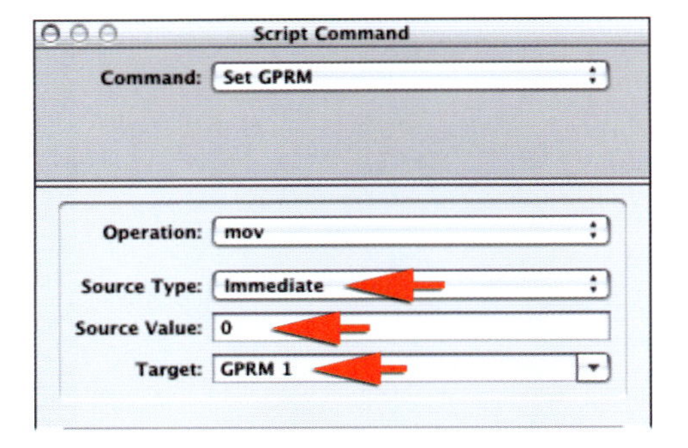

Figure 11.29 Script command — assigning a zero value to GPRM 1

Change the Source Type from GPRM to Immediate.

Leave the Source Value set to its default value of 0.

Change the Target from GPRM 0 to GPRM 1.

This is the line of code that will clear the GPRM 1 register value after a Story has finished playing.

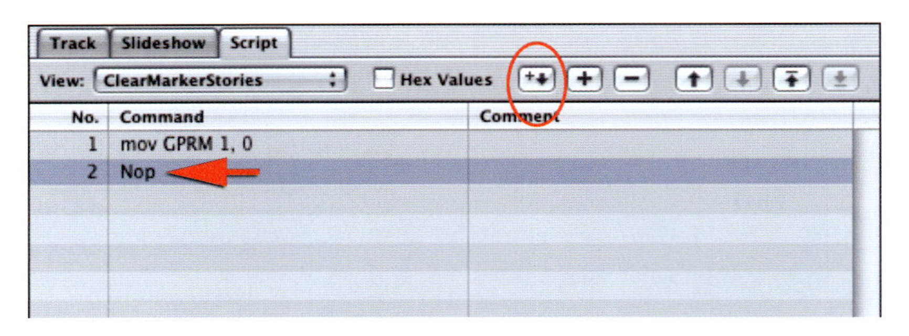

Figure 11.30 Adding additional commands to the ClearMarkerStories

Now add another line by selecting the plus sign/Down Arrow button in the button bar of the Script tab.

Select the Nop command, and in the Script Command Editor, change Nop to Set GPRM.

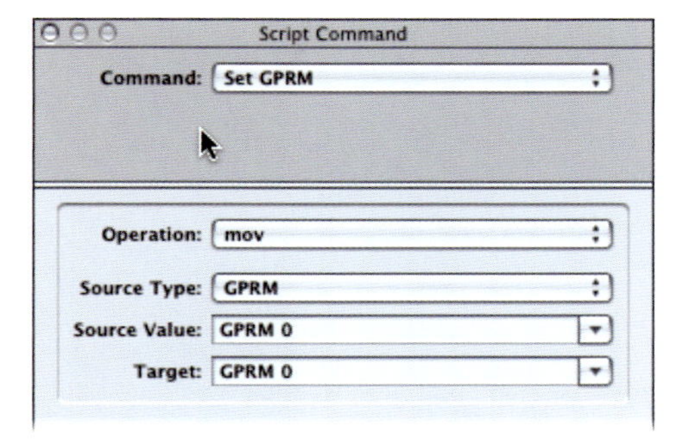

Figure 11.31 Script command — Set GPRM

Change the Source Type from GPRM to SPRM (System Parameter Register Memory).

All DVD players have a series of registers that hold various variables about the player itself, such as what language you wish to read your menus in, or a parental level you might have set. Other variables are interactive and based on things you are doing as you use the DVD player.

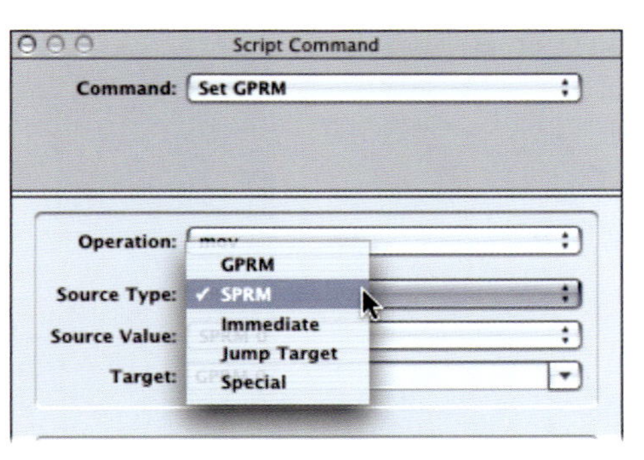

Figure 11.32 Script command — copy SPRM value to GPRM

Change the Source Value from SPRM 0 to SPRM 8.

The SPRM 8 register holds the button number in multiples of 1024. When the viewer selected Story 1 in the Chapter menu, the DVD player stored that information as a value of 1024 in the SPRM 8 register. Because these buttons are stored as values in multiples of 1024, Button 2 would be two multiples of 1024, or 2048. Button 3 would be three multiples of 1024, or 3072. Button #4 would be 4096. These multiples continue this way up to a maximum of 36 buttons on any 4:3 menu.

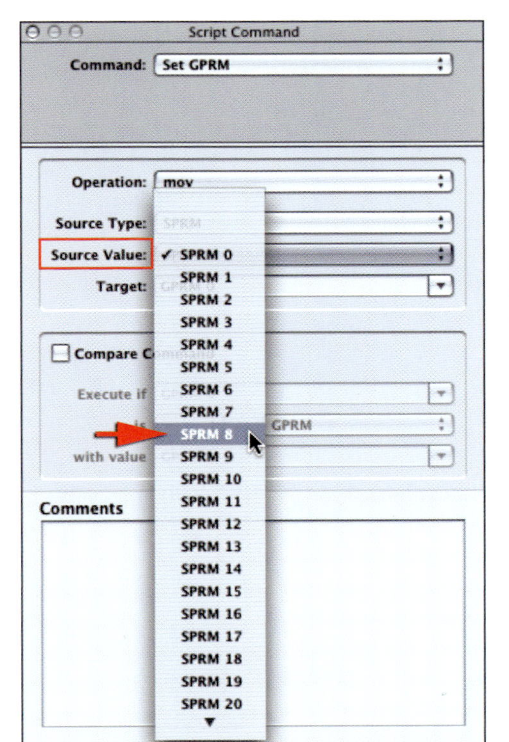

Figure 11.33 Copying the SPRM 8 register value

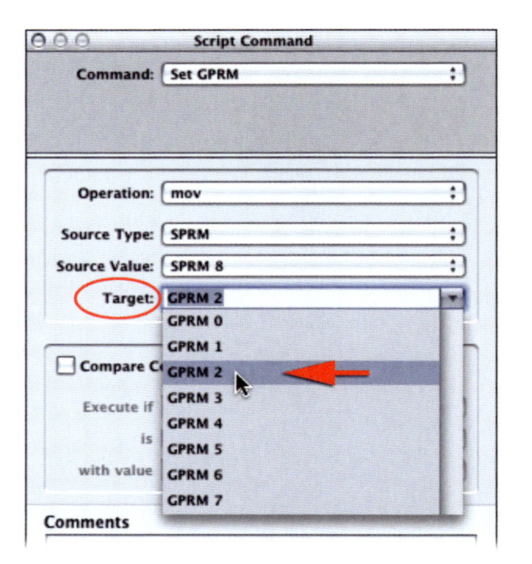

Figure 11.34 Storing SPRM 8 in the GPRM 2 register

Change the Target value from GPRM 0 to GPRM 2.

This line of code copies the value of SPRM 8, which is the number of the button multiplied by 1024, and stores that value in the register GPRM 2.

In the Script tab, add a new line of code by selecting the plus sign/Down Arrow.

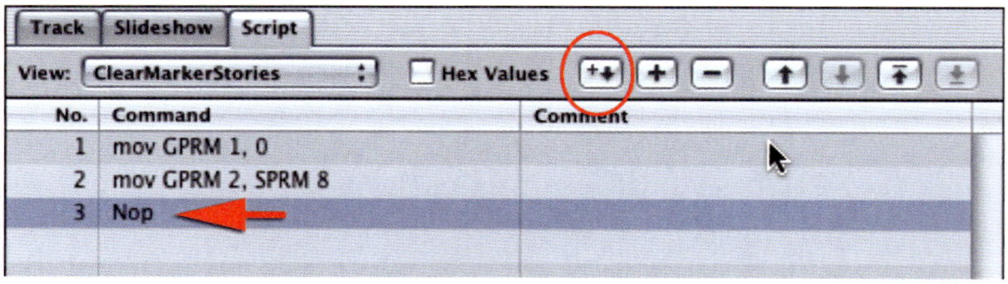

Figure 11.35 Adding additional commands in the Script Editor

Now select the Nop command in the Script tab, and then use the Script Command Editor to change the command Nop to Set GPRM.

Figure 11.36 Set GPRM

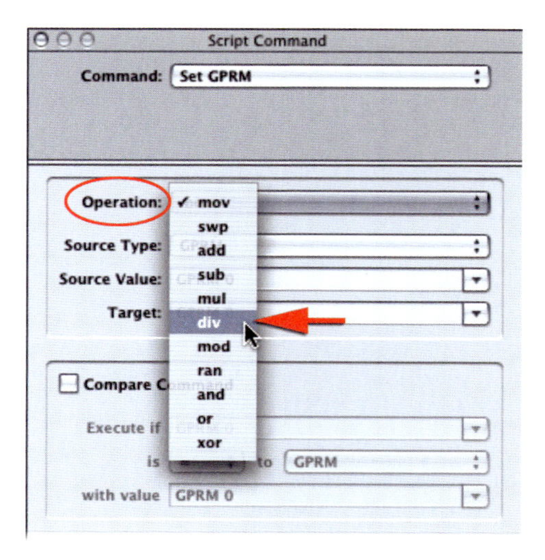

Figure 11.37 Script command — Div operation

Change the Operation from mov to div.

Mov sets register values by copying them or setting them directly through the Source Type value. You have used it several times already. This time, you are using the div operation, and just as it sounds, this operation divides one register or value into another.

Change the Source Type from GPRM to Immediate.

Change the Source Value from 0 to 1024.

Change the Target from GPRM 0 to GPRM 2.

In the second line, you had copied the value of SPRM 8 into GPRM 2. Remember that SPRM 8 holds the value of the button the user presses in the menu in multiples of 1024.

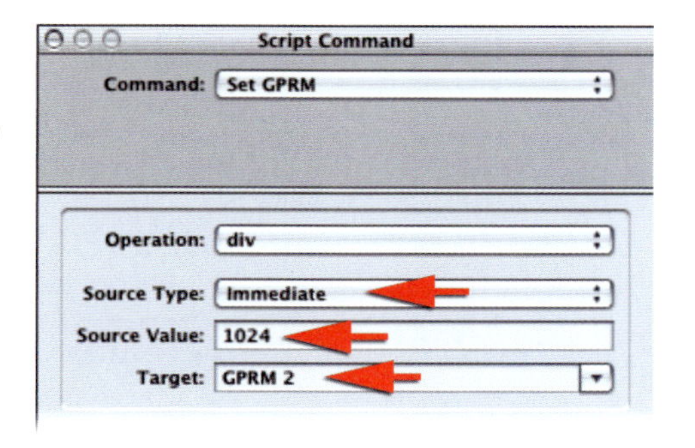

Figure 11.38 Script command — setting the div Value to 1024

In the line of code you just completed, you divided the value held in GPRM 2 by 1024. So if the viewer presses Story 1, then SPRM 8 = 1024. That is copied to GPRM 2, and you just divided GPRM 2 by 1024, yielding a value of 1.

This little song and dance translates the buttons pressed in the Chapter menu and converts them into what you will use as button targets. If the viewer presses Story 1, GPRM 2 will equal 1. If the viewer presses Story 6, then GPRM 2 will equal 6.

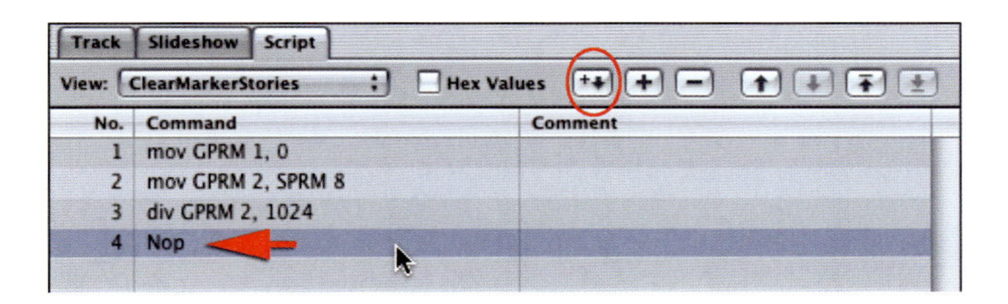

Figure 11.39 Adding additional commands to the Script Editor

Go back to the Script tab, and add your last line of code by pressing the plus sign/ Down Arrow button. Select the Nop command, and then use the Script Command Editor to change the Nop command to Jump.

Change the Jump To field from Not Set to ChapterMenu.

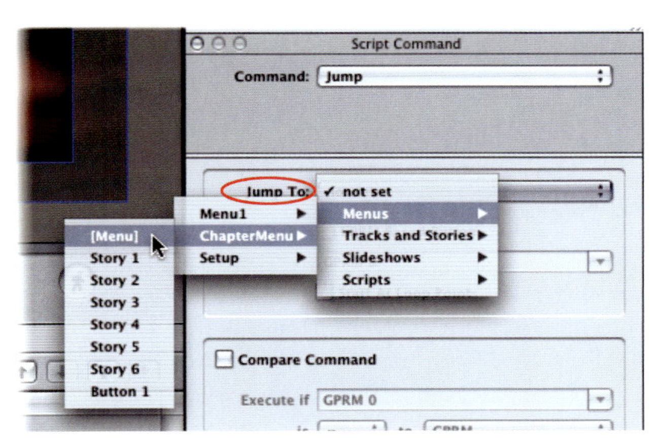

Figure 11.40 Script command — Jump

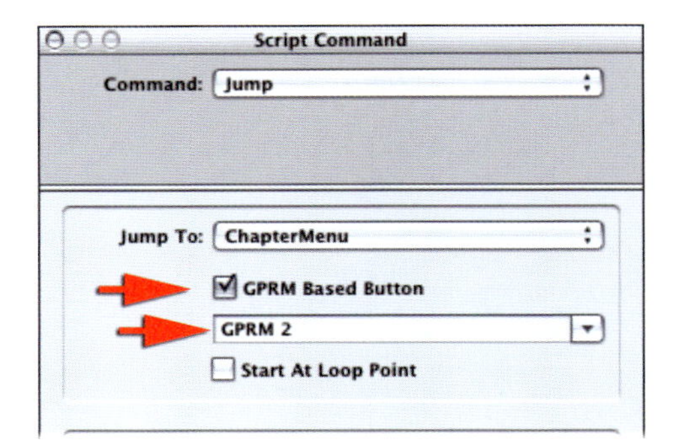

Figure 11.41 Script command — GPRM-based button

Place a check mark in the GPRM Based Button check box, and in the GPRM field below that change the value of GPRM 0 to GPRM 2.

That line of code takes that value held in GPRM 2, which is the button number you are translating, and uses those same values as button targets. The Jump command is executed, and the target is the chapter menu, and the button to highlight is whatever the value is in GPRM 2.

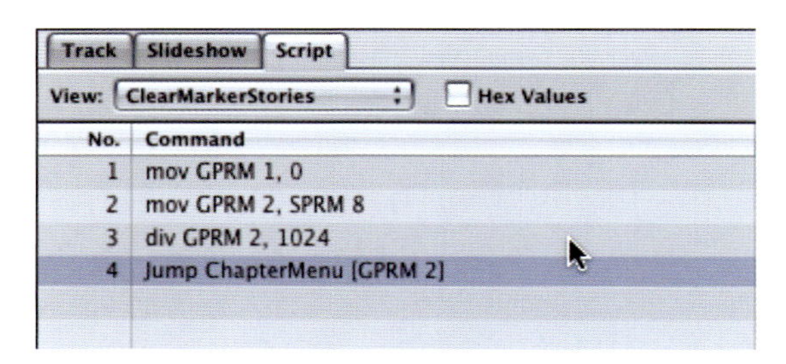

Figure 11.42 ClearMarkerStories script

You will assign this script as the End Jump to each of the six Story objects in the Outline tab.

The first line clears the value you set when the Story is told to play. Now when the Story is told to play, the DVD player uses SPRM 8 to store which button was used to play that particular Story. Line 2 takes that value from SPRM 8 and translates a copy of it into GPRM 2. Line 3 takes that number and divides it by 1024, leaving you with the original button number held in GPRM 2. Line 4 returns to the chapter menu and highlights the button number which is stored in GPRM 2.

This script is now a general purpose script which can be used by all six stories.

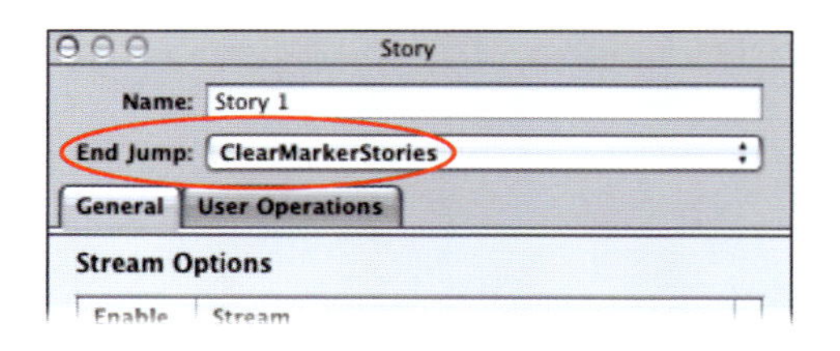

Figure 11.43 Story End Jump

Select Story 1 in the Outline tab, and then, using the inspector, change the End Jump to the script ClearMarkerStories. Now do exactly the same thing to the remaining five Story objects in the Outline tab.

The ResumeScript

You now have one more script to write, and it's a small one. This is the ResumeScript that will check the values you have applied to the tracks and stories.

Add another script to the Outline tab using the toolbar's Add Script button, and then rename this script ResumeScript. Select the Nop command in the Script tab, and the use the Script Command Editor to change the Nop command to Resume.

Place a check mark in the Compare Command check box, which causes its contents to become active and useable.

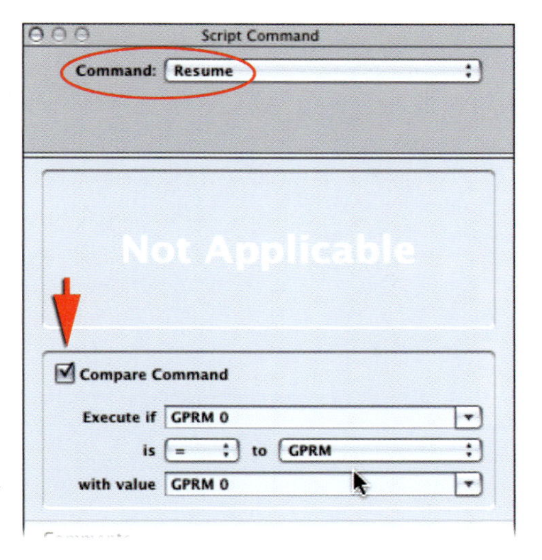

Figure 11.44 Script command — conditional resume

Change the Execute "if" field from GPRM 0 to GPRM 1.

Skip the "is" field, leaving it with an "=" sign.

Change the "to" field from GPRM to Immediate.

Change the "with value" field from 0 to 1.

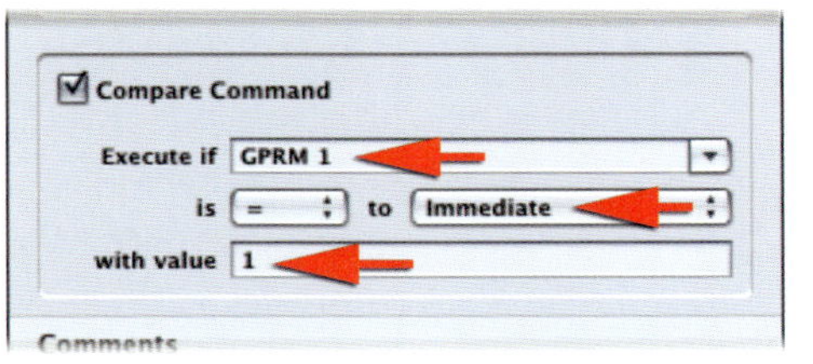

Figure 11.45 Script command — setting the value to trigger a resume

You have just issued a conditional command. You are saying resume only if GPRM 1 has a value of 1. The Set-Marker script you wrote is attached as a pre-script to each track and story, and sets a value of 1 to GPRM 1.

If the track or any story finishes playing, it will execute its End Jump. The Clear-MarkerTracks script clears GPRM 1 of its value of 1 when the track completes play. Likewise, the ClearMarkerStories script clears the same GPRM 1 of its value of 1 when a story finishes playing.

So this script is testing to current state of these GPRM 1 values. If it holds a value of 1, then a track must have never finished playing, and therefore it is okay to attempt to resume play. If the value in GPRM 1 does not equal 1, then a track or story has either finished playing or has not been played at all. In that case, this script will continue to the next line.

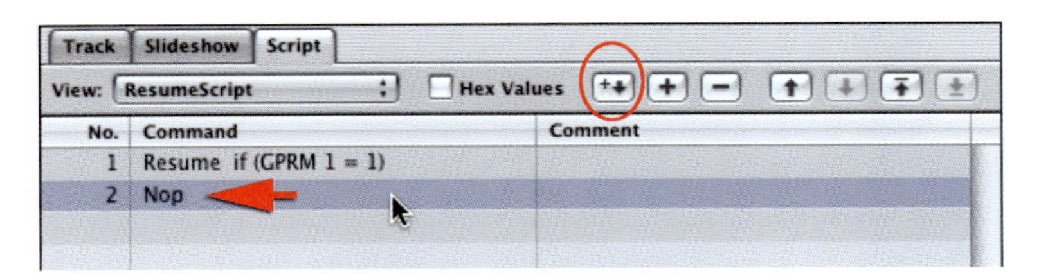

Figure 11.46 Adding an additional command

Add a new line to the script by selecting the plus sign/Down Arrow button, and then change that command from Nop to Jump using the Script Command Editor.

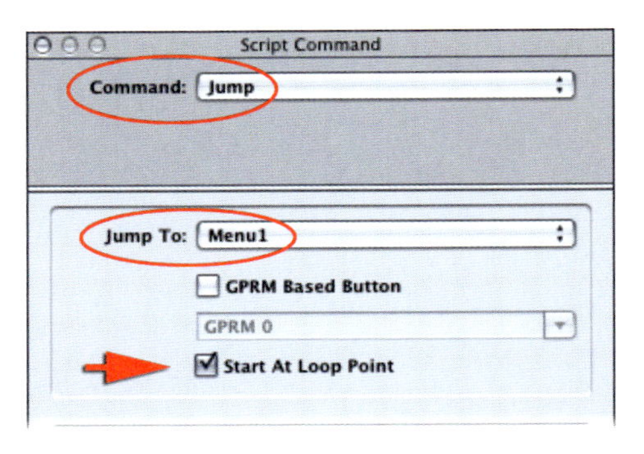

Figure 11.47

Change the Jump To from Not Set to Menu1.

Place a check mark in the Start At Loop Point check box.

Your script is now finished. Again, in line 1, if resume is possible, as indicated by the presence of a value in GPRM 1, then resume is executed. If the value has not been set or has been cleared, meaning a track or story has finished playing or has not yet been asked to play, then the conditional resume in line 1 is ignored, and the scripts continues to line 2, where the viewer is taken back to Menu1 so that a selection can be made.

Track | Slideshow | Script

View: ResumeScript Hex Values

No.	Command	Comment
1	Resume if (GPRM 1 = 1)	
2	Jump Menu1(Loop)	

Figure 11.48
Resume script

You must now assign this script to your Resume button in the Setup menu.

Using the Menu tab, change the view to Setup, and then select the Resume button. Use the inspector to set the button target to the script ResumeScript.

Save your work, and start the simulator using the Toolbar. Watch the first menu start, and when the buttons are made available, choose Start. This starts to play the Track1 object.

Now press the simulation's Menu key. You are taken back to the Menu1 object. Use the remote to navigate to the Settings button and choose that. You are taken to the Setup menu.

Choose the Spanish Audio stream. Notice the button highlight switches from the Spanish audio button to the Back button now. Press the Resume button. You are now playing the Track1 asset again; however, the background music is no longer the original score. Instead, you hear a continuous drum ensemble. This is my simulated Spanish audio.

Press Menu again, and you are returned to the Menu1 asset. Select the Settings menu again, and this time choose English for audio, and select Spanish for subtitles. Press the Resume button, and you are back watching Track1 again with the original score, and you see Spanish subtitles.

Again press Menu, and then go back to settings. Select the Subtitles Off button, and then press the Resume button. You are again playing the track exactly where you left off. This time, the subtitles are no longer showing.

Press Menu again, and this time go to the Chapter menu, and select Story 1. Allow Story 1 to finish completely. You will be taken back to the Chapter menu automatically. Press the Return button to go to the Menu1 object, and then press the Settings button to go to the Settings menu. Now press Resume. You are now taken back to the Menu1 asset, because there is nothing to resume. The story had finished playing completely.

Adjusting VTS Order

By default, when you first start DVD Studio Pro with a new project, you will notice that you have one default track asset and one default menu asset. These two assets share a single default Video Title Set, also known simply as a VTS.

Each time you add a track to the Outline tab, DVD Studio Pro essentially creates another Video Title Set on your behalf and places the additional track within that newly created VTS. So if you have just a single track asset in the Outline tab, you likely have just one VTS, called VTS1. As you add multiple tracks to your DVD project, you create VTS2, and VTS 3, and so on.

These Video Title Sets are later muxed into a collection of VOBs (Video Objects) which are stored in the VIDEO_TS folder of the DVD you play in the DVD player. These VOBs are recorded close to the core and work their way outward, in DVD-5 titles. In DVD-9 titles, these VOBs work their way outward, until they reach the layer break point, then they work their way back toward the core of the DVD in most cases.

Because you want to gain faster access to menus, and minimize the pausing effects of this layer break, there will be instances when you may decide it is best to have one track come before or after another, and thus in reality have one VTS come before or after another VTS.

Imagine that you have five tracks within your DVD project. The first of these five tracks is quite large, consuming 50 minutes of play time, while the other four tracks are each just a few minutes long.

Now imagine that one of these smaller tracks is an intro, or an information track. Each time the viewer chooses to play that track, the DVD's laser will have to travel all the way past the 50 minutes of the first track just to play the smaller track which follows the first track. This is because, as you create tracks, you define the Video Title Set order of alignment.

Take a look at this typical DVD structure created by DVD Studio Pro. The menus and the first track together with its assigned Story objects are combined into the first Video Title Set. VTS_01_0.VOB is the location of the menus, and the track and stories are stored in VTS_01_1.VOB and greater, depending on the storage requirements of the track you have defined as that first track.

My Info track, since it is my second track in the Outline tab, would then be defined as VTS_02_0.VOB as the menu VOB, and VTS_02_01.VOB as the location of the track I have defined in that track object.

Because my first track is over 50 minutes in length, it required more storage than the second track, which is just a few minutes in length, and thus you see it as multiple VOBs with the _1, and _2, and so forth in the file structure. VTS_01_1.VOB,

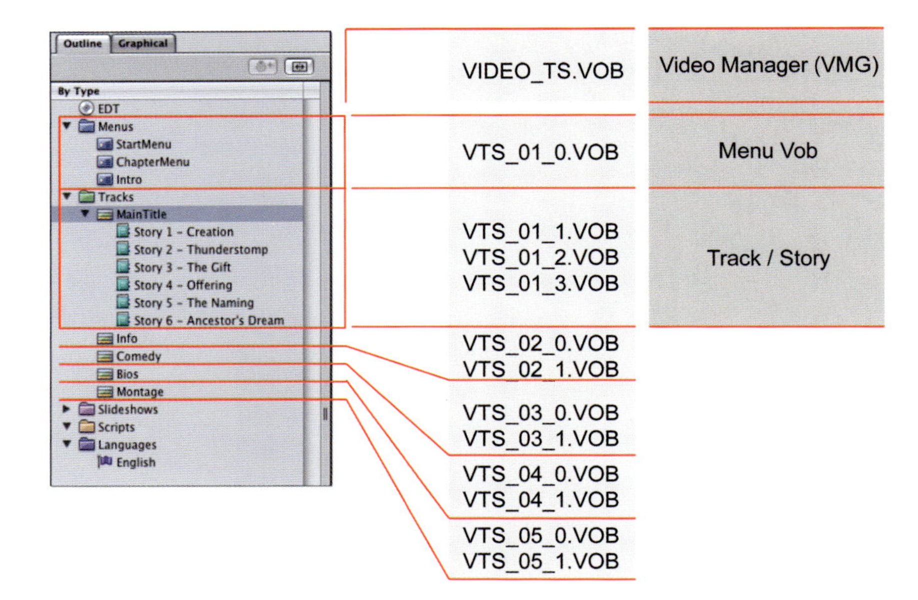

Figure 12.1 VOB structure compared with Outline tab

VTS_01_2.VOB, and VTS_01_3.VOB would represent my first track, and since the second track is just a few minutes, it requires far less space and is represented only as VTS_02_1.VOB for its track, and VTS_02_0.VOB for its menu VOB, which would be almost nonexistent in size.

If I place all my smaller tracks before the one larger track, I can gain faster access to each track from the menu since less distance is covered to get to the first VOB of each of the tracks overall.

Adjusting the VTS Order in the Outline Tab (Version 3)

You can click and hold the track asset and drag it to the lowest position in the Outline tab, thus telling DVD Studio Pro to mux that track asset as the last Video Title Set, and not the first.

Prior to DVD Studio Pro 4, this was all that was required in order to change the order in which the Video Title Sets were muxed into the final build of your DVD. However, this has changed in DVD Studio Pro 4.

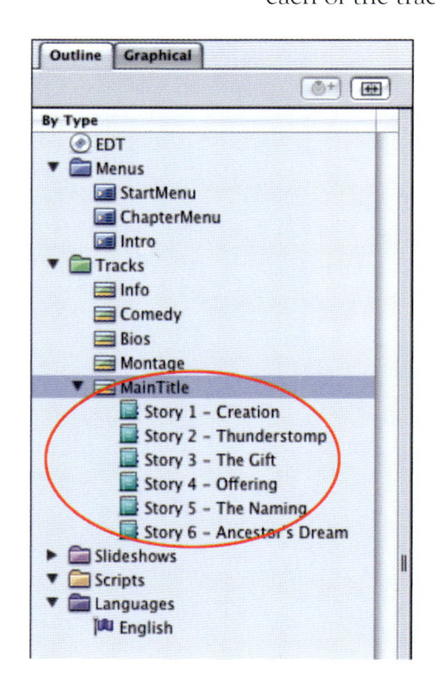

Figure 12.2 Stories associated with MainTitle Track object

Adjusting the VTS Order in the Outline Tab (Version 4)

In DVD Studio Pro 4, you have a more flexible VTS architecture which no longer follows this simple method of altering the order in which your tracks are muxed into the final Video Title Sets.

In the upper-right-hand corner of the Outline tab, you now have two added buttons that tap into two new features. The button to the far right, in the upper-right-hand corner, is the Alternate Type and VTS View button. Select that button to change the view of the Outline tab from its default view to the VTS view.

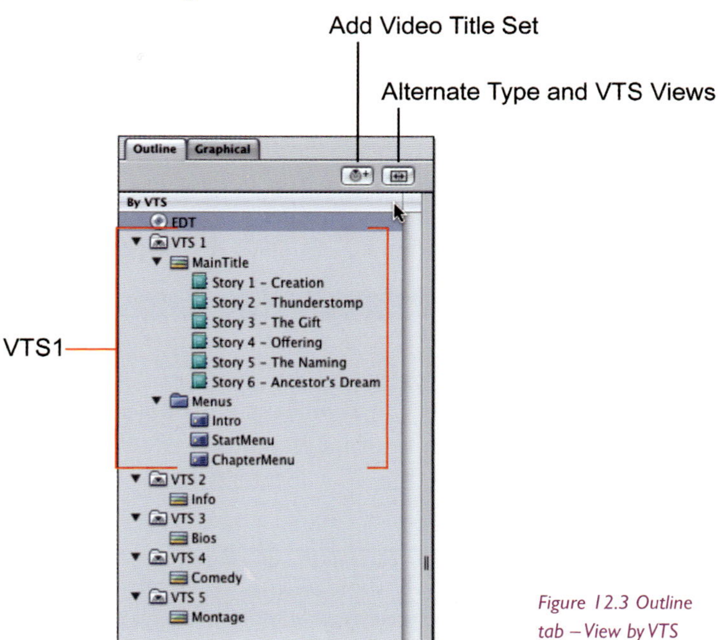

Figure 12.3 Outline tab – View by VTS

The default Menu 1 and Track 1 assets are defined as VTS1. If you keep your menus consistent in terms of video or audio type, they will automatically remain in VTS1. Inconsistencies, such as placing PCM audio in one menu and AC3 audio in another, will cause that menu to be placed in another VTS, such as VTS2, or perhaps another VTS, depending on how many menus have differences.

By using the same video and audio standards in my menus, I can keep them all in VTS1. But how do I move my tracks and stories so that they are after all my smaller tracks?

I will select the Add Video Title Set button, and then I will drag the MainTitle track asset from the VTS 1 object into the newly created VTS 6 object. Notice the little pin icon that is now placed on the track object inside the VTS 6 object. This is telling me that this track and its stories will now be muxed as the VTS 6 VOB, placing my largest asset after the smaller assets in the VTS 1 through VTS 5 objects.

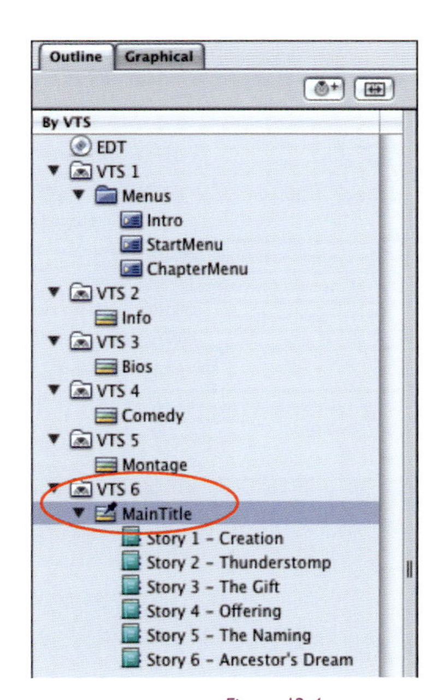

Figure 12.4 Designating a VTS

Layer Break Considerations

The VTS order you create can in some cases help you create a better experience for the viewer of your DVD. This is especially true when authoring DVD-9 titles. You already know that VTS order can speed up or slow down navigation, but VTS order can also help you define the best possible layer break, and in one case, create a layer break that the user will never actually have to view in transition at all.

There are DVD-9s that contain a single main title that is long enough that the layer break will need to be placed at some point within that main title. There are also DVDs that will have more than one track of just 45 minutes to 60 minutes, as is common with the increasingly popular television shows now being sold on DVD. In those cases, it may not be necessary to set a layer break within one of the episodes being played; rather instead, place the layer break in a small track that sits between the two episodes.

DVD-9 Layer Breaks with Less Than 60 Minutes of Continuous Playtime

When considering a DVD-9, there is a simple rule you must follow. Layer 0, the first layer of Side A, must be larger than Layer 1 of the same side A. A Dual-Layer means there is one side, and two layers. That side is defined as Side A, and its layers as Layer 0, and Layer 1.

The reason Layer 0 must be larger is because of the way the DVD Video will switch layers. Layer 0 starts from the inner core of the DVD Video, and plays outward, until it reaches its layer break, then it will use OTP (Opposite Track Path), which means Layer 1 begins at that outer edge where the layer break left off on Layer 0, and work its way back toward the core of the DVD Video. Because of this, Layer 0 must take the laser farther toward the outer edge before the return trip back to the core, else Layer 1 would run out of physical distance.

An easy way to think of this is to imagine a one-hour show on Layer 0, the first layer, and then imagine a two-hour show on Layer 1. Layer 0 starts from the core, and works outward the distances needed for 1 hour. On the return back to the core, you then would have just 1 hour again, since that is as far out as you have been taken before the laser plays backward toward the core. So a 2-hour Layer 1 is not possible if Layer 0 is only 1 hour.

In the example in Figure 12.5, I have VTS 1 at the top, which contains the menus. This is because the menus will interact with the Video Manager located at the core of the DVD; and thus keeping the menus close to the Video Manager will decrease disc access because those assets are close neighbors.

Notice that all the Video Title Sets leading up to and including VTS 6, which is Episode 1, are all set before my layer break in VTS 7. Only VTS 8, which contains Episode 2, is after the layer break, and thus smaller than Layer 0.

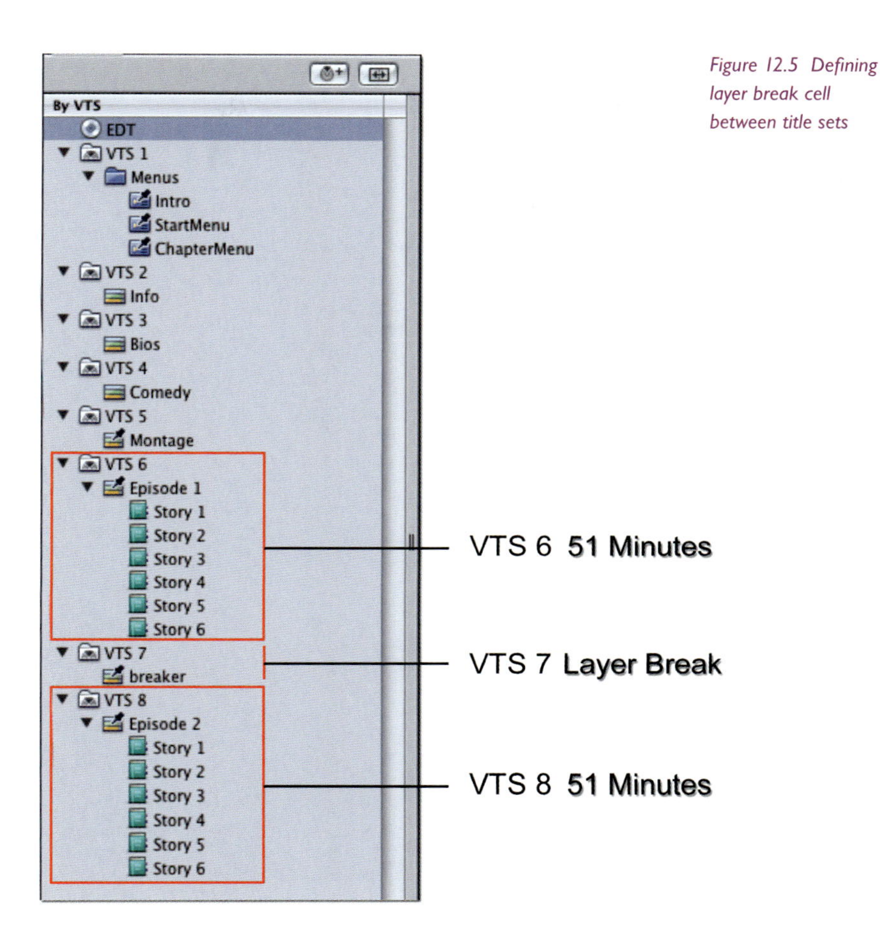

Figure 12.5 Defining layer break cell between title sets

Though I use an example of time to describe distance, I do that to make the rule simple to understand. In reality, time is not the only issue. All things being equal, meaning if my two episodes were encoded with equal bitrates for video and audio, then time can easily be used to judge distance, but the true benchmark is how many sectors the episode actually consumes.

The maximum layer size of a DVD-9 is approximately 2,074,496 sectors. How many minutes can fit in this space depends on what bitrate you use to encode your assets. When creating my DVD-9, I noticed that I got all the way to VTS 6, which includes my first 51-minute episode, which happens to be encoded at 6.5Mbps, using CBR (Constant Bit Rate). That took my estimated DVD size to 3.1GB. Adding the second episode of another 51 minutes encoded the same way brought this project to 5.4GB. In this situation it is easy to see that the layer break will do nicely between the two episodes.

Clearly Layer 0 will be larger than Layer 1, and neither will exceed the maximum sector size. I know this because my largest layer is only 3.1GB, which doesn't even come close to the maximum sector size I am allowed.

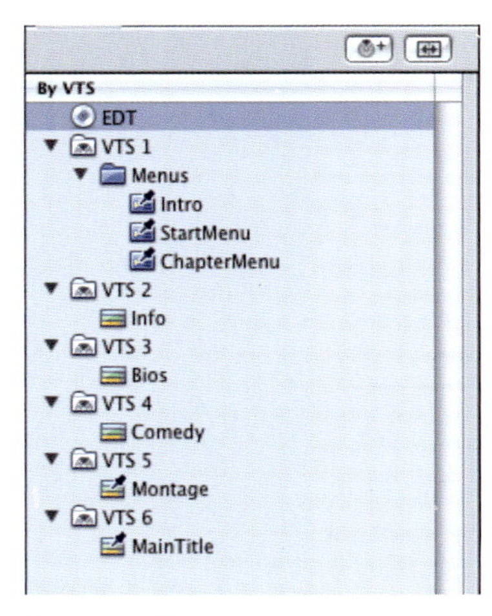

Figure 12.6 Classic VTS layout for DVD-9

DVD-9 Layer Breaks with Greater Than 90 Minutes of Continuous Playtime

The typical DVD-9 you will author will likely have a main title with 90 minutes or more being used in the main title.

As shown in the Outline tab, I have placed my MainTitle asset in VTS 6, so that the menus are better able to interact with all the assets my DVD has to offer. A chapter marker or a specific layer break marker will be set at some point in the MainTitle asset, which in this case is close to two hours in length, and combined with the other assets that precede it, extend the storage requirements of this DVD to pass 6GB, thus requiring me to define a DVD-9 and set a layer break.

Building and Formatting

Building and formatting your final project is the act of translating the project you create inside DVD Studio Pro to the media you create, whether it be a DVD-R for playback, or a DLT for mass replication, or even a muxed VIDEO_TS folder on the hard drive for further testing before you commit to a DVD-R or a DLT tape.

The first step is building your project. The build process is what actually translates the DVD Studio Pro project into a muxed set of VOBs, IFO, and BUP files you see on any common DVD.

A VOB (Video Object) is a single file which contains several streams of video, audio, and subpicture all multiplexed together.

An IFO file contains information about its accompanying VOB, such as the number of and type of streams.

A BUP file is a backup of the accompanying IFO file.

The formatting process takes the build files and formats them to TAPE, IMAGE, or DVD-R media (of some type) such as DVD-R, DVD+R, or DVD+R DL (Double Layer).

Setting the Build Preferences

You can pre-set a location for your build files. Open the Preferences, and then select Destinations.

If the Macintosh you are using has more than one hard disk, it's always a good idea to build your project on that secondary drive, rather than the build drive.

Change the Show field to Build / Format, and then select the Choose button to choose a directory where you will store your build files.

Select OK to leave the Preferences and return to the application.

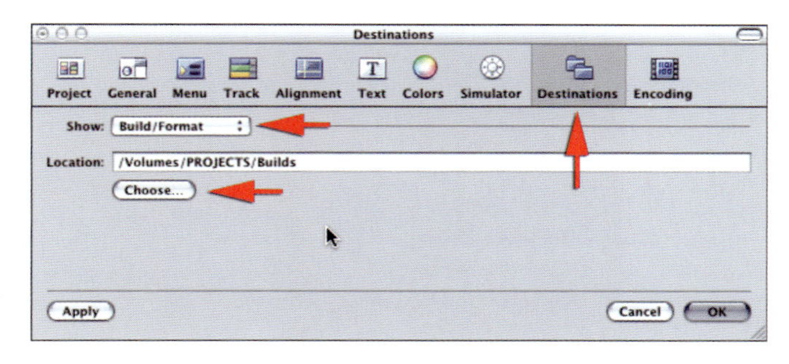

Figure 13.1 Preferences > Destinations — Setting the Build folder location

Building Your Project

When you are ready to build your project, use the Toolbar to select either Build, or Build and Format. I like to do these separately because I like to test the build files before I commit them to DVD-R, or DLT Tape.

Note: There is a function called Burn, which I have skipped over. Burn is a process that combines the Build and Format into a single function. Burn can only be used when burning directly to DVD recordable media. Burn cannot be used to write a DLT.

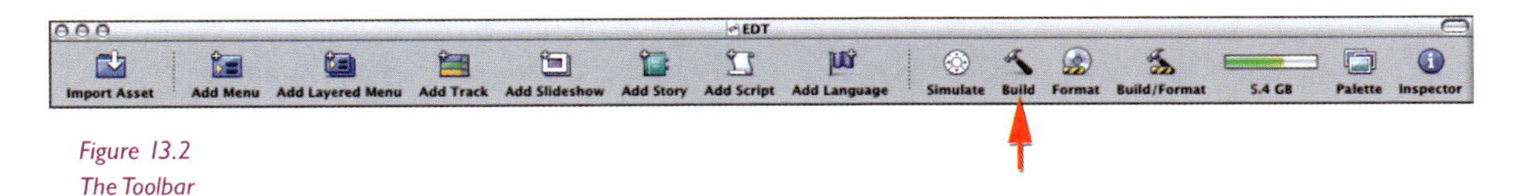

Figure 13.2 The Toolbar

Separating the Build and Format is easy. Just use Build all by itself by selecting Build in the Toolbar.

Testing Your Build

You can test the build before you commit to DVD-R or DLT by using Apple's software DVD player to play the contents of the Build folder. Open Apple's software DVD player, and using the pull-down menus, select File > Open DVD Media.

Figure 13.3 Testing the Build files

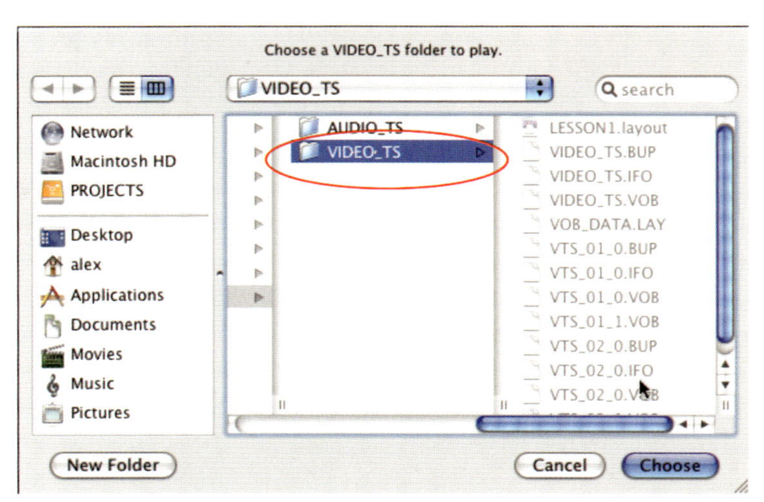

Figure 13.4 Locating the Build files

Use the file finder to locate the VIDEO_TS folder where you built your DVD project, then select Choose.

Next, select Play on the software remote control to begin playing the Build files directly from the hard drive. Once you are satisfied with your DVDs functionality, you're ready to begin the format process.

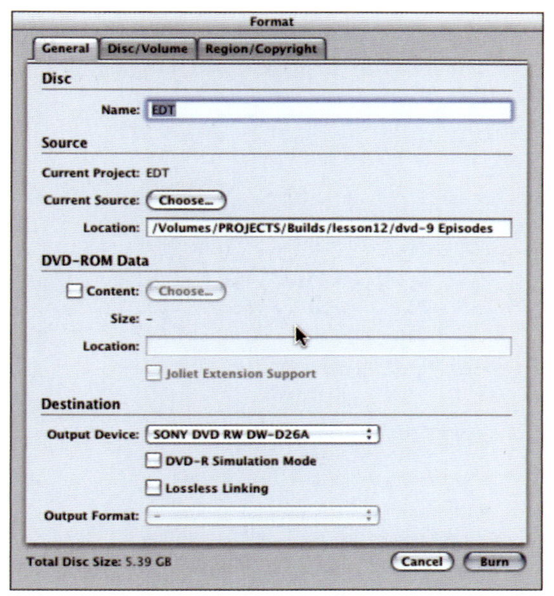

Figure 13.5 Format palette — General tab

Formatting

To get started, select the Format button in the Toolbar. The build location of the project should be in the Current Source field of the General tab of the Format window. If for any reason it is not, locate the folder that contains the VIDEO_TS folder where your project has been stored and click the Choose button.

Formatting for DVD-R Media Types

If this is for personal use, you are likely using an Apple SuperDrive as your DVD burner. If you have a more modern Macintosh with a SuperDrive that supports +R Double Layer media, then you may burn a DVD-9 project directly to DVD+R DL media from DVD Studio Pro.

For DVD-R media types, select the Output Device field, then choose your DVD burner if it isn't already selected by default.

Formatting for DLT

If your project needs to go to a replicator, then most of the time it is a good idea to format your project on DLT tape or to a hard disk if your replicator offers such a service. These days, replicators have many options. The best idea is to ask your replicator what various kinds of media it will accept.

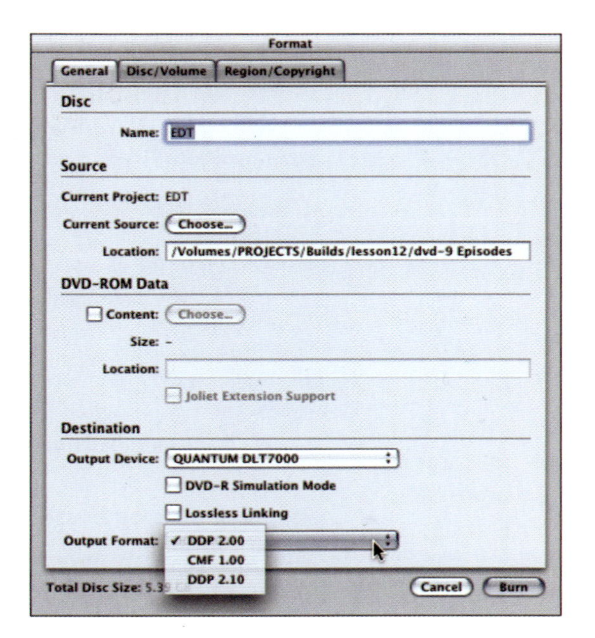

Figure 13.6 Setting the Output format

Select the Output Device and choose your DLT tape device if you have one connected to your authoring Macintosh.

Change the Output format to your replication company's standard. Most are happy with DDP2.0, but again, this is a question you should ask of your replicator.

DDP stands for Disc Description Protocol and was developed by Doug Carson and Associates, Inc. (DCA). DDP2.0 is a standard protocol designed to write a DVD image. A DVD image is written to DLT tape using the DDP or the equivalent description protocol such as the Cutting Master Format (CMF) standard.

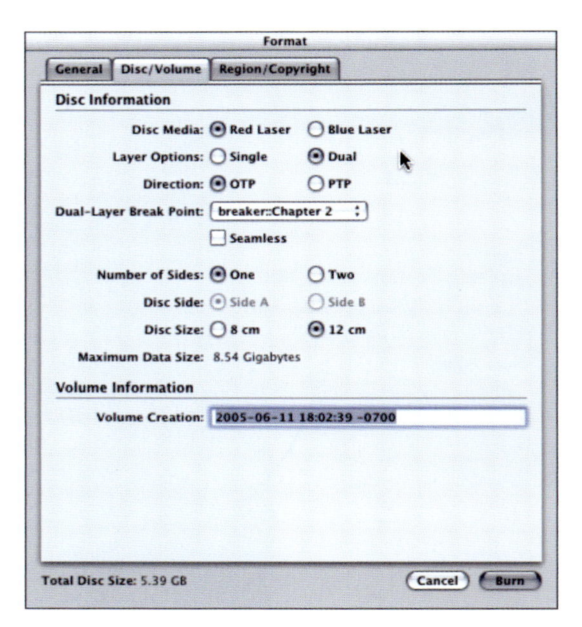

Figure 13.7 Non-seamless layer break

Setting the Disc / Volume Properties

Using the Disc / Volume tab, I will select Red Laser, because my project is intended for non-HD DVD standards using the UDF 1.02 standard rather than the UDF 2.50 standard for HD types.

My project is a DVD-9, so I will select the Dual option in the Layer Options field. This enables the Direction option. I will use OTP (Opposite Track Path), which means as the media begins to play near the core of the DVD starting with Layer 0, the first layer, it will extend to the layer break point toward the outer edge of the DVD until it reaches that point. Playback then switches layers to Layer 1 where it will play from the outer edge back toward the core.

Setting the Layer break

The Dual-Layer Break Point is required to be greater than half of the DVD's contents but still cannot exceed the maximum sector size of Layer 0.

There are three basic ways to set a layer break:

1. Predefine a layer break within a track that you know will be an ideal location for such a break.
2. Choose the Automatic option, allowing DVD Studio Pro to determine the best location for you.
3. Choose from any of a number of possible layer breaks by selecting the Dual-Layer Break Point pop-up menu and traversing the track assets until you find a chapter marker you would like to use as a layer break.

Predefining a Layer break within a Track Asset

Locate a track that you believe to be ideally located for your layer break. See Chapter 12, Adjusting VTS Order, for more information about ideal locations. Once you have that track opened in the Track tab, select an existing chapter, or create a marker at the

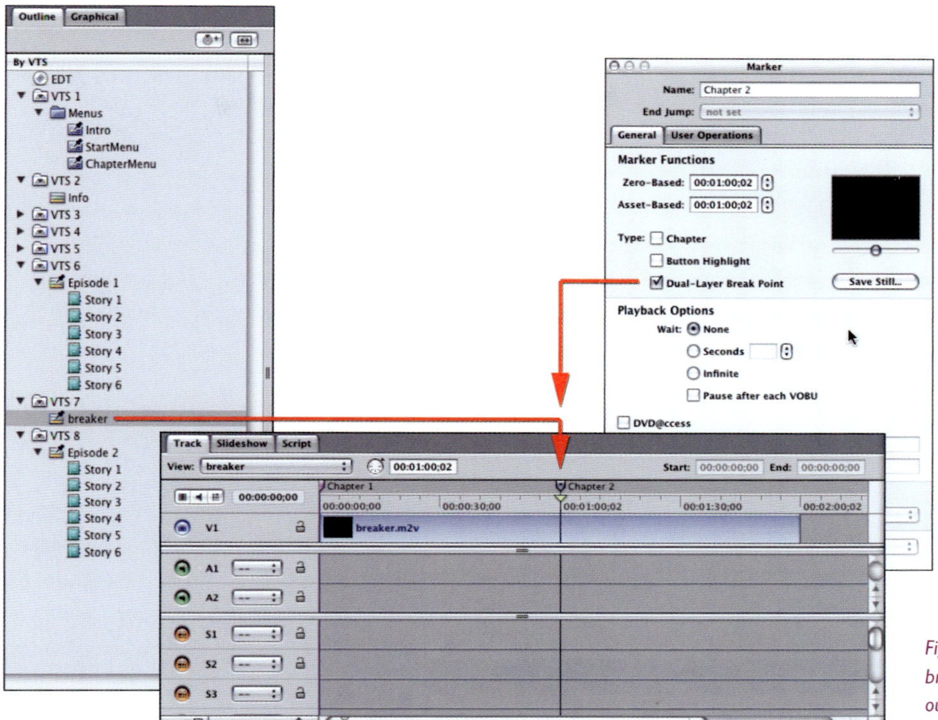

Figure 13.8 The layer break cell and VTS outline

Figure 13.9 Selecting an available layer break

location where you would like the layer break to occur.

Select the marker itself in the timeline, and open its inspector. Under the General tab of the marker's inspector, set the Type field to Dual-Layer Break Point.

A dual-layer break point may also be set as a combination chapter and dual-layer break point.

Automatic Dual-Layer Break Point

To set the Automatic Dual-Layer Break Point, simply take the default Automatic option.

Choosing a Dual-Layer Break Point

You may set a layer break by selecting the Dual-Layer Break Point pop-up menu and traversing the chapters until you find a suitable layer break. Suitable layer breaks are bold, whereas those not suitable are grayed and are not an item you may select.

Region / Copyright

The Region / Copyright tab allows you to assign region control and to protect the DVD via CSS encryption or Macrovision analog copy protection.

Playable Regions

If this DVD is intended for personal use, or being formatted for DVD-R, check all the boxes making this DVD region-free.

If the DVD is more for commercial use and you are formatting to DLT, you may wish to restrict certain regions. To restrict a region, simply remove the check mark from that region, and format to Hard Drive, IMG, or DLT tape.

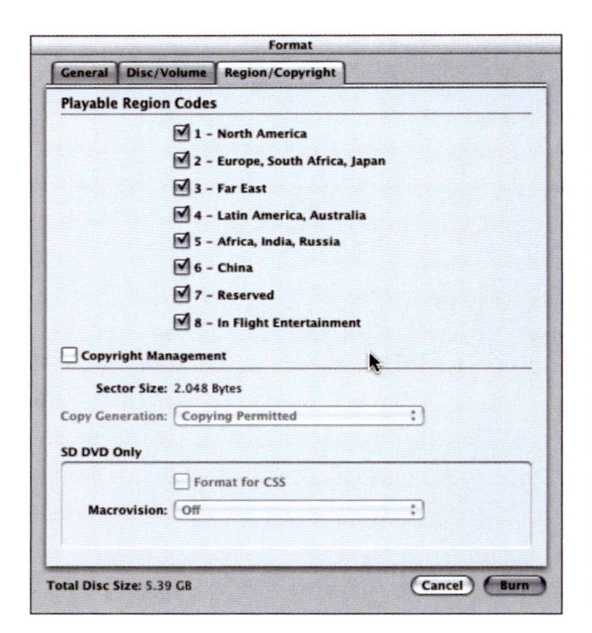

Figure 13.10 Flagging all regions for playback

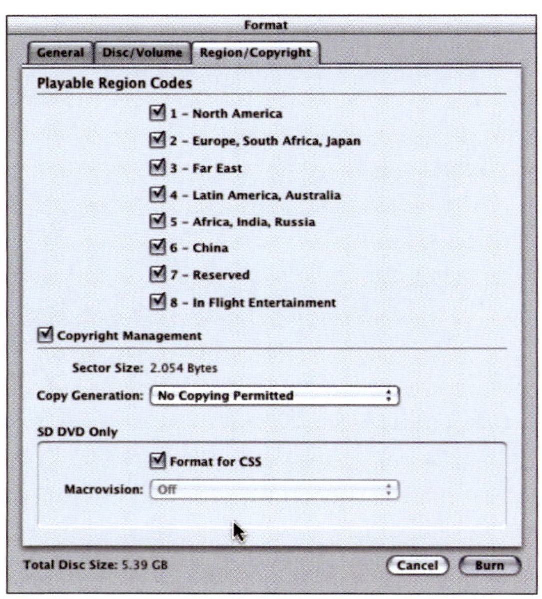

Figure 13.11 Adding copyright management and formatting for CSS

Copyright Management

If you are replicating your DVD and formatting to Hard Drive or DLT tape and you would like the replicator to add CSS encryption, then place a check mark in the Copyright Management box, and choose No Copying Permitted in the Copy Generation field, and then select Format for CSS.

Now select Format, and, depending on your selected Output Device, you'll either create a single IMG file, a directory with Layer0 and Layer1 DDP or CMF images, a DVD-R of some type, or a DLT with one tape or two, depending on DVD-5 or -9 outputs.

Index

C

T